PSYCHOLOGY UPDATES

Daniel Goleman

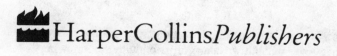HarperCollins*Publishers*

PSYCHOLOGY UPDATES By Dan Goleman

ISBN: 0-06-042375-7
90 91 92 93 94 9 8 7 6 5 4 3 2 1

About the Author

Daniel Goleman combines a background in psychology and journalism. His graduate degrees from Harvard are an MA in Clinical Psychology and Ph.D in Personality and Development. His research at Harvard—some for his dissertation, some while a junior faculty member—involved psyphysiological studies of the effects of meditation and relaxation on stress reactivity.

His academic interests span psychology's "hard" and "soft" areas, from psychophysiology and states of consciousness, health and stress coping, psychological disorders and psychotherapy, to personality and development.

Since 1975, when he joined the staff of *Psychology Today* as a writer and editor, Dr. Goleman has been one of the country's leading translators of research psychology to the general public. The articles in this collection are from his weekly writing in the Science section of the *New York Times*, where he has covered psychology since 1984.

In recognition of the excellence of his writing, the American Psychological Association has given Dr. Goleman four media awards, including one in 1988 for Lifetime Achievement. He has also received national awards for his writing from the American Psychiatric Association, the National Association for Mental Health, and the Alliance for the Mentally Ill. He was twice nominated for the Pulitzer Prize for his articles in the *New York Times*.

Preface: To the Instructor

Like any science, psychology is in a continual state of evolution and growth. Old assumptions give way to new findings and hallowed theories are challenged by new views as the conventional wisdom evolves.

This process of change presents a special challenge to the instructor in introductory psychology. How do you capture the state of a field in flux? That dilemma is reflected in the textbooks you use. Of necessity, they outline the state of the field at a given point in time, not as it is in the moment.

Timeliness

No matter how recently your textbook was published, the data it reviews will necessarily be dated by the time you use it in your course. The lag between the growing edge of findings in psychology and what a textbook can cover is inevitable. The articles in this collection are breaking news, covering much of the research that will be included in the next edition of your textbook.

The articles have been selected to help you keep your course as up-to-the-minute as possible. As such, they are meant to complement any text you might be using, by filling in the inevitable gap between the state-of-the-art when the book was written, and the cutting edge of the newest and best research.

Balance and Brevity

Many current controversies in psychology are covered in these articles, and I have made a concerted effort to cover both sides of the issue by including the major views. That is the journalist's mandate: not to advocate, but to portray an issue evenly. I go to the main figures in the field and distill the essence of what they tell me.

Writing for a newspaper also demands that I be brief, though meaty. The articles must hit on the main points of a topic, with enough background and context, without losing the general reader. That means being short and to the point.

Readability

These articles offer something more than topicality: they are engaging. Because I write them for readers of a daily newspaper, they must speak to the tacit concern of every newspaper reader: what does this have to do with my life or my understanding of my world? This journalistic requirement means that students will find each article couched in the terms that make the finding most relevant to their lives.

The articles are written for newspaper readers—not just of the *New York Times*, where they first appeared, but for readers throughout the United States and English-speaking world, in the hundreds of papers where they are regularly reprinted.

That means that they are written and edited to be easily understood. All specialized terms are defined immediately at their first use, for instance. The sentences are simple and direct. And the vocabulary is at a junior high to high school level, with an occasional vocabulary stretcher included from time to time.

Topic Arrangement

For this collection, I've arranged the articles to fit the standard organization of introductory texts. Under each topic heading there are five to eight articles. Since each articles stands alone, you can assign only those you choose to supplement a given chapter in the main textbook you are using.

The topics by which articles are grouped are those of a generic introductory text: The Brain and Nervous System; States of Consciousness; Sensation and Perception; Learning and Memory; Cognition and Thought; Emotions; Motivation; Infancy and Childhood; The Life Span; Continuity and Change; Adolescence, Adulthood and Aging; Personality, Individual Differences, and Intelligence; Health, Stress, and Coping; Psychological Disorders; Psychotherapy; Sex and the Sexes; Social Psychology.

Usefulness

You can, of course, use the articles flexibly, tailoring them to the unique needs of your course and teaching style. For instance, you can easily pick and choose to match them to the needs of a given topic; you may prefer, say, to assign articles from the health section along with your textbook chapter on emotions.

This collection of articles could also be used as a supplement to higher level courses where the overlap in topics makes for ample coverage. By assigning a selection of articles, you could easily use this collection as a supplement to, for example, Research Methods or Developmental Psychology. Other courses this collection can easily fit include Health; Personality and Adjustment; Social Psychology; or Cognitive Psychology.

In the course on experimental psychology or research methods, for instance, the articles can be assigned so students can assess the validity of the methods use. Or students might be posed the problem of designing a test of their own to support or refute the ideas in the article. And each article can be a prompt for students to consider how psychologists use research to tackle questions.

The topicality of the articles make them ideal, too, for use in introductory courses for non-majors, where the emphasis is more oriented toward applying psychology to life than to theories or method.

USING THIS BOOK IN YOUR COURSE

No matter the specifics of the course your teach, there are a variety of ways you might use these articles:

- *Provoke Discussion These articles invariably describe the implications for everyday life of psychological research. Students readily find the connections to their own lives when data is presented in this format, whether it is on the meaning of the link between the thalamus and amygdala for their emotional memories, or how attributions about failures can sabotage a career or help them succeed.*

- *Raise Methodological Issue. Most articles highlight the methods of at least one psychological researcher. This gives you the opportunity to raise a range of questions that will give your students a grasp of research fundamentals. Is that approach the best for answering the question at hand? What are other methods you might use? Do the findings raise questions for further research?*

- *Library Research. Each article includes information on the source of the research on which it is based: the main author, the journal, and the year of publication. This means you can give as-signments that will lead students to use Psychology Abstracts in tracking down the journal article, so gaining a working familiarity with basic library research skills.*

- *Update Your Text. The articles chronicle the most recent work of the best researchers in psychology. As such, they can be used as updates from the field, fresh bulletins reporting psychology's latest findings and ideas.*

- *Elicit Reactions. Each article can be the basis for small group discussion on implications of research or a reaction paper. Many describe controversies that lead to pro or con papers or discussions.*

- *For Assignments. Each article can be the basis of a term paper, with further library research. Or students can draw on the articles and compare them with the same material in their text. Assignments might include: How does the article expand, clarify, or contradict what the text says?*

- *Amplify Topics. Many of the readings provide more detail on areas only briefly touched on in introductory texts. The articles can bring added depth to these topics, particularly "hot" areas in which there is continuous, ongoing research.*

To the Student

These articles were written with someone like you in mind; curious about psychology, but without any special technical knowledge. You can use them in many ways, in addition to the assignments your instructor gives you.

Perhaps the most enjoyable approach is simply to browse, spending some time with the topics that particularly intrigue you: psychological disorders, personality and intelligence, sex and relationships, or the brain, for instance.

Each article is written with you, the reader, in mind. You'll find that they make explicit the implications for your life or for understanding yourself or other people better.

You can read, for example, about the usefulness of a good argument in a romantic relationship—if you know how to fight fair. Or how men and women have different expectations about sex on a date, and how to avoid the difficulties that can present. Another article describes the limits of the kind of intelligence measured by I.Q. tests, and an alternative kind of savvy that seems more crucial to success in life.

Another way you can use these articles is to give yourself a sense of the many directions in which psychology, as a science and profession, is growing these days. If you are interested in a psychology major or a career in the field you'll find these articles a useful guide to the areas of the field that you find of most personal interest.

However you use these articles, I hope you'll enjoy them!

Table of Contents

The Brain

How does the brain create the mind? That fundamental question of brain science is finding new answers, as psychologists examine the basic building blocks of the brain's operation. In "Investigations of the Brain Finding Clues to the Mind," researchers are turning to studies of simple brain processes to find the key to the complex ways the brain gives rise to mental events.

Are you left-handed? The unique arrangement of the brain in left-handers sometimes makes a person have special talents, such as for math. But the prenatal brain chemistry that gives rise to left-handedness may also create a risk of problems such as near-sightedness and migraine headaches, according to research described in "Left vs. Right: Brain Function Tied to Hormone in the Womb."

The brain does not stop changing and growing in childhood; in a very real sense its growth continues into life's later years. That does not mean that new brain cells form, but that they continue to add to the complexity of their interconnections—at least if we lead a stimulating life. The evidence for this is in "New Evidence Points to Growth of the Brain Even Late in Life."

It's not that you are what you eat, but that what you eat affects how you are. That is the conclusion from research linking certain nutrients in foods to changes in the levels of brain chemicals and to changes of mood. The links between what you eat and how you feel are due to some nutrients causing the brain to trigger the production of specific brain chemicals, as is described in "Food and the Brain."

Are the psychological differences between men and women based in the brain? Some may be, according to the findings in "Subtle Differences Found in the Brain Anatomy of Men and Women." But of what importance these anatomical differences between the sexes might be is a controversial issue.

The power of emotions to override rational decisions may be explained by a discovery about how the brain is arranged. One part of the brain, the amygdala, can register emotional events before the neocortex, where thought occurs. As is explained in "Brain's Design Emerges as a Key to Emotions," this means that key aspects of a person's emotional life, like primitive fears, can operate largely independent of rational thought.

Investigations of the Brain Finding Clues to the Mind

April 22, 1986

Where is memory? What is thought? Or will? How does the brain create sorrow? In short, how does the brain create the mind?

Answering these questions is the goal of much of neuroscience and psychology.

"The mind is what the brain does," said Stephen Kosslyn, one of the leading researchers.

The newest efforts in the long, frustrating quest to link brain to mind are based on the belief that the grander notions of what the mind does have in some ways been a barrier to clear understanding. Instead, the current investigators say, it is necessary to start all over again and look at mental activity in the most fundamental ways, slowly building on many hard-won small observations. On their own terms, they are making headway.

Neuroscientists and cognitive psychologists alike are heralding a coming revolution in their ability to decipher the brain's involvement in the mind.

The beginnings of this revolution are necessarily humble, focusing at a very mechanical, nuts-and-bolts level.

"Consider the immense complexity of the problem," said Harold Hawkins, a psychologist at the Office of Naval Research, which is sponsoring some of the new work. "The brain contains somewhere between 10 billion and 100 billion neurons, each of which receives information from 1,000 to 100 thousand other neurons, and sends information to a like number. Even the simplest mental act, like reading the letter 'A,' requires the activity of many millions of neurons spread through many parts of the brain."

One of the most provocative findings deals with the mechanics of a relatively complicated state of mind; the exercise of will. The research seems to stand common sense on its head. The ordinary understanding of the sequence involved in a simple decision is: first, one decides, then the mental decision leads the brain to trigger the action.

Wrong, according to findings by Benjamin Libet, a neurophysiologist at the University of California at San Francisco. His research, reported in 1986 in *The Behavioral and Brain Sciences,* shows that appreciable brain activity precedes all voluntary acts. The activity not only seems to trigger the acts, but—most surprising—it also precedes the instant at which a person decides to act.

In other words, the sequence is: brain activity, followed by the conscious decision to act, followed by the act.

In Dr. Libet's study, the volunteers' brain activity was measured as they spontaneously moved a finger. The timing of the decision to act was made by the volunteers' noting the position of a revolving spot at the moment they became aware of the intent to move the finger.

The brain activity began, on average, 350 milliseconds, or about a third of a second, before the volunteers noted the decision to move the finger. The finger actually moved about 150 milliseconds after that.

Brain Decides for the Mind

This, in Dr. Libet's widely debated interpretation, means that the brain actually decides for the mind, rather than the brain executing some conscious decision the person makes. What most people think of as "free will," in his view, is actually an illusion, occurring after the brain has made a decision to act.

However, Dr. Libet has also found there is time to cancel the decision during the one-tenth to two-tenths of a second between the person's awareness of intent and the action itself. It is in the mind's ability to "veto" the brain's decision that free will resides, in his view—a conclusion that has been greeted with skepticism from some philosophers, who view his data as a trivial base for drawing grand conclusions.

Even among psychologists, Dr. Libet's research is seen as a bare beginning in tracing the brain's role in intention, a mental act that pervaded all human activity. For some researchers, the Libet studies are not as interesting for what they suggest about free will as what they imply about impulse and self-control.

'Signal' for Wrong Actions

In related work, researchers are seeking to find out whether the brain sends a signal on whether an action about to be taken will be correct or incorrect. Emmanuel Donchin at the University of Illinois has been using a computerized brain measure called the "evoked potential" to search for just such a brain signature that errors are about to be made. If a reliable brain indicator can be found, it might be possible, for example, to monitor the brain of a jet pilot and signal him just before he is about to make a mistake.

When a person makes a simple error, such as moving the wrong hand, there is brain activity present for both the correct and the incorrect response, according to research Dr. Donchin and his colleagues reported in *the Journal of Experimental Psychology.*

In Dr. Donchin's research, the brain activity of volunteers was monitored while they squeezed one of two bulbs held in each hand in response to letters flashed before them. When they made an error, the correct and incorrect responses seemed to compete in the brain for a fraction of a second before the error was actually made.

Seeking a Simple Path

The simplicity of Dr. Donchin's and Dr. Libet's research is typical of the new approach to studying the brain and mind. The connections between the brain and mind are so complicated that, for now, the research has been able to examine only the most elementary mental tasks. In contrast, much of the earlier work connecting mind and brain focused on "localization," finding specific areas in the brain that seem to be the site for particular mental functions such as speech. The search for localization is now seen as too narrow.

"It is too simple to see a given place in the brain as where a mental act occurs," said Stephen Kosslyn, a cognitive psychologist at Harvard. "The new understanding is that specific networks of cells distributed throughout the brain are highly involved in each component of a mental act."

Thus, he and other cognitive psychologists are re-examining the very categories they use to describe the mind. Such terms as "memory," they say, are simply too vague and sloppy to be useful. For that reason, these scientists prefer to look at ever smaller connections between the brain and its thought, perception and behavior.

Basic Units of Mind

"The everyday, common-sense categories are the wrong way to describe what happens at the level of brain activity," said David Rumelhart, a cognitive psychologist at the University of California at San Diego. "We've had to ask an entirely new question: How can mental events grow out of a system like the brain? It forces us to come up with biologically plausible models of the mind."

In *Parallel Distributed Processing* (M.I.T. Press), a book about the theory, Dr. Rumelhart and John McClelland propose that what is stored in memory is not specific facts or events, but rather the relationships between the various aspects of those facts or events as they are encoded in groupings of neuronal cells or patterns of cell activity. For instance, a painting may be evoked in the mind as a collection of its parts—its colors and shapes—or as part of a genre rather than its details.

Act of Shifting Attention

Memory, then, is not so much a copy of experience as the storage of the connections between aspects of experience. And, in this view, learning entails mastering the proper strengths of the connections between them. Knowledge accumulates by the progressive association of these connections, not by isolated impressions.

Many researchers consider Dr. Rumelhart's new way of looking at the mind in terms of the simplest mental acts to be the most helpful approach yet in guiding studies linking the brain and mind. This kind of research may have important implications for understanding how people learn and thus how best to teach them.

If memory in the brain seems elusive, another researcher has taken on an equally subtle act of the brain: shifting attention. Michael Posner, a psychologist at Washington University in St. Louis, has studied what he calls "covert attention," what the mind does when, for example, a driver whose eyes are fixed on an approaching intersection shifts his attention to cars coming from the right and left.

With a model that describes these attentional shifts in terms as simple as those used by Dr. Rumelhart, Dr. Posner, watching the electric activity of the brain among other things, has been able to observe attention shifting in specific patterns and rhythms. This work, like the other cognitive work, is groundbreaking because it is a first step toward watching the brain direct acts of the mind.

Similar work has been done by Dr. Kosslyn, the Harvard psychologist, who has been able to pinpoint the different sorts of brain activity involved in reading a map. His effort, too, has been to reduce broad categories of thinking into discrete units.

"Picturing something in your mind involves at least four major mental acts," Dr. Kosslyn said. "There is forming the image, fixing it in your mind, scanning it, and seeing it move in various ways."

And each of these mental acts, he says, can be further broken down. For example, forming the mental image entails bringing to mind the parts of the image, interpreting how they should be combined and finding the right relationships between them. All of that, of course, occurs automatically.

A person's scanning of a map—whether by looking at it or by picturing it in his mind—involves a network of neurons that range through the parietal lobes of the cortex, Dr. Kosslyn has found in recent research. But when a person focuses on the image of a specific site on the map, the work is done by neural networks in the ventral portion of the cortex.

New Machines Aid Quest

Thus far, Dr. Kosslyn's research has relied on tests with stroke patients, who have lesions in different parts of the brain, to see what abilities those lesions impair. By piecing together evidence from different patients, he has sketched a picture of the parts of the brain involved. But that technique—which neuropsychologists have used for years—does not render a detailed and dynamic picture of the intact human brain in operation. And it is such a detailed picture of the brain that the new approach seeks.

For that reason, Dr. Kosslyn is beginning to use an apparatus that will allow him to map the brain's activity moment-to-moment throughout the cortex. The machine, called a "BEAM," is a sophisticated computerized electroencephalogram. It is one of a recent generation of devices for monitoring the human brain that is making the new work possible.

"For the first time," said Dr. Kosslyn, "we have the concepts to guide us in looking at how the brain makes the mind, and the tools that allow us to look."

Another promising instrument is the magnetoencephalogram, which monitors brain activity by measuring changes in the brain's magnetic field. Using this device, researchers at New York University have discovered specific networks of cells that respond to different musical notes.

"The separation between mind and brain has seemed a bar to progress in psychology," Dr. Posner has written in an essay on psychology in the 1990's. He believes overcoming that barrier will be "a major accomplishment of the next generation of psychologists."

Left vs. Right: Brain Function Tied to Hormone in the Womb

September 24, 1985

Scientists are tuning into the internal dialogue carried on between the right and left hemispheres of the brain, and their findings are offering clues about the underlying causes of mental deficits such as dyslexia and mental gifts such as mathematical genius.

Each of the brain's hemispheres has, in a sense, its own personality, the researchers are discovering. They are also finding that widespread notions about the right and left hemispheres are largely wrong.

The location in the brain of various capacities matters so much to neuroscientists because it is crucial to understanding the link between the brain and thinking. But the differences also point toward explanations for puzzles that seem far removed from the mind, including the high incidence in left-handed people of migraines, allergies and autoimmune disorders such as rheumatoid arthritis.

Left-handed people present researchers with a special challenge to sorting out how the brain is organized, particularly in determining what role each hemisphere plays. Left-handers display quite a different pattern of brain organization than right-handers. For example, in right-handed people the brain center that controls speech is located in the left hemisphere; in left-handers the speech center may be on either the right or the left half of the brain—or spread over both.

Handedness, researchers have found, is a matter of degree. About one person in 10 is fully left-handed. But as many as 20 percent of nonleft-handers are somewhat ambidextrous, so that, for example, they may write with one hand and strike a match with the other. These people, many of whom may consider themselves right-handers, may have brains with some measure of the anomalous organization found in outright left-handers.

Many researchers have been intrigued by a new, daring theory about left-handedness and the brain that at first seemed farfetched but has gained credibility as evidence mounts. The theory was proposed by Norman Geschwind, who was an eminent neurologist at Harvard Medical School.

Dr. Geschwind's theory, parts of which were published posthumously, proposes that the unusual brain organization found among left-handers signifies alterations that occurred in the developing brain of the fetus. These changes affect the anatomy and organization of the cerebral hemispheres, and have an important impact on the immune system.

Earlier this year, in a special series of articles in *the Archives of Neurology,* Dr. Geschwind and Albert Galaburda, a neurologist at Harvard Medical School, set out theory and evidence. They propose that variations during pregnancy in the level of testosterone, a male sex hormone, alter the way the fetal brain takes shape by changing the locations to which cells migrate. The levels of testosterone can be altered by such factors as the amount of stress the mother undergoes.

"The male brain matures later than that of the female, and the left hemisphere matures later than the right," Dr. Geschwind and Dr. Galaburda note. For that reason, they contend, the left hemisphere in men is especially vulnerable to irregularities.

Should testosterone changes result in the left hemisphere becoming less developed, the right hemisphere may become correspondingly more highly developed, according to the theory. This enrichment of the right hemisphere allows it to become the site of the centers for language and handedness, activities that the less-developed left hemisphere cannot support so well.

The result is a person who is more likely to be left-handed, since the right hemisphere controls the left half of the body. That also explains, the theory says, why left-handers, unlike right-handers, have more variation in where the brain centers are located for such things as speech—and many left-handers are more prone to problems like dyslexia and stuttering that depend on the operation of these brain centers.

"Probably most, if not all, individuals with developmental learning disorders have anomalous dominance," even though most of them are not totally left-handed, according to an article by Dr. Geschwind.

The variations in brain organization among left-handers are not all bad, however. While some parts of the brain are relatively underdeveloped, others can be more highly developed, notably that for spatial tasks. One sign of this, the theory notes, is the greater number of left-handers among architects and mathematically gifted children.

The effect of testosterone on brain development is more pronounced for boys than for girls, which, according to the theory, accounts for the higher incidence among males not only of left-handedness but also of such problems as dyslexia and stuttering.

The same hormonal influences that shape brain development also can affect the developing immune system, according to the theory. This results in a higher rate of certain medical problems.

In a study of 3,000 people, 280 of whom were recruited from among the customers of a specialty shop for left-handers in London, Dr. Geschwind found the links his theory predicted between left-handedness, learning disorders and disease. The study, done with Peter Behan, a neurologist at the University of Glasgow, is reported in *Cerebral Dominance,* edited by Dr. Geschwind and published by Harvard University Press.

Left-handers, the study showed, were two-and-a-half times more likely than right-handers to suffer from such auto-immune disorders as rheumatoid arthritis and ulcerative colitis, and 10 times more likely to have learning disabilities. They also reported migraine headaches twice as often and allergies 11 times more often than did right-handers.

Other investigators have recently confirmed the relationship between left-handedness, learning disabilities and immune diseases. Dr. Marcel Kinsbourne, director of the division of behavioral neurology at the Eunice Kennedy Shriver Research Center in Boston, studied more than 1,500 children and their families. Some of the children were enrolled in a school for the learning disabled and the rest were from regular schools.

"The left-handers had a much higher rate of learning problems than did the right-handers, as well as a higher rate of immune diseases," Dr. Kinsbourne said. "What's more, those right-handers with a near relative who was left-handed also had a high rate of immune disorders, which suggests a genetic factor is at play."

A specific genetic link between severe reading disabilities and immune disorders has been discovered by Bruce Pennington, a psychiatrist at the University of Colorado Medical School. Dr. Pennington studied genetic markers in nearly 100 members of eight families in which there was a three-generation history of reading disabilities.

"There was a very high rate of auto-immune diseases among these families," Dr. Pennington said in an interview. "We found that both dyslexia and the susceptibility to immune disorders were linked to chromosome 15."

"No one expected this finding; neurologists and immunologists both think this is the craziest result in the world," Dr. Pennington said. "Geschwind's is the only theory that explains how all this might hang together."

"Dr. Geschwind's theory is a very provocative, though tentative, suggestion," said Michael Gazzaniga, a neuropsychologist at Cornell Medical College. "It's very intelligent and worthwhile, and more people ought to do the research that is needed to test it."

One factor that may allow for greater variation among left-handers in how their brain is organized is that, compared to right-handers, they have a larger corpus callosum—the bundle of tissues that connects the right and left halves of the brain. According to a report last month in Science, the corpus callosum of left-handers is, on average, about 10 percent larger than that of right-handers, a difference estimated to represent as many as 25 million nerve fibers.

"The left-handers' large corpus calossum seems to allow for greter communication between the halves of the brain, and a more diffuse spread of the brain centers that control such mental functions as speaking, comprehending spoken language, and the perception of faces and of melodies," according to Sandra Witelson, a psychologist at McMaster University in Hamilton, Ontario, who did the research.

Dr. Witelson's discovery is the fruit of a unique research program in which cancer patients volunteer to undergo an exhaustive, 30-hour battery of neurological tests, and consent to a brain autopsy after they die in which more than 100 anatomical features are studied.

"Right-handers have a sharp division of labor between the hemispheres, with centers for linear mental activity on the left hemisphere, and those for spatial activity on the right," Dr. Witelson said in an interview. "In left-handers these brain centers are more spread across the hemispheres, with the greater size of their corpus callosum presumably allowing better communication."

This spread, clinical evidence has long suggested, gives many left-handers an advantage in recovering from certain kinds of brain damage, such as stroke.

"Left-handers can show little loss from brain damage when it is in a center that is spread across both hemispheres," said Dr. Witelson in an interview." A right-hander, on the other hand, is more likely to suffer destruction from the same damage to a given brain center, such as for speech, because the center is localized in only one hemisphere and is more easily knocked out."

Some investigators suspect that the corpus callosum, and its transfer of information from one hemisphere to the other, may play a key role in problems such as stuttering and dyslexia. Richard Davidson, a psychologist at the University of Wisconsin, reported in a recent issue of the journal *Brain and Language* that dyslexics show some signs of problems in the transference of information between the hemispheres.

Old Theories Misguided

The new findings are challenging widespread ideas about the brain's hemispheres. Researchers observe that the most often repeated ideas about the hemispheres are misguided.

"The popular cant that the right brain is better than the left" at seeing the big picture all at once is unfounded, according to Dr. Gazzaniga, a leading researcher in the field. "In fact, the left hemisphere is more responsive and more active than the right during most every mental activity," he said.

"The left hemisphere is also better at complicated spatial tasks, for which the right hemisphere was supposedly superior, Dr. Gazzaniga said.

One sharp distinction between the hemispheres that has held up is that in right-handers the left brain is dominant when it comes to taking in information that is sequential—such as language—or when timing is crucial, such as in the rhythm of music or Morse code. The right half is dominant in simple spatial tasks, such as recognizing faces, or in perceiving patterns, such as a musical melody or recognizing an object by touching it.

But most mental processes coordinate the hemispheres so that both are involved. For example, the idea that the left half of the brain is the seat of logical thought, while the right half governs intuitive perception, is seen as naïve by those who study the brain's hemispheres. Both halves of the brain, they say, are interwoven in mental activities as complex as logical thinking and intuition.

And while the right hemisphere has been touted as offering a much needed antidote to the problems supposedly created by the too logical left hemisphere, new data suggest that, in some ways, the left hemisphere is far more positive than the right. According to an article by Dr. Davidson in Psychophysiology, depressed people have a higher level of activation in the front portion of the right hemisphere than do people who are not depressed.

"The frontal region of the right hemisphere is the seat of negative emotions, such as disgust and sadness, while the left is where happiness is localized," Dr. Davidson said.

New Evidence Points to Growth of the Brain Even Late in Life

July 30, 1985

Evidence is building that development and growth of the brain go on into old age. It was once thought that the brain was fixed by late childhood, according to innate genetic design.

As long ago as 1911, however, Santiago Ramón y Cajal, a pioneering neurobiologist, proposed that "cerebral exercise" could benefit the brain. But a scientific consensus that the brain continues to bloom if properly stimulated by an enriched environment was long incoming.

"Over the last decade, neuroscientists have become impressed by the degree to which the structure and chemistry of the brain is affected by experience," said Floyd Bloom, director of the division of neuroscience and endocrinology at the Scripps Clinic and Research Foundation in La Jolla, Calif. The new research seeks to provide a more detailed understanding of that phenomenon.

Investigations at several different laboratories have shown that environmental influences begin while the brain is forming in the fetus and are particularly strong in infancy and early childhood. Among the most striking new evidence is a report published in a recent issue of Experimental Neurology showing that even in old age the cells of the cerebral cortex respond to an enriched environment by forging new connections to other cells. Marian Diamond, a professor of physiology and anatomy at the University of California at Berkeley, led the team of researchers who did the study.

In Dr. Diamond's study, rats 766 days old—the equivalent in human terms of roughly 75 years—were placed in an enriched environment and lived there until they reached the age of 904 days. For a rat, an impoverished environment is bare wire cage a foot square with a solitary occupant; an enriched one is a cage a yard square where 12 rats share a variety of toys, such as mazes, ladders and wheels.

The elderly rats, after living in the stimulating environment, showed increased thickening of the cortex. This thickening, other research has shown, is a sign that the brain cells have increased in dimension and activity, and that the glial cells that support the brain cells have multiplied accordingly.

The brain cells also showed a lengthening of the tips of their dendrites, the branches that receive messages from other cells. This increase in the surface of the dendrites allows for more communication with other cells.

Previous studies have shown that enriched environments changed brain cells in a number of ways, these among them. While the specific effects differ from one region of the brain to another, in general the enriched environment has been generally seen to regulate growth in the bodies of nerve cells, an increase in the amount of protein in these cells and an increase in the number or length of dendrites. In more fully developed dendritic spines, a part of the dendrite that receives chemical messages from other brain cells is induced to further growth.

Moreover, as in the new study, the thickness of the cortex was seen to increase, in part because of an increase in the numbers of glial cells needed to support the enlarged neurons. Dr. Diamond's studies on the older rats show that many, but not all, of these effects continue into old age.

These changes, in Dr. Diamond's view, mean that the cells have become more active, forming new connections to other brain cells. One sign of what the increased brain cell activity signifies for intellectual abilities is that the rats in the enriched environment became better at learning how to make their way through a maze. Indeed, Dr. Diamond and other researchers recently examined specimens from Einstein's brain. The tissue samples, from parts of the cortex presumed critical for mathematical skills, seemed to have usually large numbers of glial cells.

More Neural Flexibility

What does all this mean for the aging brain? "There is much more neural flexibility in old age than we had imagined," said Roger Walsh, a psychiatrist at the University of California Medical School at Irvine, who has done research similar to Dr. Diamond's. "The changes in brain cells have been found in every species investigated to date, including primates. They certainly should occur in humans as well."

"In my work," Dr. Walsh added, "I've found that an enriched environment in late life can largely compensate for brain cell deficiencies from earlier deprivations."

"We've been too negative in how we view the human brain," Dr. Diamond said in an interview. "Nerve cells can grow at any age in response to intellectual enrichment of all sorts: travel, crossword puzzles, anything that stimulates the brain with novelty and challenge."

Still, there seem to be limits to the degree to which the brain can respond to experience. Richard Lerner, in *On the Nature of Human Plasticity* (Cambridge University Press), notes, for example, that the impact of environmental enrichment on brain cells seems to diminish with age, although it continues into old age, an effect Dr. Diamond has noted in her research.

The effects of enriched environments on the brain are but part of a larger investigation of the impact of life's experiences on the brain, and the picture is not always positive.

"Brain plasticity can operate for better or for worse," said Jeannine Herron, a neuropsychologist at California Neuropsychology Services in San Rafael. Dr. Herron has organized a conference to be held later this month at which Dr. Diamond and other researchers will describe their findings.

Tests on Vision of Kittens

Perhaps the most frequently cited example of how experience—or the lack of it—can have a negative effect on the brain is the work of David Hubel. Dr. Hubel, who will also speak at the California conference, won a Nobel Prize for his research on the visual cortex.

As part of his research, Dr. Hubel showed that if the eye of a growing kitten is kept shut so that it is deprived of its normal experience, the cells that would ordinarily register what that eye sees will develop abnormally.

The notion that certain experiences go hand in hand with the growth and development of the brain has been demonstrated in other research, as well. For example, Arnold Scheibel, a professor of anatomy and psychiatry at the University of California at Los Angeles, has found that the cells in the speech centers of infants undergo a growth burst in which they form many new connections to other cells, just at the time the infant is beginning to respond to voices, be-

tween 6 and 12 months. Between 12 and 18 months, as the infant begins to grasp that words have meanings, this growth accelerates.

Part of this explosion of growth, Dr. Scheibel proposes, may be primed by the infant's interactions with adults, who stimulate the centers for speech by talking to the infant.

The main changes that occur during this growth in the cells of the speech centers are in the dendritic ensemble, the projecting branches of the cell that spread to send and receive messages from other cells. "The dendritic projections are like muscle tissue," Dr. Scheibel said. "They grow more the more they're used." "Even in adulthood," he added, "if you learn a new language, it's dendritic fireworks."

Responses to Injury

The brain's ability to adapt to circumstances can also be seen in its response to injury. Patricia Goldman-Rakic, a neuroanatomist at Yale University Medical School, is one of many researchers who have shown that brain cells, within limits, can rearrange themselves to compensate for a brain injury.

"The new connections that occur after an injury to the brain show that the brain's anatomy is not rigidly fixed," Dr. Goldman-Rakic said in an interview. "The uninjured cells reroute how they grow and interconnect. This ability is most prominent during infancy, when neurons are still growing. It doesn't go on forever, but we don't yet know precisely at what point in later life the brain no longer can compensate in this way. We need to more fully understand normal brain maturation first."

Norman Geschwind, a noted neuroanatomist at Harvard Medical School who died earlier this year, had been pursuing evidence suggesting that the experiences of a mother can have a lasting effect on the structure of the developing fetus's brain.

In a series of articles published posthumously in the most recent issues of *Archives of Neurology,* Dr. Geschwind, with Albert Galaburda, a colleague at Harvard Medical School proposes that the infant brain is shaped in crucial ways by the level of testosterone, a male sex hormone present in the intrauterine environment at different stages of fetal development.

At crucial points in the growth of the fetus, brain cells are formed and then migrate to the part of the brain ordained by a genetic plan. In certain parts of the brain these patterns of migration can be affected by the presence of sex hormones, particularly testosterone.

Testosterone levels in the fetus can vary with such factors as the amount of psychological stress the mother feels, maternal diet and possibly even the season of the year.

The main effects of testosterone according to Dr. Geschwind and Dr. Galaburda, are in the areas of the brain that control such skills as speech, spatial abilities and handedness. One of the key effects of testosterone is in determining the side of the brain on which the centers that control such skills will be located.

When the process goes awry, according to the theory, the result can be problems such as dyslexia, on the one hand, or unusual talents, such a mathematical giftedness, on the other.

These effects are more marked among males, in part because the brains of males develop more slowly than those of females, and in part because testosterone plays a direct role in the growth of certain areas of the male brain. The unusual patterns of brain formation are most common the theory holds, among left-handed males.

Before his death, Dr. Geschwind found from autopsies of people who had severe dyslexia in childhood that the parts of the cortex that control speech had abnormal cell development along the lines predicted by his theory.

Food and Brain: Psychiatrists Explore Use of Nutrients in Treating Disorders

March 1, 1988

Links between compounds in the food people eat and the levels of certain chemicals in their brains are leading some psychiatric researchers to suggest that nutritional supplements might be used as psychiatric drugs.

Carbohydrates like those in spaghetti, for instance, can increase the level of a brain chemical that can lift depression. And the amino acid tyrosine, a recent scientific report shows, can buffer the mental and physical effects of extreme stress.

The current issue of the journal *Integrative Psychiatry* is largely devoted to reports that consuming concentrated amounts of substances ordinarily found in food can affect depression, bulimia and mania, as well as less serious problems, like insomnia. Several of the findings, though still controversial, are already in use in the treatment of these and other psychiatric problems.

Although a few foods appear to directly affect moods and functioning—particularly carbohydrates when eaten without any protein—the psychiatrists that use this approach say most people would not benefit by changing their diets. Researchers are finding that these nutrients affect the brain when taken in a pure form and not mixed with others that appear in, say, chicken á la king.

The new approach comes from research that shows in great detail just how the foods we eat affect the brain, and how a given meal raises or lowers specific neurotransmitters, the chemicals that transmit signals between brain cells. "The ability of a meal's composition to affect the production of brain chemicals distinguishes the brain from all other organs," said Richard Wurtman, a psychiatrist at Massachusetts Institute of Technology, who has been the leader in the new research. "The crucial compounds that regulate other organs are largely independent of whatever was in the last meal we ate—but not the brain."

Within hours after a meal, the levels of certain neurotransmitters vary according to the levels of carbohydrates or proteins that were consumed. That fact, Dr. Wurtman proposed, provides the psychiatrist with a novel strategy: to use food, or substances concentrated from it, as they would drugs. The approach is widely seen as tentative, though promising. The studies are now largely at the exploratory stage, and many psychiatrists regard the approach as unproven.

Psychiatric researchers who are following Dr. Wurtman's lead are focusing on mental disorders thought to involve deficiencies in the specific brain chemicals most affected by foods. The nutrients that affect these brain chemicals are mainly among the amino acids found in all protein.

Researchers have discovered that a handful of amino acids have the unique property, once they are digested and enter the blood, of readily crossing the barrier between the brain and most compounds in the blood. Most of the research has focused on two of these amino acids, tryptophan and tyrosine.

Tryptophan affects the neurotransmitter serotonin, while tyrosine affects the catecholimines, dopamine, norepinephrine and epinephrine, also neurotransmitters. The work also focuses on choline, which acts on acetylcholine, another neurotransmitter. Choline is not an amino acid, but is found in the food substance lecithin.

The new approach is sometimes called "precursor therapy," because once these nutritional substances reach the brain they act as precursors, signaling the brain to make more of certain chemicals.

One of the most recent uses of nutrients focuses on tyrosine as an antidote to sudden, extreme stress. Tyrosine's effect in the brain is to increase dopamine and norepinephrine, two common brain chemicals.

Work by Dr. Wurtman had shown that immediately after a stress test, laboratory rats had depressed levels of norepinephrine. But when the rats were given tyrosine supplements before the stress, there was no decrease in norepinephrine.

Soldiers Under Stress

Inspired by the findings, researchers at the United States Army Research Institute of Environmental Medicine in Natick, Mass., led by Louis Banderet, a psychologist, tested the effects of tyrosine supplements on soldiers under physical conditions that became progressively harsher. The research was reported in the proceedings of a NATO conference on enhancing the performance of troops.

At the most extreme, the test conditions simulated being taken suddenly to an elevation of about 15,500 feet, and being exposed, in light clothing, to a temperature of 60 degrees, similar to being on a Colorado peak on a chilly spring day. While the temperature was not terribly uncomfortable, the sudden increase in elevation produces hypoxia, a drop in the oxygen available to the brain.

Tests showed that the soldiers who received tyrosine performed better at mental tasks that simulated, for instance, charting coordinates on a map, translating messages into a code and making complex decisions. The soldiers who took tyrosine also had a significant edge in alertness and quick response.

In addition the soldiers who had taken tyrosine were in better moods; they were less anxious or tense, and felt their thinking to be clearer than did the others. Moreover, they suffered less from the purely physical rigors of the test.

Consumed in Pure Form

The combination of physical ease and mental agility under stress produced by tyrosine, the researchers suggest, gives it a distinct advantage over both stimulant drugs, which typically make patients jumpy and tense, and tranquilizers, which usually reduce alertness.

One general advantage of nutrients like tyrosine over psychiatric drugs is their potential for significantly affecting brain activity with a minimum of undesirable side effects. Very often the nutrients have their effect on the brain in about the same dose as a person would consume in normal eating.

However, for these nutrients be most effective, they must typically be consumed in a pure form rather than as part of a normal meal.

This is because after one eats, choline and those amino acids in the food that can affect neurotransmitters must compete with each other for access to the limited biochemical channels that allow them to cross from the blood into the brain. For instance both the tyrosine and the choline in an egg vie for entry into the brain.

But if the amino acids or choline are consumed singly and in concentration, they enter the brain in concentrated doses, and so can have the potent, drug-like effects that psychiatrists are seeking to use.

The one exception is the amino acid tryptophan, which increases production in the brain of the neurotransmitter serotonin. Tryptophan is unique among amino acids in how it is affected by carbohydrates. Eating carbohydrates causes the body to secrete insulin, which in turn prompts amino acids in the blood to be taken up into muscle. Tryptophan, however, is unaffected by insulin; it remains in the blood and is free to cross into the brain with little or no competition.

Studies have shown that tryptophan is the most likely reason that a meal heavy in carbohydrates often makes people drowsy. Many of the brain structures rich in serotonin play a role in triggering the onset of sleep.

Research by Bonnie Spring, a psychologist at Texas Tech University in Lubbock, has shown that carbohydrates—a plate of pasta, for instance—tend to make women sleepy and men calmer.

Because of its sleep-inducing ef-

fects tryptophan has been used for several years as a way to help insomniacs fall asleep. The pure tryptophan works most effectively when it is taken with a high-carbohydrate snack—a piece of fruit, say, rather than a glass of hot milk, which has protein that would compete with the tryptophan.

Serotonin also influences mood and appetite, and some psychiatric uses of tryptophan under study focus on conditions in which the craving for carbohydrates is associated with depression. For instance, this combination is common among those who suffer from seasonal affective disorder, a pattern of depression that comes and goes with winter.

And victims of bulimia go on eating binges, typically of desserts like cake, after which they use purges to keep their weight down. Many bulimics are also depressed.

Dr. Wurtman believes that in each of these disorders the desire for carbohydrates is, as he puts it, "the brain's way of medicating itself," by increasing its levels of serotonin.

A treatment for depression has been based on the action of tryptophan. It uses doses of pure 5-HTP, the substance that tryptophan converts to in the brain. In several European countries, 5-HTP is used by psychiatrists as an antidepressant.

Clinical studies have shown that 5-HTP is effective for many depressed patients, especially when given in combination with certain antidepressant drugs, according to Herman van Praag, chairman of the department of psychiatry at Albert Einstein Medical School in New York City, and one of the early researchers on psychiatric applications of nutrients.

Subtle but Intriguing Differences Found in the Brain Anatomy of Men and Women

April 11, 1989

Researchers who study the brain have discovered that it differs anatomically in men and women in ways that may underlie differences in mental abilities.

The findings, although based on small-scale studies and still very preliminary, are potentially of great significance. If there are subtle differences in anatomical structure between men's and women's brains, it would help explain why women recover more quickly and more often from certain kinds of brain damage than do men, and perhaps help guide treatment.

The findings could also aid scientists in understanding why more boys than girls have problems like dyslexia, and why women on average have superior verbal abilities to men. Researchers have not yet found anything to explain the tendency of men to do better on tasks involving spatial relationships.

The new findings are emerging from the growing field of the neuropsychology of sex differences. Specialists in the discipline met at the New York Academy of Sciences last month to present their latest data.

Research on sex differences in the brain has been a controversial topic, almost taboo for a time. Some feminists fear that any differences in brain structure found might be used against women by those who would cite the difference to explain "deficiencies" that are actually due to social bias. And some researchers argue that differences in the brain are simply due to environmental influences, such as girls being discouraged from taking math seriously.

The new research is producing a complex picture of the brain in which differences in anatomical structure seem to lead to advantages in performance on certain mental tasks. The researchers emphasize, however, that it is not at all clear that education or experience do not override what differences in brain structure contribute to the normal variation in abilities. Moreover, they note that the brains of men and women are far more similar than different.

Still, in the most significant new findings, researchers are reporting that parts of the corpus callosum, the fibers that connect the left and right hemispheres of the brain, are larger in women than men. The finding is surprising because, over all, male brains—including the corpus callosum as a whole—are larger than those of females, presumably because men tend to be bigger on average than women.

Because the corpus callosum ties together so many parts of the brain, a difference there suggests far more widespread disparities between men and women in the anatomical structure of other parts of the brain.

"This anatomical difference is probably just the tip of the iceberg," said Sandra Witelson, a neuropsychologist at McMaster University Medical School in Hamilton, Ontario, who did the study. "It probably reflects differences in many parts of the brain which we have not yet even gotten a glimpse of. The anatomy of men's and women's brains may be far more different than we suspect."

The part of the brain which Dr. Witelson discovered is larger in women is in the isthmus, a narrow part of the callosum toward the back. Her findings, reported in March at the New York Academy of Sciences meeting, and published in the journal *Brain*.

Dr. Witelson's findings on the isthmus are based on studies of 50 brains, 15 male and 35 female. The brains examined were of patients who had been given routine neuropsychological tests before they died.

"Witelson's findings are potentially quite important, but it's not clear what they mean," said Bruce McEwen, a neuroscientist at Rockefeller University. "In the brain, bigger doesn't always mean better."

In 1982 a different area of the corpus callosum, the splenium, was reported by researchers to be larger in women than in men. But that study was based on only 14 brains, five of which were female. Since then, some researchers, including Dr. Witelson have failed to find the reported difference while others have.

Since such differences in brain structure can be subtle and vary greatly from person to person, it can take the close examination of hundreds of brains before neuroanatomists are convinced. But other neuroscientists say the findings are convincing enough to encourage them to do tests of their own.

Both the splenium and the isthmus are located toward the rear of the corpus callosum. This part of the corpus callosum ties together the cortical areas on each side of the brain that control some aspects of speech, such as the comprehension of spoken language, and the perception of spatial relationships.

"The isthmus connects the verbal and spatial centers on the right and left hemispheres, sending information both ways—it's a two-way highway," Dr. Witelson said. The larger isthmus in women is thought to be related to women's superiority on some tests of verbal intelligence. It is unclear what, if anything, the isthmus might have to do with the advantage of men on tests of spatial relations.

The small differences in abilities between the sexes have long puzzled researchers.

On examinations like the Scholastic Aptitude Test, which measures overall verbal and mathematical abilities, sex differences in scores have been declining. But for certain specific abilities, the sex differences are still notable, researchers say.

While these differences are still the subject of intense controversy, most researchers agree that women generally show advantages over men in certain verbal abilities. For instance, on average, girls begin to speak earlier than boys and women are more fluent with words than men, and make fewer mistakes in grammar and pronunciation.

On the other hand, men, on average, tend to be better than women on certain spatial tasks, such as drawing maps of places they have been and rotating imagined geometric images in their minds' eye—a skill useful in mathematics, engineering and architecture.

Of course, the advantages for each sex are only on average. There are individual men who do as well as the best women on verbal tests, and women who do as well as the best men on spatial tasks.

Measuring the Brain's Anatomy

One of the first studies that directly links the relatively larger parts of women's corpus callosums to superior verbal abilities was reported at the meeting of the New York Academy of Sciences by Melissa Hines, a neuropsychologist at the University of California at Los Angeles Medical School.

Dr. Hines and her associates used magnetic resonance imaging, a method that uses electrical fields generated by the brain, to measure the brain anatomy of 29 women. They found that the larger the splenium in the women, the better they were on tests of verbal fluency.

There was no relationship, however, between the size of their splenium and their scores on tests of spatial abilities, suggesting that differences in those abilities are related to anatomical structures in some other part of the brain or have nothing to do with anatomy.

"The size of the splenium," Dr. Hines said, "may provide an anatomical basis for increased communication between the hemispheres, and perhaps as a consequence, increased language abilities."

Researchers now speculate that the larger portions of the corpus callosum in women may allow for stronger connections between the parts of women's brains that are involved in speech than is true for men.

"Although we are not sure what a bigger overall isthmus means in terms of microscopic brain structure, it does suggest greater interhemispheric communication in women," Dr. Witelson said. "But if it does have something to do with the cognitive differences between the sexes, it will certainly turn out to be a complex story."

Part of that complexity has to do with explaining why, despite the bigger isthmus, women tend to do less well than men in spatial abilities, even though the isthmus connects the brain's spatial centers, too.

"Bigger isn't necessarily better, but it certainly means that it's different," Dr. Witelson said.

Other Differences Detected

A variety of other differences in the brain have been detected by the researchers in their recent studies.

For instance, Dr. Witelson found in her study that left-handed men had a bigger isthmus than did right-handed men. For women, though, there was no relationship between hand preference and isthmus size.

"How our brains do the same thing, namely use the right hand, may differ between the sexes," Dr. Witelson said.

She also found that the overall size of the callosum, particularly the front part, decreases in size between 40 and 70 years of age in men, but remains the same in women.

Several converging lines of evidence from other studies suggest that the brain centers for language are more centralized in men than in women.

One study involved cerebral blood flow, which was measured while men and women listened to words that earphones directed to one ear or the other. The research, conducted by Cecile Naylor, a neuropsychologist at Bowman Gray School of Medicine in Winston-Salem, N.C., showed that the speech centers in women's brains were connected to more areas both within and between each hemisphere.

Disdvantage in Stroke

This puts men at a relative disadvantage in recovering from certain kinds of brain damage, such as strokes, when they cause lesions in the speech centers on the left side of the brain. Women with similar lesions, by contrast, are better able to recover speech abilities, perhaps because stronger connections between the hemispheres allow them to compensate more readily for damage on the left side of the brain by relying on similar speech centers on the right.

In the current issue of *the Journal of Neuroscience*, Roger Gorski, a neuroscientist at U.C.L.A., reported finding that parts of the hypothalamus are significantly bigger in male rats than in female ones, even though the size of the overall brain is the same in both sexes.

And Dr. McEwen, working with colleagues at Rockefeller University, has found a sex difference in the structure of neurons in part of the hippocampus that relays messages from areas of the cortex.

Dr. McEwen, working with rats' brains, found that females have more branches on their dendrites, which receive chemical messages to other neurons, than do males. Males, on the other hand, have more spines on their dendrites, which also receive messages from other neurons. These differences in structure may mean differing patterns of electrical activity during brain function, he said.

"We were surprised to find any difference at all, and frankly, don't understand the implications for differences in brain function," Dr. McEwen said. "But we'd expect to find the same differences in humans; across the board, findings in rodents have had corollaries in the human brain."

Brain's Design Emerges as a Key to Emotions

August 15, 1989

The power of emotions to override even the most rational decisions may be explained by a new discovery about the brain, researchers say. The data suggest that the brain is arranged so key aspects of emotional life, like primitive fears, can operate largely independent of thought.

This arrangement may explain why certain emotional reactions, like phobias, are so tenacious despite their obvious irrationality. It may also explain other baffling facts of emotional life, such as why troubling experiences from life's earliest years can have such powerful effects decades later.

"This may explain why we have so little reflective insight into our emotional life," said Dr. Joseph LeDoux, a psychologist at the Center for Neural Science at New York University. Dr. LeDoux did many of the key studies that underlie the new view of emotion and the brain while at the Laboratory of Neurobiology at Cornell Medical Center in Manhattan.

"Dr. LeDoux has made a major discovery about the emotional side of learning, one with major implications for learned pathologies like neuroses and phobias," said Dr. Norman Weinberger, a neuroscientist at the Center for the Neurobiology of Learning and Memory at the University of California at Irvine.

The network is, so far, known largely among specialists in cognitive neurobiology, a field that specializes in tracing connections between the brain and psychological life. While further studies will be needed to verify the findings of Dr. LeDoux and their significance, other researchers have already begun to use his results in their own work. Dr. Weinberger, for instance, is applying the findings in his studies of memory problems in Alzheimer's disease.

Dr. LeDoux's research, which was done entirely on rats, included such standard techniques as cutting specific nerve pathways in the brain to see how it changed the rats' behavior.

"The architecture of the mammalian brain is basically the same in all species, but you can't do these kinds of studies on a human brain," Dr. LeDoux explained.

The new evidence suggests that certain emotional reactions occur before the brain has even had time to fully register what it is that is causing the reaction; the emotion occurs before thought. That view is a direct challenge to the prevailing wisdom in psychology, that emotional reactions follow from thoughts about a situation.

The data also call into question a longstanding view about just which brain structures link together to form the "limbic system," which regulates emotional life. The hippocampus, which has long been considered part of the limbic system, may be more involved with registering cognitive information than emotions, according to findings of other researchers reviewed by Dr. LeDoux in an article in the journal *Cognition and Emotion* this year.

His own data put another part of the limbic system, the amygdala, at the center of the primitive emotional reactions that seem to operate independent of, and prior to, thought.

Scientists had assumed that the amygdala, part of the brain that registers emotion, depended on signals from the neocortex, the thinking part of the brain, to form an emotional reaction. The work of Dr. LeDoux suggests that in many cases the amygdala triggers an emotional reaction before the thinking brain has fully processed nerve signals.

"To simplify greatly, the hippocampus seems to be the focal point for cognition and the amygdala for emotion," Dr. LeDoux said. "The hippocampus, for instance, is involved in recognizing a face and its significance, such as that it's your cousin. The amygdala adds that you really don't like him. It offers emotional reactions from memory, independent of your thoughts as the moment about something."

"Emotional reactions and emotional memories can be formed without any conscious, cognitive participation at all, because anatomically the emotional system can act independently," Dr. LeDoux said.

While other researchers had recorded activity in the thalamus or the amygdala during the moments when fear is learned, it was Dr. LeDoux who discovered the direct connection that links them during the process.

"Dr. LeDoux's research is the first to work out neural pathways for emotional response that don't go through the cortex," said Dr. Michael Gazzaniga, a psychiatry professor at Dartmouth Medical School. "It may explain why so much of emotional life is hard to understand with the rational mind."

Dr. Weinberger said, "It's the missing piece of the puzzle, showing that fear can be learned without the cortex being involved. It brings to amygdala to the forefront in studying emotions."

The prevailing view among neuroscientists is that the eyes, ears and other sensory organs transmit signals to the thalamus, and from there to sensory processing areas of the neocortex, where the signals are put together into objects as people perceive them.

The signals are sorted for meanings so that the brain recognizes what an object is and what its presence means. From the neocortex, the signals are sent to the amygdala. Thus emotional reactions usually follow from cognitive understanding.

But Dr. LeDoux has discovered nerve pathways that lead directly from the thalamus to the amygdala, in addition to those going through the cortex. That means that the amygdala can also receive direct inputs from the senses before they are fully registered by the rest of the brain.

Thus emotions can be triggered before the brain has had time to fully register just what it is that is being responded to. This is most pronounced in an emergency, when an instant response is required.

"The amygdala is just one synapse away from the thalamus, while the hippocampus is several additional "synapses away," Dr. LeDoux said. That means a difference of as much as 40 milliseconds, about a twenty-fifth of a second, in the time it takes a sensory signal to reach the amygdala as compared with the hippocampus," Dr. LeDoux said.

That time gap allows the amygdala to respond to an alarming situation before the hippocampus does. For instance, if in the corner of your eye you see what looks like a snake, it is the amygdala that sends the signal of alarm that makes you jump. You react even before the hippocampus has had time to figure out if it was actually a snake or a piece of rope.

This arrangement has had great survival value in evolution, Dr. Le-Doux believes. He observes that in more primitive species, like birds, fish and reptiles, the connections between the thalamus and the amygdala play a major role in mental life.

"This primitive, minor brain system in mammals is the main system in nonmammals," Dr. LeDoux said. "It offers a very rapid way to turn on emotions. Those extra milliseconds may be lifesaving, which is a powerful advantage in evolution. But it's a quick and dirty process; the cells are fast, but not very precise."

The amygdala triggers what Dr. LeDoux calls "pre-cognitive emotion," feelings independent of thought.

"Pre-cognitive emotion is based on neural bits and pieces of sensory information, which have not yet been sorted out and integrated into a recognizable object," he said. "It's a very raw form of sensory information like recognizing the notes without noticing the melody."

Dr. LeDoux believes these precognitive emotions may be at work in many areas of human mental life. For instance, they may explain the nature of the emotional life of infants, and the lifelong persistence of emotional patterns formed in infancy.

"A tremendous amount of learning takes place during the first two years of life, yet we have little if any conscious recall from those years," Dr. LeDoux said. The reason it is so hard to remember experiences from those years, he believes, is because the hippocampus is not fully mature at birth, while the amygdala is more fully formed during the first years of life.

That may also explain why the emotional experiences of life's earliest years, which psychoanalysts have long pointed to as key to later emotional life, are both so potent and so difficult to understand rationally.

As psychotherapists have long known, emotional memories—like deep fears or resentments—are particularly persistent and hard to counter. Dr. LeDoux is soon to publish research showing that these robust emotional habits are formed and stored in the amygdala.

In an article this month in *The Journal of Cognitive Neuroscience,* Dr. LeDoux reports a study with laboratory rats that were taught to fear a flashing light by having it paired with a shock. Ordinarily, once the fear is learned, it can be gradually extinguished by regular displays of the lights without the shock; this process typically takes several weeks.

When some of the rats had their visual cortexes removed, they still learned to fear the lights—evidence that it is the connection to the amygdala that is crucial in forming such fears. When those same rats were shown the lights without the shock for several weeks, they retained fearfulness, unlike rats whose brains had the cortex intact.

"This may explain how phobias are formed in humans, and why they can be so tenacious," Dr. LeDoux said.

"In people who have gotten over a phobia, a single scary experience can sometimes suddenly bring it back in full force," he said. "That means the phobia had not been lost to emotional memory, even though the behavior had been extinguished."

The implications of Dr. LeDoux's work for psychotherapy are in offering a neuroanatomical explanation for phenomenon long observed.

"Once your emotional system learns something, it seems you never let it go," Dr. LeDoux said. "What therapy does is teach you to control it. It teaches your cortex how to inhibit your amygdala. The propensity to act is suppressed, while your basic emotions about it may remain in a subdued form."

The psychoanalytic view that the unconscious mind has profound influence in mental life also finds support in Dr. LeDoux's work. "While some emotional memories may reach consciousness, there are many emotional memories that lead to actions, but which we do not consciously remember," Dr. LeDoux said.

He cited a study showing that people formed preferences for geometric shapes flashed so quickly that they were not aware of having seen them. His own work suggests that the amygdala may be involved in such preferences.

States of Consciousness

Just as our bodies are ready to sleep every night, they are also primed to take a mid-afternoon nap, sleep researchers are concluding. The natural nap time comes between two peaks in alertness, one in the morning, one in early evening. "You Never Outgrow Your Need for Naps" tells how sleep researchers have used a variety of techniques to determine that the body's biological rhythms are geared to an afternoon nap.

What do dreams mean? Since Freud, people have been interpreting their dreams in terms of the psychological issues in their lives. But, as is pointed out in "Do Dreams Really Contain Important Secret Meaning?" the interpretation depends largely on a person's theoretical bias. And some sleep researchers believe that the contents of dreams are essentially random, with no specific meaning.

How well can you concentrate? If you focus with full absorption on something you are doing, you may enter "flow," a euphoric and naturally occurring altered state of consciousness. The key to entering flow is to pay full attention to what you are do-ing. The research covered in "Concentration Is Likened To Euphoric States of Mind" suggest that the flow experience may come more easily to those who are readily hypnotized and that it puts the brain in a state where efforts come with a minimum of exertion.

Hypnosis is the center of controversy among researchers. Some say that there is no such thing as a hypnotic state—that the "state" is due to influences such as suggestion and the willingness of the hypnotic subject to comply. Defenders say that there is experimental evidence that hypnosis is more than that. "Hypnosis Still Provokes Some Skeptics" details the arguments on both sides.

Perhaps one of the more convincing pieces of evidence for the power of hypnosis is the research reviewed in "Hypnosis Can Suppress Brain's Perception of Pain." In this study, people who are easily hypnotized showed a unique brain response under hypnosis. Brain measures suggest that their response to pain was genuinely blocked under hypnosis, rather than that they were pretending not to feel pain.

You Never Outgrow Your Need for Naps

September 12, 1989

The human body was meant to have a mid-afternoon nap, according to a new consensus among sleep researchers who are studying the biological rhythms of sleep and alertness.

The judicious use of naps, sleep researchers now say, could be the key to maintaining alertness in people such as truckdrivers and hospital interns, where the urgent need for alertness does battle with a building drowsiness.

And apart from such extreme situations, studies are finding that, understandably, an afternoon nap can significantly increase mental alertness and improve mood, particularly in the large number of people who sleep too little at night.

The focus on naps among sleep researchers came almost accidentally, as they have sought to track the cycles of sleepiness and wakefulness throughout the 24 hours of the day.

To the surprise of researchers, over the last decade a wide range of studies, using methods ranging from brain wave recordings to sleep diaries, converged on the same conclusion: there is a strong biological readiness to fall asleep during the mid-afternoon, even in people who have had a full night's sleep.

"It seems nature definitely intended that adults should nap in the middle of the day, perhaps to get out of the midday sun," according to William Dement, director of the Sleep Disorders Clinic and Research Center at Stanford University.

Dr. Dement made his observation in a preface to *Sleep and Alertness: Chronobiological, Behavioral, and Medical Aspects of Napping,* the first collection of scientific studies of napping, published last month by Raven Press.

Until recently, naps were largely ignored by researchers, who routinely instructed the volunteers they observed in sleep laboratories to avoid taking naps during the day. The strongest evidence that the body has an inherent need was not published until 1986.

The studies were done by Scott Campbell, now at the Institute for Circadian Physiology in Boston, with other sleep researchers at the Max Planck Institute in Munich.

In that study the researchers put volunteers in a "time-free" situation—an underground room isolated from all clocks and evidence of day and night—for weeks at a time. Unlike most previous sleep studies, the volunteers were told they could sleep wherever they wanted.

When left to their own natural sleep rhythms, all took naps. The volunteers tended to sleep in two periods, one a long session at night, the other a shorter period of one or two hours in the afternoon.

Because the body's circadian rhythms tend to move people in a time-free environment to a 25-hour day, the actual timing of the naps changed as the days went on. But on average the naps began about 12 hours after the middle of the main period of sleep.

That timing holds, too, for normal afternoon naps, according to researchers. Thus someone who slept from midnight to six A.M. would be most highly primed for a nap at around three in the afternoon.

"Their study gave us the first conclusive evidence that the afternoon nap is internally generated by the brain as part of the biological clock for sleep/wake cycles," said Dr. Roger Broughton, a professor of neurology at the University of Ottawa.

It was in 1975 that Dr. Broughton first proposed the then-radical notion to sleep researchers that naps are a natural part of the sleep cycle. He speculated that the body's built in sleep rhythm included, in addition to a major period at night, a smaller period of sleep in the afternoon.

Dr. Broughton's proposal opposed the conventional wisdom in the field, which saw naps as either a sign of laziness or a social artifact, irrelevant to the scientific study of sleep. But as scientists began to review their data for what it said about naps, the evidence mounted. The Sleep Research Society held its first scientific session on naps in 1981.

Apart from the "time-free" study, Dr. Broughton cites several other lines of evidence pointing to the importance of naps. One is that babies, who begin by napping frequently through the day, usually have developed the habit of a single afternoon nap just before they give it up entirely at school age.

Another is that in cultures where there is the custom of a siesta, its timing is always in the midafternoon. In addition, studies of people in America who often take naps show that its timing is most often during that same midafternoon period.

Other evidence Dr. Broughton cites is that there is a well-documented drop in people's performance at work in midafternoon, along with a simultaneous increase in accidents due to sleepiness. That natural rise in sleepiness in midafternoon, he believes, is at play in the fact that the midafternoon period is also when the highest number of deaths occur.

In more recent research, reported in the newly published collection, Peretz Lavie, a sleep researcher at the Technion-Israel Institute of Technology in Haifa, found another kind of evidence for the need to nap. In Dr. Lavie's studies, volunteers are kept on a 20-minute sleep/wake cycle, where they sleep for 7 minutes and stay awake for 13 minutes, for several days at a time. This allows Dr. Lavie to determine how quickly, if at all, they can fall asleep at different times throughout the day.

Dr. Lavie found that, in addition to the regular nighttime propensity to go right to sleep, there is a midafternoon peak in people's readiness. That heightened sleepiness falls between morning and early evening peaks in alertness, during which time it is much harder to go to sleep, even in someone who has been deprived of sleep the night before.

In the late morning and early evening, in fact, the volunteers tended to have trouble falling asleep. But when their usual bedtime or midafternoon approached, they readily fell asleep when given the chance, sometimes within a minute.

The morning and evening peaks in alertness, according to Dr. Dinges, are periods when mental performance is naturally enhanced, while the midafternoon drop in alertness sees a decline in intellectual functioning, along with increased drowsiness.

Though many people believe that midafternoon drowsiness is caused by eating a heavy lunch, research shows that to be largely a myth. The middafternoon dip in alertness occurs whether or not people eat lunch, according to Dr. Broughton, and depends purely on the time of day rather than on eating.

To be sure, naps are easily skipped. Because the urge for an afternoon nap is appreciably weaker than the need to sleep at night, naps can be suppressed when they are inconvenient, though the cost is increased drowsiness, Dr. Broughton said.

Indeed, while the afternoon siesta has been common in many cultures around the world—particularly those in tropical climates—it seems to be waning around the globe, a victim of industrialization. In a review of surveys of sleep habits in countries around the world, Wilse Webb, a psychologist at the University of Florida, and David Dinges, a sleep researcher at the University of Pennsylvania, found that as countries became industrialized, the government outlawed siestas.

Still, other studies show the nap to be alive and well in America. According to Dr. Webb, surveys involving more than 10,000 people found that the average number of naps taken by Americans of all ages is one or two a week. About a quarter of people never nap, while a third nap four or more times a week.

Napping, understandably, is most common in groups like college students and retired people, who have more opportunity in their daily schedules than working people.

Most afternoon naps are between a half hour and an hour-and-a-half, the studies found. Despite legendary catnappers like Thomas Edison and Winston Churchill, naps under 15 minutes are uncommon.

One reason, according to Dr. Dinges, may be that naps of just a few minutes reach only the first stage of sleep, in which dreamlike images appear. Such light sleep, unlike deeper stages of sleep, may do little to enhance mental alertness after the napper awakens, Dr. Dinges said.

Such short naps have been studied far less than naps of ordinary length, which have salutary effects. "If you didn't get enough sleep the night before, an afternoon nap will improve your alertness and give you a feeling of more energy, so you can take on more tasks," Dr. Dinges said. "After napping, people not only feel better, but do significantly better on tests of mental performance."

Among the mental abilities sharpened by naps are the capacity to pay sustained attention to a task and to make complicated decisions. These improvements are greatest in people who have gotten too little sleep the previous night. For those who have slept enough the main benefit from naps is an improvement in mood rather than intellectual ability, Dr. Dinges said.

During naps, most sleep is in the deepest stages, characterized by slow, regular brain waves, according to Dr. Dinges. Relatively little of a nap is spent in the phase of sleep during which most dreaming occurs.

Because the sleep in an afternoon nap is so deep, people who are awakened abruptly sometimes experience "sleep inertia," an intense grogginess and confusion which, at its most severe, produces extreme disorientation.

"It normally doesn't matter, unless you're in an emergency mode like a firefighter or fighter pilot, and have to begin performing immediately," said Dr. Dinges. "It's best to awaken from a nap gradually, and give yourself a few minutes before engaging in anything very important."

The longer someone has gone without sleep, the stronger the brain's need to fall asleep suddenly, and the greater the inertia and confusion on arising, Dr. Dinges added.

For that reason he recomends that people whose jobs demand they stay awake for a day or more at a time—such as medical interns—take a nap both at night and during the afternoon, during which their duties are covered by someone else. That way there is minimal danger that they will make a mistake because of sleepiness or sleep inertia.

"Cutting back the hours of medical interns from 100 to 80 hours a week is not going to help much if they have to stay awake for a day or more at a stretch," said Dr. Dinges. "It would make more sense to give them regular naps, instead."

Do Dreams Really Contain Important Secret Meaning?

July 10, 1984

Ever since Freud first proposed that dreams were the "royal road to the unconscious," it has been standard clinical practice to assume that dreams bear meaningful psychological messages, though often in bizarre disguise.

In recent years some researchers and neuroscientists, using new, sophisticated techniques for measuring brain activity during sleep, have attacked that understanding. They assert that dreams are essentially mental nonsense that have no psychological significance whatsoever. Their conclusions have provoked widespread argument in the field because they suggest that all therapeutic uses of dreams may be much less valid than had been thought. But already there are some signs of compromise.

Wherever the argument may ultimately lead, the new data and theories even now are prompting some clinicians to modify their understanding of the role of dreams in mental life.

In general, researchers divide sleep into two principal phases: rapid eye movement, or REM sleep, and non-REM sleep. Dreams are associated with REM sleep.

The body and brain are in a unique state during REM sleep. The eyes move back and forth under the closed lids, hence the name. Brain waves are in many ways similar to those during the waking state. At the same time, the major muscles of the body are in a kind of paralysis, so that they move little, if at all.

In sleep research, volunteers are monitored for eye movements, brain waves and other biological functions during the night. To investigate dreaming, the volunteers are awak-

ened when these indicators signal REM sleep. About 80 percent of the time a sleeper awakened from REM will report being in the middle of a dream. In the remaining cases, for the most part, the wakened subject will report some other mental activity, such as vague thoughts, but with no visual image or sense of a dream.

The classic Freudian view of dreams held that dreams are upsetting impulses that the mind has disguised.

"The psychological work done in dreams is to disguise these impulses so they won't be disturbing, and to keep the sleeper from waking," Dr. Morton Reiser, chairman of the Department of Psychiatry at Yale University and a former president of the American Psychoanalytic Association, explained in an interview. "In a nightmare, the disguise is inadequate; the disturbing material breaks through and the person wakes up."

"Dreams are useful in therapy," he added, "because they harbor clues to the psychological issues and earlier conflicts in a person's life."

Although Dr. Reiser takes a psychoanalytic view toward dreams, he is one of those who is able to reconcile it with the new brain research.

Within the school that places great value on dreams, there are many approaches to finding the psychological message of a dream, each reflecting different theoretical outlooks. A Freudian will find one kind of meaning in a dream, while a Jungian will find another, and a Gestalt therapist will find still another meaning. But all would agree that there is meaning to be found, even if they may disagree as to exactly what that meaning might be. And many say each

and every element of a dream—a given image or sensation, say—has significance.

But the view that dreams have psychological meaning at all has come under strong attack from neuroscientists.

Strong Attack on Theory

One of the strongest attacks comes from a theory published last year in the journal *Nature* by Francis Crick of the Salk Institute in La Jolla, Calif., and Graeme Mitchison of Cambridge University. Dr. Crick, who won a Nobel Prize as the co-discoverer of DNA, has turned his attention to brain research.

Dr. Crick and Dr. Mitchison propose that REM sleep is the occasion for the brain to eliminate mental activity that might interfere with rational thought and memory. Their view holds that during a day the brain makes many more connections between brain cells than are needed for efficient thinking and memory.

The function of dreams, they say, is to "unlearn" or purge the brain of these unneeded connections. According to this view, what goes through the mind during a dream is merely the result of a sort of neural house-cleaning.

This theory, they say, explains some facts about dreams that the opposing view cannot. For example, newborn infants have a great deal of REM sleep, but presumably suffer none of the psychological conflicts or upsetting impulses that Freudian theory says leads to dreams. But, Dr. Crick and Dr. Mitchison say, infants have the same need as adults to rid the brain of accidental or meaningless connections, and thus they have dreams.

The implications of the Crick-Mitchison theory goes beyond dream meaning. They say it also suggests that it may be damaging to recall one's dreams because doing so might strengthen neural connections that should be discarded. Most dreams, Dr. Crick and Dr. Mitchison note, are never remembered. In their view, this is as it should be. "We dream in order to forget," they write.

A different view with similar implications has been offered by Christopher Evans in his book *Landscapes of the Night: How and Why We Dream,* published posthumously by Viking this month. His theory also implies that dreams do not have the psychological meanings that therapists find in them, but Dr. Evans comes to his conclusion on a different basis than that of Dr. Crick and Dr. Mitchison.

Dr. Evans, a psychologist and computer scientist, proposes that dreams are the brain's equivalent of a computer's inspection of its programs, allowing a chance to integrate the experiences of the day with the memories already stored in the brain. His theory is based in part on evidence that dreaming consolidates learning and memory.

The contents of a dream, according to Dr. Evans, are fragments of events and experiences during the day which are being patched into related previous memories. "Dreaming," he writes, "might be our biological equivalent to the computer's process of program inspection."

Such conclusions have been challenged by the work of two researchers at Harvard Medical School, Robert McCarley and J. Allan Hobson. Studies of the brain, they say, show that there is a "dream state generator" that repeatedly stimulates the cortex during REM sleep. This "generator," located in the brainstem—specifically in the so-called giant pontine cells of the reticular formation—sends random signals to higher brain centers that control such functions as vision, hearing, balance, movement and emotions, the researchers say.

The contents of a dream, the theory holds, are the product of this random activity, which the higher brain centers try to weave into a coherent story, just as is done with experiences—during waking life.

Dr. McCarley and Dr. Hobson see their theory as contradicting the Freudian view that dreams are psychological in origin, being caused by unfulfilled impulses arising from psychological conflicts. The bizarreness of dreams, they say, is not a disguise for such conflicts, but simply reflects the random nature of brain activity caused by the dream generator.

"Dreams are like a Rorschach inkblot," Dr. Hobson said in an interview. "They are ambiguous stimuli which can be interpreted in any way a therapist is predisposed to. But their meaning is in the eye of the beholder—not in the dream itself." That idea, it can be argued, is borne out by clinical examples collected by others that show how different therapists interpret the same dream differently.

Dr. Hobson has engaged in a series of public debates with psychoanalysts in which he challenged the view that dreams have psychological meaning.

Dr. Reiser of Yale is one of those who has debated Dr. Hobson. "McCarley and Hobson overextend the implications of their work when they say it shows that dreams have no meaning," he said. "I agree with them that their work refutes Freud's idea that a dream is instigated by a disguised wish. Knowing what we do now of brain physiology, we can no longer say that."

"The wish may not cause the dream," he added, "but that does not mean that dreams do not disguise wishes. The brain activity which causes dreams offers a means whereby a conflicted wish can give rise to a particular dream. In other words, wishes exploit—but do not cause—dreams."

Dr. Reiser's view stems from a growing body of evidence that seems to show that dreams serve a major role in psychological life.

Typical of this line of research is the work of Rosalind Cartwright, a psychologist at Rush-Presbyterian-St. Lukes Medical Center in Chicago. In an article to appear next month in the journal *Psychiatry,* Dr. Cartwright presents findings suggesting that dreams are connected with adjustment to major life crises, in this case divorce.

Dreams of Women Explored

Dr. Cartwright compared the dreams of women who were recently divorced and also depressed with two other groups, one made up of women who had just been divorced but showed no signs of depression, and the other consisting of married women who said they were not contemplating divorce.

She found that the depressed women had an unusual pattern of REM sleep, including an earlier onset, longer duration and more intensely visual first REM period of the night, "as if these patients can't wait to dream."

Of more significance psychologically, though, is what the different groups of women dreamed about. The depressed women, in Dr. Cartwright's view, rarely dealt with marital issues in their dreams. And while those divorced women who were not depressed frequently dreamed of themselves in the role of wife or former wife, the depressed women almost never appeared in those roles in any of their dreams.

The divorced women who were not depressed had the most anxious dreams of all, with the level of anxiety in their dreams increasing as the night progressed. The identical pattern has been found in a group of patients judged successfully treated in psychotherapy.

The depressed women, who had less overall anxiety in their dreams, with anxiety decreasing over the course of the night, duplicated the pattern of psychotherapy patients who failed to improve.

These results, in Dr. Cartwright's view, support the view that dreams are "safety valves," allowing the dreamer to deal with upsetting psychological issues.

A blend of the seemingly opposing views that, on one hand, dreams are composed of random elements, and that, on the other, they hold psychological meaning, has recently been proposed by Martin Seligman, a psychologist at the University of Pennsylvania.

Building on the work of Dr. McCarley and Dr. Hobson, Dr. Seligman accepts that the stuff of dreams consists largely of random visual hallucinations and unrelated feelings activated by the brain's dream generator. But, Dr. Seligman says, these random elements are woven into a meaningful fabric by cognitive activity that goes on continuously, day and night.

Indeed, sleep researchers have found that when people are awakened during non-REM sleep, they still report having thoughts, but not dreams.

According to Dr. Seligman, this stream of thought operates much the same during the night as it does during the day. "In my research, subjects who were asked to tell a story about random slides constructed plots similar in form to their dreams. For example, people whose dreams were tightly knit constructed tightly knit stories about the slides," Dr. Seligman said in an interview.

Dr. Seligman's theory holds room for both camps. The raw stuff of dreams may be random, but "subconscious motivation may influence the way we integrate the elements of a dream," he said.

Many clinicians, familiar with the debate over dreams, agreed in general with Dr. Seligman's proposal, al-though they differed over particulars. "There are vastly more elements—images, ideas, actions and the like—in a dream than we can deal with in analysis," said Dr. Reiser. "The way the dreamer connects those elements gives them their meaning. That's how the mind exploits the brain in a dream."

"But there is lots of 'noise' in a dream," he added. "When you find the signal—that is, the significance—in the dream, it leads you to issues in the person's life. Those parts of the dream we can't make sense of may be the random noise. Often what seems most obscure on the surface is what finally reveals a deeper meaning."

"The therapists's art is finding that signal in the noise," he said.

Concentration Is Likened To Euphoric States of Mind

March 4, 1986

The seemingly simple act of being fully absorbed in a challenging task is now being seen as akin to some of the extravagantly euphoric states such as those sought in drugs or sex or through the "runner's high."

New research is leading to the conclusion that these instances of absorption are, in effect, altered states in which the mind functions at its peak, time is often distorted and a sense of happiness seems to pervade the moment.

Such states, the new research suggests, are accompanied by mental efficiency experienced as a feeling of effortlessness.

One team of researchers describes these moments of absorption as "flow states."

According to Mike Csikszentmihalyi, a psychologist at the University of Chicago, "flow" refers to "those times when things seem to go just right, when you feel alive and fully attentive to what you are doing."

The understanding that deep absorption can be transporting will not come as news to those who readily sink into rapture at a symphony or while reading poetry, but the new research adds precision in defining the circumstances that evoke such heightened awareness.

The Chicago research on flow, which has been under way for more than a decade, began with a study of people performing at their peak. Basketball players, composers, dancers, chess masters, rock climbers, surgeons and others were asked to describe in detail times when they had outdone themselves. One of the elements that was invariably present in these descriptions was full absorption in the activity at hand, an attention that was finely attuned to the shifting demands of the moment.

Along with a full absorption, people in flow described a set of experiences that, taken together, suggest an altered state of consciousness. These include a distortion in the sense of time, so that events seem either to go very quickly or very slowly; an altered sense of one's bodily sensations or sensory perceptions, and a fine precision in gauging one's responses to a changing challenge.

With a group of colleagues at Chicago, and another group at the University of Milan Medical School, Dr. Csikszentmihalyi most recently has been studying the circumstances that draw people into the flow state. In one study, 82 volunteers carried beepers that would remind them, at random times throughout the day, to record what they were doing, how concentrated on it they were and how they felt. The volunteers ranged from assembly-line workers and clerks to engineers and managers.

"People seem to concentrate best when the demands on them are a bit greater than usual, and they are able to give more than usual," Dr. Csikszentmihalyi said. "If there is too little demand on them, people are bored. If there is too much for them to handle, they get anxious. Flow occurs in that delicate zone between boredom and anxiety."

No Easy Formula

There is no easy formula for getting into the flow state, but some circumstances make its occurrence more likely, according to the research. If a situation is boring, for example, somehow making it more challenging may lead to flow. One assembly-line worker in the Chicago research, for example, had a job in which he simply tightened a set of screws all day long. But after several years he was still experimenting with ways to shave a few seconds from his time, a challenge that kept him engrossed.

On the other hand, if things are overwhelming, sometimes simplifying a complex job into manageable pieces can bring that alignment of skill and challenge that evokes a flowing concentration. And simply making the effort to pay attention, even if a struggle at first, can on occasion give way to flow.

"Most jobs have a ceiling built in—you can learn them in a few days," said Dr. Csikszentmihalyi. "Your skills for them increase rapidly, but the challenge doesn't change, so you get bored. Many people are bored much of the time, and their attention is totally scattered. When their concentration drops, so does their motivation and confidence."

"The fine focus during flow cuts out all irrelevant thoughts and sensations," Dr. Csikszentmihalyi said. "There is a mental recruitment where everything aligns in an effortless concentration, sort of a mental overdrive."

In that way, this level of concentration resembles meditation in which the desired result is often a feeling of envigoration and relaxed alertness. The essence of medition is simply to focus attention.

2 Kinds of Attention

The "flow" state studied by the Chicago researchers needs to be distinguished from the strained concentration that is brought to bear when, for example, a person has little interest in the task at hand and must force attention. These two kinds of attention—effortless and strained—have been found to have distinctly different underlying patterns of brain function, according to findings by researchers at the National Institute of Mental Health.

The research on attention and brain activity has, in the past, revealed seemingly contradictory findings, some studies finding that full concentration increased cortical arousal, and others finding a decrease. Dr. Hamilton's research showed that the effortless concentration typical of flow brought about a lowered cortical arousal. When more effort was put into concentration, on the other hand, it seemed to increase cortical arousal.

"There seems to be a difference between effortful and effortless attention," said Jean Hamilton, a psychiatrist in Washington, who did the research with Monte Buchsbaum, a psychiatrist now at the University of California Medical School at Irvine.

The studies show that the strained concentration involves greater activity by the brain, almost as if it is in the wrong gear for the work demanded.

The scientists are finding a number of individual differences among people in their abilities to become absorbed and to make the most of it when they do.

"The ability to become completely immersed is necessary for productivity, but not sufficient," said Auke Tellegen, a psychologist at the University of Minnesota. "You also need the capacity for mental constraint, so you don't just get swept away by impulse. Many people who are prone to

absorption don't have the mental discipline that allows them to be productive."

Similarity to Hypnosis

One of the most suggestive pieces of evidence linking deep concentration to other kinds of altered states is its similarity to hypnosis.

Dr. Tellegen and others have done research showing that people who easily become absorbed in, say, fantasy or a painting, are more readily hypnotized than are those more impervious to such pleasures. And research reported in *The Journal of Personality and Social Psychology* shows that people who are given to rapt absorption are also susceptible to altered states of consciousness.

"There is a group of people who readily get so absorbed in things that they become lost in them, or in their thoughts or fantasies, for that matter," said Ronald Pekala, a psychologist at Center and Jefferson Medical College in Pennsylvania, who did the research on altered awareness with another psychologist, Krishna Kumar. "It is these same mental processes that seem to get intensified during hypnosis."

The people who are easily hypnotized, although they may become readily absorbed in some things, have to struggle as much as anyone else when it comes to endeavors that are not so enjoyable, Dr. Pekala has found. But when he simply asked them to sit quietly for a few minutes with their eyes closed, they frequently reported feelings approaching an altered state, including a rapturous joy, a sense of some profound meaningfulness, vivid imagery, and an al-

tered sense of time, all accompanying a deeply absorbed attention. Such people, Dr. Pekala believes, may go through much of the day lost in a pleasant, reverie-like state.

Although it may not be possible to force oneself into a feeling of absorption, it seems possible to learn to enter that state of mind more easily. Ellen Langer, a psychologist at Harvard University, has been studying the effects of what she calls mindfulness, a state of active attention that seems to have much in common with flow.

One of the ways Dr. Langer has increased people's mindfulness is straightforward and simple. She has them think about what is going on from as many vantage points as possible. "We taught people to watch television mindfully by asking them, to watch shows as though they were someone else—a politician, or an athlete or a criminal," Dr. Langer said. "The point is to break through people's assumptions with an active attention that stimulates their thinking."

Dr. Langer has found that mindfulness has both psychological and health benefits. In a series of studies conducted among elderly patients in nursing homes, Dr. Langer and her colleagues have discovered that compared to patients who did not receive the mindfulness training, these patients had lower blood pressure and, in a three-year follow-up had fewer physical ailments, better overall health and a better mortality rate.

Meditation training, Dr. Langer has found, produces similar effects. "We're trying to achieve the same goal as meditation, but in a Western way," Dr. Langer said. "We try to get people to see the moment more creatively by paying more active attention."

Hypnosis Still Provokes Some Skeptics

March 31, 1987

A fierce scientific debate is focusing on whether hypnosis involves a special state of awareness or, as challengers claim, is simply one person seeking to please another by cooperating with suggestions made to him.

While this battle has been fought for decades, its implications are growing more serious as the use of hypnosis as a clinical tool flourishes as never before. The debate has reached a new level of scientific sophistication as researchers use new tests to investigate, among other things, whether a person under hypnosis sees solid or transparent images, and whether hypnotically induced amnesia is real or feigned.

The debate is more than one of semantics. Even though subjects in hypnosis may report that they have reached an altered mental state, researchers have yet to identify any differences in brain activity that invariably accompany hypnosis.

The origins of hypnosis go back to religious healing rituals and trance states, according to Barry Brilliant, a historian of hypnosis. The modern practice began with Franz Anton Mesmer, an 18th-century Viennese physician who called hypnosis "animal magnetism" and used it as a cure for a wide variety of medical and psychosomatic problems. Then as now, some scientists condemned it. By the time Freud studied—and abandoned—hypnosis, the practice was under heavy scientific attack.

It was not until 1958 that, largely through the efforts of Milton Erickson and other psychiatrists, the American Medical Association acknowledged its usefulness as a therapy.

Hypnosis generally begins when the hypnotist directs the subject to narrowly focus attention on a particular object or sound. This seems to cause the subjects to become susceptible to suggestion.

"Most experts agree that hypnosis is an altered state of consciousness involving highly focused attention and heightened absorption and imagery, increased susceptibility to suggestion, and closer contact with the unconscious," said Erika Fromm, a psychologist at the University of Chicago, and an expert on the clinical uses of hypnosis.

The challengers question that view. "I prefer to look at hypnosis as a person attuned to the demands of a situation who wants to please the hypnotist by having the experiences suggested him—or seeming to have them," said Nicholas Spanos, a psychologist at Carleton University in Ottawa, the chief critic of the prevailing views.

He is joined in his critical stance by a handful of persistent and influential critics who have produced a stream of papers to refute the prevailing view. For example, Theodore Sarbin at the University of California at Berkeley argues that the hypnotic subject is not in a trance but is merely playing a role.

Because Dr. Spanos has conducted dozens of experiments to test the origins of hypnotic effects, his attack is the strongest scientific challenge to date. It takes up the thread of an earlier challenge mounted by Theodore X. Barber, Dr. Spanos's mentor and one of the first modern psychologists to argue that everything that happened under hypnosis could go on without any hypnotic induction.

"Good hypnotic subjects frequently behave as if they have lost control over their behavior," according to Dr. Spanos. He said they act that way because it fits their preconceptions about what it means to be hypnotized.

Challenge to Three Phenomena

In the latest round of the battle, Dr. Spanos challenged the three phenomena most often cited as proof that hyponosis invokes a unique mental condition: hypnotically-induced amnesia, pain-reduction and "trance logic," an obliviousness to the logical contradictions of what a person does under hypnosis. Dr. Spanos, writing in the March, 1987 issue of *The Behavioral and Brain Sciences,* reviewed dozens of studies—including many of his own—that seem to show that all three of these effects can be explained in terms of social factors including role-playing and reactions to subtle clues from the hypnotist.

But despite the evidence in support of Dr. Spanos' charges, major figures in hypnosis research who responded in the journal said they were unpersuaded by his arguments.

"It seems implausible to assume that a person who has hypnosis as the only anesthetic for major surgery, childbirth, extensive dental work," or other major operations "reports little or no pain merely to meet the demands of the situation, that is, to fool or to please the hypnotist," wrote Martin Orne, a psychiatrist at the University of Pennsylvania, with two colleagues.

"Before the 19th century, all major

surgery was done without anesthetics," said Dr. Spanos. "Anecdotes suggest that you can get the same effects without hypnosis. Physicians sometimes found they could reduce pain with simple suggestions such as, you'll feel no pain. And there is less pain in surgery than most people think—most organs are insensitive to pain."

Not everyone can be hypnotized; many researchers consider hypnotizability to be a sort of psychological talent, one which combines the ability to become deeply absorbed with an active imagination. The most vivid hypnotic phenomenon, such as trance logic and hallucinations, are found only in those susceptible to hypnosis.

"About 97 percent of people can be hypnotized to some extent," said Dr. Fromm. "And about 8 percent of people are extremely talented at it."

Dr. Spanos, though, sees "talent" at hypnosis as being little more than a sharpened sensitivity to subtle cues and an openness to suggestion. Dr. Spanos said that hypnotists typically do not ask outright that the subject do something, but rather suggest indirectly that it should happen. For instance, instead of saying "Imagine there is a cat in your lap," the hypnotist suggests it by saying there is a cat in the person's lap, implying that he should perceive it. The subtlety of these cues, Dr. Spanos argues, accounts for the variation in the extent to which people are susceptible to hypnosis.

"Many people miss the hidden commmand, and so fail," said Dr. Spanos. "If the hypnotist suggests their arm is rising, they just wait for it to rise instead of having it do so."

Nearly 30 years ago, Dr. Orne, one of the major experts on hypnosis, introduced the concept of trance logic, which he described as the tendency to fuse everyday reality with imaginary perceptions in a manner that ignores everyday logic. In his original research, Dr. Orne had highly suggestible hypnotic subjects look at a chair in which a person had been sitting and "see" the person still sitting there. He also asked another group of people to pretend they had been hypnotized and simulate the same experience.

Thinking Under Hypnosis

When instructed to look at the actual person, who was standing behind them, some of those who had been hypnotized reported an odd effect: they could look back and forth at the real person standing there and his image in the chair. Those who were pretending to be hypnotized, on the other hand, often pretended that the actual person was somebody else or was not there at all, Dr. Orne said. These findings suggest that there is something about the way people think under hypnosis that is different from normal thought, he said.

But Dr. Spanos, based on his own and other research on trance logic, draws a different conclusion. He has found that when people who are not hypnotized are asked to imagine an image with their eyes open, they find it quite difficult to evoke a crisp, solid image. If they can call to mind an image, it typically is transparent. His interpretation is that this is just what happened in Dr. Orne's trance logic experiment: the people who were hypnotized reported two images—the transparent, imaginary one and the real person—because of subtle cues suggesting that is what they should do, cues those who simulated hypnosis did not have because they did not receive the same implicit cues.

But in a rejoinder to Dr. Spanos, David Spiegel, a psychiatrist at Stanford Medical School, points to his own research showing that hypnotic hallucinations can be objectively measured. In Dr. Spiegel's study, reported in *the Journal of Abnormal Psychology,* volunteers were hypnotized and told to imagine a cardboard box blocking their view of a television screen. Those volunteers who were highly hypnotizable showed a marked change in the evoked potential, a measure of brain activity. The change, according to Dr. Spiegel, was compatible with one that would occur if their view of the screen had actually been blocked, but not with merely imagining the box.

"It is not just compliance or pretense," said Dr. Spiegel. "It is actually happening in the brain."

Pattern of Forgetfulness

Among other scientific reports of behavior that seems unique to hypnosis, Dr. John Kihlstrom, a psychologist at the University of Wisconsin, found that people who had been hypnotized—but not those who simulated it—showed a pattern or forgetfulness like that of amnesia caused by disease.

Nevertheless, researchers have been unable to find any measurable differences in the brain or body of people under hypnosis that appear uniquely and consistently during hypnosis. Instead, they find patterns that vary according to whether the hypnotist has suggested deep relaxation or intense activity.

"There won't be a psychophysiological correlate of hypnosis for a long time, if ever," said Dr. Kihlstrom "But that does not mean that hypnosis is not a special state of focused attention. It's like rapid eye movements and dreams: dreams were real before the discovery that rapid eye movements accompanied them."

Most of Dr. Kihlstrom's research has been about hypnotically-induced amnesia. But with colleagues at Wisconsin, Dr. Robert Nadon and Dr. Richard Davidson, he is undertaking a new study to see whether the right hemisphere of the brain is particularly active during hypnosis in highly hypnotizable people. "I don't expect the experiment to prove the psychophysiological reality of a hypnotic state," he said, "but rather to link hypnosis to what is known about cognitive neuropsychology," particularly memory.

Use in Law Enforcement

As the nature of hypnosis is argued, its use by law officers to refresh the memory of witnesses to crimes is also under serious challenge. Although these memories are often reliable, witnesses' hypnotically refreshed memories have sometimes been proved false, even though the witnesses were convinced of their truth. Dr. Orne chaired a panel of the Council on Scientific Affairs of the American Medical Association that strongly recommended against the practice.

Despite all the objections to hypnosis, its use in psychotherapy has grown with great speed in recent years. Indeed, clinicians who use hypnosis point out that the question of whether there is anything special about a hypnotic trance is not necessarily relevant to its clinical use, where what matters is how well it seems to work.

There are more than a half-dozen professional associations for hypnotists who are not regulated in the way other medical specialities are. Officials of these groups, citing attendance at workshops and other indicators, said they believed that the numbers of therapists and others using hypnosis has more than doubled in the last 10 years.

Most therapists who use hypnosis are undisturbed by the debate. "There are at least six major theories of what hypnosis is, from role playing to dissociation to an altered state," said Jeffrey Zeig, director of the Milton H. Erickson Society in Phoenix. "Your theoretical lens determines what you see in hypnosis. Seen most broadly, hypnosis involves all of those."

Hypnosis Can Suppress Brain's Perception of Pain

June 22, 1989

Hypnosis can suppress the brain's perception of pain, a new study has found.

The results lend strong support to the clinical use of hypnotic suggestion, deep relaxation and other non-medical techniques as alternatives to pain-killing drugs. One of the most widely used of such alternatives, for example, is controlled breathing in childbirth.

The findings indicate that the pain-reducing effects of the technique are more than simple suggestion or the wish of patients to be cooperative, as some skeptics have proposed.

If there is pain in the body, people naturally pay attention to it, said Dr. David Spiegel, a psychiatrist at Stanford Medical School, who did the research. "But you don't have to," Dr. Spiegel said. "If you focus on some other sensation, it can mute your perception of the pain."

Strength of Responses

He added: "Learning to focus elsewhere is a cognitive discipline that can be learned. One way to teach it is hypnosis."

Stories of overcoming pain, which have the ring of the miraculous or fantasy about them, are legion among professionals who use hypnosis to relieve suffering. But scientific studies have been inconsistent regarding the effectiveness of hypnosis in blunting perceptions.

The current study involved only a small number of patients, and not all the volunteers responded to the hypnosis. But the results are considered significant because of the strength of the responses. The research was published in the June 1989 issue of *The American Journal of Psychiatry,* the official publication of the American Psychiatric Association.

The hypnotic technique used in Dr. Spiegel's experiment is virtually the same as one he often teaches to patients who have chronic pain.

In the study, volunteers were given the instruction under hypnosis that a local anesthetic was spreading from their fingers to their hand and on to the forearm, making the whole arm feel as though it were immersed in a cool mountain stream.

Then the volunteers' brain waves were measured while they received a series of 110 mild electrical shocks. The shock intensity was calibrated for each of the volunteers so it was "just below their pain threshold," Dr. Spiegel said, comparing it to the sensation of being snapped on the arm with a rubber band.

Analysis by Computer

"They would feel it and not like it, but it wouldn't be intense discomfort," he said. Previous studies have shown that the brain responds to such stimulation in the same way that it does to serious pain.

In the study, the brain's response was measured using a method called the "evoked potential," in which a computer analyzes brain waves to detect the brain activity produced by a given stimulus. The activity is measured in two ways. First, the test analyzes brain activity produced by the intensity of the stimulus. The brain reacts within a tenth of a second to the stimulus; the more intense the stimulus, the larger the brain's response will be.

Second, the test measures a response to the stimulus. At three-tenths of a second after the stimulus, the brain's response is determined by psychological factors. If the stimulus is surprising, for instance, or if the person has to make some active response to it, then the brain's response in that time period will be greater.

Dr. Spiegel found that the hypnotic instructions significantly reduced both parts of the response to a pain stimulus. "Their response was substantially reduced, enough to show hypnosis could markedly reduce the sensation of pain," he said.

The findings add credibility to a large body of anecdotal reports of individual patients whose pain was relieved by hypnosis. For example, Dr. Spiegel, tells of one young cancer patient of his who had a grapefruit-size tumor. Dr. Spiegel said that despite medication, the patient was suffering with intense pain.

When the patient was asked where he would rather be, his answer was surfing. Dr. Spiegel then hypnotized the patient, suggesting that he imagine in great detail that he was out on the ocean surfing.

"His pain took a secondary place in his awareness," Dr. Spiegel said. "He was off pain medications within two days."

Previous Study on Perception

One of the strongest earlier studies regarding the effectiveness of hypnosis in blocking perception of any kind was conducted by Dr. Spiegel and colleagues and published in *The Journal of Abnormal Psychology* in 1986. Participants were given the hypnotic suggestion that a cardboard box was blocking a television screen. The researchers found the suggestion was enough to sharply reduce the brain's perception of what was on the screen.

The new study applies that same approach to blocking tactile sensations like pain. Its main advantages over previous studies of pain reduction and hypnosis is in the brain-wave measure used and in the particular hypnotic instructions given.

Some previous studies of hypnosis and pain used suggestions that people would not feel anything. When the patients felt sensations, they were surprised and their reactions were even greater than they might have been otherwise, Dr. Spiegel said.

To avoid this, Dr. Spiegel suggested that the subjects think of something else—the numbness—which would in effect block the discomfort.

But the hypnosis did not work for everyone. In general, about 10 percent of people are easily hypnotized and about 10 percent do not seem to be susceptible to hypnotic suggestion.

Dr. Spiegel's experiment involved 20 people, 10 of whom were easily hypnotized and 10 who were not susceptible to hypnotic suggestion. Only volunteers who were easily hypnotized showed the effect; there was no reduction of pain in the others.

"For the bulk of people, there's a continuum, where the effects of hypnosis are less dramatic," Dr. Spiegel said. "For many of these people, there might not be complete pain reduction, but there would be some."

He sees his results as supporting the use of other nondrug techniques for handling pain, including biofeedback and deep muscle relaxation.

"There are two components to pain: the sensation itself and how much attention you pay it," Dr. Spiegel said. "People compound their pain with their anxiety. If you can focus on something else instead, it relieves the pain."

Sensation and Perception

The sense of touch seems to play a special role beyond its importance in sensory perception. Being touched, gently and regularly, seems to prime the hormones that make infants grow more rapidly, according to the research in "The Experience of Touch: Research Points to a Critical Role." And beyond that role, touch seems essential in helping infants (and probably adults) relax—a sign of another effect on the brain of key kinds of touch.

The sense of vision involves more than creating the perception of something we are seeing. It also entails the kinds of mental images that float through the mind when, say, you try to visualize a map of some place. "Mental Images: New Research Helps Clarify Their Role" reviews how mental images are being measured, and the vital roles they are being found to play in mental life.

The ability to sense bodily sensations tells us when we may be sick. But for some people who seem to have a hyper-sensitivity to the body's aches and twinges, even normal sensations can make them alarmed they are ill. That can lead them to become hypochondriacs, chronically complaining about imaginary illnesses, according to the research described in "Behind Abnormal Fears, Normal Aches and Pains."

The senses of taste and smell combine to give us our sense of the flavor of what we eat. But our experiences shape that sensory reality into food preferences and dislikes. "What's for Dinner? Quirks and Cravings" reviews much of the research on how food likes and dislikes are formed.

High tech has created an entirely new perceptual illusion: the sense that you are in a completely different place than you actually are. The illusion arises when your sense of vision, hearing, movement, and touch receive signals from a distant robot instead of from their immediate surroundings. Just how this illusion works, and the many useful applications it has, are described in "New Breed of Robots Have the Human Touch."

The Experience of Touch: Research Points to a Critical Role

February 2, 1988

The experience of being touched, new research shows, has direct and crucial effects on the growth of the body as well as the mind.

Touch is a means of communication so critical that its absence retards growth in infants, according to researchers who are for the first time determining the neurochemical effects of skin-to-skin contact.

The new work focuses on the importance of touch itself, not merely as part of, say, a parent's loving presence. The findings may help explain the long-noted syndrome in which infants deprived of direct human contact grow slowly and even die.

Psychological and physical stunting of infants deprived of physical contact, although otherwise fed and cared for, had been noted in the pioneering work of Harry Harlow, working with primates, and the psychoanalysts John Bowlby and Renee Spitz, who observed children orphaned in World War II.

The new research suggests that certain brain chemicals released by touch, or others released in its absence, may account for these infants' failure to thrive.

The studies on the physiology of touch come against a backdrop of continuing research on the psychological benefits of touch for emotional development.

In some of the most dramatic new findings, premature infants who were massaged for 15 minutes three times a day gained weight 47 percent faster than others who were left alone in their incubators—the usual practice in the past. The massaged infants also showed signs that the nervous system was maturing more rapidly: they became more active than the other babies and more responsive to such things as a face or a rattle.

"The massaged infants did not eat more than the others," said Tiffany Field, a psychologist at the University of Miami Medical School, who did the study. "Their weight gain seems due to the effect of contact on their metabolism."

The infants who were massaged were discharged from the hospital an average of six days earlier than premature infants who were not massaged, saving about $3,000 each in hospital costs, Dr. Field said.

Eight months later, long after their discharge, the massaged infants did better than the infants who were not, on tests of mental and motor ability and held on to their advantage in weight, according to a report by Dr. Field in *The Journal of Pediatrics*.

"The standard policy in caring for premature infants has been a minimal-touch rule," Dr. Field said. Word of her continuing findings and others that support them has led to a change in this policy in some hospitals.

Babies born prematurely are kept in incubators and fed intravenously. They had been touched as little as possible because they had been observed becoming agitated when someone approached or handled them. The agitation sometimes put a dangerous strain on their tiny lungs, putting the infants in danger of hypoxia, an inability to oxygenate the blood.

However, Dr. Field found that a light massage of the babies' backs, legs and necks and gentle movement of their arms and legs proved to have a tonic effect, immediately soothing them and eventually speeding their growth.

Dr. Field had decided to try massages because of findings by Saul Schanberg of the department of pharmacology at Duke University.

Beta-Endorphin Inhibited

The strongest evidence is from studies of other mammals, but it seems to apply to humans. Dr. Schanberg's studies of infant laboratory rats showed that a particular pattern of touch by the mother rat—particularly licking—inhibited the infant rat's production of beta-endorphin, a chemical that affects the levels of insulin and growth hormone.

The slowed production of beta-endorphin did not depend on the presence of the mother; researchers were able to induce it by simulating the stroke of the mother's rough tongue with a wet paintbrush.

While levels of beta-endorphin decreased in response to licking, the levels rose when the infants were taken from their mothers. If the separation persisted, the infant rats' growth was stunted.

But resumption of the mother's touch, even when simulated with a brush, again lowered the beta-endorphin levels and quickened growth.

"We believe that the brain effects we found in rats will also hold for humans, because the basic neural and touch systems are the same," Dr. Schanberg said.

He hypothesizes that the touch system is part of a primitive survival mechanism found in all mammals. Because mammals depend on maternal care for survival in their early weeks or months, the prolonged absence of a mother's touch—more than 45 minutes in a rat, for instance—triggers a slowing of the infant's metabolism, and thus a lowering of its need for nourishment. Such a reaction heightens its chances of surviving until it is once again in contact with the mother.

While the slower metabolism is beneficial in the short term, it stunts growth if very prolonged. According to Dr. Schanberg, part of the response in rats, which includes huddling down and becoming still, is a change in metabolism that conserves the store of energy and slows the rate of growth. The mother's touch, however, reverses the process, so that growth resumes at normal rates.

In related findings, physical contact with the mother appears essential to reducing the release of hormones by an infant when subjected to stress, according to Seymour Levine, a psychologist in the department of psychiatry at Stanford University Medical School. When infant rats or monkeys are separated from their mothers, activity in the pituitary-adrenal system rises, a response that is also typical for humans under stress. In Dr. Levine's studies, physical contact with the infant's mother lowered this stress response.

Beyond Mere Proximity

Contact and touch have a significant role in the infant's ability "to regulate its own responses to stress," Dr. Levine said. His work does not allow him to separate touch in itself from the more general effect of the mother's presence, but he theorizes that in humans a touch-induced reduction of stress hormones may account for the soothing effects of skin-to-skin contact.

In an article published in *Child Development,* Dr. Schanberg and Dr. Field review data indicating that it was touch, rather than mere proximity or motion, that regulated infants' growth rate.

Other research suggests that all babies benefit from touch, not just the premature infants Dr. Field studied. Research by Theodore Wacks, a psychologist at Purdue, showed that in-

fants who experienced more skin-to-skin contact had an advantage in mental development in the first six months of life.

The Best Kind of Touch

Such findings have encouraged the formation of some infant massage groups outside of hospitals, for parents to learn the best ways to massage their babies. The best stroke for an infant, Dr. Field said, is gentle, firm and slow. If the touch is too light, it can overstimulate and even irritate an infant.

Different areas of an infant's body respond differently to touch. If a parent wants to soothe an infant, gentle strokes or light massage on its back and legs will relax it. On the other hand, stroking a baby's face, belly or feet tends to stimulate it.

"In most parts of the world, people massage babies," said Dr. Field. "The Western countries are about the only place this is not routine."

The primacy of touch in infancy, experts say, is tied to touch, which is the most mature sensory system for the first several months of life.

"It's the first way an infant learns about the environment," said Kathryn Barnard, a professor of nursing at the University of Washington. "About 80 percent of a baby's communication is through its body movement. It's easier to read a baby's communication with skin-to-skin contact."

Conveying Subtle Needs

Babies resort to crying when their needs become urgent, while they use movements to show more subtle feelings and needs, Dr. Barnard said.

Her research has shown that the more a mother holds her baby the more aware she is of the baby's needs. And Barnard found that those infants who were held more showed superior cognitive development as long as eight years later, apparently because they were more alert.

"We touch each other too little," Dr. Field said. "Body contact is very

beneficial between parents and children right up to adolescence."

Psychological Development

While a warm touch is part of loving contact and is difficult to separate from it, research is suggesting that touch has an importance over and above other expressions of affection and that its presence has consequences for psychological development.

For instance, physical contact is the ultimate signal to infants or small children that they are safe. When a small child is frightened, for instance, the most effective way to calm him is for someone he trusts to hold him; simply being there or reassuring him is not enough, touch researchers believe.

In addition, "how—and whether—parents touch their children may influence how they feel about their bodies," said Sandra Weiss, a professor in the department of mental health and community nursing at the University of California Medical School at San Francisco.

In a study of how families of children 7 to 10 years old play together, Dr. Weiss found that rough-housing seemed to give children more positive feelings about themselves and a more accurate sense of their bodies. To measure the perceptions, the children are asked what they like about their bodies, then they are asked to draw a body.

"The physical play gives a child the message, 'I like to be close to you; it's fun to be around you,'" Dr. Weiss said. "It affects both their feelings about themselves and about how they are put together."

Individual Differences

People differ, however, in the intensity of physical contact they find comfortable. While some of the difference may be an innate property of the person's nervous system, some of it may be shaped by the experience of being touched or not being touched.

Work in rats by Marion Diamond, a professor of anatomy at the University of California at Berkeley, showed that those who had more tactile experience had better-developed nerve cells in the area of the cortex that processes the sensations of touch. Lack of that experience, however, led to a decrease of the richness of connection and size of those brain cells.

"People who touch little, as opposed to those who like to cuddle," Dr. Diamond said, "probably experience the same effect. Those who have had little physical contact over the years might become hypersensitive to such touch, so that they found it physically uncomfortable."

Mental Images: New Research Helps Clarify Their Role

August 12, 1986

Mental images can be so fleeting, lasting in some instances mere hundreths of a second, that even the person creating the image may be unaware that a picture has come and gone. For scientists this imagery has been so elusive that studying it seemed a most unpromising pursuit.

But recent progress in understanding the nature of imagery has given vitality to an area of research that probes a central act in the life of the mind.

Einstein said his most original ideas came to him in mental pictures, not in words or numbers; Aristotle said that thought is impossible without images. Nevertheless, it was only in the early 1970's that there was much serious scientific interest in such images, and only very recently that some of the most significant discoveries have been made.

The researchers have learned that some people's minds jump and seeth with imagery while others are relatively quiescent.

"About three percent of people cannot seem to get any mental pictures at all, and about three percent are superb at it," said Stephen Kosslyn, a psychologist at Harvard University, who has done much of the new research.

Psychologists have also identified the skills that underlie the creation of imagery and believe that these skills can be sharpened to serve in an array of mental endeavors including not only visual activities such as design but also problem solving and logic. Some of the other important findings point to the most common uses of images in daily life and, sweeping away some long-held assumptions,

suggest the location in the brain where images are formed.

Many of the recent advances are based on the discovery that mental images can be measured. Using computerized measuring techniques, researchers are now able to time, to within thousandths of a second, the specific steps involved when the mind pictures something. They have learned, for instance, that the mind perceives images in ways similar to those it uses in processing actual vision. For example, it takes as long to scan an imaginary map as it does to scan an actual one.

A project recently completed at Harvard established which kinds of images are important in daily life, and their relative frequency. The Harvard study, by Dr. Kosslyn and Carol Seger, one of his students, asked people to keep a diary in which they made detailed reports every hour of their mental images.

More than 80 percent of the images were in color. In about 40 percent the images faded in and out, shrank and expanded or acted in other ways impossible in real life.

For some people the images are not just visual. Their images were multimodal, involving smells, tastes, sounds, or touch. One person reported that virtually all his images involved several senses.

The diary entries showed that the subjects ordinarily used mental images in six principal ways.

The most common use of the images, about a third of all those reported, was for making a decision or solving a problem. It was very common, for instance, for someone getting dressed to picture himself or her-

self in one set of clothes rather than another. One of the more frequent ways multimodal images were used was in deciding what to eat: people pictured, smelled and tasted the alternative dishes in their minds.

About a quarter of the images were used to help understand a verbal description. While listening to someone else, for example, people would picture in their minds what the words they were hearing represented. Such images also play a key role in reading; people reported mentally picturing scenes they read about.

People also reported using images to change their feelings, particularly to get in or out of a particular mood, or to motivate themselves. Some imagined themselves thinner to help themselves stay on a diet.

People also reported using mental images to help explain or describe something; for instance, they would visualize a scene at the previous night's party to describe it to a friend.

While rehearsing with mental images is frequently used in the training of athletes and others for peak performance, this was one of the less common day-to-day uses of images reported in the diary study. When it was reported, people said their images were used to improve a skill, such as a swimming stroke, or to prepare for something, such as asking for a raise, by rehearsing in their minds what it would be like to go through it.

Since the ancient Greeks, techniques have been taught that used images as an aid to memory. But the diary study found this use to be one of the least common. While people did occasionally report using images to jog memory—for instance, by vizualizing one's keys to help remember where they were left—Dr. Kosslyn said he believed that this is one of several vastly underused ways in which the use of mental images could be helpful.

"Most people could be very much better at their use of mental images for such things as solving problems or remembering names, but it just does not seem to occur to them at the time," said Dr. Kosslyn. "Imaging abilities are vastly underdeveloped in most of us."

Dr. Kosslyn said that first it was important to understand the role of imagery and then to practice using in cases where it is known to be helpful.

"People differ greatly in their ability to get pictures in their mind," said Robert Wechsler, a psychologist at Wright State School of Medicine in Cleveland, who uses imagery to help patients cope with pain and speed recovery after surgery. Patients suffer less from pain, he has found, if they can put it at a psychological distance. So he teaches patients to see the painful part of the body as separate. Sometimes it is helpful to imagine the injured part as actually healed.

"With training and a bit of practice, people can improve immensely in the capacity to use images," said Dr. Kosslyn. "For most all of us it's one of the underused abilities of the mind."

Some psychologists hope that the experimental work will help improve the practical applications of imagery.

Among the key abilities for imaging that Dr. Kosslyn described in *Visual Cognition,* published by the M.I.T. Press, are finding and putting the separate parts of a mental picture together properly and scanning it, moving it around, zooming in on one part of the picture or panning to see more of the whole.

Some, but not all, of the important imaging abilities specified in Dr. Kosslyn's theory appear to be controlled by the left hemisphere of the brain, according to research by Martha Farah, a psychologist at Carnegie-Mellon University, published in the journal *Neuropsychologia.*

Not only does this finding refine the established map of the mind but it helps explain the mysterious loss of ability to form mental images some people suffer after some accidents.

This finding also contradicts the widespread assumption that, in most people, the left side of the brain controls verbal abilities, while the right side specializes in images. The exact location of images has long mystified researchers. The new studies suggest that it is not in one place but in several.

"If you think of imaging as a single ability and look for a part of the brain that controls it, you simply do not find such a place," said Dr. Farah.

In examining patients who had lesions in their left hemisphere, Dr. Farah found that their mind's eye was blind: they simply could not bring to mind a mental image. There was no impairment, though, in their ability to perform tasks involving spatial skills, such as solving a maze.

In conjunction with Michael Gazzaniga of Cornell University Medical College, Dr. Farah studied patients who had had the connections between their right and left hemisphere surgically severed in order to control extreme epilepsy. She found that the left hemisphere, rather than the right, was able to perform the imaging tasks that had been impaired in the patients with damage to the left hemisphere.

Even pure logical deduction, for many people, can involve mental pictures, according to work by Janelien Huttenlocher, a psychologist at the University of Chicago. Dr. Huttenlocher's research resolved a long-standing debate over whether images played a role in logical thinking. While some philosophy texts actually encouraged translating certain logical puzzles into visual symbols to help come to a solution, some psychologists maintained that except for a few special cases, logical thought involved words, not pictures.

Dr. Huttenlocher found that people relied on images in solving a wide range of logical problems, particularly those involving syllogisms. She found that people resort to images, for example, when they are given a set of premises such as "John is smarter than Bill and Susan is smarter than John" and they are asked to decide whether Susan is smarter than Bill.

In describing how they came to their decision, many of the people Dr. Huttenlocher studied said they often solved the problems by such means as imagining a line and placing dots along it to represent each person, with dots further to the right representing a smarter person. The more complicated the syllogism, the more useful were the mental images.

Behind Abnormal Fears, Normal Aches and Pains

November 29, 1988

Hypochondriacs do have something different about them, but it is not the elusive diseases that they are convinced they suffer.

Instead, new research suggests that hypochondriacs are unusually sensitive to all kinds of bodily sensations, providing constant nourishment for their irrational fears of disease.

For hypochondriacs, almost imperceptible tingles or aches, the body's normal creaks and groans, can become obsessions.

"What might be a minor twinge or soreness to most of us is a severe, consuming pain to the person who amplifies sensations," said Dr. Arthur Barsky, a psychiatrist at Harvard Medical School. "These are people who amplify all forms of distress."

Not all people who have this hypersensitivity become hypochondriacs, according to Dr. Barsky's theory. But some, the hypochondriacs, overreact to the physical sensations, seeing them as signs of serious medical disorders.

"They scrutinize trivial and transitory symptoms that others might dismiss as insignificant, and react to these perceptions with apprehension and alarm," Dr. Barsky said. "They readily attribute what they notice to disease rather than to aging, overexertion or emotions."

Helping hypochondriacs realize they are over-reacting to normal sensations plays a major role in a new treatment Dr. Barsky has developed. The treatment does not seek to end hypochondriacs' sensitivities. Rather it helps patients live with the sensations more easily, and it helps them stop seeking medical assistance where none is needed.

The approach overcomes what had been formidable obstacles to helping hypochondriacs, who as a group are notoriously difficult patients. They typically follow an unhappy route from doctor to doctor and test to test, all in pursuit of an ever-elusive diagnosis. Convinced that they are suffering some physical disorder, they refuse psychological treatment.

Dr. Barsky does not try to convince hypochondriacs that they are not feeling ill. "Their experience of the symptom is not likely to change," he said. "What can change is what they make of that experience."

As a result, Dr. Barsky urges the patients to accept the inevitability of living with some degree of discomfort, so they will give up their fruitless search for medical solutions.

"These people have not reconciled themselves to the fact they have to live with some kind of symptoms," Dr. Barsky said. "They have the fantasy there will be a discrete answer to what's bothering them, and a real cure. The paradox for them is that they can't get better psychologically until they accept that they won't get better medically."

Some evidence supporting Dr. Barsky's approach comes from a study of 115 patients who came to a walk-in clinic at Massachusetts General Hospital complaining of upper respiratory tract infections. The study was published in *Psychosomatic Medicine* in Fall, 1988.

Quick to Sense Hunger

Dr. Barsky and his colleagues found that patients who complained of symptoms far more severe than medically indicated in an examination also tended to be the most sensitive to physical stimulation. They said they were very disturbed by loud, sudden noises, easily made uncomfortable by heat or cold and quick to sense hunger.

Other researchers said Dr. Barsky's use of this hypersensitivity to identify those most likely to be hypochondriacs is a promising approach.

"He's on the right track," said Dr. Monte Buchsbaum, a research psychiatrist at the University of California at Irvine who has studied the brain systems that control perceptual sensitivities. "A test that would allow us to identify patients with an overly sensitive nervous system could become a positive indicator for the diagnosis of hypochondria. That would be helpful in screening them out."

As Dr. Z. J. Lipowski noted in the November, 1988 issue of the *American Journal of Psychiatry,* studies show that 5 percent to 30 percent of patients seeking treatment are hypochondriacs or, in the term now current in psychiatric diagnosis, "somatizers."

Many such patients are actually depressed, said Dr. Lipowski, a psychiatrist at the University of Toronto School of Medicine.

Others, Dr. Barsky said, may have a real medical problem, "but they are unduly distressed by their symptoms."

Influence of Parents

One factor that may lead hypersensitive people to become hypochondriacs, some researchers believe, is having had a parent who was overly attentive to their childhood illnesses. For instance, a study started in the early 1960's found that the more attentive a child's parents were to any symptoms the child had, the more the child became preoccupied with them. When the same children were studied 16 years later, those who had learned in childhood to be vigilant for signs of medical problems were more likely to be hypochondriacs as adults.

"The more attention you pay to a symptom, the more intense it gets," Dr. Barsky said.

In one study by Dr. James Pennebaker, a psychologist at Southern Methodist University, men walking on an exercise treadmill listened either to a tape of city sounds or to the sound of their own breathing. After getting off the treadmill, those who heard their own breathing reported a large number of symptoms, such as headache and racing heart, even though there were no physiological differences between the groups.

Sensations That Verify Belief

In an even simpler experiment, Dr. Pennebaker asked volunteers to spend one minute either concentrating on any sensations of nasal congestion, or to sensations of free breathing. Those who were asked to notice the congestion were more likely to judge their noses to be stuffy.

"Simply telling a hypochondriac he is not really sick is not effective," Dr. Pennebaker said. "Such a person always has some sensations which can verify the illness belief he holds."

In Dr. Barsky's treatment, patients meet in small groups for eight weeks for a course on "the perception of physical symptoms."

Study of Dental Pain

One of the first lessons deals with how paying attention to symptoms intensifies them.

The patients are told about a study in which people undergoing dental extractions were asked to rate pain every 20 minutes, or just after two hours. "For those who rated the pain every 20 minutes, the pain was much more severe," Dr. Barsky said. "Our patients learn that's what they're doing to themselves."

Another important lesson in the course deals with how people's beliefs about illness convert normal or minor aches into medical symptoms in their own minds.

"What you think is going on in your body matters immensely," Dr. Barsky said. "If you see normal aches and pains as medical symptoms, then they become ominous and alarming."

Learning 'Practical Strategies'

Patients also learn to use their ability to concentrate on bodily sensations in a more positive way. Instead of focusing on their aches they concentrate on the natural flow of their breathing in a meditation exercise. They are encouraged to use such techniques when they find themselves preoccupied with the sensations they take to be symptoms.

One common insight gained by those in the course is that their pursuit of a medical cure has kept them from learning to deal more positively with the sensations that bother them. "We talk about how to cope with something like chronic low-level back pain, or constant fatigue," Dr. Barsky said. "Patients learn practical strategies like conserving their energy, or how to relax."

Dr. Barsky does not seek a cure in the usual sense. "People's symptoms don't get better," he said. "But they aren't bothered by them as much."

'The Worried Well'

In 1988 editorial in the *New England Journal of Medicine,* Dr. Barsky argued that hypochondria may be increasing as a paradoxical effect of improvements in medical care. "Having come to imagine that somewhere there is a treatment for almost everything that ails us," he wrote, "we experience refractory symptoms as a mistake, an injustice, a failure of medical care."

This attitude encourages people to continue searching for a cure, even when there is nothing medically wrong to be cured. In his book *Worried Sick,* published by Little, Brown, Dr. Barsky cited statistics showing that since the 1930's the average number of visits made by Americans to physicians has doubled, to an average of five per year. While there is good reason to seek care for what may be signs of illness, the statistics indicated that there was no serious medical condition found for as many as 60 percent of the visits.

"People are more willing to consult physicians for conditions that were previously thought unsuited for medical treatment," such as minor back pain or upper respiratory infections, Dr. Barsky wrote in the *New England Journal of Medicine.* "This encourages a cultural climate of alarm and hypochondria, undermining feelings of well-being. It is harder to feel confident about one's health when sensations one had assumed to be trivial are protrayed as ominous, when every ache is thought to merit medical attention."

What's for Dinner? Psychologists Explore Quirks and Cravings

July 11, 1989

Psychological factors lie at the heart of many eating problems, from children who refuse anything but hot dogs to people who gain weight the moment they go off a diet, researchers are finding.

New studies also show that some of the tactics parents use to get their children to eat a proper diet can backfire, leading children to rebel and establishing lifelong habits that can frustrate later attempts to eat a healthful diet.

The findings are part of a body of research indicating that psychological and social factors play a larger role than had been thought in determining a person's choice of foods, but that, even so, biology sometimes confounds people's best intentions, particularly when it comes to trying to lose weight. And the findings are shedding new light on an area that nutritionists, food scientists and biologists, have explored for decades.

Just how people select an adequate diet from the array of foods available to them remains somewhat of a mystery.

In the first year of life, infants generally regulate what they eat in accord with their body's nutritional needs, according to studies by Dr. Leann Birch, a psychologist at the University of Illinois. For instance, at six weeks, babies given a formula that was diluted with excess water drank more of it, so that they got the amount of nutrients they needed.

But as early as age 2, social forces begin to influence eating and can eventually lead to quirky food preferences. Parents, inadvertently, are often the cause.

"The universal parental tactic of offering children a reward if they fin-

ish a certain food—you can have some cake if you finish your peas—might work in the short term," said Dr. Birch. "But in the long run, it makes children dislike the food they had to finish," because it suggests that there is something wrong with the food they are being coerced to eat.

On the other hand, the tactic leads children to like even more the food used as the reward, which too often is a rich dessert. But there are limits to the foods that can be made more appealing by using them as rewards. "When we told 2-year-olds, finish your cake so you can eat your peas, they thought that was a real sidesplitter," Dr. Birch said.

Another way parents can distort their children's sense of how much food they need to eat is by using adult portions to judge how much of a certain food a child "should" eat.

"A 2-year-old only needs two teaspoons of peas, not a half cup," Dr. Birch said. "It can be destructive to make a child finish everything on his plate, especially if the portions are too big. Coercion backfires. If you focus on external factors, like how much food is left on the plate, or what time it is, then children get out of touch with their internal cues for when they are hungry and when they are full."

Researchers at Duke University found that many people who were prone to obesity as adults, continually going on and off diets, were oblivious to their body's cues for hunger and satiety. These people tended to have had parents who used coercion to get them to finish their food, or who were sticklers for eating only at certain times.

"If your parents say it's not time to eat yet when you tell them you're

hungry, or insist you finish what's on your plate when you're already full, it can lead you to look to externals to decide when and how much to eat, and that creates lifelong weight problems," Dr. Birch said. "Natural eaters, in contrast, eat when they're hungry and stop when they're full. They rarely have weight problems."

Trying Strange Foods

Social pressure has a great effect on children's food preferences, Dr. Birch has found. In experiments with 2-to-5-year-olds, a child who disliked a specific food was seated at a table for a snack with three children who liked that food. After several days of seeing the other children eat the disliked food, the child who once avoided it started to prefer it, even weeks later.

In general, children prefer familiar foods and are reluctant to try strange ones. But parents should be more persistent, Dr. Birch said. Accepting an initial "I don't like it," means the child may never even try the food. But in experiments Dr. Birch has found that getting a child to taste a strange food will eventually make it familiar and preferred. "It may take 10 times," she said.

While many people believe that the body will naturally develop a craving for food containing the nutrients it needs, the human senses of taste and smell cannot directly detect the presence or absence in a food of most major nutrients. Proteins, carbohydrates, fat and vitamins cannot be detected by the human nose or tongue. Only salt and sugar, among basic nutrients, are directly tasted.

No Sensory Receptors

What people think of as "taste" is mostly smells of substances that happen to accompany nutrients in various foods.

"The problem is that even though we need protein, fat, starch and vitamins, humans have virtually no sensory receptors for these nutrients," said Dr. Linda Bartoshuk, a psychologist at Yale University who studies the perception of taste.

In the 1940's, scientists discovered that if people were deprived of salt or sugars, they would develop cravings for them. But the specific cravings turned out to be limited to salt and sugars. The notion that other nutritional deficiencies create specific cravings was disproven in the 1950's by experiments in which rats were deprived of a nutrient, then offered a range of foods.

"They don't choose foods with the nutrient they've been deprived of," said Dr. Bartoshuk. "Instead, they just choose any food that is novel. Whether they get what they need is hit-or-miss."

But once they find a food with the missing nutrients, animals and people tend to prefer it, at least for a while. Nutritional deficiencies tend to create physical discomfort, which the proper food remedies. "When animals are deficient in a given vitamin, for instance, there's some evidence that they explore many foods until they hit upon the right one, and tend to eat it until they feel better," said Dr. Gary Beauchamp, a biopsychologist at Monell Chemical Sciences Center, a research institute in Philadelphia that specializes in studies of taste, smell and food sciences.

One current theory holds that people tend to develop lasting preferences for foods that have made them feel better by correcting a nutritional deficiency.

Developing Food Aversions

This kind of preference is a form of conditioning that seems to shape many food preferences. Often it works in the reverse direction, making people averse to a given food. Someone who gets sick after eating a meal will often develop a strong distaste for whatever food in the meal had the most distinctive flavor, whether or not it had anything to do with the sickness.

One theory holds that this is behind many of the food aversions children develop. Because tastes are so distinctive for children and because they come down with colds and the flu relatively often, there are many opportunities for aversions to develop.

Despite the importance of psychological and social factors, biology remains a dominant force in many eating problems. Indeed, many of the dietary problems of modern life stem from the persistent force of biological mechanisms that once served people well. "Fat, sugar and salt are bad for us only as an artifact of civilized life," said Dr. Beauchamp. "In evolution they were all beneficial" because except in times of plenty—such as modern life—these essential nutrients are hard to get in nature.

In a recent experiment, Dr. C. Peter Herman, a psychologist at the University of Toronto, and his colleagues found that people who are hungry, though not starving, paradoxically tend to become more finicky in what they eat, preferring better-tasting food, which generally means food that is high in fats and sugars.

"We're born liking sweet foods," said Dr. Bartoshuk. "In evolution, we needed the energy of sweet-tasting, sugary foods, especially during times of scarcity."

Other discouraging news for dieters comes from research by Kelly Brownell, a psychiatrist at the University of Pennsylvania, corroborating earlier findings. In work with rats that were repeatedly put on diets and then taken off, he found that their metabolic rate tended to fall each time, becoming progressively lower. A lower metabolic rate means the body burns fewer calories.

"It's unfortunate for dieters," said Dr. Logue. "The body is not designed to lose weight."

The body also works against the effectiveness of crash diets on other ways, research is showing. Studies by Dr. Herman, a psychologist at the University of Toronto, suggest that people who are chronic dieters unintentionally increase their craving for high-calorie foods as they cut back on what they eat. Thus when they go off the diet, they will tend to choose foods that are higher in calories, and so tend to build up their weight again.

Effects of Artificial Sweeteners

Scientists have also learned that one modern food substitute, artificial sweeteners like saccharin, has the unintended consequence of increasing hunger. Although studies confirming this were done with rats, the implications for humans is that people who use saccharin to lose weight are inadvertently increasing their hunger, leading them to eat more.

"The taste of any sweets, even artificial sweeteners, makes the body release insulin, which in turn leads more food to be stored, rather than be released as available energy," said Alexandra Logue, a psychologist at the State University of New York at Stony Brook, who wrote *The Psychology of Eating and Drinking* (W. H. Freeman, 1986). "That makes less energy available for immediate use, so the body craves more food to get the energy."

New Breed of Robots Have the Human Touch

August 1, 1989

Engineers are developing machines that they say will fulfill a dream of robotics: devices that can handle situations with the deftness and dexterity of humans in places too dangerous for humans. The machines are being developed for use with toxic waste, in nuclear plants, deep under the ocean, in outer space, by police bomb squads and even on the battlefield.

"The idea is being there without going there," said John D. Merritt, an experimental psychologist and consultant in Williamsburg, Mass., who is a developer of the new approach.

The designers say a person operating one of the new machines wears a helmet that receives visual and auditory signals. These signals give the operator the illusion of being in the machine and seeing and hearing precisely what it sees and hears. At the same time, the machine mimics the operator's every move. The design allows people to direct the machines at a distance with nearly the same precision they bring to tasks immediately at hand, the engineers say.

Strictly speaking, the new machines are not robots. They are called "teleoperators," referring to the fact that their operation is directed by a person at a distance. The perceptual illusion that makes the person experience the sensation of being in the same place as the distant robot is called "telepresence."

While wearing the helmet, an operator looks directly into two tiny television screens that show what the teleoperator is looking at rather than what is actually in front of the person.

"You forget where you are," Mr. Merritt said. "You assume you're in the location where the machine is. If in the process you have the robot approach you, you'll see yourself as though you were someone else entirely."

One appeal of teleoperation is that it allows an expert to work in a dangerous setting while staying safe.

Mark Friedman, director of the Human-Machine Interactions Laboratory at the Robotics Institute at Carnegie-Mellon University, said, "There are certain applications where telepresence makes the most sense: where you need high levels of human judgment, inventiveness and precision, but where it's too dangerous to go."

Some of the strongest interest in teleoperators has come from the nuclear industry, where some experts see the devices as the answer to the problems of working with radioactivity.

"Since the operator can be in a safe environment while the robot goes into the dangerous area, the nuclear industry is very interested," said Lee Martin, director of Telerobotics International, in Oak Ridge, Tennessee. "The biggest growth in the use of teleoperators is going to be in nuclear cleanup and waste handling. It will grow even more as we have to dismantle and refurbish plants."

'A Better Way'

"Now many of those tasks are done by people in protective suits who can only enter a radioactive zone a fixed number of times, and then can never go there again," he said. "It's extremely expensive. Telerobotics offer a better way."

Several teleoperation systems are under development in the United States. One of the more advanced ones is at the Naval Ocean Systems Center, a Navy research site in Hawaii. Another will be designed for NASA for use in building and maintaining the planned space station. Projects are also under way in France and Germany; Japan has made teleoperators the focus of an eight-year national project based at Tsukuba Science City, a Government-sponsored research center.

Of the several versions of teleoperators now being developed, the more advanced mimic most precisely the sensory input to the brain.

"The closer you come to duplicating the human experience, the more easily your mind transposes into the zone as though you were there," said John White, president of Remotec, a concern in Oak Ridge.

Teleoperators being designed for use with the space shuttle may make it unnecessary for crew members to do any tasks themselves in space, said John Molino, president of the Tech-U-Fit Corporation in Alexandria, Virginia. "We're now testing six prototype tasks, such as locking in place the modules that will be used to build the space station."

The version being tested has a special glove that duplicates the pressures and forces on the hands of the robot. But the teleoperator need not hear, since there is no sound in space.

Overcoming Tough Problems

Such teleoperators promise to solve several problems that have stymied researchers in robotics. One is that no computer has been able to simulate the workings of the human visual and auditory system, let alone coordinate them with lifelike movement.

Thus robots that rely on computers to direct them have failed at all but the simplest perceptual tasks. Teleoperators get around the problem by having a person, rather than a computer, direct the machine. Another problem solved by the teleoperators is the relative lack of precision in three-dimensional tasks like digging a hole in which a person directs a robot's armature while viewing the task on a television screen.

Even so, the best teleoperators are not yet on par with a person's abilities in the same situation. None, for example, have a sense of smell, and their sense of touch lacks some of the sensitivity and dexterity of the human hand. Further, potential customers complain that commercial units now available lack state-of-the-art sensors.

The most advanced teleoperators use dual video cameras mounted about as far apart as a human's eyes. Each camera sends an image to one eye. That arrangement creates a crispness in depth perception that is lacking from an ordinary television picture.

In tests comparing the speed and dexterity of people using each arrangement, teleoperators were about twice as fast on simple tasks as were people operating the robot arms by watching a television screen, now the most common method. The advantage became greater the more the tasks required spatial cues, like looping a cable through rings.

A New Precision

"Where things are in three-dimensional space comes through poorly on a TV screen," Mr. Merritt said. "But it comes through with precision when you recreate the sensory inputs of someone as though they were there."

The focus in developing teleoperators is to approach ever more closely the exact combination of messages that the human brain normally receives from the senses. In seeking to duplicate the sensation and movements of the person operating the device, researchers have had to make several subtle adjustments.

One was to have the video cameras positioned about four inches ahead of the neck pivot point, simulating the relationship of the eyes to the skull's pivot point around the spine. The teleoperator duplicates the movements of the operator's torso, neck, head and arms. By mimicking human movements, the teleoperators blend cues for movement with those for sounds and sights.

Researchers are now studying the way different senses work together. For instance, they are trying to determine how distance perception is informed by sounds.

"The next generation of teleoperators will be based on sensory fusion, the idea that the operator gets complementary data from many senses," said Ralph C. Gonzalez, a professor of electrical and computer engineering at the University of Tennessee, and president of Perceptics, a firm in Oak Ridge.

Mr. Merritt said, "If you don't create a robotic perceptual system that mimics precisely the sensory inputs to the brain, it will make subtle differences that can be disorienting or disturbing to the person operating it." For example, an added-nuance in perception is having the microphones placed not just on the sides of the robot's "head" but also in a simulated ear.

"It's not enough just to have a microphone," he said. "You want to imitate the pattern of acoustic stimulation at the eardrum that your brain experiences as real. Ideally, each person who ran the teleoperator would have their own set of imitation ears, molded to the precise shape of their own, which their brain is used to."

Learning and Memory

B. F. Skinner has been the leading thinker in behaviorism for close to four decades. Now in his 80s, he reflects on the continued uses of his thoeries of learning for understanding the complexities of human behavior. In "Embattled Giant of Psychology Speaks His Mind," he defends his views and responds to critics.

While B. F. Skinner is the leading proponent of the study of observable behavior, Jerome Bruner is one of the founders of cognitive psychology, which focuses on studying the workings of the mind, such as memory. In "Leading Psychologist Expands the Boundaries" Bruner shows what people's life stories can reveal about how memory works and the importance of narratives.

How well do you remember the things that have happened to you in your life? And how accurately? The answers may surprise you. "In Memory, People Re-Create Their Lives to Suit Their Images of the Present" covers research showing that we are all biased in recalling permanent memories, painting a rosier picture of our past than was actually the case.

Another bias in memory comes from the fact that we tend to see ourselves at the center of the events in our lives. This somewhat skewed view of reality is a universal trait, the consequences of which for better and worse are shown in "A Bias Puts Self at the Center of Everything."

Do you sometimes worry that you are forgetting things? That worry is increasingly more common as people grow older. But most people worry about it more than they need to: it's just that we don't realize how common forgetfulness actually is. The research in "Forgetfulness Is Seen Causing More Worry than It Should" explains why worries about forgetting are so prevalent.

Embattled Giant of Psychology Speaks His Mind

August 25, 1987

B. F. Skinner is a creature of carefully shaped habit. At the age of 83, he has fashioned a schedule and environment for himself that is in perfect keeping with his theories of behavioral reinforcement.

Dr. Skinner's personal Skinner box—his own self-contained environment of positive reinforcements—is his basement office in his home here, a 1950's flat-top set among charming New England-style saltboxes.

"I spent a lot of time creating the environment where I work," Dr. Skinner said as he recently led a visitor through the home where he and his wife, Yvonne, live. "I believe people should design a world where they will be as happy as possible in old age."

Burrhus Frederic Skinner, the chief architect of behaviorism, uses the office to marshal a crusade against what he sees as grave mistakes in psychology that have left his own once preeminent theories in decline.

Behaviorism holds that people act as they do because of the rewards and punishments—positive and negative reinforcements—they have received. The mind and such things as memory and perception cannot be directly observed, and so, in Dr. Skinner's view, are unworthy of scientific study.

Much of Dr. Skinner's efforts now aim at meeting two major challenges to behaviorism: brain science, the study of links between brain and behavior, and cognitive psychology, the study of how the mind perceives, thinks and remembers and how goals and plans influence behavior.

During the recent visit, Dr. Skinner, known to colleagues as Fred, was in the midst of preparing a talk to be given at psychology's major annual convention.

It is to maximize his productivity in such writing, and to conserve energy in his later years, that Dr. Skinner has designed this environment. He sleeps in the office, in a bright yellow plastic tank just large enough for the mattress it contains, a small television and some narrow shelves and controls. The bed unit, which bears some resemblance to a sleeper on a train, is one of those used by the Japanese in stacks in tiny hotel rooms, Dr. Skinner explained.

The office-bedroom suits Dr. Skinner's habits well: he goes to bed each night at 10 P.M., sleeps three hours, then rolls out of bed to his nearby desk, where he works for one hour. Then he goes back to bed for another three hours, getting up to begin his day at 5 A.M.

Positive Reinforcement: Music

In these early morning hours Dr. Skinner puts in about three hours of writing, which he considers to be his main work. After his writing, he walks a mile or so to his office at Harvard University, where he answers mail and attends to other business. And then, for reinforcement, he spends the afternoon listening to music—which he loves—on the quadrophonic tape deck in his office.

This schedule, with its work output and rewards, allows Dr. Skinner to continue to act as the undisputed leader of modern behaviorism. As such, he fights a continuing battle for his ideas on many fronts, many of which he touched on in the wide-ranging interview.

"I think cognitive psychology is a great hoax and a fraud, and that goes for brain science, too," Dr. Skinner said. "They are nowhere near answering the important questions about behavior."

Dr. Skinner is still vigorous in arguing his cause. In addition to the speech opposing cognitive psychology he is giving at the annual meeting of the American Psychological Association, next month he will publish in the *American Psychologist* an article attacking not only cognitive psychology, but also other enemies of his brand of behaviorism: humanistic psychology and other nonbehaviorist psychotherapies.

Humanists, Dr. Skinner writes in his article, have attacked behaviorism as undermining people's sense of freedom and have denounced its claims that the environment determines what people achieve. And, he writes, psychotherapists—apart from those who practice a behaviorist approach—rely too much on inferences they make about what is supposedly going on inside their patients, and too little on direct observation of what they do.

The use of punishment is another issue Dr. Skinner still feels impassioned about. He is an ardent opponent of the use of punishment, such as spanking, or using "aversives"—such as pinches and shocks—with autistic children.

"What's wrong with punishments is that they work immediately, but give no long-term results." Dr. Skinner said. "The responses to punishment are either the urge to escape, to counterattack or a stubborn apathy. These are the bad effects you get in prisons or schools, or wherever punishments are used."

One of the ways Dr. Skinner feels behaviorist techniques have been under-appreciated is in the failure of teaching machines to find wide acceptance in the schools. The machines, which can be computerized, break a topic into small, manageable concepts, and methodically teach each so a student gets the reinforcement of knowing he has mastered it before moving on to the next.

The learning devices had a great advantage over the classroom teacher, according to Dr. Skinner. "Schools were invented to extend a tutor to more than one student at once," Dr. Skinner said. "That's O.K. with three or four, but when you have 30 or more in a classroom, the teacher is no longer able to give the student the reinforcement of a 'right' before moving on to the next task."

Such machines are widely used now in industrial education, but are not widely used in schools.

Rewards of Work

Dr. Skinner continues to act as a social philosopher, a role he played most prominently with his 1948 book *Walden Two*, which described a behaviorist utopia. In a 1986 article in *the American Psychologist* in which he examined "What is Wrong With Daily Life in the Western World." Dr. Skinner charged that common practices had eroded the natural relationship between what people do and the pleasing effects that would reinforce their activities.

For instance, in Dr. Skinner's view, fixed salaries, do not reinforce workers because they are paid whether or not they do more than the minimum job. If workers were paid on a commission or by the piece, their pay would be a direct reinforcer for their labors, and they would work with more effort and pleasure, according to behaviorist principles.

Another aspect of modern life Dr. Skinner criticizes, in all seriousness,

is labor-saving devices such as dishwashers or frozen dinners, which he sees as depriving people of the small satisfactions that accomplishing something brings. "We've destroyed all the reinforcers in daily life," said Dr. Skinner. "For example, if you wash a dish, you've accomplished something, done something that gives you a pleasing result. That is far more reinforcing than putting the dishes in with some powder and then taking them out again."

The device for which Dr. Skinner may be most famous, the original "Skinner box," was a large, glass-enclosed, climate-controlled baby crib with equipment to keep infants amused and well-exercised. Dr. Skinner is still pained by the rumors that his daughters, who used the box, became psychotic or suicidal as a result. Today one daughter is an artist and writer living in London, and the other is a professor of educational psychology at Indiana University; both are married.

When Dr. Skinner first began in the 1930's and 1940's to develop the principles of what he calls "radical behaviorism"—to distinguish it from the earlier theories of Pavlov and Watson—he argued that a scientific psychology could only study behavior that can be directly observed. For that reason, Skinnerian behaviorists have studied the laws of learning through observing responses such as the pecking of a pigeon, and avoided the "black box" of the inner workings of the mind.

In recent decades, though, advances in devices for monitoring faculties such as attention have spurred studies linking the brain and mental activity. If he were starting his research today, Dr. Skinner was asked, would he avail himself of these techniques?

"If I had it all to do again, I would still call the mind a black box," Dr. Skinner said, "I would not use any of the new techniques for measuring information processing. My point has always been that psychology should not look at the nervous system or so-called mind—just at behavior."

For Dr. Skinner, the mind is irrelevant to understanding why people be-

have as they do. In his view, most assumptions about mental life made by laymen and psychologists alike are based on fallacies. In his address before the American Psychological Association, he argued that all the words that describe mental activities actually refer to some behavior.

"No one invented a word for mental experiences that comes from the mind," Dr. Skinner said. "They all have their roots in a reference to action."

"To contemplate, for instance, means to look at a template, or picture. 'Consider' comes from roots meaning to look at the stars until you see a pattern. 'Compare' means to put things side by side to see if they match."

"All the words for mental experience go back to what people do." Dr. Skinner continued. "Over thousands of years, people have used these terms to express something that goes on in their bodies. But these are action terms; they do not mean that these things are going on inside the mind."

"The cognitive revolution is a search inside the mind for something that is not there," Dr. Skinner said. "You can't see yourself process information: information-processing is an inference from behavior—and a bad one, at that. If you look carefully at what people mean when they talk about the mind, you find it just refers to how they behave."

One of the major disputes between the cognitive and behaviorist viewpoints is whether a person's actions are guided by goals and plans, or whether they are a result of that person's history of rewards and punishments. For Dr. Skinner, there is no question. "Behavior is always reinforced behavior," he said.

Despite their differences with other points of view, behaviorists are influential in many psychology departments, and the school of thought remains prominent, particularly among those who are trying to apply its principles in areas like psychotherapy, industrial motivation and remedial education. From the 1930's through the 1960's, behaviorism dominated academic psychology in the 1960's the so-called cognitive revolution began and would go on to sweep psychology.

There is no precise estimate of the numbers of behaviorists, although there are 1,228 members of the division of the psychological association that is devoted to behaviorist research and applications. The strong holds of behaviorism tend to be in colleges in the South and Midwest, according to Kurt Salzinger, a psychologist at Polytechnic University in Brooklyn who is the new president of the behaviorist division.

Dr. Skinner concedes that behaviorism is on the decline while the cognitive school of thought is increasingly popular among psychologists.

There is now a move afoot to reconcile the two approaches.

"Behaviorism was right in saying the task of psychology is to account for what people do, but wrong in ruling out talking about what's going on in the head that generates what people do," said Stephan Harnad, one of the editors of a collection of Dr. Skinner's major papers, along with more than 150 comments by leading scholars. The book is scheduled to be published this winter by the Cambridge University Press.

"That left behaviorists only able to talk about a person's history of rewards and punishments," Dr. Harnad said. "But that accounts for almost nothing of what we can do—our perception, our being able to remember something and our speech. This calls for a cognitive theory."

As the field evolves, an increasing number of behaviorists are violating Dr. Skinner's tenets by studying mental activity. "My major research now is a collaborative project with a cognitive scientist," said Richard Herrnstein, a psychologist who is a former colleague of Dr. Skinner at Harvard University. "We're studying how organisms perceive shapes; we're doing studies of pigeons, humans and computers. I'm pretty comfortable with much of the cognitive school and I consider myself a behaviorist."

Leading Psychologist Expands the Boundaries

October 20, 1987

After a lifetime of finding unexpected paths into the mind, Jerome Bruner has embarked on a new tangent; as usual, he is discovering it as he goes.

This time, the eminent psychologist is listening to people tell their life stories. Their words and images—the framework they use to view the seemingly unconnected events in their lives—shape the way they experience life itself, he believes.

For Dr. Bruner, this is but the most recent journey outside the boundaries of his field. Each time, the field has eventually caught up with him. In his long career as a psychologist and teacher, Dr. Bruner has often balked at prevailing views, striking out on his own into unexplored terrain.

After close to three decades as a professor of psychology at Harvard and then another eight years at Oxford, Dr. Bruner, 72 years old, is the George Herbert Mead Professor at the New School for Social Research and a fellow of the Institute for the Humanities at New York University. His dual posts reflect the most recent twist in his career: his efforts to bridge the gap between psychology and the humanities.

"Jerome Bruner is the only real intellectual in modern cognitive psychology," said Eric Wanner, a psychologist and president of the Russell Sage Foundation in New York City. "He has tried very effectively to say to the field that a less narrow psychology is possible, one that speaks to the great questions of intellectual life, such as how we make order out of our experience."

The Framework of Life

In his most recent research, Dr. Bruner and his colleagues have been asking people to tell, in a half-hour, the story of their lives. Analyzing the words and constructions people use, Dr. Bruner has found a strong relationship between the form of the life story and its contents. For instance, a young woman with a strong sense of home and family life used metaphors about space and place in 37 of the first 100 sentences she spoke, he said.

In telling their life stories, Dr. Bruner said, people create their own plot lines, establishing the framework in which they live and will live. These life stories reveal what they feel is significant, now and in the future.

Writing in a 1987 issue of *Social Research,* Dr. Bruner argued that the ways people tell their stories "become so habitual that they finally become recipes for structuring experience itself, for laying down routes into memory," and finally for guiding one's life.

In his 1987 book, *Actual Minds, Possible Worlds* (Harvard University Press), Dr. Bruner makes the case that the narrative of the poet and storyteller is one of two major modes of thought, logical argument is the other. Cognitive psychologists—those who investigate the way the mind digests information—who devote themselves to constructing computer-like models impoverish psychology. "Basing a view of the mind on compute-ability leaves too much out of the story," he said. "It rules out things like beliefs, desires, expectations, emotions and intentions."

Man and Chemicals

Dr. Bruner told of his own life recently in a conversation with a visitor to his Greenwich Village office, where he works with his wife Carol Fleisher Feldman, a psychologist at New York University and CUNY.

When he was 9 years old, Dr. Bruner recalled, he saw a display in the American Museum of Natural History of a model of a man, next to which were piles of all the various chemicals found in the human body. The sign nearby said, "Man is nothing but these chemicals."

"I thought to myself, 'that misses all the mystery of how it works together,' " Dr. Bruner said. That childhood experience was reflected again and again in his career of searching out the mysteries in the mind.

His work has led Dr. Bruner to dialogues with playwrights and novelists, historians and philosophers. His recollections are peppered with references to giants in other fields with whom he has had crucial encounters and friendships: Ernst Gombrich, the art historian; J. Robert Oppenheimer, the physicist; John von Neumann, the mathematician; A. R. Luria, the Russian neuropsychologist; Claude Levi-Strauss, the anthropologist, and W. H. Auden, the poet.

Drawing on the Humanities

Psychology—particularly cognitive—has become too sterile and narrow in its view of the psyche, Dr. Bruner feels. He looks to a cross-fertilization with philosophy, the arts and literature to offer psychology a richer view of the human mind.

That view is controversial, but controversy has marked Dr. Bruner's career. He has repeatedly emerged as a spokesman for minority views that originally met fierce opposition, though many are now taken for granted.

One of Dr. Bruner's first major contributions came during the 1950's, in demonstrating that perceptions are not mental photographs but rather images shaped by the meaning to the individual of what is perceived. In one famous study, for instance, children were asked to estimate the size of coins. Poor children exaggerated their size; well-to-do children did not.

"We started to see perception as active, rather than passive, as had been assumed," Dr. Bruner said. "I was a visiting scholar at Princeton's Institute for Advanced Studies about that time, and found physicists deeply interested in the same question. As one put it, physics was 5 percent observation and 95 percent speculation. They saw that the models you build determine what you look for, how you interpret what you see, and what you do not see."

Dr. Bruner's study, and others like it, gave rise to a movement that was then called the "New Look" in psychology, which focused on such factors as how people's intentions or emotions affected their perception. Although at the time the New Look was assailed by behaviorists and experimental psychologists alike, its descendant—cognitive psychology—thrives today.

Findings Have Borne Him Out

"Back then there was no theory of a mechanism that could explain Bruner's idea that factors like intention could shape perception," said Dr. Wanner. "But recent work showing there are many very rapid stages in the mind's processing of information have borne him out."

The next issue that Dr. Bruner took on was a challenge to the notion, then prevalent, that from infancy on children's learning is shaped entirely by what happens to them. "Infants were assumed to be blank slates, who had to learn even the most basic dis-

tinctions," Dr. Bruner said. "Their world was supposed to be a buzzing, blooming confusion."

In one key study, Dr. Bruner and his colleagues had two-week-old infants suck on a rubber nipple with sensors inside while they gazed at a slide of a motherly woman's face. How they sucked on the nipple controlled whether the slide was in focus or fuzzy. Their sucking patterns showed that the infants knew when the picture was in and out of focus, and would suck to control it.

How Babies Learn

While the finding may seem trivial, its implications were great. To Dr. Bruner, it suggested that from the outset infants have a directing sense of intention that guides their intellectual development. Babies were not the passive learners that had been assumed; they were active participants in learning.

That insight, says Dr. Bruner, gave him the idea that became the seed of the Head Start programs for preschool children. "When kids live in an impoverished environment that gives them little or nothing back for their efforts to learn, they give up," said Dr. Bruner. Dr. Bruner was one of those psychologists who conceived the program, and was on the Presidential board that organized it.

In Dr. Bruner's thinking, one of the strongest influences on people's perception comes from the culture they live in. This point was brought home for him in studies done in Senegal in the 1960's, by members of the Center for Cognitive Studies, which he founded in the mid-1960's at Harvard.

"We found that in cultures apart from places like Cambridge, Massachusetts, and suburban Geneva, where Piaget did his work, kids did not pass through the sequence of cognitive development that Piaget thought was invariant," said Dr. Bruner. Instead, mental abilities Piaget saw as developing in later stages of childhood, were present in some

form very early. "What was missing altogether from Piaget's thinking was the influence of culture on people's ways of knowing," Dr. Bruner said.

It was this insight that made the work of a Russian linguist, Lev Vygotsky, appealing to Dr. Bruner. "As Vygotsky saw, culture is passed on as the child learns to see the world as the adult does."

Theories of Language

Following Vygotsky's lead, Dr. Bruner began to study how infants acquire language. At the time—he had just come to Oxford, in 1972—the field was torn between a view put forth by B. F. Skinner, which said that children learn language through imitation and reinforcement, and that of Noam Chomsky, which held that children were born with an innate "program" for learning language, that guides their language learning.

Dr. Bruner's work showed the crucial role in language learning of the multitude of small interactions between mother and child, a duet that allows the infant, for instance, to focus his attention on the topic of his mother's comments. His findings and arguments are summed up in *Child's Talk,* published recently by Norton.

What the infant learns before he can speak, Dr. Bruner concluded, is what language is used for. The infant, with the careful, though automatic cooperation of his caretakers, learns the conventions that make an utterance a request a year before he learns how to frame it as a sentence. In mastering the building blocks of language, in Dr. Bruner's view, children are learning the ways of their culture.

To be sure, Dr. Bruner has not been alone in making these contributions. But more often than not his has been the most eloquent voice in arguing the new position.

Some psychologists have accused him of not doing the systematic studies that would prove his new ideas. "He has often done the initial key work that opened up a new field, but he is not the kind of plodder who plows the field," said Dr. Wanner.

In Memory, People Recreate Their Lives to Suit Their Images of the Present

June 23, 1987

Scientific inquiry into personal memory is revealing the forces that create, distort and sometimes erase the images that constitute each person's autobiography.

Sorting through the fiction and fact with which each of us paints the canvas of our lives, the new research is saying with new precision which aspects of a person's memory are likely to be most accurate and which aspects skewed or even erroneous. It examines the periods of life best remembered, those most often lost and the factors that shape or contaminate memory. Through such findings researchers are coming to understand more about the strands from which a personal past is woven.

"Most people would be quite surprised at how malleable their memory is—even those memories they feel most certain about," said David C. Rubin, a psychologist at Duke University.

Dr. Rubin's research has shown that people remember some parts of their lives far more easily than others. Remarkably, the pattern of past memories tends to be the same for everyone. For instance, from middle age on, most people have more reminiscences from their youth and early adult years than for the most recent years of their lives.

Evidence on how the present paints the past is emerging in other research revealing people's propensity to forget parts of their life that no longer fit with their current images of themselves. This became clear in a study of the early home life of 310 men and women who as children had been so troubled they were treated in a child guidance clinic. Researchers who tracked the children down some 30 years later discovered that those who had adjusted well in adulthood had fewer memories of the painful events of childhood than did those who were currently suffering from emotional problems.

For the well-adjusted adults, the forgotten facts of childhood included family dependence on welfare and being in the care of foster parents or in a home for delinquents.

"They have become conventional people after a troubled and disadvantaged childhood; they like to look back on life as though it were always that way," said Lee Robbins, a sociologist in the department of psychiatry at Washington University in St. Louis, who published the study in *the American Journal of Orthopsychiatry*.

The bias in memory can work both ways, Dr. Robbins pointed out. A present predicament can sensitize a person to parts of his past. For instance, one study showed that people with arthritis were more likely than their nonarthritic siblings to remember that a parent had also suffered from the disease.

Similarly, research by Gordon Bowers at Stanford University and others has shown that depressed people, for example, remember sad events from their past more easily than happy people, while happy people recall more pleasant moments.

When it comes to the emotional facts of childhood, people from the same family can remember almost opposite circumstances. In another study Dr. Robbins compared the childhood memories of patients being treated for alcoholism or depression with those of their siblings, who were no more than 4 years older or younger. At her time of the study, the subjects were 30 to 50 years old.

Dr. Robbins found that the pairs of siblings agreed 71 percent of the time on such factual matters as whether the family had moved or whether the parents yelled at each other during arguments. But when the siblings were asked to say how often these things had occurred, the level of agreement fell dramatically, to 47 percent.

And when the memories were of matters that required a value judgment or inference—such as whether a parent was hard on the children, whether a mother hid her anger, or whether the father's drinking embarrassed the family—the level of agreement plummeted to as low as 29 percent.

Implications for Therapy

The findings have strong implications for psychotherapy, where the patient's recall of his past is often central. "A clinician relies heavily on the ability of people to tell about their past," said Dr. Robbins. "But their answers are likely to be highly colored by their current view of themselves. And the vaguer the question—for instance, how happy was your childhood?—the more open to inaccuracy the answer will be."

And because memory is so malleable, there may be a danger that a psychotherapist will cause a bias in his patient's memories by searching for particular kinds of events, according to Donald Spence, a psychoanalyst at Rutgers Medical School. "The patient's memory is fragmented already," he said. "If the therapist suggests something simply by asking about it, he may color the patient's recollection so that he weaves it into his memory."

Dr. Spence cites a study of mothers whose children had been seen at a well-baby clinic 15 years earlier. The mothers were asked to tell when the child had reached developmental milestones such as talking and walking. Their answers tended to be earlier or later than was actually the case, depending on what they had gleaned was better from child experts like Benjamin Spock.

While most alterations in memory have no deeper meaning, some are seen as having clinical significance. Freud saw biases and holes in memory as a clue to a person's deepest conflicts. Psychoanalysis tries to get past a patient's "screen memories"—false memories that hide painful truths—and retrieve a better understanding of those truths.

"Although there is much forgetting that is simply forgetting, a rule of thumb is that the more psychodynamically important a memory is, the more prone it is to warping or forgetting altogether," said Theodore Shapiro, a psychoanalyst and professor of psychiatry at Cornell Medical College.

The relationship between disturbing events and their repression is suggested by a study of 53 women who, as children, had been victims of incest. The earlier, longer and more violent the incest, the more it had been forgotten, according to a report by Judith Lewis Herman, a psychiatrist at the Women's Mental Health Collective in Somerville, Massachusetts. The extent of the incest was known because the women studied had been able to find independent corroboration of their experiences.

Apart from the impact of emotions and conflicts on memory, the lifelong contours of personal memory itself are uneven, with some periods of life standing out while others recede, according to research by Dr. Rubin of Duke, reported in *Autobiographical Memory,* a collection of articles he edited that was published in 1987 by Cambridge University Press.

The spontaneous memories of those in their later years, Dr. Rubin reports, fall off steadily over the most recent two to three decades, but increase for the two to three decades before that and then recede again through childhood. Seventy-year-olds thus tend to remember more from their 30's than from their 50's.

"It seems to be that reminiscence flows more freely about the period in life that comes to define you: the time of your first date, marriage, job, child," according to Dr. Rubin, who discovered the effect in an analysis of data from five studies. "It's not that life is duller from 40 to 55 than from 20 to 35, but that the patterns are more stable, and so less memorable."

The one period of life that virtually no one remembers are the years before the age of about four. While Freud attributed this childhood amnesia to the repression of infantile sexuality, some of the memory researchers today believe this is because mental abilities used to cue memory—language, for instance—have not yet matured.

The nature of a person's earliest memory is coming in for special scrutiny. Alfred Adler, one of Freud's disciples, proposed that the earliest memory a person has, reveals the person's overall psychological stance in life. These early memories are seen by many psychoanalysts as retrospective inventions or convenient selections that express some psychological truth about one's life. Patients' earliest memories sometimes shift over the course of psychotherapy as psychological conflicts become resolved, according to clinical studies.

The relationships reflected in those memories, in this view, repeat themselves in a wide range of situations in the person's life. Evidence that the earliest memories play such crucial roles comes from a study by Jacob Orlofsky, a psychologist at the University of Missouri at St. Louis, published in 1987 in the *Journal of Personality and Social Psychology.* College students were tested on the degree to which they had reached an adult identity, and those levels were compared against their earliest memories.

Those students who had reached fullest psychological maturity—having achieved commitments after a period of doubt and searching—tended to have early memories reflecting such themes as striving and mastery. This was also true of students who were still searching on the way to full maturity.

But those students who had adopted their parents' values without independently seeking an identity had early memories that reflected such dependence. Their memories revolved around themes of a need for nurturance and safety, and of complying with authority to maintain closeness.

A Fast 'Forgetting Rate'

Not surprisingly, people's memories are better for the out-of-the-ordinary, special moments of their lives than for the mundane, according to new data on which events survive best in memory. In the study by William Brewer, a psychologist at the University of Illinois, students carried beepers and wrote down what they were doing and thinking about at random moments when the beepers went off.

Most of the events were soon forgotten. The students' best recall for what they had been doing was when they were reminded what they had been thinking; the students forgot about 20 percent of the events just one week later and could not recall half of them two months later.

The students' worst recall was when they were simply told the time and date—a week later, they could recall only a third of the events and two months later just 15 percent.

"The forgetting rate was much faster than had been expected," said Dr. Brewer.

The best-remembered moments were those that were exciting, unusual, or novel, like the first date with a particular person. "The events of everyday life are unremittingly dull, and people have little memory for there specifics," Dr. Brewer said. "These are the events that vanish in memory."

A Bias Puts Self at Center of Everything

June 13, 1984

Nothing, wrote Walt Whitman "is greater to one than one's self is."

Whitman's words in "Song of Myself" are true for people not only in the obvious ways, researchers are now affirming, but also in a multitude of subtle forms that have not previously been known.

Psychologists are discovering that the personal bias with which people perceive the world is far more extensive than had been thought. Although it has long been understood that egocentricity in some individuals results in a distorted view of reality, research suggests that a somewhat skewed view of reality is a virtually universal trait and that it affects each person's life far more significantly than had been realized.

"In a way, we're all a little like paranoids, who experience everything that goes on around them as having to do with themselves," Anthony Greenwald, a psychologist at Ohio State University, said in an interview. "To a lesser degree, everyone tends to see events as more centered on themselves than is actually the case. People experience life through a self-centered filter."

This propensity, which Dr. Greenwald calls the "egocentricity bias," is said to skew all of perception, from how people initially construe what happens to them, to how they finally recall it from memory.

Though the new concept of egocentricity bias already has substantial support in the social science community, many clinicians see a danger in over-emphasizing it, a risk in becoming simplistic. They point out that it is but one of many ways to understand the rich and complex fabric of the self. But for social psycholo-gists, the notion is a useful way to put within a larger framework a disparate variety of behavior.

For example, in one experiment testing the egocentric bias, Miron Zuckerman, a psychologist at the University of Rochester, found that in group discussions people consistently exaggerate their own importance.

The study, reported in *The Journal of Personality,* showed that people see themselves as having attracted more attention from other members, as having more impact on other people's opinions, and as being the object of others' comments, much more than was the case. In essence, the results suggest that, in an informal group, each person present may be seeing himself as at its center.

Dr. Greenwald, in the *Handbook of Social Cognition* (Erlbaum), published in 1984, reviews extensive evidence for the egocentricity bias. Moreover, he says, it leads to an illusion of control over events in people's life over which, objectively, they have none at all. This illusion gives lottery players, for example, the sense that their ticket has a far greater probability of being selected a winner than it has.

Another sign of the egocentricity bias is people seeing themselves as the target of other's actions, which in fact have nothing to do with them. In the view of Robert Jervis, a political scientist at Columbia University, this misperception occurs frequently among decision-makers in international politics.

"What's most important to America is the East-West struggle, and we tend to see it at work in cases where local concerns are more directly the cause—say, in El Salvador," Dr. Jervis said, "This seems to be even more true for the Russians, who, for example, see the West as being behind the trouble in Poland, downplaying local dissatisfaction."

The egocentricity bias also leads people to reinterpret events to put themselves in a favorable light, according to Dr. Greenwald. He coined the term "beneffectance" for this tendency, which is commonly seen in people's readiness to take credit for success, but not for failure. He coined the word to avoid the negative connotations of the alternative terms, 'egoistic' and 'self-serving.' Dr. Greenwald sees beneffectance as a normal phenomenon, which should not be judged negatively. The word is a compound of beneficence, in the sense of being beneficial, and effectance, a special psychological term for competence.

Beneffectance, in his view, is very common. "For example, if you talk to students after they've gotten their grades back on an exam," Dr. Greenwald said, "and ask them if it was a good test of their abilities, they'll say it was if they did well. But if they did poorly, they'll tell you it was a rotten exam."

The effect shows up, too, in the language people use to describe events such as these. For example, when fans of a team describe a victory, they are likely to couch it as "we won." A defeat, however, more often is put, "they lost."

The most pronounced effects of egocentricity bias are in memory. A large number of studies show, for example, that it is far easier for people to remember information if it somehow refers to themselves.

"If people are asked to remember

events from 5 or 10 years ago," Dr. Greenwald said, "they will recall what happened to themselves much more readily than they can remember the general events of the day."

People fabricate and rewrite memory, Dr. Greenwald says, to enhance their importance in the events they recall. "The past," he writes, "is remembered as if it were a drama in which one self was the leading player."

"The egocentric bias in memory is not just fairly common, it's universal," according to Dr. Greenwald. The reason, he says, is that it simply is more efficient to organize experience in terms of what happens to oneself than in any other format.

"There does not seem to be a choice," he said. "The mind is organized to perceive and store information in terms of the egocentric bias. It serves as an essential cognitive function: the bias organizes our experience in a stable and consistent way so that we can later recall it. The self is like the indexing system of a library. Once you arrange information according to one system—what happened to me—if you switch systems you'd be completely lost."

That may account for the amnesia most people have for their very early years, Dr. Greenwald suggests. "The inability to remember life's earliest events may be due to the fact that one's sense of oneself is so very different in adulthood than it was in the first years of life. It's a bit like trying to find a book in a library using the card catalogue from an old index, after the books have been arranged by a new indexing system."

The egocentricity bias seems to diminish when people become depressed, and its presence may well be a sign of mental health, some researchers believe. For example, in one study where people rated their contribution to a task over which they actually had little control, depressed people were realistic in acknowledging their lack of involvement in the outcome. Nondepressed people, however, overestimated the credit due them.

The self-enhancing bias of nondepressed people, reveals, according to one researcher, the "illusory glow" with which people view their involvement in the world—a glow that is lost in depression. When depressed patients improve, the "illusory glow" returns.

Although the egocentricity bias may well be an indispensable fixture of the mind, as Dr. Greenwald notes, at its extremes it can be a symptom of mental disorder, like paranoia. When, then, is egocentricity healthy, and when is it a sign of pathology?

Psychiatric diagnostic manuals list egocentricity as a common distortion in certain mental disorders. For example, writing in *Cognitive Approaches to Stress* (Guilford), Aaron Beck describes the egocentricity of a patient with chronic anxiety in terms that could, to some degree, apply to most other people as well. "He views all events as though he were the central character in a drama; the behavior of all the other characters has meaning only insofar as he relates it to his own 'vital interests.' He personalizes events that are essentially impersonal and perceives confrontations and challenges when others are conducting their own lives—oblivious of him," Dr. Beck said.

"At its extremes, egocentricity is a frequent symptom of mental disorders," Dr. Beck said in an interview. "For example, an overly anxious person, if he hears a siren, will think, 'Something is wrong with someone in my family.' A paranoid, of course, will think, 'They're after me.' If something goes wrong, a depressed person will think, 'It's my fault,' and if something goes well, a manic person will take the credit."

How, then, to make the distinction between pathological and normal?

"It's partly a matter of degree," Dr. Beck said. "The mild, positive personalization of events is normal, but in mental disorders it becomes quite extreme and overgeneralized. Most telling, perhaps, is that people become quite rigid in their egocentrism, even in the face of evidence to the contrary that would ordinarily convince someone that they were overdoing it."

"Part of therapy is to loosen the patient's overuse of egocentricity, so he doesn't interpret absolutely everything as relevant to himself in some distorted way, and so he can assess evidence objectively to see he is not always the target of what goes on around him," Dr. Beck said.

The normal person may well be aware of his or her egocentricity, or at least be able to recognize and deal with it in the face of reasonably convincing evidence. Reality and illusion must not be so far apart, in other words, as to inflict harm, or, perhaps in the end, deep tragedy.

Forgetfulness Is Seen Causing More Worry Than It Should

July 1, 1986

Moments of forgetfulness are among those small blows to self-esteem that can lead people to worry about declining intelligence or impending senility.

New research should be reassuring. It documents how very common forgetfulness is, what it is that people tend to forget most often and how the fear of forgetfulness influences the way people shape the world around them. At the same time, it shows how durable memory can be.

For the last century, most memory research has been conducted in laboratories, concentrating on technical aspects of memory that are removed from ordinary life. As research psychologists have left the laboratory to study memory in the real world, they have learned more about the effects of forgetting on the daily lives of just about everyone.

They have learned, for example, that virtually every healthy person finds himself standing from time to time in a room having completely forgotten why he is there. And while some people's memories are, indeed, worse than others, researchers have found, it is only sudden and severe memory loss that may indicate a problem.

"Most people think their memories are much worse than you find they actually are when you go out and observe them," said Ulric Neisser, a cognitive psychologist at Emory University who is a leader in the new work.

Dr. Neisser was one of the first researchers to study the kinds of forgetfulness that affect people in their daily lives. Freud, of course, looked at memory lapses as clues to deeper problems, but current study is focusing on forgetfulness itself, and thus brings new hard data to the understanding of a common experience. With Douglas Herrmann, a psychologist at Hamilton College, Dr. Neisser surveyed more than 200 people to determine which lapses occurred most frequently.

Among those that had the highest frequency were being introduced to someone at a social gathering and forgetting the person's name a few minutes later; awakening in the morning with the strong sense of having just been dreaming but being unable to remember a single detail, and forgetting to bring up a point in a conversation.

Much less frequent were such lapses as going out somewhere and realizing that one has left something behind, or having to ask the date.

Although healthy people often complain about how bad their memory is getting, researchers say, that may be because they have no idea how frequently other people suffer the same lapses. The research by Dr. Herrmann and Dr. Neisser and others is a step toward establishing with some precision what is a normal degree of forgetfulness and what is a sign of trouble.

Although the research shows that memory lapses in healthy people are far more common than most people realize, clinicians recognize that more extreme memory lapses can be symptoms of problems ranging from depression to Alzheimer's disease or overmedication.

"Memory loss is normal," said Jack Botwinick, a psychologist at Washington University in St. Louis. "It becomes abnormal if it disrupts your life."

People's memories for what they have learned can be surprisingly long-lasting. Harry Bahrick, a psychologist at Ohio Wesleyan University, studied 1,000 people who had learned Spanish in high school or college, and found that most of what they forgot was lost in the first three to five years after finishing their language courses. Of the Spanish that remained, little was forgotten for the next 25 years.

Challenging Link to Age

Dr. Bahrick's work challenges the notion from experimental studies that there is a gradual, continuous loss of memory as time goes on. "If you retain knowledge for five years, it seems you'll remember it for another 25," Dr. Bahrick said.

While some kinds of memory do decline with age, memory for names and faces does not seem to be especially vulnerable to the passing of years. Thirty-five years after graduation from high school, Dr. Bahrick has found, people could recognize the names and faces of about 90 percent of their classmates. Fifty years after graduation, they could still identify 70 to 80 percent of them.

When professors were tested for memory of former students, those who were 75 years old when tested did about as well, or poorly, as those who were 36.

Another kind of memory that age does not seem to diminish is what researchers call "prospective memory"—remembering to do something at the right time. This memory ability, psychologists now say, is every bit as important as being able to recall events from the past, or "retrospective memory," which has come under much more intensive scientific scrutiny.

Maturity Seems to Help

In a study of how well people remembered to keep an appointment, a group of volunteers ranging in age from 65 to 75 were far better at remembering to make a telephone call at a certain time than were a group of college students. There was only one lapse among the older people, but 14 among the college students.

Organizing one's life so as to remember to do things seems to be one of those skills that comes with maturity, according to John Harris, a psychologist at Cambridge University, who did the research. He found that the older people in the study had learned to rely on memory aids, such as writing notes to themselves.

"There is a tendency for those who trust their memories and make comments such as 'I've got an internal alarm' to be more likely to miss an appointment," Dr. Harris said.

Although the young people were, in Dr. Harris's words, "a little cocky" about their memories, they complained more than the elderly did about not being able to remember things. Among the most common complaints of the young was of having completely forgotten to do things they had promised to do.

Perception vs. Memory

Some kinds of forgetfulness, researchers are finding, are not problems with memory so much as with perception. Yvette Tenney, a psychologist at the Boston Veterans Administration Hospital, asked people to think of times they had misplaced something, only to find it later. The discovered object was frequently in a place where the person had already looked, but had not noticed it.

Older people, Dr. Tenney found, reported such failures to notice a "lost" object more often than younger

people did. Dr. Tenney interprets the results as indicating that there is a slight decrease in perceptual efficiency with aging, which can make older people think their memory is worse than it actually is.

"When I look in a file and can't find what should be there, I always go back and look again," said Dr. Neisser, commenting on Dr. Tenney's results. "I find that I missed something the first time because it didn't quite look the way I expected it to; I saw it but I didn't recognize it."

To be sure, "forgetting" can be convenient, a way to shirk onerous obligations or to avoid troubling feelings, as Freud observed. In a recent study of one variety of repression, researchers at the University of Pennsylvania, Columbia, and Yale investigated instances in which people momentarily forgot what they were about to say in a psychotherapy session.

Nervousness Before Forgetting

Careful analysis of the tape recorded conversations leading to the lapses showed that the patients gave signs of increasing nervousness just before forgetting. More significant, when they later remembered what it was that had slipped their mind, it almost invariably had to do with insecurities about their relationship with the therapist, a troubling topic to bring up.

The patients remembered the forgotten thought in more than two-thirds of the instances, usually within a minute. If they were unable to remember within two minutes, they rarely could retrieve the thought at all.

Such clear records of real-life forgetting are eagerly sought by researchers who are trying to study forgetting outside the laboratory. One difficulty in studying everyday memory, the researchers complain, is that they cannot rely on asking people how good their memory is. People whose memories are quite poor often report that it is very good, simply because they have forgotten about having forgotten. On the other hand, many people whose memories are excellent are troubled by those few

times they have forgotten to do something, and so exaggerate in their minds the frequency with which they forget.

Researchers have found they can get around this difficulty, in part, by having people keep logs of memory lapses, writing them down on the spot when they realize they have occurred. Of course, those that completely slip by are never recorded. Another method is to check people's own reports against those of spouses or co-workers, on the theory that people are more accurate in reporting other people's lapses than they are in reporting their own.

Organization and Memory

As researchers examine day-to-day memory more closely, they are finding that it explains much about how the man-made world is set up. How people arrange their possessions—from just what is where on their bulletin boards, to which drawer they use for the egg beater—is determined by their need to prime their memories.

"We structure our surroundings, in large part, so that it acts as a memory aid," said Donald Norman, a cognitive psychologist at the University of California at San Diego. "People make a sort of natural map of their world by putting things in places that fit their habits. When there is no fit between where things are and what you need them for, then memory is more likely to fail."

In research done at the Xerox Corporation on how people arranged their desks and offices, for example, it was found that their reason for having seemingly haphazard piles of books and papers around was to help them remember what to do or where to find things.

The more obvious and visible an object, the more urgent is its claim on the person's memory. "If you want to find something on someone else's desk, you should decide how important it is to them," Dr. Norman said. "If it is of great importance, you look in the more obvious or frequently used places, like the top drawer."

Memory, too, plays a role in the design of man-made objects. "One of the basic rules of good design is that a user should immediately recognize and remember how to use an article, whether a blender or a computer," Dr. Norman said. "The more often he has to ask, 'How do I work this?' the poorer the design."

"I have a fancy European car with 112 different controls, counting all the different radio knobs, the windows and so on," Dr. Norman said. "I picked it up at the factory, and a guy sat beside me and showed me everything just once. That was enough— that's good design. But I still can't remember how to use my phone for all the things it can do, like call forwarding; there's nothing in its design to remind me."

Thinking and Language

The unconscious is taking a new importance in psychology, as research into how information flows through the mind shows the unconscious to be the site of a far larger portion of mental life than even Freud envisioned. "New View of Unconscious Gives It Expanded Role" reviews a growing body of research showing that the unconscious mind understands and responds to meanings, forms emotional responses, and guides most of our actions.

"Freudian slips," those revealing slips of the tongue, are coming in for a new interpretation, as cognitive psychologists bring more systematic methods to the study of mental processes. "Do 'Freudian Slips' Betray a Darker, Hidden Meaning?" tells of research suggesting that most slips are benign, simple and innocent mistakes that give clues to the inner workings of how the mind registers and responds to information.

The capacity to deceive ourselves is one byproduct of the way the mind pays attention and remembers what it takes in—or fails to. The lies we tell ourselves are often motivated by the desire to avoid unpleasant feelings, such as anxiety or sadness. "Insights Into Self-Deception" describes a range of experimental findings that suggest just how the mind can deceive itself.

Creativity is a bent of mind that is not reserved just for those who make brilliant contributions to the arts. Anyone can be creative in how he or she meets the challenges of daily life. Studies of the ways ordinary people display a flair for innovation in everyday work and leisure—and what circumstances unleash the creative spirit—are summarized in "A New Index Illuminates the Creative Life."

Laughter is one aid to creativity. When thinking follows the same ruts, it stifles creativity. But a good joke can jog the mind into new ways of looking at a problem, according to the research reviewed in "Humor Found in Aid Problem-Solving."

What do babies think is going on when they look at TV? Do they see anything more than pretty patterns and colors? "TV's Potential to Teach Infants" discusses research showing that even before infants can talk, they can follow what is happening in a show like "Sesame Street," and even learn by watching.

New View of Unconscious Gives It Expanded Role

February 7, 1984

Suddenly, psychology is excited again about the unconscious.

For decades mainstream research psychologists suppressed the notion that crucial mental activity could take place unconsciously. Indeed, through the 1950's, these experimental psychologists largely ignored any such entity as "the mind," focusing instead on observable behavior. Even in the 1960's when the resurgence of cognitive psychology legitimized the study of how the mind registers information, the unconscious was still slighted outside psychoanalytic circles.

But now, in what one researcher calls "a silent revolution," experimental psychologists are taking the unconscious seriously in the wake of new and compelling evidence that the unconscious is the site of a far larger portion of mental life than even Freud envisioned. The main studies show that the unconscious mind may understand and respond to meaning, form emotional responses and guide most actions, largely independent of conscious awareness. And the research evidence extends beyond the laboratory to such real-life situations as an operating room. Researchers have verified, for example, that what patients hear while under anesthesia can affect their subsequent behavior and, ultimately, their health.

The findings imply that, despite the subjective experience of being in conscious control of feelings and thoughts, decisions and actions, people are piloted far more than they know by the unconscious mind.

"An enormous portion of cognitive activity is nonconscious," said Emmanuel Donchin, director of the Laboratory for Cognitive Psychophysiology at the University of Illinois. "Figuratively speaking, it could be 99 percent; we probably will never know precisely how much is outside awareness."

The methods that have conferred a new respectability on the unconscious offer a textbook case of how experimental psychology—perhaps the most rigorously "scientific" field of psychology—proceeds. By carefully isolating a small piece of behavior and experimenting with it under highly controlled conditions, psychologists can confirm or reject theories with far-reaching implications.

A case in point is the work of Anthony Marcel, a psychologist at Cambridge University, whose research has generated much of the current excitement about the unconscious.

Dr. Marcel stumbled into research on nonconscious perception inadvertently. He was studying reading, by flashing words rapidly on a screen and asking children to say what they were; some of the words were flashed so rapidly that they could not be read. Dr. Marcel was struck by some odd results. For words that could not be read, the children would sometimes guess a word similar in meaning, such as "queen" for "king."

Dr. Marcel remembered that the same "clever mistake" had been observed in certain aphasic patients, brain-damaged people who are unable to utter words that they in fact do know. To follow up, he began a series of experiments on what he now calls "unconscious reading." Dr. Marcel would, for example, "mask" a word by flashing it in a nonsense context, so confusing, his subjects did not even know that they had seen it. Then he asked which of two words looked or meant the same as the one masked. If, say, the unseen word was "blood," the look-alike might be "flood"; the related meaning, might be "flesh." Although they had not the least idea what word they had seen before, the subjects were right in their guesses an astonishing 90 percent of the time.

"Once we have learned to read," Dr. Marcel concludes, "the meanings of words can register without consciousness. Indeed, much of perception is automatic and independent of conscious intention or awareness."

He has found a parallel role for nonconscious processes in "blindsight," a curious phenomenon occurring in certain people who have lost their sight because of lesions in the brain instead of damage to the eye.

Dr. Marcel placed an object in front of such a patient and asked him to reach for it, meanwhile tracking his movements with high-speed movie cameras. The film showed that the patient did not grope; instead he reached directly for the object, his preparatory motions fine-tuned to its specific location, shape and size.

"They thought I was mad, at first, because they couldn't see a thing," says Dr. Marcel. "But when they finally tried it, they reached for the object perfectly. It turns out their vision is, in a sense, superb, but they don't know they can see."

Dr. Marcel believes both blindsight and the masked-word effect show there can be understanding without conscious awareness. Further, he believes the unconscious mind has unique properties that bear little direct relation to what people subjectively experience. "Conscious perception proceeds according to our rational beliefs about the world and

Thinking and Language

our minds, while nonconscious perception probably does not," he adds.

In Dr. Marcel's view, the nonconscious mind has far greater capacity than the conscious, and so can handle a much larger array of possibilities. For example, what pops into awareness when one reads is the appropriate meaning selected for a word, according to its context, out of all the possible meanings that the word can have. And one is wholly unaware of whatever procedure the mind may use in selecting that one meaning.

Other researchers concur with Dr. Marcel in granting the unconscious mind a primary role in mental life. For example, Robert Zajonc, a psychologist at the University of Michigan, argues that the unconscious mind can form likes or dislikes before the conscious mind even knows what is being responded to.

Dr. Zajonc came to his conclusions through experimental techniques similar to Dr. Marcel's, in which people were shown geometrical forms so fast they were unaware of having seen them. Later, they preferred these shapes to forms they were genuinely seeing for the first time. This suggests, says Dr. Zajonc, that emotions can sometimes operate unconsciously, completely separately from cognition—feelings need no reasons.

"In many cases," says Dr. Zajonc, "when people explain why they've made a decision, they are simply rationalizing, attributing what sound like reasonable bases for what is in fact a murky, unknowable process."

One of the more controversial claims coming out of the new research is a challenge to the notion of conscious volition, or will.

Benjamin Libet, a professor of physiology at the University of California in San Francisco, has conducted research measuring brain waves. His subjects are instructed to flex a hand spontaneously, and with the aid of an electronic device they are able to register the millisecond at which they become aware of their intent to move. That moment is generally two-tenths of a second before the movement actually occurs.

In a recent article in the journal *Brain,* Dr. Libet reports that measure-ments of the subjects' brain waves show that the brain starts to initiate the act about four-tenths of a second before a person is aware of wanting to do it. "This means," Dr. Libet said in an interview, "that you don't initiate voluntary actions consciously, but decide to make them somewhere in the brain outside of awareness. The part of the mind that becomes aware of a decision to act is not the part that decides; a person's decisions come to him already made."

Dr. Libet's research and interpretations rankle both philosophers and fellow brain researchers. For example, Dr. Donchin agrees with Dr. Libet's results, but not the interpretations he gives them.

But, in Dr. Donchin's view, these results do not challenge the notion of free will. "For one thing, what do you mean by "'the person'?" he asks. "Some place in the nervous system responds before the movement occurs, but whether the person is aware at that point may be unknowable. We still don't have a precise measure of the instant at which something passes into awareness."

Although it may be difficult to draw the precise border between conscious and nonconscious, other researchers are fascinated by what that elusive line means for how the mind orchestrates behavior. For example, Donald Norman, a cognitive scientist at the University of California at San Diego, sees that borderline as crucial for understanding how errors occur.

Such slips might be called "Post-Freudian"; they are innocuous, like putting your money in a candy vending machine when what you really wanted was coffee. "Such errors," says Dr. Norman, "are unconscious. They happen only with well-learned routines."

"The channel of conscious awareness is narrower than the unconscious, but more powerful," Dr. Norman says. "The beginner pays full attention to a task. But as a person masters a task, he pays less and less attention to doing it; it goes on smoothly, in the unconscious. That leaves more of his awareness free for other tasks."

"When an error in an automatic routine occurs, it enters conscious-ness," Dr. Norman says. "One of the main functions of consciousness seems to be making repairs in routines where a slip has occurred. Otherwise, it's handy to have most of what we do go on outside consciousness, so we don't have to be bothered with it."

Dr. Norman says when Dr. Marcel first tried to publish an article on his research in the journal *Cognitive Psychology* just four years ago, "reviewers simply refused to believe" the results. "But now they've been so widely replicated that just about everyone takes them seriously," he says. "He opened a door, even for the most traditional experimental psychologists to studying nonconscious processes."

"Marcel's work has brought a new interest in a line of research that dates back to the 40's," says Matthew Erdelyi, whose book on Freud as a cognitive psychologist will be published this fall. "There were hundreds of studies done on what was called perceptual defense. For example, they found that when a dirty word was flashed, subjects would not be able to say what it was, but their sweat response showed a strong reaction."

"Twenty and 30 years ago, when these studies were reported, the *zeitgeist* in psychology was unreceptive," Dr. Erdelyi adds. "Interest waned. But the new research by Marcel and others shows the same effect, though with neutral words; stimuli that register outside awareness have a measurable effect on behavior. It has opened the door for new, serious research on the unconscious."

For example, Howard Shevrin, a psychologist at the University of Michigan has duplicated the perceptual defense effect using a sophisticated brain measure called the evoked potential. Dr. Shevrin finds that people have stronger brain responses to emotionally loaded words than to neutral ones, even when they are totally unaware they have seen any word at all.

The new acceptance of the unconscious by the rigorous experimentalists of the field will no doubt be reasuring to therapists who have used subliminal techniques such as taped suggestions for weight loss or enhanced self-esteem.

Still, when experimental psychologists speak of the unconscious, they do not necessarily mean the same by the term as Freud did.

In his 1905 book *The Interpretation of Dreams,* Freud proposed a model of the mind quite prescient in its similarity to the most modern models, with information first registering in a nonconscious realm before becoming conscious. But in Freudian pariance today, the "unconscious" has come to carry a large load of special attributes such as being the repository of anxiety-arousing memories.

The new view of the mind's architecture may allow ample room for the Freudian unconscious, but for most experimental psychologists, the Freudian notion is still unverified.

"Making the distinction between the conscious and unconscious parts of mind is just the start," says Michael Posner of the University of Oregon. "The next step is to ask, do they differ in their operations? Freud argued that they do. Whether he was right or not is still an open question."

Not all cognitive psychologists are swayed by the current wave of interest. One skeptic is Ulric Neisser, whose 1967 book *Cognitive Psychology* was the field's manifesto. "Even though more researchers than used to, now believe that unnoticed things make fleeting contact with the mind and have effects," he says, "I don't know if this has any significance for the real world."

Do "Freudian Slips" Betray a Darker, Hidden Meaning?

November 27, 1984

Freudian slips are in trouble. A new body of psychological research now suggests that they are generally not "Freudian" at all; that for the most part they do not, as the old master would have us believe, bespeak some hidden message from the unconscious.

Consider some cases in point. The phone rings in the office. A harassed, preoccupied man picks up the receiver and bellows, "Come in!" At a copying machine, a clerk stands counting copies: "... 9, 10, jack, queen, king." A jogger, just finishing her run, tosses her shirt into the toilet instead of the laundry hamper.

Freud read hidden meanings in every slip. But the new school of thought holds that the vast majority of slips are devoid of ulterior motives or meanings; though some may, indeed, be motivated by unconscious conflicts, more often than not, a slip is just a slip.

The new work is leading to a better understanding of why people make mistakes.

A Freudian analysis of such mistakes is "not required for the understanding of the mechanisms that underlie slips," according to Donald Norman, a cognitive psychologist at the University of California at San Diego, who is one of those at the forefront of the recent work. The single most common type of slip seems simply to be the intrusion of a strong habit; for instance, standing at a friend's door trying to unlock it with one's own housekey. In a study of such mistakes, for example, 40 percent were found to be habitual sequences that were easily recognized as pertinent to some other activity that was more frequent, recent or familiar than the intended actions.

The parallel case for the tip-of-the-tongue involved a more familiar word that repeatedly came to mind instead of the word that was sought. Such familiar blocking words occurred 60 percent of the time.

The new work relegates Freud's explanations to the background, seeing them as applicable to a minority of slips. The emerging theory favors what its proponents see as a more parsimonious explanation, which does not need to invoke the ideas of psychoanalysis. Instead, it puts them in terms of the understanding of the mechanisms of mind that has emerged in recent years from cognitive psychology. Cognitive psychologists study how the mind registers information and directs activity.

The new research follows decades of neglect. But the last five years has seen a surge of renewed interest, motivated not so much by an interest in Freud's theory as by the compelling need to understand the minor lapses that, in modern times, can lead to major disasters; for example, errors by a jet pilot or air traffic controller. Such catastrophes, in the words of one researcher, "tend to be due to quite commonplace slips and lapses which in more forgiving circumstances would pass largely unremarked."

The new model does not entirely rule out the kinds of causes Freud found for such slips. Indeed, in the view of some researchers, it actually provides a framework for predicting the mental circumstances under which people will be most prone to so-called "Freudian" slips, as well as to neutral errors.

Psychoanalysts, however, argue that the cognitive approach omits crucial evidence for the meanings to be found in slips. "A hidden determinant would be found even for the most seemingly innocuous slip, if it were investigated with psychoanalytic methods," according to Dr. Charles Brenner, an eminent psychoanalyst who has written extensively on the topic.

"The unconscious determinant may not be guilty or bad, but it will be one that makes sense in the person's mental life," he added in an interview. "But since these researchers refrain from using the psychoanalytic method, they can never put Freud's claims to the test."

Dr. James Reason, a psychologist at the University of Manchester in England, has been one of the first major investigators since Freud to collect and analyze actual slips. In one study, for example, Dr. Reason had volunteers report all instances of having a word on the tip of the tongue over the course of several weeks. Dr. Reason classifies the inability to bring to mind a sought-after word as a variety of slip. On the basis of this and other studies, he estimates that adults experience an average of two to three such incidents each week.

One striking fact emerging from his research, says Dr. Reason, is that slips and errors of all sorts seem to have a high degree of uniformity, regardless of the domain of activity in which they occur. Thus, slips of the tongue share much in common with lapses in memory and with errors in physical actions. The lawfulness of these errors has become the basis for a new theory that sees a single, global mental process at work across a wide variety of mental processes.

The research and Dr. Reason's theory are summarized in *Everyday Memory, Actions and Absent-Mindedness,* published in 1984 by Academic Press.

People differ widely in their susceptibility to slips, according to studies by Donald Broadbent at Cambridge University. Some evidence, for example, suggests that people with obsessive personalities are relatively invulnerable to slips.

Mistaken Words and Actions

What's more, people prone to one kind of mistake—such as slips of the tongue—seem equally prone to all other kinds; for example, to mistaken actions and forgetting names as well. This fact, in Dr. Reason's view, points to a general factor exerting influence across all aspects of mental function.

That factor, in Dr. Reason's view, is a failure to suppress competing choices. To select one action—speaking a word, making a movement—the mind must simultaneously suppress a potentially huge variety of alternatives. When the mind fails to suppress an alternative, a slip occurs.

Attention, according to Dr. Reason and others in the field, is the critical factor. The more attention one gives to an act, the less likely there will be an unintended alternate response. When attention lags, alternate responses are more able to replace the intended one, and slips become more probable.

Dr. Norman gives the example of having decided not to take another bite of a delicious and very rich cake, and, after a brief lapse of attention, the cake somehow is eaten anyway.

Investigators at Oxford University found that people who are generally anxious make more slips. The Oxford researchers interpret this finding, too, in terms of attention rather than psychodynamic causes. They propose that the anxious person's worries and preoccupations compete for attention with whatever else may be his task at hand, and so make him prone to slips.

At such times, in Dr. Reason's view, the most probable slip is simply some well-learned action akin to the one that was actually intended, not a slip with some hidden message. Indeed, he finds that most slips are the substitution of a better-learned response for one that is less familiar, though intended.

Dr. Reason's theory fits well with other, independent lines of research. For example, linguists have been interested in slips for reasons of their own. Their main concern is to detect errors that creep into a text in the course of it being passed along from version to version; for example, by a typist or printer's mistake.

A More Familiar Word

One of the most common kinds of errors linguists have identified is what is called "banalization," the replacement of an intended word by an erroneous one that is more familiar or simpler.

Even though cognitive scientists, including Dr. Reason, see the vast majority of slips as innocuous, they readily allow that some may have the hidden causes and meanings Freud saw in them. The most convincing work in this regard has been that of Bernard Baars, a psychologist at the State University of New York at Stony Brook.

In an ingenious series of studies, Dr. Baars has been able to induce and study Freudian slips experimentally. His technique, in essence, is to have his volunteers repeatedly give one kind of response, such as word-pairs with the same pattern of beginning letters. Once these responses have become habitual, Dr. Baars switches the response they are to give. Often the volunteers do not fully adjust to the new demand, and make a mistake.

Those mistakes, he finds, are likely to be slips of the Freudian variety if the person is preoccupied with some feeling he is repressing, such as anger or sexual interest. For example, male volunteers found to be high in guilt about sex were likely to give a sex-related slip when the experimenter was an attractive woman. Instead of giving the response "lice-legs," for instance, they said "nice-legs."

Dr. Baars's findings do not, in his view, contradict the new models of slips, but extend them to handle unconsciously motivated ones as well. "If a person is mentally primed with a given emotion or set of needs," he said in an interview, "should he then make a slip, it is more likely to be of the sort Freud talked about, and for the reasons Freud gave."

"Nevertheless," Dr. Baars added, "these slips are a special case of the failure of an editing capacity of the mind that is far more general than Freud saw. With every action, the mind has to edit out competing alternatives; when the editing fails there is a slip. The vast majority of these alternatives, and the slips they lead to, are neutral, not Freudian."

Freud Foresaw Explanations

Freud himself foresaw many of the alternative explanations of slips given by cognitive psychologists and belittled them as shallow. He contended that these cognitive explanations simply indicate when a slip is likely, but do not give a sufficient explanation of their true causes.

"Such psycho-physiological factors as excitement, absent-mindedness and disturbances of attention will clearly help us very little toward an explanation," Freud wrote. "They are only empty phrases, screens behind which we must not let ourselves be prevented from having a look."

Insights into Self-Deception

May 12, 1985

The woman spoke about her father only after being reassured she would not be identified, because, in his time, the man had been famous. Even now, some 25 years after his death, the woman's voice was halting as she talked about her father's alcoholism and about how her family had somehow managed not to know how troubled he was.

"After my father died, we would find bottles of liquor hidden around the house, behind books, in the backs of closets. And, looking back, I can remember how poppa was always 'taking a nap,' as my mother would say. Sometimes he would get very loud and angry with my mother and push her around. She'd tell my little sister and me that he was 'in a mood,' and, without another word, she'd take us by the hand outdoors for a walk.

"He was an alcoholic, but somehow we stayed oblivious to it all. Once, after I was grown and married myself, I got up the nerve to ask my mother about it all. She denied it out-and-out." To this day, her mother has refused to admit the truth about her husband's drinking.

Family therapists have described this sort of denial and cover-up as "the game of happy family." It is just one aspect of the larger phenomenon of human self-deception, the nature of which as only now beginning to be understood by cognitive psychologists. The scientists' work explains how and why people lie to themselves. And patterns emerge from the scientific evidence that would seem to indicate that, just as individuals and families deceive themselves, so do larger groups of people, so do whole societies. The new research reveals a natural bent toward self-de-

ception so great that the need for counterbalancing forces within the mind and society as a whole—forces such as insight and respect for truth—becomes more apparent than ever.

The theme of buried secrets is so familiar and ancient in literature that it attests to the universality of the experience. The story of Oedipus revolves around such secrets. Willy Loman's tragic fall in "Death of a Salesman," testifies to the explosive potential of family secrets unmasked. Ibsen called this sort of secret a "vital lie," a myth that stands in place of a disturbing reality.

To acknowledge that it is commonplace for people to lie to themselves is not to understand why or how unpleasant truths can be buried so effectively. Freud explained it by proposing a range of psychological defenses, but his speculations came long before the detailed mapping of the mind's mechanics by cognitive psychologists, researchers who study how the mind perceives, processes and remembers information. Working in the laboratory with new techniques for measuring perception and memory, researchers have been able to sketch a scientific model of the mind, one that shows how and why self-deception can operate with such ease.

Among the major discoveries that have contributed to the modern understanding of the mind's architecture, and the place of self-deception in that design, are the following.

There is now firm scientific evidence that the unconscious mind plays an immensely potent role in mental life. The evidence includes the startling phenomenon known as

"unconscious reading," in which, as psychologists at Cambridge University in England have shown, a person unconsciously registers the meaning of words that are presented to him in such a way that he has no conscious awareness of having seen them at all. The premise that most mental processes go on prior to awareness—and may never reach awareness at all—has now come into widespread acceptance among cognitive scientists.

Recently, psychologists at the University of Wisconsin have obtained evidence—for the first time ever—that suggests there is a specific mechanism in brain function associated with psychological defense of repression. The transfer of information from one half of the brain to the other, they have found, is the point at which upsetting emotional experience may be blocked from awareness.

Self-deception itself is coming to be seen in a more positive light by psychologists, who find that it can serve people well as a psychological basis for self-confidence and hope. Researchers at the University of California at Berkeley have found that, in certain medical situations, those patients who deny the seriousness of medical risk fare better than those who dwell on it. This is not to say that self-deception is always to the good. But it may be that people fall prey to self-deception with such ease precisely because it has an appropriate, even essential, place in the ecology of mind.

Although researchers are exploring self-deception by probing deep into the mechanics of the mind, the phenomenon itself can easily be observed in everyday life and at several levels of human activity. The roots of self-deception seem to lie in the mind's ability to allay anxiety by distorting awareness. Denial soothes. Freud saw that the mind, with remarkable claraity, can deny a range of facts it would rather avoid and then not seem to know that it has done so.

At a dinner party, for example, a young woman commented on how close she was to her family, how loving family members had always been. She then went on to report, as evidence of their closeness, "When I disagreed with my mother she threw whatever was nearest at me. Once it happened to be a knife and I needed 10 stitches in my leg. A few years later my father tried to choke me when I began dating a boy he didn't like. They really are very concerned about me," she added, in all seriousness.

While the self-deception here is obvious, it often takes much more subtle forms, such as those that psychoanalysts track—defense mechanisms like denial and repression. All such mental maneuvers are part of a psychological calculus in which painful truths and soothing denials are the main variables. In the game of happy family, for instance, the rules call for twists of attention to bolster the pretense that nothing is wrong. Such psychological charades require that family members orchestrate their attention in an exquisitely coordinated self-deception.

As the Scottish psychiatrist R. D. Laing put it, "I have never come across a family that does not draw a line somewhere as to what may be put into words, and what words it may be put into." The line directs attention *here* and away from *there*. The rule works best when family members are not aware it exists at all but simply respect it automatically. In Dr. Laing's words. "If you obey these rules, you will not know that they exist."

Synchronized denial can take place in groups of all kinds. We slip so easily into group membership, as Freud saw, because we have learned the art of belonging as children in our families. The unspoken pact in family is repeated in every other group we will join in life. Part of the price of membership, of being valued as part of a group, is to honor the implicit rules of shared attention and shared denial.

Such orchestrated self-deceptions were at work, for example, among the group that planned the Bay of Pigs invasion. Irving L. Janis, a psychologist at Yale University, studied in detail how the plans were laid for that fiasco. It was a textbook case of the collective defenses that Janis has called "groupthink."

Essentially, when groupthink is at work, group members hobble their seeking of information in order to preserve a cozy unanimity. Loyalty to the group requires that no one raise embarrassing questions, nor attack weak arguments, nor counter softheaded thinking with hard facts. "The more amiable the esprit de corps among the members of a policymaking group," Janis has observed, "the greater is the danger that independent critical thinking will be replaced by groupthink."

Looking back, Arthur Schlesinger Jr., who was then on the White House staff, observed how the meetings in which the Bay of Pigs plan took shape went on "in a curious atmosphere of assumed consensus." Yet, he suspects that had a single person voiced a strong objection, President Kennedy would have canceled the plan. No one spoke up. In a post-mortem, Theodore Sorenson, who had been special counsel to President Kennedy, concluded that "doubts were entertained but never pressed, partly out of fear of being labeled 'soft' or undaring in the eyes of their colleagues." The rationalization, erroneous, as it turned out, that there would be a mass uprising against Castro once the invasion began, kept the group from contemplating such devastating information as the fact that Castro's army outnumbered the invading force by more than 140 to one.

The same dynamics that shunt discomforting facts from attention in groups operate in society at large. When some aspects of the shared reality are troubling, a semblance of cozy calm can be maintained by an unspoken agreement to deny the pertinent facts, to ignore key questions.

Take the case of Argentina in the late 1970's. While the military junta was in control there, the unaskable question within the society was: "What happened to the 10,000 or so political dissenters who mysteriously disappeared?" When the democratic regime took over in 1983, the unaskable question was the first to be asked. The answer, of course, pointed the finger of guilt at the junta itself.

To understand such self-deceit, whether individual or shared, cognitive psychologists focus on the mechanisms of the mind. A key element in the mind's architecture is rather dramatically represented by the phenomenon known as "blindsight." Certain functionally blind people—sightless as the result of stroke or brain injury rather than damage to the eye—have the uncanny ability to reach with accuracy for an object placed in front of them, even though, before they reach, they can not say where it is, or whether it is there at all. If asked to reach for the object, they will say it is impossible, since they cannot see it. But if they can be persuaded to try, they will find it with a sureness that amazes even themselves.

Blindsight is such a startling ability that some experts refuse to believe it can happen. Its authenticity is still hotly debated among cognitive scientists, some of whom are uncomfortable with the implication that only part of the mind can be aware of something. They argue that blindsight must be due to some form of cheating or sloppy research. One of those who defends blindsight is Anthony Marcel, a psychologist at Cambridge University. Dr. Marcel is more comfortable with blindsight than are some of his colleagues partly because he has done other experimental work that shows in normal people the mental capacity that seems most jarring in blindsight: that one part of the mind can know something, while the part that supposedly knows what is going on—awareness—remains oblivious.

Dr. Marcel had been doing studies of how people read when he chanced upon a strange effect. In his experiments, he would rapidly flash words on a screen, displaying them in a visual context so confusing they could not be read. When he asked his subjects to guess at the words that they thought they hadn't read, he was struck by a pattern of "clever mistakes." Often, the subjects would guess a word with a closely related meaning: "day," for instance, might have been the word on the screen, and "night," the subject's guess.

Intrigued, Dr. Marcel began to flash words in such a way that observers did not even know that any describable image had been presented. Then he would project a pair of words and ask his subjects to guess which of the words meant or looked the same as the one they had not been able to perceive. He found that people guessed right more often than could be predicted by chance.

The results of these and subsequent studies involving the perception of words from strings of letters—Dr. Marcel calls these "unconscious reading"—make sense only if we adopt a rather radical premise in terms of how we normally think about the mind. Much consequential mental activity goes on outside awareness.

The whole process of recognition, sorting and selection takes a fraction of a second. Emanuel Donchin of the University of Illinois, a leading researcher in the field of cognitive psychophysiology, has done a great many studies using the evoked potential, a sophisticated brain-wave measure, to track the timing of the mind's operations. "In our research, we find that the mind recognizes a word within the first 150 milliseconds of seeing it," says Dr. Donchin. "But nothing shows up in awareness, as the subject reports it, for another 100 milliseconds or so, if it shows up at all."

At any given moment, then, most of what impinges on the senses, and most of the thoughts or memories that might come to mind as a result, never do come to mind. A huge amount of mental effort goes into sorting through and selecting a slim thread of consciousness from an immense array of mental candidates for awareness. The evidence is that the vast majority of possible thoughts and perceptions that might enter awareness are blocked from consciousness. There is a filter at work, and an intelligent one at that.

There are compelling reasons for this arrangement in the design of the mind. Awareness would be far too cluttered were the flow of information not vastly reduced by the time it arrived. If too much gets through, awareness is swamped by irrelevant information, as happens, in different forms, during anxiety attacks and in schizophrenia.

"Awareness is a limited capacity system," Dr. Donchin explains. "We don't know—and don't need to know—about most of the stuff the mind does. I have no idea how I search memory or get grammatically correct sentences out of my mouth. It's hard enough to handle the little that reaches awareness. We'd be in terrible shape if everything were conscious."

The existence of an intelligent filter raises the question of just what intelligence guides the filter's operations. The answer seems to be that what enters through the senses gets a thorough, automatic scan by memory itself. There are several kinds of memory, and this crucial gatekeeper's task seems to be performed, in part, by "semantic" memory, the repository of meanings and knowledge about the world. Semantic memory filters experience so that those messages that reach awareness are primarily those that have pertinence to current mental activity.

Donald A. Norman, a cognitive psychologist at the University of California at San Diego, who was one of the first to propose this design of the mind, argues that perception is a matter of degree. The judgment of relevancy is orchestrated by "schemas," the term psychologists use for the packets in which the mind organizes and stores information. All the contents of the mind are sorted into schemas; a train of association in thought is a road map through loosely connected schemas.

Schemas and attention interact in an intricate dance. Attention to one facet of experience—it is lunchtime, say, and you are hungry—activates other relevant schemas—thoughts of nearby restaurants, say, or of what is at hand in the refrigerator. The schemas, in turn, guide attention. If you walk down the street with these sche-

mas active, your focus will be on the restaurants, not the other kinds of shops on the street; if you go to the refrigerator, your attention will fix on the cold cuts, not on the roast for the evening meal. Schemas choose this and not that; they determine the scope of attention. The interplay between attention and schemas puts them at the heart of the matter of self-deception. Schemas not only determine what we will notice; they also can determine what we do not notice.

Ulric Neisser, a psychologist at Emory University who wrote *Cognitive Psychology,* the volume that put the discipline on the intellectual map, makes the point with an elegant, straightforward demonstration. He made a videotape of four young men playing basketball. The tape lasts just one minute. About midway, an attractive young woman carrying a large white umbrella saunters through the game. She is on the screen for four seconds.

Neisser showed the tape to visitors to his laboratory, who were asked to press a key whenever the basketball was passed between players. When Neisser asked afterward if they had seen anything unusual, very few mentioned the woman with the white umbrella. They had not noticed her; the schema guiding their viewing fixed attention on the ball. When Neisser then replayed the tape, they were astonished to see the woman.

I once asked Neisser whether there might be schemas that, in effect, say "do not notice that."

"Yes," said he, "I'm sure there are, at several levels. It probably starts from cases like the woman with the umbrella. People don't shift their attention from the task at hand. But the mechanism would be much the same when you have pretty good suspicion of what's over there if you were to look, and you'd rather not deal with it. And you don't look; you don't shift your attention. You have a diversionary schema that keeps you looking at something else instead."

This kind of schema has a special potency in the mind. It operates on attention like a magician misdirecting his audience. Just such a mechanism seems to have been at work in classic study conducted by Lester Luborsky, a psychologist at the University of Pennsylvania School of Medicine. Dr. Luborsky used a special camera to track people's eye movements while they looked at pictures. His apparatus allowed him to tell precisely where their gaze fell at each moment.

Some people gave a remarkable performance. When he had them look at pictures that were partly sexual in content, they were able to avoid letting their gaze stray even once to the sexual part of those pictures, though, presumably, their peripheral vision could detect it. Thus, when they looked at a drawing of the outline of a woman's breast, beyond which there was a man reading a paper, their eye did not fix on the woman at all, but focused only the man and his paper. Later, when asked to describe the picture, they had no recall of the sexual aspects; as it turned out, these people were particularly anxious about sexual matters.

"I think there's a lot of this kind of repression in everyday life," says Dr. Neisser, "lots of limits and avoidance in thinking about or looking at things. We all do that. There may be some painful experience in your life which, when you start to think about, you simply decide at some level not to pursue. So you avoid using your recall strategies. You could probably get pretty skilled at it, at not remembering what's painful."

In what may be the most telling results to date on the roots of self-deception, a team of researchers have pinpointed a brain mechanism associated with at least one defensive maneuver, a prospect Freud himself envisioned and then abandoned because of the primitive state of the brain sciences of his time.

The first step in this breakthrough was accomplished by Daniel A. Weinberger, now a psychologist at Stanford University, while he was still a graduate student at Yale. Dr. Weinberger was able to show that certain people, whom he called "repressors," consistently denied being anxious. In research on stress, he contended, they were being misclassified as being very low in anxiety, when, in fact, they displayed all the physical and behavioral signs of tension.

Dr. Weinberger presented college students identified as repressors with sexual or aggressive phrases. He would confront them, for instance, with "the prostitute slept with the student," or "his roommate kicked him in the stomach." He then asked them to free-associate from the phrases and found that their repression was obvious. Unlike other students who did the same task, the repressors offered associations that downplayed or avoided altogether the sexual or hostile tone of the phrases. At the same time, measurements of their heart rate, perspiration and forehead muscle tension revealed that they were, in fact, agitated.

There is, of course, the question of how conscious the repressors were of their self-deception. Were they lying about their feelings, or actually unaware of them?

An answer to that question has been suggested by very recent research. Richard J. Davidson, a psychologist at the University of Wisconsin who had been a collaborator of Dr. Weinberger, carried the investigation one crucial step further. Dr. Davidson, working with Jonathan Perl and Clifford Saron of the State University of New York at Purchase, and using an ingenious technique, has been able to show that repressors suffer from a faulty transfer of information from one half of the brain to the other.

Dr. Davidson's experiments employed a device that, by means of a precise arrangement of lenses, projects a word so that it is seen by only that part of the retina that sends signals to the right hemisphere. Then the brain passes the information to the left. In a right-handed person, this means that the right hemisphere, which can register the meaning of words, must transfer the information to the speech center in the left before the person can speak that meaning.

Dr. Davidson had repressors free-associate to negative emotional words, many of which were sexual or hostile in meaning. When he presented these words to the right hemisphere, he found that a significant time elapsed before the subjects could utter their responses. Among those who study brain response, this slower reaction time is interpreted to mean

that there is a deficiency in the transfer of information, in this case from the right to the left hemisphere. Of most significance was the specificity of the lag; It was for the negative words—which presumably posed a psychological threat—not for neutral or positive words. And the lag showed up only when the words were presented to the right hemisphere, not when shown to the left.

These findings take on special significance in light of the fact that the right hemisphere is strongly believed to be a center for emotions, such as fear and anxiety. Thus, in theory, when repressors experience anxiety, their emotional center in the right brain sends that information to the verbal center in the left over the same faulty circuits. In short, the entire pattern suggests that the repressors's denial of his anxiety is associated with deficient brain function centering on the transfer of information from the right to the left hemisphere. The findings suggest that the repressor is not lying about his lack of agitation, but is actually less aware of it than are most people. The same mechanism, Dr. Davidson believes, may operate whenever people repress threatening information.

A range of research suggests a decidedly positive role for certain kinds of self-deceit. For example, in research at a hospital near San Francisco, Richard S. Lazarus of the University of California at Berkeley found that patients who avoided thinking about the surgery they were facing fared better afterward. Dr. Lazarus's colleague, Frances Cohen, interviewed patients about to undergo elective surgery, such as for gall bladder problems. Some patients, they found, were extremely vigilant about what would happen—and what might go wrong—during surgery, even reading medical texts to discover fine details of the procedure. Others completely ignored such facts, relying instead on faith that things would go right.

The avoiders, the researchers found, recovered more quickly after the surgery, and with fewer complications. In a similar study, researchers at the University of North Carolina have found that those patients who similarly avoided thinking about forthcoming dental surgery showed more rapid healing afterward.

Avoiding what is painful, to a great extent, seems to serve a positive function. There is a growing body of research evidence that shows there to be a pervasive mental tendency for people to ignore or forget unpleasant facts about themselves and to highlight and remember more easily the pleasant ones. The result is an illusory glow of positivity. When people become depressed, the illusion that things are better than a neutral weighing of facts might suggest disappears. Hope, the crucial mainstay in the face of all adversity, depends to a great extent on the same illusion. In short, self-deception, to a point, has a decidedly positive place in the human psyche.

Nevertheless, Dr. Lazarus is quick to point out that the context makes all the difference. "You shouldn't assume denial is necessarily good," he observes. "The presurgical patients had nothing to gain from their vigilance. Take, by contrast, the case of a diabetic; he's got to monitor his sugar levels constantly. If he denies his problem, he's in great trouble."

If there is a lesson to be drawn from the new research, it is the urgent need for compelling antidotes to self-deception. The more we understand how natural a part self-deceit plays in mental life, the more we can admit the almost gravitational pull toward putting out of mind unpleasant facts. And yet, as in the case of the diabetic cited by Richard Lazarus, there is often danger in giving in to denial, whether that denial is individual or collective.

Psychotherapy seeks to heal by exposing, not suppressing, hidden truths, and the therapist's stance is no different from that of the investigative reporter, the ombudsman, the grand jury or the whistle-blower. Each bespeaks a willingness to rock the boat, to bring into the open those facts that have been hidden in the service of keeping things comfortable.

We live in an age, we say, when information has taken on an import and urgency unparalleled in history. A mark of democracy, we maintain, is that information flows freely. It is totalitarian authority that must choke off alternative views and suppress contrary facts. Censorship seems the social equivalent of a defense mechanism.

Now that cognitive psychology is showing how easily our civilization can be put at risk by burying our awareness of painful truths, we may come to cherish truth and insight, more than ever before, as the purest of goods.

A New Index Illuminates the Creative Life

September 13, 1988

The propensity for inventive flair is the subject of new studies by psychologists who are investigating the role of creativity in the everyday lives of ordinary people.

The studies seek to take the study of creativity out of the laboratory and to focus not just on brilliant achievements in the arts and sciences but also on creative acts in all realms of life, from gardening to running a business. Some of the studies are using a newly developed index of creativity to evaluate how inventive people are both at work and at leisure.

One goal of the research is to better understand just what allows a person's inventiveness in certain areas to blossom at some points in life, and to identify factors that stifle or encourage inventiveness.

"Creativity is a fragile phenomenon, easily crushed," said Teresa Amabile, a psychologist at Brandeis University, who is studying the social circumstances that tend to enhance or inhibit creativity. "But if you understand what inhibits it, then you also know how to create the situations where it can flourish."

In the new studies, researchers see creativity in the use of new or unusual elements in a way that is meaningful to others, rather than completely idiosyncratic. This broad view of creativity allows its recognition in, say, teaching or the deal-making of a financier, as well as in those endeavors traditionally regarded as creative, such as writing or painting.

Scientists using the index to study creative acts in life have found a new twist in the popular belief that madness goes hand in hand with creativity. They have found that, while a propensity for an exalted state of ela-tion often does spur creative acts, it is usually not those with manic-depressive disease who are the most highly creative. Instead, it tends more often to be family members who have no overt symptoms of the disorder.

Studies by Dr. Amabile and other psychologists are pinpointing how to overcome blocks to creativity and how to free the creative impulse to find its fullest expression. They find that being watched while working, for instance, or having to produce on demand tend to stifle creativity.

The index, developed at Harvard Medical School by Ruth Richards, a psychiatrist, and Dennis Kinney, a psychologist, is applied by using a structured interview to evaluate people's lives for two aspects of creativity.

Peak creativity assesses the major enterprise of a person's lifetime that is most outstandingly innovative; it is seen as reflecting a person's innate capacity for creativity when circumstances are most favorable. A second scale evaluates the breadth of innovation in all areas of a persons's life over time, which is seen as reflecting the motivation or propensity for creativity.

Based on a study of lifetime creativity in 461 men and women, fewer than 1 percent of people have "exceptional" creativity, while about 10 percent are high in creativity, Dr. Kinney said. About 60 percent of people fall in the categories of "moderate" to "some" creativity.

The evaluations for the Lifetime Creativity Scale developed by Dr. Richards and Dr. Kinney are based on a scoring system that scrutinizes interviews about a person's life for signs of innovativeness in both leisure and work. Details of their work were published in 1988 in the *Journal of Personality and Social Psychology.*

While virtually everyone values creativity, the picture of the exceptionally creative person shows that at its highest levels, creativity involves important sacrifices. For people at the most exceptional level, creativity is a pervasive, almost compulsive preoccupation; innovative activities dominate their lives, often to the detriment of other aspects of living. One example was an entrepeneur who spent long hours—including many weekends—at work developing a new product, often skipping meals, sometimes not getting home at night, for several years.

A high involvement with creativity is indicated by having strong, but not so all-consuming commitments to innovative efforts—for instance, a woman who invested much of her spare time teaching handicapped children to use a special device that helps them with movement and coordination, which she originally developed for her own child.

Those with moderate levels of creativity display occasional imaginative flair, but in the course of their routine work or leisure activities. A chef who came up with unusual menus at a series of restaurants displayed this level of creativity, as did an amateur dance enthusiast who won several competitions.

Those people with some creative involvement, as measured by the scale, display innovations that are quite usual, such as hobbies of knitting or photograhy, or a baker who occasionally came up with a new recipe.

And those with minor creativity, or virtually none, spent most of their lives following routines at work and as passive spectators—of television or sports, for instance—at home.

Mood Disorders and Creativity

Using the new scale, Dr. Richards and Dr. Kinney have discovered that there is an unexpected connection between manic depression and creativity, according to a study published this month in the *Journal of Abnormal Psychology*. Contrary to conclusions based on earlier research by other scientists, it is not those who have extreme manic depression who tend to be the most creative, but rather their near relatives, many of whom have very mild signs of the disorder, or who exhibit no symptoms at all,

For instance, a study of eminent writers who were instructors at the Iowa Writers Workshop had found that far more of them suffered from manic depression than was true for the population as a whole. The study, by Nancy Andreasen, a psychiatrist at the University of Iowa, is one of several that have found a strong association between outstanding creativity in the arts and manic-depression.

Dr. Andreason's study, typical of many in the past, focused only on people who had made an outstanding contribution to the arts. She did not study the relatives of the artists with less obvious forms of creativity. But by using the new scale, Dr. Richards and Dr. Kinney were able to evaluate the degree of creativity exhibited in the lives of a group of ordinary people being treated for manic-depression, their relatives, and a comparison group who had no symptoms of the disorder and no family history of it.

While those being treated for manic-depression showed significantly greater levels of creativity than did those in the comparison group, the highest levels of creativity were found in their relatives who were prone to mild mood swings or who showed no signs of the tendency at all.

"The link between creativity and mood disorders is not limited to a handful of eminent people, or to a few fields such as the fine arts, but can be seen at lesser levels in millions of others," Dr. Kinney said. "It is found not just in the 1 percent or so of people who get full-blown manic-depressive illness, but extends to the much larger number of their relatives."

'Mild Manic Feeling'

Dr. Kinney believes that mildly elated moods, as opposed to full-blown mania, facilitates creativity, and that the same genetic tendency that makes some members of a family become manic depressive may lead others to smaller mood swings that make them more creative.

"If your mood is so elevated that you become manic, you become too restless and overwhelmed by your ideas to be effective." Dr. Kinney said, "But a mild manic feeling, what we call 'hypomania,' gives people an increased energy and self-confidence along with fuller access to unusual ideas. They are more able than usual to come up with ideas that challenge the status quo, to take risks, and those are vital ingredients of a creative life."

In related research, Kay Jamison, a psychologist at the University of California at Los Angeles, interviewed several dozen eminent artists and writers and found that their most creative periods occurred when they were in just such an elated mood. And Dr. Andreasen found that the creative writers she studied were most productive during those periods when they were not suffering the more intense symptoms of manic depression.

Mild mood swings might facilitate creativity, Dr. Kinney said, because a person is more imaginative during the elated phase, but can then evaluate and criticize those ideas when feeling more sober. That combination of the fluid generation of novel ideas and a critical judgment makes for successful creative efforts.

"Many people inhibit their creativity because they judge their ideas too critically," said Dr. Richards. "You need to suspend self-judgments for a time."

But it is not enough just to have sound creative ideas; Dr. Kinney notes that the most creative people also have the drive and ability to execute their ideas. An elated mood helps there, too.

"You see that kind of unusual drive in those people who get little sleep, but always seem to have lots of energy—the tireless executive or politician, for instance," Dr. Kinney said.

To be sure, there are many routes to creativity; many among the most creative people are not prone to manic depression and are not related to people with the disorder. Many psychologists are studying the conditions that can enhance a person's creativity.

One of these is exposure to novel circumstances, such as travel to a foreign land. "Unusual experiences generate a richness of new ideas," said Dr. Kinney. "One's mind becomes a more fertile ground."

Not surprisingly, being engaged in tasks that one chooses and enjoys enhances creativity.

Extinguishing the Sparks

By the same token, studies have made clear many of the factors that extinguish the spark of creativity. For example, David Harrington, a psychologist at the University of California at Santa Cruz, found that children whose parents were more accepting of their creative efforts and other accomplishments grew up to be more creative adults than did other children.

Having to perform on command the pressure of competition, or being watched while one works also tend to dampen creativity, studies have found.

"You have to take risks to be creative," Dr. Amabile said. "Competition, evaluation and surveillance all make people prefer the safest option, hesitating to explore more creative—and risky—possibilities."

Humor Found to Aid Problem-Solving

August 4, 1987

"In America, everything is permitted that's not forbidden," a European joke has it. "In Germany, everything is forbidden that's not permitted. In France, everything is permitted, even if it's forbidden. And in Russia, everything is forbidden, even if it's permitted."

Such jokes suit the notion that much humor veils aggression, permitting the joke-teller, in Freud's words, "to be malicious with dignity." But Freud's longstanding analysis of humor as the release of repressed feelings is receding as a growing group of social scientists, for whom humor is no joke, make it the focus of serious research. In the new work, humor is seen less as disguised hostility and more as a stimulant to problem-solving and productivity, as an aid to education and as the stuff of social bonds.

Humor and its uses have been a subject of conjecture since Aristotle, and a large body of psychoanalytic literature deals with jokes. But "humor has been a neglected topic among researchers," said Donna Cooper, a psychologist at the University of Connecticut who is a consultant on the uses of humor in organizations. "Most psychologists are preoccupied with grim topics and problems; humor and the positive emotions get little interest or funding."

Of late, though, that has begun to change. Some of the more visible new research, inspired by Norman Cousins' account of how watching Marx Brothers movies and other comedy films helped him recover from a debilitating illness, deals with links between positive feelings and healing.

Less well known is recent research suggesting that putting people in a good mood by telling them jokes makes them think through problems with more ingenuity. Casual joking at work may thus improve people's effectiveness in their tasks.

"Any joke that makes you feel good is likely to help you think more broadly and creatively," said Alice M. Isen, a psychologist at the University of Maryland in Baltimore. The elation that comes from hearing a good joke, Dr. Isen has found, is similar to that which people feel when they receive a small, unexpected gift. Such elation, her research shows, facilitates innovation.

In the research, reported in 1987 in *The Journal of Personality and Social Psychology,* Dr. Isen found that people who had just watched a short comedy film of television "bloopers" were better able to find a creative solution to a puzzling problem than were people who had watched a film about math or who had exercised.

The problem posed was one frequently used in such research. People were given a candle, matches and a box of tacks and asked to attach the candle to a corkboard wall so that the candle would burn without dripping wax on the floor.

Most people who try to solve this problem fall prey to "functional fixedness," the tendency to see the objects presented them only in terms of their conventional uses. Those who were in a good mood from watching the funny film, however, were generally able to solve the problem by seeing another use for the box holding the tacks: They tacked the box to the wall and used it as a candleholder.

In other studies, Dr. Isen found that the comedy film increased people's ability to think more broadly, seeing relationships that otherwise eluded them. This is a mental skill that is important in finding creative solutions to problems and in foreseeing the consequences of a given decision. The ability to recognize complex relationships and far-flung implications has also been found, in other research, to mark the most successful business executives.

"The mind associates more broadly when people are feeling good after hearing a joke," said Dr. Isen. "They think of things they ordinarily would not and have access to a broader range of mental material. And the more ideas present in your mind, the more ways you see to connect things; you're able to see more solutions."

Beyond Satisfaction

In light of this and other research, joking at work is being appreciated as more than mere diversion. Research to be reported next month at the annual meeting of the American Psychological Association shows that the feeling of having fun at work is more important than overall job satisfaction in workers' effectiveness.

In a survey of 382 people from a wide variety of work places, David Abramis, a psychologist in the School of Business Administration at California State University at Long Beach, found that those who felt their work was fun performed better and got along better with co-workers than did those who were satisfied with their jobs but did not see them as fun.

Traditionally, psychologists have focused on people's sense of satisfaction with their jobs as a measure of their psychological adjustment to work. Dr. Abramis, though, believes that the feeling that one's work is fun is of equal importance and that job satisfaction and have fun at work are independent considerations.

A major source of fun at work, the study showed, is joking with fellow workers, according to Dr. Abramis. "If you are trying to improve people's performance at work, it is not enough to improve their job satisfaction," he said. "Increasing their sense of having a good time at work improves their performance over and above satisfaction."

Joking also has its dangers, particularly carelessness, according to Dr. Isen. "If you want a jocular environment at work, you need to make sure people keep in mind the importance of their work," she said. "If you don't, feeling good may make people sloppy where they should be plodding. But if you tell people who are feeling good that they have made a mistake, they are especially thorough in correcting their errors."

Implications for Children

Although it is a relatively new idea that joking may enhance productivity at work, humor has long been used to make learning more palatable for children, as "Sesame Street" demonstrated. At first, some educators argued that such humor was detrimental to learning, because it drew children's attention away from the serious parts of the material presented. More recently, though, interspersing humor among the serious has been shown to improve children's learning, provided the humor is of the right sort.

New research on which sorts of humor aid learning and which hinder it shows that when the humor distorts the information, it often confuses children. According to findings by Dolf Zillman, a psychologist at Indiana University, irony is particularly confusing to young children, who do not yet have the basic knowledge that would allow them to see what is true and what a distortion. Dr. Zillman cites as an example of distortion a "Sesame Street" depiction of seat belts on an airplane; when the plane turns upside down the seat-belted characters hang from the cockpit as if the belts were rubber.

Children up to fourth grade, and perhaps beyond are often confused by such distortions, Dr. Zillman reported in the *Handbook of Humor Research* (Springer-Verlag). On the other hand, he has found that humor that does not distort generally enhances children's ability to master new material. The solution he recommends is to use jokes that are unrelated to the topic at hand, rather than jokes about the information itself.

The Maturing Process

By the time students reach college age, though, humor that is unrelated to the educational topic can backfire, Dr. Zillman warns. A lecturer who habitually tells such jokes may be viewed as digressing, according to Dr. Zillman, and the joking asides seem to interfere with the students' grasp of the material presented. On the other hand, lecturers who weave into their material humor about the topic seem to be more effective.

Exactly what people find funny changes as they age, according to a survey of forty stand-up comedians performed by Lucille Nahemow, a psychologist at the University of Connecticut. "Adults of all ages respond to sexual humor," she said, "while younger audiences like aggressive humor, such as put-down jokes, and older audiences like jokes about family life."

Jokes serve an important social function in strengthening the bonds between people, researchers are finding. By laughing at the same things, people let one another know that they have a similar outlook, without having to say so. This makes jokes especially important in communicating about discomforting topics.

"Many jokes are a way to talk about troubling topics like sex and racism," according to Alan Dundes, a folklorist at the University of California at Berkeley, who in *Cracking Jokes* (Ten Speed Press) analyzes the hidden meanings of humor. By laughing at a joke, the listener tacitly signals that he shares the attitude implicit in it, Dr. Dundes argues.

"Wherever there is anxiety in a culture, you find humor," Dr. Dundes said. "In Eastern Europe, for example, you find many more jokes about politics and Russians than you do in the West, where these concerns are not so overriding."

Indeed, Dr. Dundes takes the popular jokes of a people as a barometer of their hidden concerns. Of particular significance, he finds, are "joke cycles," jokes on a single topic that spring up suddenly, have many variations and are extremely popular. Thus, in his view, "Jewish American princess" jokes of the late 1970's were a reaction to feminism.

"All jokes are serious, and anything funny is at someone's expense," Dr. Dundes said. "It is hard to find a truly harmless joke, one without a serious overtone."

TV's Potential to Teach Infants

November 22, 1988

When infants as young as 10 months watch television, they are not simply staring at pretty patterns and colors on the screen. Instead, they are often engaged in learning tasks that promote their intellectual development, new research suggests.

Watching television, at least certain kinds of programs, can help infants acquire language skills, the ability to perform physical tasks and an understanding that what they are watching is akin to the rest of life around them, researchers say.

Some studies are finding that television helps teach the master skills basic to language acquisition in the same way that reading simple stories to an infant helps.

Similarly, in one dramatic new finding, scientists said that an infant can learn to disassemble a novel toy by watching a demonstration on television.

The latest research, published in the current issue of *Child Development,* also refutes an influential theory of perception, which held that one needs to acquire the understanding that a two-dimensional image, such as a painting or television image, represents three-dimensional reality. The findings with infants suggest that the ability is innate.

"The little ones can more or less learn from television as they would from a book, especially if the program is designed for it, like 'Sesame Street,' " said Mabel Rice, a psychologist at the University of Kansas. "They need a tight focus on the object, and for the object to be kept in view while it is being talked about, preferably repeatedly. You wouldn't get this if you put a baby in front of 'Dallas'."

The news that television can be a teacher for infants may come as a relief to those parents who have noticed that their infants stare with fascination at the screen long before they can talk.

Not that most infants are nearly as avid watchers of television as their older siblings. Researchers say that babies two-years-old and under generally are exposed to about two hours of television on average each day, while two- to five-year-olds watch television about four hours a day. Researchers focusing on the children older than two are particularly concerned about the number of acts of violence in children's cartoons and other programs, fearing that this encourages children to be aggressive.

Infants under one year old actually pay attention to the screen for about ten percent of the time they are exposed to it, while babies one to two watch the screen about 30 percent of the time that the television is on, according to a study by Daniel Anderson, a psychologist at the University of Massachusetts at Amherst.

"Between one and two, babies' language comprehension is way ahead of what they can say," Dr. Anderson said. "They can make sense of the kind of slow-moving, simple segments you see on 'Sesame Street,' but still may have trouble understanding the quick montage editing that is the visual language of most television shows."

Understanding at Ten Months

The youngest infants who seem to understand what they are watching on television were ten months old, the researchers said.

It is especially difficult to study the mental reactions of infants before they can talk. But in one ingenious study, by Richard Davidson of the University of Wisconsin and Nathan Fox of the University of Maryland, ten-month-olds sat on their mother's laps and watched a video recording while their brain waves were measured. The recording, lasting about a minute, was shown in two versions. In one, an actress went from a neutral expression to smiling, to laughing. In the other, she went from a neutral face to a distressed one, to crying.

When the infants saw the laughing video, their brain waves reflected a pattern that, in other research, Dr. Davidson has found associated with happy emotions. Brain activity intensified in the left front area of the cortex, the top layer of the brain, which processes complex information. But when the infants watched the sad video, their brain waves showed a lessening of activity there, which reflects unhappy emotions.

"The babies had emotional reactions that mimicked the one they watched," Dr. Davidson said. "Around this age infants become far more responsive to emotional cues in those around them, even if they watch them on television."

Dr. Rice reported in *The Journal of Child Language* that a critical language skill that television can help infants master is the matching of a name to an object. "For toddlers, one of the most basic language skills is matching a name to the thing represents," Dr. Rice said.

In Dr. Rice's research, done with Dafna Lemish, a psychologist, toddlers twelve to eighteen months old were observed as they watched television at home with a parent.

"We found that the toddlers used the television just as if it were a talking picture book," Dr. Rice said.

"The very little ones will walk over to the TV, point, and say something like, 'Big Bird,'" Dr. Rice added. "It shows they are mastering the name-thing association, one of the fundamental skills that comes with learning their first words, sometime between nine and twelve months."

Such learning from the television is enhanced if an adult watches television with the infant and talks about what they are seeing, said Gabriel Solomon, a psychologist at the University of Tel Aviv.

Apart from language, infants seem to learn how to deal with the physical world from watching television, according to additional research published in *Child Development*. In a study by Andrew Meltzoff, a psychologist at the University of Washington, babies as young as fourteen months were able to learn from watching TV how to manipulate a toy they had never seen before.

In the study, babies watched a small black-and-white television monitor. On the screen, they saw a man pick up a special dumbbell-shaped toy that could be pulled apart.

For twenty of the babies, their parents then put the same toy on the table in front of them; thirteen of the twenty immediately picked up the toy and pulled it apart, as they had seen demonstrated on television. Another group of twenty were not shown the toy until the next day. Still, eight of them also showed that they knew what to do with the toy by pulling it apart. This shows, Dr. Meltzoff points out, that babies can absorb information on the first viewing, then apply it appropriately when the opportunity arises, even when that moment is much later.

Babies in a group that watched the adult on television pick up the toy but not take it apart did more poorly on the task. Only four of ten could take the toy apart immediately after the television display and only one of ten could take the toy apart a day later.

An influential perceptual theory put forward in the 1960's by Nelson Goodman, a Harvard philosopher, held that humans have to learn the correspondence between two-dimensional representations of reality and the real world, just as in learning a language. "Our work shows that this ability is there quite early, before language," Dr. Meltzoff said. "We suspect it may be innate."

Emotion

The march of emotions in a baby's development is more methodical than you might think. While a newborn infant does not have all emotions in place, there is a developmental timetable that emotions follow as they emerge over the years. "Order Found in Develoment of Emotions" shows how their emergence is linked to the unfolding of cognitive stages.

Want to feel a litle better? Try putting on a happy face. That should evoke a happier mood, according to a theory described in "Facial Expressions Can Help Create Moods They Show." This theory holds that your facial expression adjusts blood flow to the brain, which in turn affects your mood. It's an old idea in psychology, but one with very new evidence.

Despite changes in sex roles over the last few decades, the emotional lives of men and women seem as different as ever, according to data in "Sex Roles Reign Powerful as Ever in the Emotions." While men and women seem to differ little in the actual emotions they feel, the big differences come in how they express those feelings.

People vary greatly in how intensely they experience their emotions, whether your emotions register with high or low intensity is an important factor in how you perceive and react to events. In "Key Roles are Attributed to Intensity of Emotion" research shows that whether you are excitable or unflappable is likely to be a lifelong trait of your temperament.

Much of what we communicate is expressed by a look, a gesture, or tone of voice rather than the words we speak. These nonverbal messages have a much larger importance than we might suppose. "Studies Point to Power of Nonverbal Signals" describes data showing the impact of these messages in such crucial situations as a trial, between physican and patient, and teacher and student.

Do you know when you're being lied to? Not always. Some data suggests that most of us think we're much better than we actually are at detecting the lies people tell us. "Researchers Identify True Clues to Lying" details research that pinpoints what the reliable signals of a lie really are.

Finally, a note of caution: hostility may be suicidal. "Agreeableness vs. Anger" reviews a mounting body of data suggesting that people who are quick to anger or who are mistrustful, skeptical, and snide by nature, are at greater risk for disease than are more agreeable folk.

Order Found in Development of Emotions

June 19, 1984

Babies, as everyone knows, have intense feelings from the moment of birth. But their early feelings are few, limited to the most primitive such as distress and disgust. Only with the passage of time does the full emotional panoply blossom.

And it grows, one or two feelings at a time, in a lawful, orderly fashion—a progression which scientists are tracking with greater precision than was possible before. For instance, the capacity for joy has been found to precede that for sadness by many months. And years after the development of those two come the capacities for envy and for social confidence.

Among the main practical benefits of this research, the psychologists say, should be a more realistic standard of emotional growth. Such a standard could act as an antidote to the tendency of some adults—parents and teachers foremost among them—to judge children's emotional reactions by adult standards rather than by a yardstick gauged to their actual stages of maturation. Thus, since humility typically is not part of a child's emotional repertoire until around the age of five, the seemingly outrageous bragging of a four-year-old can be seen as, in all likelihood, the most normal of expressions.

The sense of orderly emotional development in human beings has been noted in the impressions of behavioral scientists in the past. And of course psychoanalytic theory discusses aspects of this development in detail. Now it is being observed by another group of researchers, the developmental psychologists, through rigorous scientific experimentation.

Dr. T. Berry Brazelton, a Harvard University researcher and popular author on child development, expressed pleasure in the current direction of investigation.

"It's about time we started looking at emotions more carefully," he said. "Everything we know about a child shows that healthy emotional development is the key to other kinds of growth."

The new approach is a direct outgrowth of cognitive psychology, which has proven extraordinarily fruitful in uncovering the orderly stages by which intellectual capacities develop. That understanding has made it possible, among other things, to adjust expectations about childhood development to reality rather than supposition.

The burst of studies on the emotional life of children has already begun to yield insights into the nature of emotion itself, revealing the intimate interplay between feeling and thought.

The emphasis in the field of developmental psychology—which is devoted to understanding human maturation better—has long been on cognitive growth, a legacy of Jean Piaget, one of the field's founders. This emphasis is now regarded as one-sided. "Psychology's view of children had put too much emphasis on cognition alone," said Jerome Kagan, a developmental psychologist at Harvard University in an interview. "Bringing emotion into the picture corrects what had been a distorted view of human development."

Rigorous though they may be, the recent findings can sound somewhat more exact than they actually are. The moment at which a given emotion arrives can be blurred indeed.

Joseph Campos, a developmental psychologist at the University of Denver, said in an interview that "there is a controversy over the precise moment each can be said to emerge, since emotions are complex and the early signs may differ from later ones." Fear in a baby, for instance, may not be expressed in the same way that it is in a toddler.

Changing Emotional Capacity

The way in which an emotional capacity changes as a child grows is illustrated by the work on empathy by Martin Hoffman at the University of Michigan.

Infants in the first year of life, says Dr. Hoffman, can probably experience something like empathy in response to another child's distressed cry. But since very young infants do not yet clearly differentiate themselves from others, they may be unclear about whose distress they are hearing. Such infants, says Dr. Hoffman, will frequently act as though another child's distress is their own.

For example, and eleven-month-old infant who saw another child fall and start crying stared for a moment at the victim, then put her thumb in her mouth and buried her head in her mother's lap,—her usual response when she hurt herself.

"This first level of empathic distress is obviously primitive," Dr. Hoffman writes. "We call it empathy, although the child does not really put himself in the other's place and imagine what the other is feeling."

Something closer to empathy comes at around one year, when infants have a more solid sense of themselves as separate individuals and clearly can tell that the distress is someone else's. However, they still tend to confuse their own reactions and consolations with those of the other person.

Thus a thirteen-month-old who saw an adult looking sad offered the adult a beloved doll.

By about two or three years, according to Dr. Hoffman, children become aware that other people's feelings are different from their own and can respond more appropriately. And as they master language they can respond not only to immediate cues of distress such as crying, but also to the idea that another is in distress.

With the growth of their understanding children can empathize with a wider range of emotions, including complex feelngs such as betrayal. As their sophisticaion increases they can comprehend situations where, for example, a victim does not want to be helped because he would feel demeaned thereby.

Finally, by late childhood full empathy appears. Children become capable of empathy not just for a specific person's plight, but also for groups of people such as the poor or the oppressed.

The March of Emotional Growth

To test whether a given emotion is present at a certain age, researchers have had to find ways to provoke various feelings without doing their subjects harm and then to record the children's reactions.

While there is still uncertainty and disagreement about the specific signs that signify an emotion has entered a child's repertoire, there is an emerging consensus among developmental psychologists about the march of emotional growth.

At birth the infant has only the most elementary emotional life. Newborns show an expression of disgust, for example, in response to strong tastes, and show surprise in reaction to sudden changes. They also show interest, which developmental psychologists consider an emotion in its own right.

By ten months infants display the full range of what are considered the basic emotions: joy, anger, sadness, disgust, surprise and fear.

The emergence of the basic emotions during the first year or two of life seems to be programmed by a biological clock for brain development. As the appropriate brain maturation occurs, the various emotions appear in an infant's repertory.

For example, studies of brain activity in ten-month-olds show that the right frontal regions are more active during positive emotions, and the left during negative emotions. The rudiments of this brain organization may already exist at birth, according to data recently reported by Nathan Fox at the University of Maryland and Richard Davidson at the State University of New York at Purchase.

Special Circumstances

While the biological timetable determines the general rate and progression for emotional growth, special circumstances can alter it, the researchers say. Infants often do not show clear signs of fear until about seven or eight months of age. But abused infants as young as three months showed a fearful expression when a male stranger approached, according to a study by Theodore Gaensbauer and Susan Hiatt reported in *The Psychobiology of Affective Development* (Erlbaum), published in 1987.

This study suggests that the biological mechanism for fear is activated in such infants much earlier than usual, according to Carroll Izard of the University of Delaware, an expert on infants' emotions.

The three-month-old abused children also showed expressions of sadness, an emotion formerly thought to make its appearance at about eight months.

"Psychoanalytic theory held that an infant could not feel true sadness until he had formed a strong attachment to his mother or some other caretaker—by about eight months," said Dr. Campos. "Then he would feel sad when he was separated from that special caretaker." The new findings, Dr. Campos said, show that sadness, under unusual circumstances, can come much earlier. "It's a related sadness," he said, "not over separation, but over having been abused by the parent."

Intellect and Emotions

Developmental psychologists, so intensely interested in the intellectual progressions of childhood, seem to have been ideally placed to detail the subtle association between the intellect and emotions, with each new intellectual advance setting the stage for emotional ones.

Dr. Kagan, in *Emotions, Cognition and Behavior,* to be published next month by Cambridge University Press, gives as an example the results of a study done in his laboratory. One-month-old and seven-month-old infants were shown a distorted human face. The one-month-olds responded with interest to the bizarre face and rarely cried. The seven-month-olds reacted by crying and other signs of distress.

The difference, Dr. Kagan assumes, is that the older infants had a mental image of what a face should look like, to which they compared the distorted one and became distressed at the mismatch. The one-month-olds did not yet have the cognitive abilities that would allow such comparisons and so were not disturbed.

Even though an infant may display some of the signs of a given emotion, many researchers are cautious about equating that response with the full-fledged emotion as adults experience it. They say that while a three-month-old may cry and fret his distress is not the same as that of an older child because he has not developed basic cognitive skills, which begin to appear at about four months.

Dr. Kagan warns of the potential error in mistaking an observed reaction for what the child actually feels. "There is potential danger in attributing to the three-month-old the same affect state ascribed to the older child, whether the term used is surprise or fear," he writes.

Social Awareness

A major period of growth in a child's emotional life, according to Dr. Kagan, occurs around five or six years, when a child has a firm sense of himself and how he compares to others. The transition into social awareness brings with it a whole new repertory of emotions.

"The crucial new cognitive competence," Dr. Kagan writes, is the ability to compare oneself to others in such things as abilities, attractiveness, popularity and other attributes.

The feelings thus engendered are social emotions such as pride and humility, insecurity and confidence, and jealousy and envy.

In adolescence, Dr. Kagan says, the full complement of adult emotions is completed with the cognitive advance that Piaget called "formal operations." This capacity, for example, allows adolescents to examine beliefs for logical consistency.

This sets the stage for philosophical brooding on such favored adolescent topics as why, if God loves man, there is so much suffering in the world; why sexual activity can be deemed bad if it is so enjoyable, and why, if parents are omniscient, they blunder.

Contrary to their stereotype, adolescents are not especially moody, according to Dr. Kagan. "Teen-agers are no more moody than a three-year-old," he said.

Facial Expressions Can Help Create Moods They Show

July 18, 1989

Putting on a sad face or a smile directly produces the feelings that the expressions represent, according to a new theory of how emotions are produced.

This view elaborates on ideas proposed more than a century ago by Charles Darwin and William James, the philosopher and psychologist. It holds that facial expressions are not just the visible sign of an emotion, but actually contribute to the feeling itself.

The theory does not propose that facial expressions are more important than thoughts or memories in prompting emotions. But it points to the physiology of facial expression as a cause of emotions in its own right.

The theory has been gaining gradual support over the last decade among psychologists. Two of the strongest pieces of evidence were published separately in scientific journals this month.

In one, researchers found that simply inducing people to place the muscles of their face in the pattern of a given emotional expression elicited that feeling. In the other, researchers showed that facial expressions affected the temperature of blood flowing to the brain, providing a possible, although disputed, mechanism for regulating emotions.

Effect Seen as Modest

To be sure, no one suggests that putting on a happy face can cheer up someone who is in mourning. The effects of facial expression are seen as modest, though consequential. In lieu of any other strong feeling, the theory holds, a given expression can induce the mood it portrays.

While the weight of evidence now strongly shows that facial expression can influence mood, there is debate over what physiological mechanisms might be involved, as well as just how important the phenomenon is in emotional life.

"I'm not saying that all moods are due to changes in the muscles of the face, only that facial action leads to changes in mood," said Dr. Robert Zajonc, a psychologist at the University of Michigan and a leading proponent of the new theory.

"Of course there's more to emotion than that, but this is a significant part of the story, too," he said.

Dr. Zajonc's theory holds that as certain facial muscles relax and tighten, they raise or lower the temperature of blood flowing to the brain. These changes in temperature, in turn, affect the activity of brain centers that regulate emotion.

The link between expression and emotion was demonstrated most recently in an article published in 1989 in the *Journal of Personality and Social Psychology*. A team of psychologists at Clark University in Worcester, Massachusetts, showed that simply having people put their facial muscles in a configuration typical of a given emotion produced that feeling.

In the study, volunteers were given instructions like this, for fear: "raise your eyebrows, and open your eyes wide. Move your whole head back, so that your chin is tucked in a little bit, and let your mouth relax and hang open a little."

Volunteers Not Told

Similar instructions were given for anger, disgust and sadness. But the volunteers were not told that the study was testing emotion or that the facial movements were to mimic a specific expression.

By and large, the different expressions produced the moods they portray. While making an expression of disgust, for example, the volunteers reported feeling more disgust than anger, fear, or sadness.

In another study, German researchers were able to induce happy feelings by having people hold a small pen clenched in their teeth, imitating a smile. When the people held the pen in their protruding lips, imitating a pout, they felt unhappy.

In Dr. Zajonc's study, volunteers repeated vowel sounds over and over, those of a long "e," which forces a smile, and "ah," which imitates part of the expression of surprise. Both induced pleasant feelings. But a long "u" and the German vowel "ü" both put volunteers in their worst mood.

In 1984, Dr. Paul Ekman and other psychologists at the University of California Medical School at San Francisco published an article in the journal *Science* showing that when people mimic different emotional expressions, their bodies produce distinctive physiological patterns, such as changes in heart and breath rate, for each emotion.

The findings have revived a long-standing debate in psychology over the mechanics of emotional life, one that traces its roots to Charles Darwin, who published a major treatise on facial expression and emotion in 1872. Darwin asserted that facial expressions played important roles in prompting the feelings that accompany it.

His view was given its most influential support by William James, in 1884, although he also acknowledged that the idea seemed to run counter to most people's experience.

Over the years, however, these views fell out of favor among psychologists, who generally believe that emotions follow from thoughts, and that facial expression are the final result of feelings, not their cause.

The case that facial expression determines mood, along with a detailed proposal for the biological means, is made in 1989 issue of the *Psychological Review* by Dr. Zajonc.

Dr. Zajonc's theory hinges on the fact that all biochemical processes in the body change their rates as the temperature in the immediate region of the body changes. This includes the activity of neurons and neurotransmitters, the brain's chemical messengers.

Regulating Temperature

The internal carotid artery, which provides the main supply of blood to the brain, flows through the cavernous sinus. This part of the sinus is laced with veins from the face. As the facial muscles stretch and tighten, Dr. Zajonc contends, the blood flow to the cavernous sinus changes.

This, in turn, raises or lowers the temperature of blood flowing into the brain, particularly the hypothalamus, a structure that regulates both emotion and the body's reactions to heat and cold.

For instance, a smile tightens muscles primarily in the cheek, and the broader the smile, the tighter those muscles become. This in turn tends to decrease the flow of blood to the cavernous sinus, thus cooling the blood that flows to the brain, the theory holds. Unhappy expressions, like a frown or scowl, tighten different sets of facial muscles, which tend to allow more blood into the cavernous sinus. This heats the blood that flows to the brain.

"The hypothalamus is profoundly involved in emotional life," Dr. Zajonc said. "But it also regulates the temperature of both the brain and the body. Its dual role is indicated, for instance, by its involvement in shivering, which occurs both in fear and in freezing, or in sweating, which is seen during anxiety or excitement, as well as in reaction to excessive heat."

Dr. Zajonc points to a range of studies suggesting that raising the temperature of the brain causes unpleasant feelings, while cooling it leads to pleasant ones.

Enthusiasm for Dr. Zajonc's conclusions is not universal.

"I think the theory is completely wrong," said Dr. Henry Schutta, chairman of the neurology department at the University of Wisconsin. "There's nothing in the anatomy to support it. For instance, there are no special sensors in the cavernous sinus that would allow it to regulate temperature so finely.

"And although standard anatomy texts show the carotid artery going straight through the cavernous sinus, dissections find that it often runs to the side," he added.

On the other hand, said Dr. Joseph LeDoux at the Center for Neural Science at New York University, "Dr. Zajonc's evidence is very compelling so far, though the data aren't all in. We don't yet know the essential neuroanatomical details, but he's working in a gray area. His work on emotions is the most creative in years."

Sex Roles Reign Powerful as Ever in the Emotions

August 23, 1988

Despite two decades of assaults on sexual stereotypes, new research shows that when it comes to emotional life, men and women seem as bound as ever by traditional sex roles.

The differences are starkest in the suppression of feeling. Psychologists are finding that men generally are still more reticent when it comes to emotions like sympathy, sadness and distress, while women are more inhibited when it comes to anger and sexuality.

Yet studies are finding that men and women differ little, if at all, in the actual physiology of these feelings; the differences appear only when it comes to their expression.

Beyond the expression of feeling, men and women also differ in how they explain an emotional outburst—especially intense feelings like anger and sadness—and what the appropriate response might be.

And these differences seem destined to last. Recent studies show that parents still treat boys and girls differently in regard to their emotional life.

"The stereotypes of emotionality for men and women are as strong as ever, in spite of two decades of efforts to break them down," said Dr. Virginia O'Leary, a psychologist at Radcliffe College. Dr. O'Leary was one of several psychologists presenting findings on sex differences in emotions at a meeting of the American Psychological Association in 1988.

Some of the most compelling laboratory research shows, for instance, that when provoked, men and women had equivalent reactions in terms of heart rate and other physiological responses. But when questioned, the men usually said they were angry while the women usually said they were hurt or sad.

In a study, men and women viewed scenes of accidents and their victims. The men's faces showed no expression, while the women expressed sympathy. Physiological measures, meanwhile, showed that both men and women were equally affected by the scenes.

'Just as Angry Inside'

"Although women don't admit to feeling angry as much as do men, they may feel just as angry inside," said Leslie Brody, a psychologist at Boston University. "It's their early training that tells women not to be as open about their anger. And the same is true for men with emotions like sympathy."

Dr. Brody has reviewed much of the research on sex differences in emotion in *Gender and Personality,* published by Duke University Press. In Dr. Brody's own research, men and women are presented with situations intended to elicit various emotions. In those that elicit anger—for instance, descriptions of betrayal or criticism—men simply react with anger. Women, on the other hand, were likely to say that they would be sad, hurt or disappointed.

"Men are about four times more likely to commit acts of violence than are women, while women are about twice as likely to become depressed as men," Dr. Brody said. "When men are in conflict, they turn their anger against the other person, while women tend to turn it against themselves by taking the blame."

The inhibitions in expressing emotion seem strongest in social situations, and weakest in situations where a person is most at ease. For instance, in a study where people were asked to reveal an emotionally upsetting secret, men did so as readily as women when they could tell the secret by talking into a tape recorder or by writing in a private journal.

But in face-to-face situations, differences emerge between men and women, said James Pennebaker, a psychologist at Southern Methodist University, who did the research on confessions. "It's more threatening for men to express emotion that show they are troubled," he said.

In the emotional politics of life, the relative ease with which men express their anger may lead to unsuspected difficulties. In a survey of women who work as secretaries, the single most disliked characteristic of male bosses was anger, Dr. O'Leary said.

Sexuality is another arena where there is a marked difference between the sexes in inhibition. One study found that as many as 42 percent of women said they were not sexually aroused, even as readings of vaginal temperature showed that they were responding physiologically. The women in the study were listening to a tape of an erotic story while the measurements were made. In the same study, not a single man was unaware of his sexual arousal.

More recent studies have had similar findings, said Dr. Patricia Morokoff of the University of Rhode Island. Dr. Morokoff has found that, particularly among women with less sexual experience, there tended to be a disparity between physiological arousal and the arousal they reported, measured during both erotic films and sex fantasies.

'Ambivalent Message'

"Girls are taught to restrict knowledge of their genitals and genital responses," while boys are freer to explore their genitals, Dr. Morokoff said.

"Society presents an ambivalent message to women about sex. It is desirable to be sexually responsive with one's partner, but it is not desirable to be interested in sex for gratifiction of one's own sexual needs," she added. "One way out of this double-bind is physiological response without awareness of arousal."

For men, the greatest suppression is for a range of emotions that, in terms of gender stereotypes, are seen as "unmanly," said Dr. O'Leary of Radcliffe.

In research with Devorah Smith, a psychologist at Boston University, Dr. O'Leary found that men and women differ in the causes they attribute for emotions like anger, fear or sadness in themselves or others.

"Men are more likely to explain a strong emotion in terms of some impersonal event, something that happened in the situation, while women are more likely to see the cause as something in a personal relationship or the person's mood," Dr. O'Leary said.

"This difference between men and women has greatest implications for arguments between the sexes," she said.

"If a couple fight, the man is likely to make an instrumental response—to look for something in the situation to change and make things better," Dr. O'Leary said. "But the woman is likely to read the argument as an index of trouble in the relationship itself, and become critical of their relationship."

Dealing With Failures

The difference between the sexes in the causes they use to explain life's difficulties may be one reason women tend to be more susceptible to depression than men, said Ellen McGrath, a psychologist in New York City who addressed the psychology meeting on women and depression.

"If men fail at something, they tend to attribute it to some external cause, like the challenge being impossible, or not enough support from their boss," Dr. McGrath said. "For women, though, the tendency is to see a failure as due to something about themselves, as the result of some personal inadequacy."

The influence of sex roles on depression was reported in another study at the psychology meeting by Rosalind Cartwright, a psychologist at Rush-Presbyterian-St. Luke's Medical Center in Chicago. The research, which is continuing, involves 157 men and women who are going though separation or divorce. So far, half of the men and women in the study have become severely depressed.

Traditional Sex Roles

While the usual sex ratio for those being treated for depression shows a rate of twice as many women as men, the Chicago study found that the rates were identical for men and women.

But when the volunteers were asked questions to assess how they conform to the traditional sex roles, the two-to-one ratio emerged. Among the most traditional men and women, there were twice as many depressed women as men. Among the least traditional, the ratio was reversed.

The emotional differences seem destined to remain, researchers say, since the ways parents treat boys and girls appear to be as distinctive as ever. Studies at Pennsylvania State University have shown that parents ask their eighteen-month-old girls how they are feeling more often than they ask boys of the same age. Mothers were also found to talk to their two-year-old daughters about feelings more than they do to their two-year-old sons.

The patterns of emotional inhibition among adult men and women seem in large part attributable to how parents treat their children. Parents insist more that boys control their emotions, for instance, but with girls emphasize emotional closeness, studies have found. And research shows, too, that when parents tell stories to children, they tend to use more emotional words with girls, with one exception: they refer more to anger in stories they tell to boys.

Key Roles Are Attributed to Intensity of Emotion

March 17, 1987

Emotional intensity, a major, lifelong aspect of temperament, is emerging as a fruitful area of research that is yielding rich insights into how people experience themselves and others. Although the idea that people differ in emotional intensity is not new, the systematic new research is revealing important differences in the way that those with high and low intensity perceive, think about and react to events.

Some people, psychologists are observing, find themselves in emotional tumult even in reaction to mundane events, while others remain unperturbed under the most trying of circumstances. These levels of feeling characterize a person's entire emotional life; those with the deepest lows also have the loftiest highs, the research shows. And differences between people seem to emerge early in childhood, if not from birth, and remain a major mark of character throughout life.

Those who live lives of deep emotional intensity, researchers have found, seem to have a more complex sense of themselves and lead lives that are more complicated than do those whose emotions are less strong.

The inner lives of people at the extremes—those whose feelings burn with intensity or those who are utterly cool—are worlds apart regardless of the emotions they may express outwardly. For the emotionally intense person, events that to an outside observer seem unremarkable can take on a crucial importance. But the stolid react to even the gravest crisis with little feeling.

"One of the more emotionally intense people we studied was a woman who, for instance, was once depressed and distraught for days after she lost her pen," said Edward Diener, a psychologist at the University of Illinois, who has done much of the new research. On the other hand, he said, she became so thrilled on seeing an advertisement for a big sale on expensive women's shoes that "she hopped in her car on the spot and drove three hours to the store in Chicago."

"One of the least intense," Dr. Diener added, "was a man who, one evening, spotted a fire that had broken out in a college dorm and got an extinguisher and put it out. But instead of running, he walked to get the extinguisher and walked back to the fire. Another man, who was being treated for cancer, was so unexcitable that when he was told that the disease was in remission, he reported being somewhat happy for a day or so, then went back to his usual neutral state."

Understanding temperament with more precision can help psychotherapists better understand where normality ends and pathology begins. The new data are showing that what are considered discrete psychological disorders may, in fact, be simply the extremes of a continuum of normality.

The most highly reactive people seem to have what psychotherapists call a "cyclothymic" personality given to grand mood swings. At the extreme, he said, the tendency slides into a mild form of manic-depressive disorder.

At the other end of the continuum are people who are so imperturbable that they hardly seem to have emotions. Some of these may have "alexthymia," a term applied to those who say they have no feelings at all—or who at least cannot find the words to describe the feelings—or anhedonia, the inability to feel pleasure.

Those people whose emotions are more intense, the research is showing, seem to have more complex lives in general. "The emotionally intense people seek variety, novelty, complexity," said Robert Emmons, a psychologist at Michigan State University. "They have more varied goals in life, know more people in more different situations, and because they are doing so many different things, feel more conflict in their lives. They may want to work harder to achieve success at work, while at the same time trying to spend more time with a range of friends.

"These conflicts can be a source of stress for the emotionally intense, and may explain why they report getting more minor illnesses, like colds and flus, than do less emotional people," said Dr. Emmons.

Much of the conflict felt by the highly emotional, according to Dr. Emmons, is over whether to express or act on their feelings. "Although they may feel intensely, they do not always express themselves openly," Dr. Emmons said. "Intense people who are bottled up are in the worst situation."

Despite the conflicts and afflictions that intensity seems to bring, the emotionally intense thrive on the richness of their feelings. Research reported in 1987 in the *Journal of Research in Personality* shows that, inspite of their sufferings, emotionally intense people report as great a sense of well-being and contentment as do those whose lives lack such turmoil.

This tendency to exaggerate the emotional impact of events extends, too, to how highly emotional people assume others respond to those same events. Dr. Larsen has found that the emotionally intense tend to assume that everyone else experiences things with similar emotional urgency.

Emotional style also seems to determine what sorts of arguments a person will find more persuasive. "Highly emotional people are attuned to emotional appeals, while low-intensity people are more influenced by rational ones," Dr. Diener said.

The tendency to amplify or diminish emotions seems to appear quite early in life, according to research by Dr. Larsen. He asked the parents of 76 college students to describe what those students had been like as young children—whether, for instance, they were generally fussy, or would cry loudly if a toy were taken away, or would fight back when teased. The evaluations generally agreed with separate ratings, made by Dr. Larsen, of the students' emotional intensity as young adults.

Not every fussy baby will become an emotionally intense adult. But work by other researchers suggests that the level of intensity is largely hereditary, shows up virtually from birth, and persists throughout life. One of the earliest studies to suggest that children's temperament differed in terms of emotional intensity, among other dimensions, was that of Alexander Thomas and Stella Chess, psychiatrists who directed the New York Longitudinal Study, which studied infants beginning in the 1950's and followed them for twenty years.

In a more recent study, Ian Cesa and Laura Baker, psychologists at the University of Southern California, compared levels of emotional intensity in 75 pairs of fraternal and identical twins, and found that, in general, identical twins were more likely to be similar in temperament than were fraternal twins.

In an article in 1987 in the *Journal of Personality and Social Psychology*, Dr. Diener and Randy Larsen, a psychologist at Purdue University, report that the difference in emotional styles is closely tied to a difference in how people think about events. In one study, volunteers kept a record of their day-to-day lives and their emotional reactions; in another they were shown disturbing slides and their responses were analyzed. From studies such as these a portrait is emerging of the distinctive mental lives of those who have tumultuous or placid emotions.

For example, highly emotional people, when shown disturbing slides—a woman holding an injured, bleeding baby, for example—had an immediate thought that personalized the event, such as "What if this happened to me, or someone in my family."

The unemotional people, though, more often focused on a factual detail of the pictures; one commented about a slide of a dying man, "It looks like his pants are brand new."

"Some mental tactics used to avoid emotion are similar to the psychoanalytic defense mechanisms," Dr. Diener said. "We find that when people avoid their unpleasant feelings in this way, they pay a price: they blunt their positive feelings, too."

In addition to relating the disturbing slides to themselves, the highly emotional people tended to focus their attention on the worst part of the slide and to make a generalization about it, such as thinking about how much evil there is in the world. Such people, Dr. Larsen and Dr. Diener conclude, tend to see themselves as at the center of an emotional vortex; they overestimate the extent to which events relate to them, and become excessively absorbed in what those events mean to them.

Even the most volatile people seem gradually to mellow with age, according to a study of emotional intensity in 242 people aged 15 to 70, as reported last year in the journal *De-velopmental Psychology*. The average level of intensity, the study found, drops with each decade of life, with the most pronounced drop between early adulthood—roughly the 20's—and early middle-age in the 40's.

Some researchers believe that highly emotional people thrive on emotional-provoking situations, and the intense highs or lows that result. This idea is based on a more general theory that too high or too low a level of brain arousal is uncomfortable, producing either boredom or anxiety. As a result, this theory holds, people are driven to raise or lower their emotional arousal to optimal levels. That reasoning has been proposed, for instance, to explain the heightened social activities of extroverts, who are seen as needing social stimulation in order to increase an innately low level of central nervous system activity.

In a recent study Dr. Larsen found that, paradoxically, the more emotionally intense people had less physiological activity—as measured, for example, by heart rate—when they were at rest than did those whose emotions are less intense. In Dr. Larsen's view, this suggests that the steady diet of roiling emotions in high-intensity people satisfies a biological craving for a greater level of brain activity.

The stronger a person's emotions, the less sophisticated his awareness of emotions may be, according to Richard Lane, a psychiatrist at Chicago Medical College. In an article in 1987 in the *American Journal of Psychiatry*, written with Gary Schwartz, a psychologist at Yale, Dr. Lane points out that, apart from the intensity with which people feel their emotions, people differ, too, in the sophistication with which they are aware of them.

The levels of awareness run from an unreflective, but vivid, emotional outburst, to the sophisticated subtlety of emotional nuance typical, say, of the characters of Henry James.

Studies Point to Power of Nonverbal Signals

April 8, 1986

The nonverbal messages people send, with a look, a gesture, a tone of voice, are far more pervasive and important in the workaday world than have been generally realized, researchers are finding. But they are concluding too, that these messages are more complex and subtle than the popular accounts of "body language" that have appeared in recent years have indicated.

Such covert cues, the new data show, have a strong impact in key relationships such as those between judge and jury, physician and patient, or teacher and student.

Indeed, the tacit communication of expectations between one person and another are found, in many cases, to make all the difference between success or failure in various kinds of endeavors.

How a judge gives his instructions to a jury was perceived to double the likelihood that the jury would deliver a verdict of guilty or not guilty—even when on the surface the judge's demeanor seemed perfectly impartial. A doctor's attitude affected the course of a patient's disease; a teacher's attitude influenced the intellectual progress of students.

And findings of the new research are likely to have repercussions in areas of life where it is crucial to avoid bias, even the most subtle. For example, according to some legal experts, one consequence of the study of research on judges, if it is borne out by further research, may be to provide a more precise basis for showing when a judge may have silently biased a trial.

The judicial study, reported in the November 1986 issue of *The Stanford Law Review,* is believed to be one of the first scientific tests of the courtroom lore that the judge's attitudes, even if never openly expressed, are often crucial to a trial's outcome. One striking finding concerned trials in which the judge knew that the defendant had a record of previous felonies, a fact that a jury, by law, is not allowed to know unless the defendant takes the stand. When the judges were aware of past felonies, the Stanford study found, their final instructions to juries were lacking in warmth, tolerance, patience and competence.

The juries in these cases said they were unaware of any bias on the part of the judges, yet their verdicts were twice as likely to be "guilty" than in cases in which the charges were as serious but defendants had no record of felonies.

When videotapes were analyzed by independent raters, they found that the judges' tone of voice, rather than anything in their words or body movements, communicated the strongest, most negative messages.

"Judges can't come out and say, 'This defendant is guilty,' " said Peter Blanck, who did the study. "But they may say it subtly, nonverbally—even if that message is inadvertent."

A judge's charge to a jury is, by law, supposed to be free of such bias, and Dr. Blanck, a social psychologist who is a Stanford law student, said he believed that most of the biasing elements he found in his research were unintended. He sees his study as a first step in helping judges to neutralize their hidden messages, as well as, one day, providing lawyers with a new basis for challenging verdicts.

"If judges became sensitized to the problem, they could learn to be more impartial in their demeanor," Dr. Blanck said.

Dr. Blanck's research is one of a wave of studies assessing the subtle influence. The whole line of research owes much to the work of Robert Rosenthal of Harvard University, with whom Dr. Blanck did graduate studies before going to Stanford Law School, where he became head of The Law Review.

"Rosenthal is the pioneer in the field," said Randolph Lee, a clinical psychologist at Trinity College in Hartford, who edits *The Journal of Nonverbal Behavior.* "He was the first to find a way to measure how people send and receive nonverbal messages."

A physician's rapport with his patients, for instance, depends to a great extent on his body language, according to Dr. Rosenthal's recent studies, done with Jinni Harrigan, a psychologist at the University of Cincinnati Medical School. The research is described in *Nonverbal Communication in the Clinical Context,* published in 1986 by the Pennsylvania State Press.

The studies found that physicians who were rated as having the best rapport sat leaning toward the patient, with arms and legs uncrossed, and nodding as they talked to patients. Another sign of rapport was looking the patient in the eye from time to time, but not staring. The net effect seemed to communicate a desire to be attentive and intimate.

The meaning of a given posture or movement, Dr. Rosenthal cautions, is highly specific to a given situation. Thus, a physician who leaned back in his chair, which in many social settings would be a sign of feeling relaxed, could be seen by a patient as signaling a lack of interest.

Dr. Rosenthal, like many other researchers, is cautious in attempting to derive anything like a vocabulary of nonverbal messages from the research results. The field, he says, has suffered from popularizers who presumed to tell people exactly which movement or posture would communicate what message—a precision that the scientific data do not yet allow and may never, since much of what is communicated nonverbally means one thing within a given context and quite another in different situations.

"It's too simplistic to say that, for example, a physician is sending a message of rapport when he nods or tilts forward," said Dr. Rosenthal. "When you freeze the moment and extract one part of what is going on from it, you lose the richness of the phenomenon. When people try to equate a specific cue with a given message, it gets too mechanical."

Nonetheless, it is clearly important for everyone to know that, in one way or another, they are in almost constant nonverbal communication with others.

Tone of voice was a potentially damaging covert bias found in one study of psychotherapists with their patients. When the therapists talked to resident patients at a large private hospital, their tone was much more hostile and anxious than when they spoke with patients who lived outside the hospital.

The message received by the inpatients was comparatively pessimistic. Often it was something like, "You don't think I'm going to get that well, because I'm an inpatient," in the view of Dr. Blanck, who was one of the researchers. Moreover, when the psychotherapists talked to their supervisors about their patients, the tone of voice they used reflected the tones used with the patients.

"The nonverbal messages during therapy can be more important than what is said," Dr. Lee said.

In another setting, a study of job interviews found that the more often an interviewer touched his foot, the more likely that his hiring decision was favorable. While at first glance that result may seem curious, an explanation is provided by Dr. Rosenthal and Shelly Goldberg, a student at Harvard with whom he did the study.

When people are feeling ill at ease,

as is often the case during such interviews, they tend to sit stiffly and shift very little. One possibility, according to Dr. Rosenthal and Miss Goldberg, is that once an interviewer makes a favorable hiring decision, he becomes more relaxed and shifts position more, making it more likely that he will touch his foot, which is otherwise difficult to reach if he is sitting in a more formal position. The study is published in *The Journal of Nonverbal Behavior.*

In the 1950's, while doing dissertation research, Dr. Rosenthal discovered that, somehow, he had influenced the volunteers in his study to show the effect he expected even before he performed his experiment.

Dismayed, Dr. Rosenthal began to investigate the possibility that psychologists running experiments were on the power of their expectations alone, inadvertently leading the volunteers in their studies to show the predicted results. When, for example, Dr. Rosenthal told half of a group of testers that they were to duplicate a "well-established" result that people would judge photographs of faces positively, those experimenters found exactly that. But when the other half of the testers were told that the "well-established" result was that the judgments would be negative, that was what they found. In short, the testers' expectations swayed the results.

The same effect, Dr. Rosenthal discovered, even held when the testers were measuring how quickly rats were able to learn to find their way through a maze. Those testers who were told their rats were quick learners proved to have rats that learned the maze quicker than rats whose testers expected them to be slow. The rats in both groups were identical at the outset, but the smart ones were handled with greater care. Taking the principle that expectations become self-fulfilling one step further, in 1964 Dr. Rosenthal performed his famous "Pygmalion" experiment, in which teachers were given the names of children in their school who, supposedly, had been identified by a new test as being on the verge of blooming intellectually. The children had actually been chosen randomly.

At the end of the school year,

though, the selected children showed gains in intellectual abilities compared with the other children. Moreover, teachers perceived the children in the "bloomer" group as more appealing, adjusted and affectionate than the others.

The Pygmalion study evoked heated objections from many educational psychologists. But by 1978 Dr. Rosenthal was able to review 345 studies showing the power of the Pygmalion effect.

Many of the Pygmalion studies, he found, pointed to subtle factors. Teachers, for example, became especially warm toward the "special" students, gave more specific reactions to how they performed, taught them more difficult material and gave them greater opportunities to respond than with the other students.

"The same factors operate with bosses and their employees, therapists and their clients, or parents and children," said Dr. Rosenthal. "The more warmth and the more positive the expectations that are communicated, the better the person who receives those messages will do."

To better understand the nuances of how such messages are sent and received, Dr. Rosenthal and his colleagues designed a special videotape test, called the PONS, or Profile of Nonverbal Sensitivity. The test portrays people in a range of scenes, including nagging a child, seducing someone, and praying. The test allows the analysis of the different aspects of nonverbal messages, including facial expressions, body movements and tone of voice.

The PONS test has been used now in hundreds of studies, with thousands of people in twenty countries. The data show that women, by and large, are better than men at reading nonverbal cues and at expressing their feelings nonverbally, reports Judith Hall, a psychologist at Harvard Medical School.

One implication of the new research, Dr. Rosenthal and others believe, is for physicians' behavior with their patients. "When a physician gives up on a patient, that patient gets the most negative of nonverbal messages—too bad you're dying—which makes the patient give up hope," said Dr. Rosenthal.

Researchers Identify True Clues to Lying

February 12, 1985

People are surprisingly inept, new research shows, at detecting lies.

One reason is that most of the supposed clues to deceit, such as shifty eyes or nervousness, seldom, in fact, accompany a premeditated lie. Another reason is that people generally have not been aware of the more reliable indicators, which psychologists have only now begun to identify.

While people frequently expect a liar to give himself away through nervous gestures, for example, the new studies discern that liars are more likely to attempt to inhibit all such nervous movements, and so appear more composed. "Most liars can fool most people most of the time," according to Paul Ekman, a psychologist at the University of California at San Francisco.

Nevertheless, researchers have found that there are some specific physical signs that the purveyor of untruth cannot supress.

Lying actually takes many forms: hedges, evasions, exaggerations, half-truths, and outright falsehoods among them. Social lies—the fictional previous engagement, for example—make life work more smoothly or prevent hurt feelings, and so are tacitly ignored. Daily life is rife with lies, many benign and some malicious.

"People tell about two lies a day, or at least that is how many they will admit to," according to Bella DePaulo, a psychologist at the University of Virginia, who in one study is having people keep a daily diary of the lies they tell.

One of the consistent findings of the new research which is being conducted by psychologists at several universities, is that people think they are better detectors of lies than they really are. Dozens of studies have found that people's accuracy at detecting lies usually exceeds chance by very little. While guessing alone would give a rate of 50 percent accuracy, in the recent studies the best rate of accuracy for any group has never exceeded 60 percent, and is most often near chance.

This is true even for those in professions where lie detection is at a premium. In a study done at Cornell University, for example, customs inspectors proved no better than college students at guessing which people were trying to smuggle contraband. Likewise, a study at Auburn University in Alabama found that police detectives were no more successful in judging people lying about a mock crime than were students.

Another study found that a group of seasoned Federal law enforcement officers from the Secret Service and the Criminal Investigation Divisions of the armed forces were no more accurate in detecting deceit than were newly recruited officers who had just joined those agencies. The one difference between the groups, though, was that the seasoned officers, who averaged seven years of service, felt more confident of their ability to detect lying, even though they were no more accurate. Studies such as they have revealed that people are poor at detecting lies in large part because they base their judgment on the wrong clues. For example, in the study of customs inspectors, people were most often thought to be telling lies if they did such things as hesitating before answering questions, avoided meeting the eyes of their questioner or shifted their posture. None of these signs, though, were actually more common among those who lied than among those who did not.

Even customs inspectors, who make judgments of lying throughout the day, do not seem to become more proficient at detecting lies, Dr. DePaulo found. One major reason for this, she said, is that they get no systematic information about which of their judgments are right. Of those people they let pass without inspection, an unknown number carry contraband; of those they check, another unknown number of the guilty nevertheless evade detection.

The custom inspectors' occasional successes, Dr. DePaulo said, give them reinforcement for whatever grounds for judgment they may happen to use. "However," she added, "it is possible that their success occurred in spite of their beliefs about cues to deception—beliefs which may have actually been erroneous."

Reliable Clues Are Automatic

The same holds, in theory, for those in other occupations where the detection of lies is routine, such as courtroom lawyers, detectives or insurance investigators. However, as some of the researchers acknowledge, these laboratory tests of the ability to detect lies may not be a true indication of a person's proficiency in a true life situation, where he or she can observe and question the suspected person freely.

Much of the new data have come from the work of Dr. Ekman, who describes his research on what he claims are reliable clues to lying in

Telling Lies, published in 1985 by W. W. Norton.

According to Dr. Ekman, whose theory is generally accepted by other experts, the least dependable indicators of lying are those channels of expression that a person can control most fully. Thus, words are far less accurate clues than tone of voice, because it is easier to rehearse what one will say than it is to control the pitch of voice while saying it.

By far the most reliable clues to lying, Dr. Ekman said, are the reponses a person makes automatically, and which are subject to little or no control. Such responses are most likely during lies that are more important to the liar and in which he has an emotional stake.

For example, Dr. Ekman's research has identified certain movements of facial muscles that very few people can make deliberately. Unlike most facial muscles, these seem to be regulated by a more primitive part of the brain, which makes it nearly impossible to control them voluntarily. As a result, when that muscle movement is part of an emotional expression, people are unable to conceal it.

Three Muscle Groups Are Key

Dr. Ekman believes at least three such muscle movements are telltale signs of emotional reactions that people who are lying often try to conceal: distress, fear and anger.

The signal of distress or worry is the lifting of just the inner part of the eyebrows. "Fewer than 15 percent of people can control this movement at will," Dr. Ekman said in an interview. "Woody Allen is one; it gives him the ability to seem particularly sympathetic or vulnerable. But in most people, this movement of the brows happens only when a person feels genuine distress. It can also signal guilt. Ordinarily, this movement will appear despite a person's best attempts to conceal these feelings."

Another such reliable facial signal is for fear. In this movement the eyebrows are raised and pulled together. "Not a single person we've tested can

produce this movement deliberately," Dr. Ekman said.

The third such clue is to anger. An angry person often narrows and tightens the red margin of the lips. Dr. Ekman says this muscle action frequently appears just as someone starts to get angry, even before the person is aware of the feeling. It is, however, a subtle and fleeting movement.

Smiles, too, can belie true feelings. A feigned smile, Dr. Ekman says, is likely to be asymmetrical. Although both sides of the face make the same movements, the muscles on one side are stronger than the other, and so yield a slightly lopsided expression.

General Expressiveness Is Factor

One important factor in all this is how expressive a person is in general. People who are usually very expressive change drastically while telling a planned lie. They seem to adopt a strategy of overcontrol, according to Howard Friedman, a psychologist at the University of California at Riverside, and as a result they make fewer nervous gestures than they would ordinarily.

When people care about the lie they are telling, according to Dr. DePaulo, their reponses are generally shorter, slower, more negative, and more highly pitched that are their truthful responses. They also tend to avoid eye contact with the person to whom they are speaking, blink less and make fewer head movements and postural shifts.

While telling lies, people also seem to be prone to more problems with the fluency of their speech, according to Dr. DePaulo. They tend to give shorter and more hesitant answers, speak in a higher pitch, and make more grammatical errors and slips of the tongue.

On the other hand, when people are judging whether someone is lying, they tend to use very few of these actual indicators. Most often, people judge another person to be lying when he does such things as smiling less, shifting his posture more and taking

longer to answer a question. None of these behaviors, according to the research, is actually more common among people while telling a lie.

The research confirms that some time-honored clues to deception hold up. Dilated pupils, for example, signal emotional arousal; they are highly reliable indicators since the dilation is completely beyond a person's voluntary control. However, Dr. Ekman points out that they can be a clue to lying only when evidence of any emotion whatever would signal a lie. Further, one would have to rule out that the emotional arousal was not the sign that an innocent person is afraid of being wrongly judged to be a liar.

Several Hazards in Detection

There are several such hazards, Dr. Ekman warns, in trying to use clues such as these to detect lying. For one, he cautions that a single clue to deceit is not enough; they need to be corroborated by others. "Facial clues should be confirmed by those from the voice or body, for example," he said.

Another hazard is what he calls the "Othello error," in reference to Othello's falsely suspecting Desdemona of infidelity, which induces her to panic. "This error," Dr. Ekman said, "is due to the failure to recognize that some truthful people can become highly emotional when they are suspected of lying. Almost any emotional signal can be felt by an innocent person, including distress, fear, and anger."

Despite these ambiguities, Dr. Ekman asserts that people can be taught to improve their skills at catching lies. He suggests that past attempts by researchers to teach people to improve their lie detection skills have done poorly because until very recently there has been only the most general understanding of the specific indicators of lying.

"For example, researchers have found that there is no difference in the amount of smiling during lying and truth-telling, and so have taught people to ignore smiles when trying to detect lies," Dr. Ekman said. "But what they did not realize was that people can be taught to tell the difference between false and felt smiles. We've begun to teach people thirty specific clues to lying such as these."

"There are no absolute clues to lying itself, only to the emotions or kind of performance that accompany lies," Dr. Ekman added. "It's complex. You've got to take into account such elements as whether the lie is likely to be poorly rehearsed, or what emotion would give away the lie. Each type of lie has its unique set of clues."

There seem to be some people who are so skilled at telling lies that it is virtually impossible to catch them at it. In Dr. Ekman's view, the attributes that suggest a person may be able to lie flawlessly include having acting experience, being inventive at fabricating stories, having a good memory, and being a smooth, convincing talker.

Among the qualities that make a person a poor detector of lies, Dr. Ekman lists being biased against the suspected liar, being prone to denial and avoidance of problems, and being under the sway of highly charged feelings. These factors might make someone more likely either to miss seeing signs of lying, or to see lies where they are none.

Agreeableness vs. Anger

April 16, 1989

Hostility can be suicidal. A host of recent studies come to the same conclusion. People who are chronically hostile, who see the world through a lens of suspicion and cynicism, are particularly vulnerable to heart disease. The data also suggest that hostility increases the risk of contracting a range of other ailments as well. By the same token, amiability—plain old good-naturedness—seems to have a protective effect on health. "A cynical, mistrusting attitude is a driving force that makes people most susceptible to heart disease," says Dr. Redford Williams, an internist and behavioral medicine researcher at Duke University Medical Center. "Hostility predicts the risk not just of heart disease, but mortality due to all causes."

Not only those given to explosive fits of anger are at risk. More subtle styles of hostility—skepticism, mistrust, a propensity to make snide comments—are just as damaging. No matter how they express their hostility, antagonistic people die from heart disease in greater numbers than do their more agreeable peers.

How behavior affects health has been the subject of considerable research. Studies conducted in the United States and Europe have yielded strong evidence of a link between heart disease and Type A behavior. The emerging consensus among researchers is that hostility is the most toxic element of anger, although there is a counter view. Recently, Dr. Williams and his colleagues have made some important discoveries as to what it is about hostility that is so harmful, and how the damaging effects occur.

The connection between anger and health was brought to public attention some thirty years ago when a pair of San Francisco cardiologists, Dr. Meyer Friedman and Dr. Ray H. Rosenman, coined the term "Type A" to describe a behavior pattern that led to an increased risk of heart disease. A person displaying Type A behavior was ambitious, irritable, competitive, fiercely focused on his goals and always racing the clock. By contrast, a Type B person was easygoing, cooperative, patient and slow to anger.

Subsequent research shifted to a related issue: If people feel anger, what should they do about it? In the 1960's and early 1970's, people were encouraged to let their anger out, to "ventilate" it. By the late 1970's however, studies were showing that the net effect of such ventilation was simply to make anger a more likely response to any annoying situation.

The most recent studies by Dr. Williams and his colleagues conclude that whether anger is expressed or not is far less important than whether it is habitually felt. An occasional display of hostility is not dangerous to one's health. Certainly in urban life there are many situations where hostile feelings are bound to occur. The problem arises when hostility is chronic, that is, when it becomes a personal style.

The first clue that Dr. Williams was on the right track came in the late 1970's. He and his colleagues at Duke found that they could measure hostility with the Minnesota Multiphasic Personality Inventory (M.M.P.I.), a personality test widely used by psychologists. The subjects in the Duke study were evaluated by a face-to-face interview that tested, among other things, whether they were prone to be mistrustful of others and tended to behave aggressively.

Those who scored high on the test were 50 percent more likely to have had a blockage of their coronary arteries than were low scorers. The subjects were also evaluated to see whether they exhibited Type A behavior in general. Here, too, there was a correlation with heart disease, but it was weaker. The implication was that competitive, hard-driving people—classic Type A's—who are not hostile are less at risk than their more antagonistic counterparts.

The evidence, however, was not conclusive. Since the participants in the Duke study already had some form of heart disease, the personality traits revealed by the test might have been a consequence of the disease rather than a cause. What was needed was data showing that hostile people with no symptoms of heart trouble later developed the disease.

Some important evidence came from a study of about 1,800 healthy, middle-aged men who worked at a Western Electric plant in Chicago. The workers took the M.M.P.I. when they first enrolled in the study, in 1957, and over the following two decades their health and life styles were carefully monitored. Richard B. Shekelle, now a professor of epidemiology at the University of Texas School of Public Health in Houston, analyzed the data from that study and found that those workers who had scored in the top fifth on the M.M.P.I. hostility scale were one and a half times more likely to have had a heart attack or died from heart disease twenty years later than those with low scores.

A 1983 study of 255 graduates of

the University of North Carolina School of Medicine, conducted by Dr. Williams and other researchers at Duke and the University of North Carolina, provided even stronger evidence. Like the Western Electric workers, the doctors had taken the M.M.P.I. about 25 years earlier. But here the effect of hostility on health was more dramatic. Those with scores above the median were about five times more likely to have had a heart attack or angina or to have died of heart disease than those who scored below the median; they were also 6.4 times more likely to have died from any cause. A similar study by Dr. Williams and his research team looked at 118 lawyers who had taken the M.M.P.I. as students at the University of North Carolina School of Law. Those who scored highest on the hostility scale were 4.2 times more likely to have died three decades later from heart disease or other causes than those who were least hostile.

Dr. Williams believes that the effect of hostility on the heart was stronger among the doctors and lawyers than the Western Electric workers primarily because of a difference in age between the two groups, rather than a difference in stress levels between the professions. The Western Electric workers were middle-aged when they were first tested, whereas the medical and law students were in their 20's.

Another study done last year by Dr. Williams and his team supports this hypothesis. This time the research focused on 2,289 patients who had undergone coronary angiography—X-rays of the coronary arteries that pinpoint lesions and blockages—at Duke University between September 1974 and November 1980. It turned out that Type A patients with heart disease who were 45 years of age or younger tended to have severe blockages of their coronary arteries, while Type A patients who were 55 and older tended to have problems of a much less serious nature. The same pattern with regard to age was even stronger with patients who had scored high on the M.M.P.I. hostility scale.

"It seems that the impact of hostility on health is greatest in early adulthood," says Dr. Williams. For reasons still unknown, some people are simply biologically prone to the damaging effects of hostility, he explains. As a result, many of them die by the time they reach middle age, whereas people who are resistant to these harmful effects survive.

A recent study in Finland of 3,750 men between the ages of 40 and 59 provides evidence that hostility is especially deadly for heart patients. Of the 104 men in the study who had high blood pressure and ischemic heart disease, which involves a drop in the supply of blood to the heart muscle, those with the highest hostility levels were nearly thirteen times more likely to die or be admitted to a hospital for heart disease over the next few years than those with the lowest hostility levels.

As a result of their most recent research, Dr. Williams and his colleagues have come to a better understanding of the biological links between hostility and heart disease. When participants were given a drug that triggers the body's natural stress reaction—which involves, among other things, a rise in blood pressure—there was a notable difference between the responses of the hostile participants and the responses of the more easygoing people. When the drug was administered intravenously for long periods of time at high doses, the stress reaction of the hostile subjects was long-lasting, as might have been expected. The easygoing subjects showed a paradoxical effect, physiological relaxation.

"It's almost as though the easygoing types have an automatic cut-off switch," says Dr. Williams. In such people, the sympathetic nervous system, which prepares the body to deal with stressful situations, is able to calm down. "The hostile personalities don't have that protective mechanism," he says.

How stress leads to heart disease in hostile people is still being studied. According to Dr. Williams, certain hormones that are produced by the body as part of the normal stress reaction, such as cortisol and epinephrine, may play a crucial role. Among their many effects, these "stress hormones" cause the heart to beat more strongly and blood pressure to rise. Dr. Williams believes that when this reaction is sustained for hours or repeated day after day, year after year, there may be damage to the coronary arteries. In addition, studies have shown that these stress hormones cause fats to be released into the bloodstream, raising cholesterol levels. Since cholesterol tends to accumulate at sites of injury in the coronary arteries, this chain of events may increase a person's risk of a heart attack or angina.

Dr. Williams suspects that easygoing people are resistant to stress because they have robust parasympathetic nervous systems, the part of the nervous system that calms the body by lowering blood pressure and heart rate. To test this idea, he devised a study in which ice packs were applied to the faces of twenty people. This stimulates the "dive reflex"—a slowing of the heartbeat to conserve oxygen—which can be observed in all mammals when they dive under water. The study showed that the reflex was stronger and lasted longer in easygoing people than it did in people more given to hostility. According to Dr. Williams, this demonstrates that amiable people have a strong parasympathetic reaction following stress, and he suggests that this reaction may blunt the harmful effects of the sympathetic nervous system.

Researchers are now identifying what aspects of a hostile personality are most lethal. Kenneth A. Dodge, a psychologist at Vanderbilt University, working with Dr. Williams and his team, recently took another look at the data from the University of North Carolina law students who had taken the M.M.P.I. more than thirty years ago. When he analyzed their responses to questions about hostility, he found that three qualities were most likely to predict death from heart disease: a cynical attitude, an angry mood and an aggressive style of responding to the questions. These three factors together were stronger predictors than the M.M.P.I hostility scale.

Other researchers, working with

similar kinds of data, have reached similar conclusions. One is Paul T. Costa Jr., a psychologist at the Gerontology Research Center, part of the National Institute on Aging in Baltimore. "The toxic kind of hostility is in an antagonistic style," he says. You see it in people who are rude, condescending and uncooperative. They don't sit there fuming all the time, but they can be belittling and cynical. It's the cold-blooded variety of hostility that puts you at risk for heart disease, not the hot-blooded kind."

None of the research suggests that it is unhealthy to get angry from time to time. In fact, researchers and psychotherapists believe that expressing anger in an appropriate manner can be good for one's health.

If expressing anger can be good, is suppressing it bad? "It used to be thought that if you felt angry and did not express it, that could lead to high blood pressure and heart disease," Costa says. "In fact, those who experience anger and frustration but rarely express it are frequently diagnosed as having heart disease." But, he maintains, these diagnoses are often wrong. "When you do angiography studies, you find that these patients have little or no disease—they are just more given to complaints." The key factor in the development of heart disease is whether a person feels angry all the time, not whether he suppresses or expresses it, Costa concludes.

Despite all the accumulating evidence, not all researchers are convinced that hostility leads to heart disease. Chief among the skeptics is Dr. Ray H. Rosenman, one of the originators of the Type A concept and a cardiologist at S.R.I. International, a research institute in Menlo Park, California. He maintains that the proponents of the hostility theory ignore various studies that have failed to find a link between hostility and heart disease. And he argues that Dr. Williams and his colleagues have misinterpreted their own findings. "Their own data don't actually show that hostile behavior predicts heart disease," he says. What the data do show, in his view, is that hostile people are more prone to die prematurely from *all* causes, including cancer. According to Dr. Rosenman, the only type of behavior that has been linked conclusively to heart disease is the classic overarching competitiveness of Type A's—the kind that sends people tearing down the freeway or clawing their way up the ladder in the business world. This behavior is based, he says, on "a deep-seated insecurity that leads not just to covert hostility but also to a constant sense of time pressure."

Dr. Williams agrees that hostility is not the only psychological factor in heart disease. Stress and interpersonal conflict are also important villains, he says—but especially when they act in concert with hostility.

While researchers debate the dangers of anger, clinical programs across the country are trying to teach hostile Type A's to be more like easygoing Type B's, on the theory that this will help them live longer.

"There was one police lieutenant who was irritated so much of the time that his family joked that he got angry every thirty seconds," says Robert Allan, a clinical psychologist who is co-director of the Coronary Risk Reduction Program at New York Hospital-Cornell Medical Center in New York.

The program is designed especially for people who, like the anger-prone lieutenant, have already had a heart attack or coronary bypass surgery, or are at high risk for heart disease. Participants are helped to see just how damaging cynicism can be, and they learn techniques to help them change habits that may contribute to heart disease. Allan says he's struck by how often the patients' anger "is triggered by what they see as injustice or incompetence. They don't see that they are full of free-floating hostility; instead, they have the conviction that all their anger is justified."

"The antidote to hostility is to develop a more trusting heart," says Dr. Williams. In his book, *The Trusting Heart,* he outlines twelve steps that have been used successfully in clinical programs designed to make hostile heart patients more easygoing. Some are obvious: Learn to relax with meditation, and try to be more forgiving. Dr. Williams recommends carrying a notebook in which to write down cynical or hostile thoughts. Another suggestion is to short-circuit such thoughts by saying "Stop!" whenever they begin. People are encouraged to substitute reasonable thoughts for cynical, mistrustful ones during stressful situations. For instance, if an elevator takes a long time to come, think of a good reason why it may have stopped along the way rather than rage against some imaginary person's thoughtlessness in holding it up. Still another technique is to see things from the other person's point of view; empathy soothes the angry heart.

For some people, however, self-help may not be enough. "If you've tried all these techniques and they don't seem to be helping as much as you'd like, or if your spouse or friends say you're still hostile, then professional help may be advisable," says Dr. Williams.

Aren't the techniques Dr. Williams recommends in his book simply too gimmicky for people who are, after all, too cynical?

"All it takes is the right motivation," he says. "When people see that their hostility can lead to an early grave, they are ready to try."

Motivation

Want to get ahead in life? One of the best all-around tickets to success at just about anything, is an optimistic outlook. That is the message of the research in "Power of Positive Thinking." For instance, one key is how you handle failures, it's best to have the attitude that you'll learn from them and try, try again.

How rational is love? And can it be measured with any accuracy? That is the debate in "Psychologist Pursue the Irrational Aspects of Love." On the one hand, researchers have tried to assess love using objective questionnaires. But others argue that love is so irrational that people cannot report directly on the stirrings of their own heart.

Add to the list of human motives, like the need for achievement or power, the need for intimacy. In some people that need is particularly high.

For them friendships and relationships come first—but along with that need may sometimes come a fear of closeness, according to the findings in "Worries About Intimacy Are Rising, Therapists Find."

Is there a true aphrodisiac? In a sense, yes. The one compound that makes for sexual chemistry is the male sex hormone, testosterone. But what testosterone generates is desire—sexual performance itself, according to the research in "Chemistry of Sexual Desire Yields Its Elusive Secrets."

What is the appeal of the sensation of risk? What attracts thousands to roller coasters and "scream machines?" It's the excitement produced by the simulation of danger, research suggests in "Why Do People Crave the Experience?"

Research Affirms Power of Positive Thinking

Februay 3, 1987

Pollyana was right, new research shows.

Optimism—at least reasonable optimism—can pay dividends as wide-ranging as health, longevity, job success and higher scores on achievement tests.

Pessimism not only has the opposite effect but also seems to be at play in such psychological disorders as extreme shyness and depression.

The new research is an outgrowth of earlier work on the power of self-fulfilling prophecies. That early work concentrated largely on how individuals tend to conform to others' expectations of them, a phenomenon known as the "Pygmalion effect." If anything, researchers have found, the Pygmalion effect is more pervasive than had been thought. The new work looks at people's expectations about their own lives and finds that the power of expectations goes beyond mere achievement to visceral, emotional qualities.

"Our expectancies not only affect how we see reality but also affect the reality itself," according to Edward E. Jones, a psychologist at Princeton University, who reviewed the research on expectancy in a recent issue of *Science.*

Michael F. Scheier, a psychologist at Carnegie-Mellon University in Pittsburgh, has found that optimists handle stress better than do pessimists. In a 1987 report in the *Journal of Personality and Social Psychology,* he wrote that optimists tend to respond to disappointments like being turned down for a job by formulating a plan of action and asking other people for help and advice; pessimists more often react to such difficulties by trying to forget the whole thing or assuming there is nothing they can do to

change things—an attitude optimists adopted only when there was, objectively nothing that could be done.

In one of the more hotly pursued lines of investigation, psychologists are tracking the importance of how people explain their failures to themselves. People tend to have a habitual explanatory style, a typical way of explaining the events that befall them, according to work by Martin Seligman, a psychologist at the University of Pennsylvania.

Pessimists, Dr. Seligman has found, tend to construe bad events such as flunking an exam or giving a party that flops as resulting from a personal deficit that will plague them forever in everything they do. Others see the same setbacks more optimistically, as being due to mistakes that can be remedied. They feel they can make the necessary changes.

Most people mix a pessimistic and an optimistic outlook to some degree. The new research findings apply most strongly to those people at the extremes, who most clearly exemplify one style or the other.

Work by several researchers has shown people who tend to blame themselves for their misfortunes are more susceptible to disease. For example, George Valliant, a psychiatrist at Dartmouth Medical School, and Christopher Peterson, a psychologist at the University of Michigan, worked with Dr. Seligman to study 99 members of the Harvard graduating classes of 1939 to 1944. The Harvard men had been interviewed on their return from World War II about their war experiences, and have had physical examinations every five years since their graduation.

Those men whose postwar interviews indicated they had been opti-

mistic in college were healthier in later life than the pessimists were. "The men's explanatory style at age 25 predicted their health at 65," said Dr. Seligman. "Around age 45 the health of the pessimists started to deteriorate more quickly."

Researchers are not sure just why explanatory style should affect health. One possible answer is suggested by studies at the University of Colorado and Yale University, which found that the attitude of helplessness typical of pessimists is associated with weakening of the immune system's resistance to tumors and infection. Or pessimists may neglect themselves. Dr. Peterson at the University of Michigan has found for example, that people whose explanatory style is pessimistic smoke and drink more and exercise less than do optimists. On a checklist of health habits, they were much more careless of their health than were the optimists. And the pessimists reported twice as many colds and doctors' visits during the year as the optimists did.

Several researchers, including Dr. Seligman, have tied explanatory style to depression in the face of failure. "If you see a failure as due to something you can change, then it is not so devastating," said Craig Anderson, a psychologist at Rice University, who has studied people's explanatory style in depression, loneliness, and shyness. People are most vulnerable to these problems, he said, if they feel they can do little or nothing to change the causes of failure.

In a study of insurance agents reported in a 1987 issue of the *Journal of Personality and Social Psychology,* for example, Dr. Seligman found that how the agents explained their failures to make a sale made the difference between their becoming outstanding salesmen on the one hand, or quitting the company on the other. Those salesmen who had a more optimistic outlook, the study found, sold 37 percent more insurance in their first two years on the job than did those with the pessimistic view. The pessimists were twice as likely to quit in their first year as were the optimists.

Dr. Seligman, who has developed a test to measure explanatory style, has found that this aspect of personality is a better predictor of how people will fare at jobs like sales, where failure is part of one's daily routine, than do many tests now used in hiring people for those jobs.

"About three-quarters of the life insurance agents hired quit within their first three years," said Dr. Seligman. "Those agents with an optimistic explanatory style weather the challenges better."

The test describes in detail a dozen hypothetical good and bad events, such as having someone compliment you on your appearance, or having a date go badly. People taking the test imagine themselves in the situations and then give a reason why it might have happened. The reasons given are scored in terms of optimism and pessimism.

Using a modified version of the test, researchers have found differences in explanatory style among children as young as third grade. While there is not yet a firm theory of how people's explanatory styles are shaped, major influences seem to come from the attitudes of significant adults in a child's life, especially parents and teachers. Two studies comparing the explanatory styles of parents and their children have found that a mother's style, but not the father's, correlates highly with the styles of their children. That pattern suggests that social influence, not heredity, is at play.

"The young child listens attentively to how his primary caretaker—usually his mother—explains bad things," said Dr. Seligman.

Working with Susan Nolen-Hoeksema of Stanford and Joan Girgus of Princeton, Dr. Seligman has found that even among third- and fourth-graders, those with a pessimistic outlook are more susceptible to depression than do those with an optimistic style.

The pessimistic children also do less well on achievement tests. "It is not that they are less bright," said Dr. Seligman. "My hunch is that for a given level of intelligence, your actual achievement is a function not just of talent, but also of the capacity to stand defeat. If an otherwise bright child is doing poorly in school, he may be the victim of a pessimistic style."

Working with the dean of admissions at the University of Pennsylvania, Dr. Seligman and Leslie Kamen tested 500 members of the incoming freshman class in 1984. Using a composite of the students' high school grades and college entrance exam scores, the dean's office is able to predict what each student's freshman year grades should be. The test of explanatory style, however, was able to predict which freshman would do better than expected and which would do worse.

"College entrance exams measure talent, while explanatory style tells you who gives up," Dr. Seligman said. "It is the combination of reasonable talent and the ability to keep going in the face of defeat that leads to success. What's missing in tests of ability is a measure of motivation. What you need to know about someone is whether they will keep going when things get frustrating."

People's explanatory styles seem to be relatively stable over the course of life, according to research by Dr. Seligman and Melanie Burns, a graduate student. Through ads in almuni bulletins they found people now in their seventies and eighties who had diaries from adolescence, and they studied the diaries.

"If you were an optimistic teen, then you'll be an optimist at 80," said Dr. Seligman. "People's reactions to bad events are highly stable over a half century or more. If as a teenager you think boys shun you because you are unlovable, then as a grandparent you will talk about your grandchildren's health problems as being because the family is sickly."

But Dr. Seligman believes that explanatory style can be changed. In a recent study of depressed patients he found that cognitive therapy—a technique that identifies and corrects erroneous habits of thought—changed the style of the patients from pessimistic to optimistic, and that the change persisted one year after therapy ended.

One method used in cognitive therapy, for example, is to have people monitor their automatic thoughts in reaction to things they regret doing, and then to replace those thoughts with ones that are more realistic. Dr. Seligman gives the example of a depressed young student who came to his office ready to drop out of graduate school after getting a C on her first paper. Her automatic thoughts were, "I can't write; I'm a bad student; I don't deserve to be in school."

Dr. Seligman, after exploring with the student what some alternative possibilities might be, came up with several, among them that the class average was a C and that she needed to work harder. He then had her call the professor and ask why she got a C. The answer: the class average was a C and she needed to work harder. "She went, in her own mind, from a hopeless student, to one who could do all right if she tried harder," said Dr. Seligman.

"Drugs can make you better from depression, but they don't change your explanatory style, leaving you vulnerable to depression again at the next upset in your life," said Dr. Seligman. "I think the active ingredient in therapies that are effective for depression is a change in explanatory style.

One unresolved point as yet in the research is whether pessimists have more troubles because of their explanatory style, or have become pessimists because of their bad luck.

"I think it is probably a two-way street," said Dr. Peterson. "My research shows that pessimists make a mess of their lives; more bad things befall them like break-ups, family troubles, and failure in school. They are also more lonely and estranged from people; talking gloom and doom is a turn off. But having a life so troubled may give them good cause to be pessimistic, which makes them act in a way that invites more trouble. The question is why do some people bounce back from trouble, while others are defeated by it?"

Psychologists Pursue the Irrational Aspects of Love

July 22, 1986

How rational is love? In recent years, the mainstream of psychological research has looked at love almost as if it were a business transaction, a matter of profit and loss.

While that approach has spawned serious theories of why people fall in love, it is now coming under attack by researchers who have emphasized instead fantasy, selflessness and the inexpressible elements of love. The dispute illustrates the difficulty of trying to apply the precision of science to matters of the heart.

The most compelling new research assumes that much of the stirrings of love occur in nonverbal parts of the brain, leaving even articulate people at a loss when asked to report with accuracy how they fell in love and what it was like, and forcing researchers to tabulate mundane explanations that fall short of the soaring reality.

Still, the old approaches to love have yielded a solid body of findings by social psychologists. The major work applies exchange theory, the postulate that human relationships are based mainly on self-interest, to explain what goes on between men and women as they meet, pair off and become couples.

Much of this research has shown, for example, that people calibrate their social, physical and other assets against a potential partner's; the closer the match, the more likely they will become a pair. Exchange theory is able to predict, more or less, the stability of a couple based on the way each partner feels he or she compares to the other.

For example, one study of 537 dating men and women found that partners who felt they were getting far more in the exchange than they were giving, felt guilty and insecure, while those who felt they gave more than they got felt angry.

The "giving" was largely psychological; it could be simply being more attractive than the partner, or having more social prestige. The greater the imbalance in either direction, the more likely was the couple to break up; the more equitable the partners felt the exchange was, the more stable the couple.

"People care greatly about equity in a loving relationship," said Elaine Hatfield, a psychologist at the University of Hawaii who is one of the leading researchers on love. "It takes many forms, including the day-to-day concerns of who does what, and how cared about each partner feels. It's terribly corroding if one person feels taken advantage of. And it is just as disturbing to feel you can take advantage of your partner."

Much of the research on love has involved people filling out questionnaires, an approach many experts see as limited. "People don't always know what is really going on in a relationship, or they rewrite the past to fit their present feelings," Dr. Hatfield said.

And psychoanalysts who trace the nature of adult love to patterns of attachment between parents and their children see exchange theory as too simple to explain the complexities of love.

The most forceful critique of past research on love is an article in the *July, 1986* issue of *The Journal of Personality* by David C. McClelland, a psychologist who has just retired from Harvard University and is to assume a post at Boston University in the fall.

The mainstream view among psychologists who do research on love is too hard-boiled, Dr. McClelland complains. Psychologists have used exchange theory to reduce love to a dry formula, he asserts, weighing it in terms of how partners satisfy each other's needs. Recently, for example, that approach has led to a formal analysis of lovers' decision-making that allows the process of falling in love to be simulated on a computer.

While such theories have a place in psychology, Dr. McClelland argues, they do not capture the flavor of love. Moreover, he says, the theories are predicated on the assumption that people act from selfish concerns, trying to manipulate others to their own advantage, an assumption that does not do justice to the more sublime aspects of love.

"It's absurd to reduce love to selfishness," Dr. McClelland said in an interview.

After reading these psychological theories, Dr. McClelland said, "I wondered what had become of the ecstasies and verities described in the poetry of love. The poets don't speak in terms of selfish advantages, of love as a means-ends relationship, but about an altruistic, undying devotion."

"It's as though there have been two psychologies of love," Dr. McClelland said. The poetic vision of love is akin to the theories of those like Abraham Maslow, a personality theorist, and Martin Buber, a social philospher, who have depicted love as an experience of delight, harmony and a feeling of intense union. The mainstream research, says Dr. McClelland, has for the most part failed to capture this aspect of the experience of being in love.

Social psychologists who have done that research are, understandably, unsympathetic to Dr. McClelland's critique. They point out that the social psychology approach has contributed much to the understanding of diverse aspects of loving, from what attracts lovers to how working couples arrive at an equitable sharing of duties. Pencil-and-paper measures of love have worked, they argue.

"Surveys play an essential role in exploring a topic like love," said Dr. Hatfield, "particularly to get the big picture at the beginning, so you know what ideas you want to test with experiments."

But Dr. McClelland argues that asking people about love is only of limited value Since love is not a rational experience, he says, people's explanations are a poor guide to its mysteries.

To tap the nonrational side of the mind. Dr. McClelland does not simply ask people why they are in love. Instead, after presenting them with fictitious situations and asking them to make up stories about them, he analyzes the thoughts and fantasies in their stories, a method he developed in his earlier work on the needs for achievement and power, the research for which he is best known.

Dr. McClelland contends that feelings of love involve parts of the brain that are poorly linked to the verbal center in the left half. "When a couple in love is interviewed by a social psychologist, what he gets is their rational thoughts about why they are in love," said Dr. McClelland. "That leads the psychologist to discover prosaic left-brain type reasons for being in love; because a lover meets a person's needs, like a shovel meets the needs of a gardener."

Other reseachers agree that the present theories do not fully explain the ways of love.

"I have no argument that our knowledge of love is still incomplete," said Ellen Berscheid, a social psycholoigst at the University of Minnesota who is a researcher in the field. "The questionnaire approach simply isn't enough to fully understand love; you've got to triangulate everything you can measure about love to get a full picture."

Using methods that tap people's fantasies, Dr. McClelland and his associate, Daniel McAdams, a psychologist at Loyola University of Chicago, have identified what they call the "need for intimacy," a set of thought patterns that characterize people who are generally loving.

Dr. McAdams, applying a coding system, evaluates the fantasies of his research subjects to identify the themes that distinguish loving people. Such people, the research shows, are given to a preoccupation with themes of harmony, responsibility and commitment; a sense of surrender to fate, and the wish to escape to a situation where there can be a sharing of warm intimacy—in short, thoughts of love.

These themes, the researchers say, show up over and over in many guises in the stories told by people who say they are in love, as well as by those who are in situations—such as having seen a romantic movie—where loving feelings run high. Already the approach has yielded intriguing findings, not just about the nature of love, but also about the qualities loving people exhibit.

A link between these themes of love and mental health was reported at the 1986 meeting of the American Psychological Association by Dr. McAdams, who has done most of the research on the need for intimacy. In a nationwide study of 1,200 men and women, Dr. McAdams found that those with a high need for intimcy reported a greater sense of well-being, were happier and felt more secure than those who were lower on the measure.

In research done with George E. Vaillant, a psychiatrist at Dartmouth, Dr. McAdams evaluated the capacity for intimacy in 57 Harvard graduates from classes in the 1940's. The men, as part of a continuing study of adult development, had been periodically tested and interviewed since before they graduated.

Dr. McAdams, on the basis of sto-ries the men had made up when they were 30 years old, was able to judge their degree of need for intimacy at that age and compare it with their adjustment to life, rated when they were 47.

The higher their need for intimacy at age 30, Dr. McAdams found, the more successfully the men had adjusted to life, particularly in their enjoyment of their jobs and marriages.

The results of Dr. McAdams's research fit well with Freud's notion that the hallmarks of psychological maturity are the abilities to love and to work, as well as with more current psychoanalytic thought on the nature of healthy and unhealthy love.

Psychoanalysts say that children who are the victims of parental neglect or hostility often grow up to treat their loved ones in those ways. On the other hand, people in whom the need for intimacy is particularly strong, Dr. McAdams believes, had parents whose care for them in infancy and childhood was characterized by mutual delight and harmony. These early loving experiences, says Dr. McAdams, "beckon to be found again in interpersonal relationships throughout life."

"Our research shows that the thoughts of loving people are not as manipulative as most social psychologists have depicted them," said Dr. McAdams. "Instead we find that these people have a sort of positive passivity; they are adept at listening and letting a relationship grow naturally without manipulating it. That capacity for relinquishing control is a key to the ability to love."

"If you're too assertive and forceful, love dies," said Dr. McAdams. "As Martin Buber said, the Thou encounters me by grace."

Romance is not the only variety of love that the new measures assess. James McKay, a graduate student working with Dr. McClelland at Harvard, has found that selfless love, a caring for others without worrying about benefits for oneself, is related to good health.

Selfless love, according to Mr. McKay's research, is reflected not just by thoughts of doing things for others without consideration for a personal benefit, but also such things as a sense of humor and a lack of cynicism.

In a series of studies, Mr. McKay found that those men and women whose fantasies showed a tendency toward selfless love also reported having fewer infectious diseases than did others in the study. Moreover, an assay of their T-cells, a specialized form of disease-fighting lymphocyte in the blood, showed a pattern reflecting resistance to viruses.

These results support those from an earlier study by Dr. McClelland, in which immune function was assessed in people before and after they watched a film about Mother Teresa and her work with the poor of Calcutta in India.

In most people who watched the film, there was a significant, though temporary, rise in a measure of defense against upper respiratory infections.

And when people were asked to spend an hour recalling times they had loved or been loved, the immune measure stayed at the higher levels the entire time.

"Dwelling on love seems to strengthen this aspect of immune function," Dr. McClelland said.

Worries About Intimacy Are Rising, Therapists Find

November 3, 1987

Intimacy, that combination of self-disclosure and emotional closeness, is carrying more of a premium than ever. Since the 1950's, surveys show, more and more people have come to see intimacy—in friendship, at work and at home—as increasingly important to their sense of satisfaction with life.

Whether it reflects an increased consciousness of the matter or a genuine change in emotional circumstances or needs, psychotherapists report seeing more patients who say they have trouble developing intimacy. They are seeking a better understanding of why some people more readily develop deep attachments and others recoil from them.

"Problems with intimacy are relatively common these days," said Joseph Newirth, a psychoanalyst trainer of therapists at Adelphi University. "You see marriages in which both partners have the sense of not being known by the other, of not being noticed."

What therapists are finding, ironically, is that the very resistance to intimacy that plagues one's personal relationships is a powerful tool in psychotherapy. "A person's obstacles to being open become obvious in therapy," said Ernest Wolf, a psychiatrist and training analyst at the Chicago Institute for Psychoanalysis. "For the first time in his life, the patient becomes aware of what he has been doing in his relationships all through life."

The resistance to intimacy shows itself in therapy when patients are unreasonably hostile toward therapists, when patients distort what therapists have said or done, or when patients remain silent. Those forms of resistance become a major focus of psychotherapy because they illuminate how the patient acts in his other relationships. Such insights can go a long way toward helping patients become more intimate, therapists are finding.

For some people, the prospect of intimacy strikes outright fear or triggers an instant remoteness.

"To be intimate means being willing to be affected by someone else's feelings, to be aware of the nuances of their inner meanings and their moods," Dr. Newirth said. But people who need to insulate themselves from the emotional demands of others fear this.

Guarantees of Distance

Such people often adopt patterns in their relationships that ensure a safe emotional distance. Some people alternate between involvement and distance, breaking up and then making up over and over again, or ending relationships just as they become too intimate. Others tend to become involved with partners who have some flaw that guarantees unavailabilty; they may be married to someone else, or addicted to drugs or work.

"There are many couples in which both partners fear intimacy so that even though they may consciously yearn for closeness, when they achieve a measure of that closeness, one or the other will create distance until the distance itself triggers a new move towards one another," according to Judith Ladner, a therapist in Rosyln, Long Island.

Anxiety about intimacy, according to psychoanalytic thinking, can be traced to a poor relationship with one's parents in early childhood, such as an overly intrusive mother or too aloof father. Such parenting can leave the child feeling either wary of emotional manipulation or fearful of rejection. Such anxiety over intimacy can result in adulthood in people who are clinging and dependent, on the one hand, or withdrawn or even hostile on the other.

Men, Women and Intimacy

Some researchers now question the longheld assumption that men have less need for intimacy than do women. New data show that emotional intimacy is, on average, of nearly equal importance for the happiness of both sexes, but that there is a telling discrepancy in the place of intimacy in the emotional lives of men and women. The study, based in part on results from a national survey, is reported by Dan P. McAdams, a psychologist at Loyola University of Chicago, in the November, 1987 issue of the *Journal of Personality*.

Dr. McAdams' national study is the largest investigation of the need for intimacy to date. It is based on a new analysis of the responses of 1,208 men and women who were contacted in their homes during a national survey of mental health conducted by Joseph Veroff, a psychologist at the University of Michigan. The study, conducted first in 1957 and then again in 1976, showed that over the course of two decades people saw personal intimacy as increasingly important as a source of personal fulfillment.

Men feel almost as great a need for intimacy, on average, as do women according to a report by Dr. McAdams, published in 1987 in the *Journal of Personality Assessment*. Dr. McAdams found in a separate study of more than a thousand men and women, that although women tend to have a slightly higher need for intimacy, on average, than men, the difference is minor. What is very different, though, is how men and women experience intimacy and the psychological needs it fulfils for each sex.

For women, emotional intimacy tends to lead directly to happiness with their relationship roles, such as wife and mother, according to Dr. McAdam's results. For men, on the other hand, a sense of closeness is not as strongly related to their satisfaction with personal relationships as it is to their sense of certainty about the world in general. Instead, such intimacy seems to provide men with an emotional springboard of confidence and resilience that allows achievements in the world.

'Less Stress and Strain'

"Men who value and have intimacy more feel a secure emotional base in life," Dr. McAdams said. "They report less stress and strain in life, and are more confident about the future—troubles at work, for instance, don't upset them as much as they do other men."

To be sure, women, too, tend to feel more confident in general when they have a secure relationship, but the effect tends to be stronger for men.

Differences between men and women in how they deal with intimacy can often help explain marital tensions, according to research by Daniel Sternberg of Yale and John Gottman of the University of Washington. Women, for instance, share their feelings much more readily than do men, and it is just such emotional self-disclosure that gives them a satis-fying sense of intimacy. For many men, however, simply sharing enjoyable activities together—rather than talking over feelings—gives a sense of closeness.

Studies suggest that men who value intimacy tend to have happier marriages. Men who had a high need for intimacy at age 30—whether married or single—had the happiest and most stable marriages 17 years later, according to a study Dr. McAdams did with George Vaillant, a psychiatrist at Dartmouth Medical School.

The ability to be intimate has long been seen as key to emotional health. For instance, the psychoanalyst Erik Erikson proposed that forming intimate bonds was the crucial psychological task of early adulthood, along with finding one's identity.

With the help of a new technique for evaluating the intensity of people's need for intimacy, Dr. McAdams has been able to identify and compare those people who crave closness and those who are indifferent to it. People high in the need for intimacy, for instance, share more personal details in conversation, such as their feelings, fears, and dreams for the future, and are also good listeners, eliciting self-revelations from those they talk with.

While such people find friendship itself a paramount source of meaning in their lives, they are also especially sensitive to what they perceive as betrayals of trust in which someone breaks an implicit pact of the relationship, such as breaking a promise or telling a secret.

For those who seek psychotherapy because of problems with intimacy, there is a paradox: they may find it difficult to open up to their therapist, too. "Psychotherapy is the one place where a person is expected to share his most secret self," said Martin Fisher, a psychologist at Adelphi University, who edited *Intimacy,* published by Plenum Press.

"In psychoanalysis, it is expected that the patient will hold back, cen-soring his free associations throughout the analysis." he said. "Once he can free associate without self-censorship, he would no longer need to be in analysis. But we don't really expect people to reach such total openness—just to get much closer to it."

Advice for Couples

For couples who want to improve their level of intimacy, therapists offer more direct advice. They do not generally advocate self-conscious attempts at self-revelation, but rather urge couples to cultivate the atmosphere in which intimacy is likely to flourish. Though some of the advice may seem obvious, therapists say the steps nevertheless can restore intimacy where it has waned.

For people who find that spontaneity comes hard, it often helps to take the risk of feeling silly by trying to be more playful. An open, unabashed playfulness encourages the kind of relaxed atmosphere that more naturally leads to intimacy, the therapists say.

It helps, too, if partners in a relationship break out of the habit of asking perfunctory questions about each other, and express a real interest. "You see couples where the wife turns to her female friends because she feels her husband does not care or won't understand her feelings," said Aaron Beck, a psychiatrist at the University of Pennsylvania. "The wife needs to try again, and the husband needs to make more effort to persist in asking questions that will break through the crust of habit to the real feelings."

Another technique recommended by therapists is to encourage each partner to let the other know explicitly when they have done something that pleases them, whether it be as minor as a kind word or thoughtful gesture. This lets the partner know that he or she is appreciated and loved, and can assuage the uncertainties that keep some people from being more open.

Chemistry of Sexual Desire Yields Its Elusive Secrets

October 18, 1988

The sex hormone testosterone is a genuine aphrodisiac, with higher levels stimulating sexual desire in men and perhaps in women as well, recent research has shown. But the level of testosterone coursing through a person's body has little direct impact on sexual performance, according to the studies, which have discovered a sharp distinction between the chemistry of desire and that of the sexual act itself.

The findings on testosterone's role in erotic life are part of a series of recent discoveries emerging from laboratories as sexual desire, an urge at once elusive and compelling, yields its secrets to the cold eye of science.

While for several decades scientists have made detailed studies of the psychology and anatomy of sexual arousal itself, it is only within the last few years that desire, the harbinger of arousal, has become a focus for research. The new studies, which aim to aid therapy of individuals and couples who suffer a lack of erotic impulses, are focusing on both the biological and the emotional chemistry of desire.

"Sexual desire is an extraordinarily complicated part of life and there is an enormous range of difference," said Harold Lief, an emeritus professor of psychiatry at the University of Pennsylvania who is a pioneer in identifying and treating problems with desire.

"College students who are asked to press a wrist counter every time they have a sexual thought, fantasy or feeling may count over 300 a day, while other people report that they rarely, if ever, have a sexual desire," Dr. Lief added.

The research is focusing on two kinds of problems. One involves individuals who, perhaps because of hormonal imbalances or psychological problems, generally feel no sexual urge. The second emphasis is on the psychological and emotional interactions of couples that can destroy desire in people who, in other situations, might have strong sexual urges.

The impetus for the new studies has been the growing realization by sex therapists that many patients who had been treated for difficulties with the mechanics of sexual performance, such as impotence or a failure to reach orgasm, actually suffered from an underlying lack of sexual desire.

"Desire and arousal are two entirely different processes, each under the influence of different factors," said Gayle Beck, a psychologist at the University of Houston.

Most Common Complaint

Today problems with sexual desire rank as the most common complaint treated by sex therapists, even though it is only in the last decade that the problem was given an official diagnosis. A recent survey of 289 sex therapists found that the most common complaint of partners—in 31 percent of couples seeking sex therapy—was a discrepancy between partners in their desire for sex. The second most common complaint, reported by 28 percent of patients, was individuals troubled by either too little or too much sexual desire.

Much of the new research focuses on the biochemistry of desire, particularly the role of hormones, especially testosterone. Testosterone is often called the male sex hormone because it is more prevalent in men, although it fluctuates in the individual with time, and plays a key role in development of masculine traits. But it is also found in lesser quantities in women, in whom its levels fluctuate over the course of the menstrual cycle. Recent studies show that one of its main effects is on desire, and that, contrary to earlier assumptions, it has virtually no role in the sexual act itself.

In a study of men who suffered from extremely low levels of desire as the result of underactive gonads, doses of testosterone increased the men's frequency of sexual fantasies and restored their sexual desire. But the testosterone had no effect on the mechanics of sexual arousal, such as their genital arousal while watching erotic videotapes or fantasying.

This study and others with similar results have led scientists to conclude that testosterone regulates sexual desire. The new study, done by Julian Davidson, a physiologist, and colleagues at Stanford University, was reported in *Patterns of Sexual Arousal,* published in 1988 by Guilford Press.

"It's now very clear that testosterone is the biological substrate of desire, at least in men," Dr. Davidson said.

There is less agreement on the relationship between testosterone and desire in women. Studies by Dr. Lief and others have found that in many women sexual desire peaks in the middle phase of the menstrual period, when testosterone levels are at their highest. But other researchers have failed to duplicate the findings.

While there is uncertainty about the role of ordinary levels of testosterone in regulating desire in women, higher doses of testosterone than are normally found in the body are now used to treat the loss of desire in some women who are post-menopausal or who have had their ovaries removed, according to Dr. Lief.

Biochemistry aside, every couple who have ever been at odds know that emotional life shapes their sexual life for better or worse. New studies are pinpointing more precisely which emotions have what effects.

The most common cause of low desire, clinicians say, is marital conflict. New laboratory research shows that, like depression, anger is particularly devastating to erotic desire. Anxiety, on the other hand, can sometimes fan desire, but interferes with the sexual act itself.

In men, desire is more vulnerable to anger, while sexual arousal is more sensitive to anxiety, Dr. Beck has found in research reported at a recent meeting of the American Psychological Association. In the study, male college students used a lever to report their level of sexual desire and a gauge measured their genital arousal while they listened to tapes depicting sexual encounters.

When the tapes portrayed an angry dialogue during the sexual encounter, the students reported a sharp drop in their own levels of desire. But there was little effect on their genital arousal. Tapes designed to elicit anxiety, on the other hand, resulted in the student's having a drop in physical arousal, but none in sexual desire.

The findings suggest that conflict between a couple is more damaging to their desire for sex than would be moderate levels of stress or anxiety, according to Dr. Beck.

"Someone who is preoccupied by worries would be likely to feel sexual desire, but might have trouble getting or staying aroused," she said. "Lovemaking is vulnerable to intrusive, worrisome thoughts because it is largely a skill, while desire is more vulnerable to anger because it operates much like an emotion While an argument will dampen partners' desire for sex, they could still follow through if they were to become aroused."

Survey of 93 Couples

The judgment of what level of desire is "too low" or "too high" is, of course, a relative one. But to get a sense of what the usual range of desire is for married couples, Joseph LoPiccolo, a psychologist at the University of Missouri, and Jerry Friedman, a sex therapist in Stony Brook, Long Island, surveyed 93 couples who, on average, were 34 years old and had been married for 9 years. The survey is reported in *Sexual Desire Disorders,* published in 1988 by Guilford Press.

The men generally expressed a greater desire for sex than did their wives. More than 12 percent of the men said they preferred intercourse more than once a day, while about 3 percent of women expressed the same preference. On the other hand, about 4 percent of men and 10 percent of women said they desired sex just once a week. The most common preference was for sex three or four times a week. Fifty percent of women and 42 percent of men expressed this preference.

But desire outpaced reality. Just 2 percent of men and 1 percent of women said they actually made love more than once a day, while 12 percent both of men and of women said the rate of lovemaking in their marriage was once every two weeks or just once a month. And 3 percent of men, but no women, said they made love less than once a month.

The discrepancies between the men and women in the rates of lovemaking they reported in the survey reflects the very different perceptions of their sex life that couples bring to sex therapy.

"When a couple seeks treatment for a problem with sexual desire, I often hear, 'he's oversexed,' or, 'she doesn't love me anymore,' but I quickly learned to speak only in terms of a discrepancy in desire," Dr. Beck said. "To see one partner or the other as too highly sexed or as having too little desire is unhelpful."

There is a bias in treating couples with a discrepancy in desire, one that too easily blames the partner with the lower level of desire for the problem, said Bernard Apfelbaum, a psychologist at the Berkeley Sex Therapy Group. He points, for instance, to the onus attached to the term frigidity, a word no longer used by sex therapists. When there is a marked discrepancy between partners in their levels of desire, many sex therapists try to help the couple negotiate a compromise rather than focusing treatment exclusively on the partner with the lower levels of desire.

While there is a drop in testosterone levels in men after the 40's, aging tends to bring only a gradual lessening of desire. A sudden drop in desire more often reflects other problems, such as continual marital conflict, according to sex therapists.

"Often the problem is boredom—habituation to one's partner," said Dr. Lief. A study by Dr. Lief of post-menopausal women that compared one group married an average of 25 years with another married just 2 years found that the newlyweds had a much higher level of sexual desire than those who remained in the lengthy marriage. But the level of desire in the newlywed post-menopausal women was not as high as that of young couples.

After marital conflict, depression is the second most common cause of low desire, according to Dr. Lief. What is more surprising, though is that many of the medications often prescribed for depression can themselves inhibit desire. Not all anti-depressants lower desire, and those that do affect only certain people. The problem is most likely in those drugs that affect dopamine, a brain chemical that interacts with testosterone. Lowered sexual desire can be a side effect of many other drugs, including some prescribed to control anxiety, for psychosis and for hypertension.

Scientists say that a promising research frontier for sex therapists is the interaction between emotions and chemistry, especially levels of testosterone and other sex-related hormones. But so far, too little evidence is available to draw firm conclusions.

Sex therapy for too little desire almost always focuses on the quality of the couple's relationship. Apart from out-and-out conflict, difficulties such as the fear of emotional closeness in one partner, or a difference between partners in how much emotional intimacy they feel is comfortable can also cause problems with desire. Often what seems to be a loss of desire is a disguised form of anger, part of a power struggle between the couple, Dr. Lief said.

Paradoxically, some partners first experience a sudden drop in desire when they get married or in some other way move toward a major commitment. In such cases, the partners typically have idealized each other creating a romantic universe in which neither has any flaws, said David Scharff, a psychoanalyst at George Washington University Medical School. But at the point of deeper commitment, the partners may begin to see each other more realistically discovering traits in each other that do not fit their idealization.

People at this point may also want more than ever to reveal their true selves to the partner because they want to be accepted completely. This may cause the partner to feel he or she is with a different person than imagined.

Loss of Sexual Interest

In some people, the loss of sexual interest occurs while dating, as they become more deeply involved emotionally with their partner. This problem, which Freudians have called the "Madonna/whore complex" when applied to men's views of women, arises in members of either sex when their overly moralistic conscience make them unable to love and have sex with the same person.

The tactics of therapy generally take the obvious route of tackling the problem, such as depression, that is blocking desire. "If a couple is having marital problems, for instance, in therapy we deal with the disharmony, while encouraging the expression of all the affection and tenderness the couple feel for each other," said Dr. Lief. "The rest happens naturally."

Why Do People Crave the Experience?

August 2, 1988

Why do people submit themselves to roller coasters and their mutations, the "scream machines" that seem so ubiquitous on the summer landscape?

Some clearheaded analyses of the allure of wild rides are emerging as scientists study why certain people seek the thrill of great velocities, upside-down suspensions, and other sensations that the human body can read only as pure torment.

The roller-coaster question touches on some complex physiological issues. New research suggests, for instance, that the craving of thrills may be hare-wired into those who thrive on the level of primitive brain activity that physical danger stimulates.

Another appeal is that roller coasters, in simulating true danger, provide the illusion of mastering a great peril. It is a deeply satisfying feeling in which mock danger provides the exhiliration of self-affirmation.

Fear is the key component, as has been shown in research into more dangerous activities like skiing and parachute-jumping.

"If you ask accident-prone skiiers if they are scared when they are on a high-risk slope, they'll say they wouldn't bother to ski the slope if they weren't scared," said Seymour Epstein, a psychologist at the University of Massachusetts.

"They want a slope that terrifies them," he said. "Parachuters say the same thing. After you take the plunge there's an immense relief and sense of well-being in facing a fear that doesn't materialize."

That kind of exhiliration is particuarly appealing to a personality type, aptly known as "thrill-seekers," people who have been studied by Frank Farley, a psychologist at the University of Wisconsin. People who are high in that trait, Dr. Farley said, "seek variety, novelty, intensity and risk."

"Not everybody goes on scary rides like roller coasters, or comes back a second time if they try it," Dr. Farley said. "It's those with the thrill-seeking personality who come back again and again. They like adventure, like high diving and hang gliding."

Underlying the propensity for physical thrills, Dr. Farley believes, may be a neurological need for the biochemical state that comes from intense physical excitement.

One theory holds that the brains of thrill-seekers are usually at a lower level of arousal compared with most other people. This theory holds that the sense of danger and the physical extremes of a roller coaster ride prime a neural network at the base of the brain called the reticular activating system, which in turn heightens the level of activation throughout the rest of the brain.

"They feel fully alive when something raises their level of brain arousal," Dr. Farley said of thrill-seekers.

Another theory, put forth by Marvin Zuckerman, a psychologist at the University of Delaware, proposes that those who need to seek out intense stimulation, the roller coaster being a prime example, have an imbalance in a brain chemical, monoamine oxidase, which has also been implicated in some forms of depression. Excitement seems to change the levels of the chemical in some people, lifting them from torpor to elation.

Heightened concentration is at play, too. "Being totally absorbed is in itself pleasurable," Dr. Epstein said. "Complete concentration that blanks out everything else temporarily relieves you from all conflicts. Even if it's scary, its a way to drive out disturbing thoughts."

Dr. Epstein added, "It makes you feel very alive to be so scared. When you react to something that demands your full attention so forcefully, all your senses engage. It's a very different feeling from being in your usual semiawake state."

Individual Differences: Personality and Intelligence

The old controversy about whether nature or nurture determines personality has been answered by a unique approach. "Major Personality Study Finds That Traits are Mostly Inherited" recounts a study of identical twins who were separated in infancy and reared apart. Personality tests given the twins as adults show that a high proportion of many personality traits seem to be due to their common genetic inheritance.

Do our personalities change as we grow through life? Not much, when it comes to the major traits, according to the data reported in "Personality: Major Traits Found Stable Through Life." The findings challenge theories that emphasize stages in adult life in which people undergo great personality shifts.

Some theories of personality hold that a child's experiences of family life leave a deep imprint on personality. That would suggest that the children who grow up in the same household would be subject to the same influences. Not so, according to the findings in "Each Sibling Experiences Different Family." Instead, there seems to be as many "families" as there are children—each child having a unique experience.

The roots of satisfaction in life may be far simpler than we're led to believe. In "Meaningful Activities and Temperament Key in Satisfaction With Life" the sources of contentment are found not to be such things as how much money one makes or

achieving a long-held goal, but simpler factors, such as feeling what you do is meaningful. And some people seem to be born with a temperament that leaves them feeling more satisfied with life.

The earliest theory of personality, psychoanalysis, has had great staying power since Freud first proposed it at the turn of the century. But skeptics have long challenged psychoanalysts to produce rigorous research that would lend it scientific support. That research is at last underway in "Is Analysis Testable as Science, After All?"

One striking limit of intelligence tests is that they are poor predictors of just who will end up succeeding in life—for instance, being most satisfied with relationships, most respected by professional peers, or making the most money. IQ tests do predict well who will excel in school. But "New Scales of Intelligence Rank Talent For Living" describes the research that is leading to a new kind of intelligence scale.

Beyond their inability to predict life success, intelligence tests are being faulted as testing too narrow a band of intelligence. Social perceptiveness or musical talents, for instance, reflect important kinds of intelligence ignored by IQ tests. People can be gifted in many more ways than is measured by the standard tests, according to evidence reviewed in "Rethinking the Value of Intelligence Tests."

The fact that many minority

groups do not do as well, on average, as do members of the white majority is due to many causes. Poverty and the effects of discrimination are two. But the findings in "An Emerging Theory on Blacks' I.Q. Scores" tells a different story. Data from around the world suggest that something akin to India's caste system may be at work.

Major Personality Study Finds That Traits Are Mostly Inherited

December 12, 1986

The genetic makeup of a child is a stronger influence on personality than child rearing, according to the first study to examine identical twins reared in different families. The findings shatter a widespread belief among experts and laymen alike in the primacy of family influence and are sure to engender fierce debate.

The findings are the first major results to emerge from a long-term project at the University of Minnesota. Since 1979, more than 350 pairs of twins in the project have gone through six days of extensive testing that has included analysis of blood, brain waves, intelligence and allergies.

The results on personality were published in the *Journal of Personality and Social Psychology*. Although there has been wide press coverage of pairs of twins reared apart who met for the first time in the course of the study, the personality results are the first significant scientific data to be announced.

For most of the traits measured, more than half the variation was found to be due to heredity, leaving less than half determined by the influence of parents, home environment and other experiences in life.

The Minnesota findings stand in sharp contradiction to standard wisdom on nature versus nurture in forming adult personality. Virtually all major theories since Freud have given far more importance to environment, or nurture, than to genes, or nature.

Even though the findings point to the strong influence of heredity, the family still shapes the broad suggestion of personality offered by heredity. For example, a family might tend to make an innately timid child either more timid or less so. But the inference from this study is that the family would be unlikely to make the child brave.

The 350 pairs of twins studied included some who were raised apart. Among these separately reared twins were 44 pairs of identical twins and 21 pairs of fraternal twins. Comparing twins raised separately with those raised in the same home allows researchers to determine the relative importance of heredity and of environment in their development. Although some twins go out of their way to emphasize differences between them, in general identical twins are very much alike in personality.

But what accounts for that similarity? If environment were the major influence in personality, then identical twins raised in the same home would be expected to show more similarity than would the twins reared apart. But the study of 11 personality traits found differences between the kinds of twins were far smaller than had been assumed.

"If in fact twins reared apart are that similar, this study is extremely important for understanding how personality is shaped," commented Jerome Kagan, a developmental psychologist at Harvard University. "It implies that some aspects of personality are under a great degree of genetic control."

The traits were measured using a personality questionnaire developed by Auke Tellegen, a psychologist at the University of Minnesota who was one of the principal researchers. The questionnaire assesses many major aspects of personality, including aggressiveness, striving for achievement, and the need for personal intimacy.

For example, agreement with the statement, "When I work with others, I like to take charge," is an indication of the trait called social potency, or leadership, while agreement with the sentence, "I often keep working on a problem, even if I am very tired," indicates the need for achievement.

Among traits found most strongly determined by heredity were leadership and, surprisingly, traditionalism or obedience to authority. "One would not expect the tendency to believe in traditional values and the strict enforcement of rules to be more an inherited than learned trait," said David Lykken, a psychologist in the Minnesota project. "But we found that, in some mysterious way, it is one of traits with the strongest genetic influence."

Other traits that the study concludes were more than 50 percent determined by heredity included a sense of well-being and zest for life; alienation, vulnerability or resistance to stress, and fearfulness or risk-seeking. Another highly inherited trait, though one not commonly thought of as part of personality, was the capacity for becoming rapt in an aesthetic experience, such as a concert.

Vulnerability to stress, as measured on the Tellegen test, reflects what is commonly thought of as "neuroticism," according to Dr. Lykken. "People high in this trait are nervous and jumpy, easily irritated, highly sensitive to stimuli, and generally dissatisfied with themselves, while those low on the trait are resilient and see themselves in a positive light," he said. "Therapy may help vulnerable people to some extent, but they seem to have a built-in susceptibility that may mean, in general, they would be more content with a life low in stress."

The need to achieve, including ambition and an inclination to work hard toward goals, also was found to be genetically influenced, but more than half of this trait seemed determined by life experience. The same lower degree of hereditary influence was found for impulsiveness and its opposite, caution.

The need for personal intimacy appeared the least determined by heredity among the traits tested; about two-thirds of that tendency was found to depend on experience. People high in this trait have a strong desire for emotionally intense realtionships; those low in the trait tend to be loners who keep their troubles to themselves.

"This is one trait that can be greatly strengthened by the quality of interactions in a family," Dr. Lykken said. "The more physical and emotional intimacy, the more likely this trait will be developed in children, and those children with the strongest inherited tendency will have the greatest need for social closeness as adults."

No single gene is believed responsible for any one of these traits. Instead, each trait, the Minnesota researchers propose, is determined by a great number of genes in combination, so that the pattern of inheritance is complex and indirect.

No one believes, for instance, that there is a single gene for timidity but rather a host of genetic influences. That may explain, they say, why previous studies have found little connection between the personality traits of parents and their children. Whereas identical twins would share with each other the whole constellation of genes that might be responsible for a particular trait, children might share only some part of that constellation with each parent.

That is why, just as a short parent may have a tall child, an achieve-ment-oriented parent might have a child with little ambition.

The Minnesota findings are sure to stir debate. Though most social scientists accept the careful study of twins, particularly when it includes identical twins reared apart, as the best method of assessing the degree to which a trait is inherited, some object to using these methods for assessing the genetic component of complex behavior patterns or question the conclusions that are drawn from it.

Further, some researchers consider paper-and-pencil tests of personality less reliable than observations of how people act, since people's own reports of their behavior can be biased. "The level of heritability they found is surprisingly high, considering that questionnaires are not the most sensitive index of personality," said Dr. Kagan. "There is often a poor relationship between how people respond on a questionnaire and what they actually do."

"Years ago, when the field was dominated by a psychodynamic view, you could not publish a study like this," Dr. Kagan added. "Now the field is shifting to a greater acceptance of genetic determinants, and there is the danger of being too uncritical of such results."

Seymour Epstein, a personality psychologist at the University of Massachusetts, said he was skeptical of precise estimates of heritability. "The study compared people from a relatively narrow range of cultures and environments," he said. "If the range had been much greater—say Pygmies and Eskimos as well as middle-class Americans—then environment would certainly contribute more to personality. The results might have shown environment to be a far more powerful influence than heredity," he said.

Dr. Tellegen himself said, "Even though the differences between families do not account for much of the unique attributes of their children, a family still exercises important influence. In cases of extreme deprivation or abuse, for instance, the family would have a much larger impact—though a negative one—than any found in the study. Although the twins studied came from widely different environments, there were no extremely deprived families."

Gardner Lindzey, director of the Center for Advanced Studies in the Behavioral Sciences in Palo Alto, California, said the Minnesota findings would "no doubt produce empassioned rejoinders."

"They do not in and of themselves say what makes a given character trait emerge," he said, "and they can be disputed and argued about, as have similar studies of intelligence."

For parents, the study points to the importance of treating each child in accord with his innate temperament.

"The message for parents is not that it does not matter how they treat their children, but that it is a big mistake to treat all kids the same," said Dr. Lykken. "To guide and shape a child you have to respect his individuality, adapt to it and cultivate those qualities that will help him in life.

"If there are two brothers in the same family, one fearless and the other timid, a good parent will help the timid one become less so by giving him experiences of doing well at risk-taking, and let the other develop his fearlessness tempered with some intelligent caution. But if the parent shelters the one who is naturally timid, he will likely become more so."

The Minnesota results lend weight and precision to earlier work that pointed to the importance of a child's temperament in development. For instance, the New York Longitudinal Study, conducted by Alexander Thomas and Stella Chess, psychiatrists at New York University Medical Center, identified three basic temperaments in children, each of which could lead to behavioral problems if not handled well.

"Good parenting now must be seen in terms of meeting the special needs of a child's temperament, including dealing with whatever conflicts it creates," said Stanley Grossman, a staff member of the medical center's Psychoanalytic Institute.

Personality: Major Traits Found Stable Through Life

March 24, 1987

The largest and longest studies to carefully analyze personality throughout life reveal a core of traits that remain remarkably stable over the years and a number of other traits that can change drastically from age to age.

The new studies have shown that three basic aspects of personality change little throughout life: a person's anxiety level, friendliness and eagerness for novel experiences. But other traits, such as alienation, morale and feelings of satisfaction, can vary greatly as a person goes through life. These more changeable traits largely reflect such things as how a person sees himself and his life at a given point, rather than a basic underlying temperament.

One of the recently completed studies followed 10,000 people 25 to 74 years old for nine years. Another involved 300 couples first tested in 1935. The studies are joined by a new analysis of more than two dozen earlier studies of lifetime personality and a study of twins that looks at the genetic contribution.

The recent work poses a powerful challenge to theories of personality that have emphasized stages or passages—predictable points in adult life—in which people change significantly.

The new research is "a death knell" for the passage theories of adult personality, in the view of a researcher who conducted one of the new studies. "I see no evidence for specific changes in personality due to age," said the researcher, Paul T. Costa Jr. "What changes as you go through life are your roles and the issues that matter most to you. People may think their personality has changed as they age, but it is their habits that change, their vigor and health, their responsibilities and circumstances—not their basic personality."

But the new work has not made converts of the theorists who see adult life through the framework of passages. Rather they assert that simple pencil and paper tests cannot discern the richness inherent in the maturing personality. A theory proposed by Daniel Levinson, a psychologist at Yale University, suggests a series of sometimes troubled transitions between psychological stages; Erik Erikson coined the term "identity crisis" for the difficulties some young people have in settling on a life course.

Proponents of the most recent studies say, however, that the notion of passages, built on clinical interviews, was never objectively tested.

Some of the strongest evidence for the stability of the core personality throughout adulthood comes from a study by Dr. Costa and Robert McCrae, psychologists at the National Institute on Aging in Baltimore. They interviewed thousands of people in 100 places throughout the United States in 1975, and again in 1984.

The researchers found virtually no change in the three key personality traits. Their report in the *Journal of Gerontology* asserts that a person who was calm and well-adjusted at 25 years of age would remain so at 65, while a person who was emotionally volatile at 25 would be about the same at 65. Their findings represented averages, however, and could not reflect the changes in some individuals that might have been brought on by, for instance, psychotherapy or a personal catastrophe.

Only the Form Changes

"There is no evidence of any universal age-related crises; those people who have crises at one point or another in the life tend to be those who are more emotional," said Dr. Costa. "Such people experience some degree of distress through most of life; only the form of the trouble seems to change."

A mellowing in midlife, found by other studies, has now been shown to relate more to a muting of some of a person's more extreme feelings than to any change in the overall pattern of personality.

The new studies find no increase in irritability with aging. "The stereotype that people become cranky and rigid as they age does not hold up," said Dr. Costa. "The calm, outgoing, adventurous young person is going to stay that way into old age, given good health. Those who are dogmatic and closed to experience early in life remain that way."

The greatest changes in core personality occur in childhood and from adolescence to early adulthood, according to Dr. Costa. "After 25, as William James said, character is set in plaster," he said. "What does change is one's role in life, and the situations that influence your temporary behavior one way or another."

Support for Dr. Costa's large study comes from a recent study of twins that found an important genetic influence on the three main traits. Early childhood experiences, the investigators concluded, are not the main influence in shaping the most persistent of personality traits, though they may shape them to some degree, as they do all personality.

In this study of 203 pairs of twins at Indiana University, the researchers, Michael Pogue-Geile and Richard Rose, administered a personality test when the subjects were 20, and again when they were 25. The researchers were looking to see whether fraternal twins changed in the same ways as identical twins in that time, which is one of the stages of turbulent transition proposed by some theorists. If a particular trait is genetically determined it will tend to change more similarly in identical twins than it will in fraternal twins.

There was evidence of significant genetic influence on the three main personality traits of anxiety or emotionality, friendliness and openness to new things.

Life experience also shaped these basic traits. But it had a far greater influence on other personality traits, including alienation, morale and feelings of satisfaction. These traits change so much over the course of adult life that there is virtually no relationship between their levels when a person is in his 20's and when he is in his 60's, according to James Conley, who studied 300 couples who were tested in 1935, 1955 and 1980, when the researchers were able to interview 388 of the original 600 men and women.

"If you try to predict how alienated or satisfied with life people will be in their later years from how they seem in college, you will fail abysmally," he said.

Dr. Conley is among those finding that the three basic traits change little over a lifetime. In addition to the study of couples, he has reviewed data from more than two dozen other long-term personality studies.

Some personality traits may make certain crises in life more probable. For instance, the study of couples suggests that specific combinations of personality in a marriage are explo-

sive. Over the course of 45 years, the highest probability of divorce occurred in those marriages where both the husband and wife were emotionally volatile and the husband had little impulse control.

"The evaluations in 1935, by five friends, of the personalities of an engaged couple was highly predictive of which marriages would break up," Dr. Conley said. "If you have a couple with emotional hair triggers, and where the husband philanders, gambles, drinks, or loses jobs, a break-up is almost certain. Some marriages broke up right away: some took 45 years to end. Data from younger couples suggests that today the dangerous combination of personalities is the same, except now it can be either the wife or the husband whose impulsiveness triggers the trouble."

Walter Mischel, a psychologist at Columbia University, wrote an influential article in 1968 arguing that the variation in expression of a given trait from situation to situation is so great that the notion of personality traits itself was of little use in accounting for how people behave.

Variations With Situation

"There is lots of evidence for the stability of some traits, such as extroversion, over time," Dr. Mischel said in a recent interview. "But the same person may be quite outgoing in some circumstances, and not at all in others."

Kenneth Craik, a psychologist at the University of California at Berkeley, said, "The belief for 10 to 15 years after Mischel's critique was that the situation determined far more than personality about how people behave." "Now, within the last few years," he said, "personality and situation are seen by most researchers as having about equal influence."

Researchers are concluding that the influence of one situation or another on how a person acts may also create the impression that personality itself changes more than is the case; apparent changes in personality may actually reflect temporary circumstances.

"Any trait can vary with the moment," said Seymour Epstein, a personality psychologist at the University of Massachusetts at Amherst. "You need to look at the person in many situations to get a stable rating of that trait."

And people seem to differ in how much situations affect their actions, according to research by Mark Snyder, a psychologist at the University of Minnesota. In *Public Appearances, Private Reality,* published recently by W. H. Freeman & Company, Dr. Snyder reviews evidence showing that some people are virtual chameleons, shaping themselves to blend into whatever social situation they find themselves, while others are almost oblivious to the special demands and expectations of differing situations, being more or less the same person regardless of where they are.

The situation-oriented, Dr. Snyder has found, are skilled at social roles. At a church service, they display just the right combination of seriousness and reserve; at a cocktail party they become the friendly and sociable extrovert.

Those less affected by situations are more consistent in their behavior, putting less effort into role-playing. They have a smaller wardrobe, wearing the same clothes in more situations, than do the situation-oriented.

It is as though each type were playing to a different audience, one inner, the other outer, says Dr. Snyder.

Those adept at situations flourish in jobs where they deal with a range of different groups, Dr. Snyder reports.

Each Sibling Experiences Different Family

July 28, 1987

Behavioral scientists studying personality differences between siblings have discovered what they describe as the overriding influence of a unique "micro-environment" in the family for each child.

The research suggests that, in a sense, there is not a single family, but rather as many disparate families as there are children to experience them.

"We used to assume that a family offered the same environment to all its children," said Gene Brody, a psychologist at the University of Georgia. "Now we are searching for what creates different environments for children in the same household." Robert Plomin, a behavioral geneticist at Pennyslvania State University, and Denise Daniels, a psychologist at Stanford University's School of Medicine, report that environmental influences affecting "psychological development operate in a manner quite different from the way most psychologists thought they worked." In an article in the July, 1987, issue of *Behavioral and Brain Sciences,* they review their own recent work, as well as ten years of careful studies that used twins, adopted children and other siblings to separate the influences of genetics and environment on how children develop.

"All the psychological theories point to the family as the basic unit of socialization," Dr. Daniels said. "If so, you would expect children from the same family to be largely similar. But it is really quite the opposite. The assumption that the family environment operates the same for all children in it does not hold up."

In a commentary on the article, Sandra Scarr, a psychologist at the University of Virginia, wrote, "Up-per-middle-class brothers who attend the same school and whose parents take them to the same plays, sporting events, music lessons and therapists, and use similar child-rearing practices on them, are little more similar in personality measures than they are to working-class or farm boys, whose lives are totally different."

Siblings have been found to display a small degree of similarity in personality, but the limited similarity appears to result entirely from shared genes, rather than from shared experience, the researchers report.

Thus, of far greater concern are the larger differences they found among siblings. And the unique aspects of each child's experience while growing up appear to be more powerful in shaping personality than what the siblings experience in common. The finding has spurred new, intensive research to pinpoint the often subtle disparities in how children are treated within a family, disparities that now loom larger than ever.

Factors previously thought to be significant in shaping personality, particularly the order of birth, are being found to matter little. "There is a tiny effect for birth order," Dr. Daniels said. "You know almost nothing about a kid from knowing if he is the oldest or the youngest."

Instead, factors ranging from a child's perceptions about parental affection and discipline, to the friends a child chooses, are coming to the forefront of a range of studies.

"We are searching for the life events that make the major difference in how children turn out," Dr. Daniels said. She has developed a scale on which siblings compare themselves to one another on such factors as pa-rental love, control, attention and favoritism, sibling jealousy, and one's popularity with peers.

Several patterns have emerged already, according to results published by Dr. Daniels in *The Journal of Personality and Social Psychology.* For example, the sibling who experiences more closeness to the father also tends to be the one who expects to achieve more in an occupation. And the shyer siblings experience less antagonism from brothers and sisters, while more sociable ones feel closest to other siblings.

This finding gives new import to complaints often voiced by patients in psychotherapy that a sibling was treated better or worse than the others. Moreover, the key differences in the family environment may be more obvious to children themselves than to their parents, according to research published by Dr. Daniels and others in *Child Development.*

Those differences—and the different perceptions of them—may be a source of friction in the family. "We've found that to the extent that a parent treats children differently, the children will be more hostile later, when they are alone," Dr. Brody said.

The differences Dr. Brody has found are often very subtle—in the number of compliments, smiles and affectionate touches, or scolding remarks, frowns and dirty looks, for instance.

The child himself has a large influence on these differences, according to Stella Chess, a psychiatrist at New York University Medical Center. To a child who is difficult—slow to adapt to change, with intense moods—parents may react with confusion, guilt and frustration, Dr. Chess says. To one who is easygoing, parents are more likely to respond with pleasure and a sense of approval.

"Parents may make the same demands on two children with different temperaments and the effects on the children will be different," Dr. Chess said. "Parents may expect their child to adjust quickly and easily to beginning school, but this may only be possible for the child who responds to new situations positively and adapts quickly to new change."

The new work on personality builds on recent research—such as studies done at the University of Minnesota of identical twins reared apart—that indicate a genetic basis for 30 to 60 percent of a given personality trait. The other factors responsible for the trait, it was assumed, were family environment and, to a far lesser degree, peers, teachers and other influences outside the family.

The importance of the family per se in shaping personality and other traits, though, is now being seen in a different light, largely because of studies comparing the personality traits, emotional problems and intelligence of adopted children raised from infancy in the same family. The assumption was that any similarity in personality among such children might be largely attributed to some common influence from the family.

But a study to be reported in *The Journal of Personality and Social Psychology* found that the correlation among the children in any given family was close to zero for personality, and only slightly larger for I.Q.

"We found very little evidence for the influence of a common family environment," said John Loehlin of the University of Texas. Dr. Loehlin's studies of identical twins and fraternal twins raised in the same families show that virtually all their personality similarities are due to shared genes. The twins' differences in personality, the studies showed, were due to experiences that they did not share. Similar results have been obtained in ten other studies of twins, including a Swedish investigation of 12,000 adult twin pairs.

A Sharing of Attitudes

Siblings seem to share attitudes, such as religiousness or conservatism, far more than they share personality traits like extroversion and neuroticism, according to Dr. Loehlin.

The new research also may illuminate why only one child in a family may become mentally ill in adulthood. In schizophrenia and depression, as in personality, apart from genetic factors, "the most important influences on psychopathology lie in the category of nonshared environment," according to Dr. Plomin and Dr. Daniels.

"Most psychological studies have included only one child from a given family, not siblings," Dr. Daniels said. "It was only when behavior genetics started to study children within the same familly that the finding emerged that the family itself had a trivial effect on how children turn out. The sometimes subtle differences experienced or perceived by children in the same family are the environmental factors that drive development—not the similarities."

So far, family "micro-environments" remain little understood, although family therapists and researchers in behavior genetics are familiar with their emerging importance. "The notion of each child having his own micro-environment in the family is a new idea, just six or seven years old, and spreading slowly," Dr. Brody said.

Limited Findings So Far

Many behaviorial scientists still assume that a family affects its children mostly identically. And other experts contend that the findings—limited so far to American middle-class families—will not be supported when studies are extended to include, say, Eskimo or poor urban families.

Meanwhile, psychologists studying micro-environments hope that their research will one day help explain why one child in a family has psychological or social problems while others do well. But even these researchers caution that the new work does not imply that parents should treat all their children exactly the same.

"Treating kids identically can have negative effects," Dr. Brody said. "For example, if one child is able intellectually, while another is not, you do not want to hold them to the same expectations. The best approach is to match your response to each child's strengths."

Meaningful Activities and Temperament Key in Satisfaction with Life

December 23, 1986

Some of the most widespread beliefs about the quest for satisfaction with life are misleading or dead wrong, psychologists have found.

Achieving a long-held goal, for instance, seems to be less satisfying than simply avoiding unpleasantness from day to day.

And while financial security, a happy marriage and fulfilling social activities are all related to contentment, they and similar factors are weak predictors of who will be satisfied with life and who will not. Altogether, such factors explain less than 30 percent of people's reports of satisfaction.

Instead, temperament, which changes little over the course of life, is emerging as an unexpectedly strong determinant of how satisfied people report they are. Even stronger is how much time people are able to spend doing things they find most meaningful, are most competent at, and take the most pleasure in.

Inquiry about these factors seems most useful in understanding the many exceptions to the prevailing wisdom on what makes for happiness; retirees who live on a pittance but are happy with life, the widowed who feel their lives are full even though they are alone, or victims of debilitating illness who nevertheless retain their spirit and enthusiasm.

In one of several such studies, involving 600 men and women who were first tested in the late 1930's, psychologists at Wesleyan University have found that initial personality evaluations were excellent predictors of people's satisfaction with life 45 years later.

Those who were neurotic in their 20's tended to be unhappy 45 years later, while those who were extroverted in youth tended to be happier in their later years, according to a report by James Conley and Richard Marsh, the Wesleyan psychologists. Similar findings on the lifelong effect of temperament on life satisfaction have been reported by researchers at the National Institute of Mental Health and at the University of California at Berkeley.

In this and in other research, psychologists studying satisfaction do not speak of a precisely defined concept.

Instead, they tend to employ one or another of the numerous rating scales available. The scales ask people to reflect on how contented they are with a variety of common experiences, such as friendships, sex, work and health, and rate them from, say, "delighted" to "terrible." The result is presented as a life-satisfaction rating.

Researchers at Berkeley studied men who were tested as teen-agers in the 1920's and then 50 years later. The teen-agers who were rated as having a more pleasant temperament—as being more cheerful, warm and unresenting of demands—were found, when tested again in their 60's and 70's, to be more satisfied with their jobs and with the overall course of their careers. Teen-agers who had been rated as, for instance, more hostile, thin-skinned and distrustful were less satisfied with their work life in their later years.

The data were collected as part of a longitudinal study at Berkeley's Institute of Human Development and

published in a recent issue of *Administrative Science Quarterly*.

Despite these findings, experts say, negative personality factors of youth need not doom one to a life of dissatisfaction. "Lots of people change and become happier as time goes on; therapy or a good marriage can do it," said Ed Diener, a psychologist at the University of Illinois who is an expert on the research on satisfaction. "Learning to take direct action to handle your problems, rather than just stewing about them, and talking them over with people are two of the most effective ways to change."

Temperament aside, the Wesleyan research showed that men and women tend to differ in some of what leads to satisfaction with life. While for both sexes a divorce in later adulthood led to low levels of satisfaction, childlessness was strongly associated with unhappiness in elderly women, but not in the men. The researchers say that childlessness may be a less important factor for women in the future.

For men, more than women, a serious emotional problem or a bout with alcoholism was likely to mean less satisfaction in old age. But having had more social activities outside their own families meant the men were more likely to be satisfied.

For the women, more than the men, the quality of ties to their children, the frequency of sexual relations and level of education in early life were closely tied to levels of satisfaction in old age. Elderly women who felt their childhood families had little emotional closeness were less likely to be content.

Health and Social Life

The new research adds these psychological factors to an already long list of circumstances that social scientists, in surveys of thousands of people, have found to predict satisfaction with some accuracy.

Health, for instance, is the strongest of these, according to a review in the *Journal of Gerontology* of 30 years of such research. Other major factors include a full social life, an adequate income, a fulfilling marriage and pleasing housing.

In sum, the main research has found, perhaps to no one's surprise, that being neurotic, sick, poor, lonely and the like contribute to dissatisfaction with life. But statistical analysis shows these factors account for only about 30 percent, on average, of what matters for satisfaction, according to a critique by Daniel Ogilvie, a psychologist at Rutgers University. He is seeking ways to understand the large numbers of exceptions to these rules; the many men and women who are pleased with their lives despite hardships, or those who complain regardless of seeming advantages.

"What is true of people on the average does not explain the many, many exceptions," he said.

Dr. Ogilvie's research leads him to challenge the common belief that satisfaction is reached when long-held goals are met, rewards reaped, or ideals attained. Such achievements, his work shows, have less effect on satisfaction than does simply avoiding roles in life in which one experiences undesirable feelings like dependence or selfishness.

"The amount of time a person spends avoiding the undesirable parts of himself is a far better gauge of how satisfied he feels in life than is how close he feels to his ideal self," said Dr. Ogilvie.

His findings challenge another long-held belief in psychology, that satisfaction is strongly related to how close a person feels himself to be to his ideal self-image.

For Freud, the person's ideal self was an aspect of the superego, a creation of the infantile mind built from images of untarnished parents, heroes and heroines, and times when one

was "good." Karen Horney, an early psychoanalytic theorist, postulated that the ideal self-image haunts the neurotic with the "tyranny of the should," an inner recitation of failings and faults that all indicate the person is falling short of what the person feels, deep down, he or she should be.

Carl Rogers developed a widely used method that helps a person clarify the specifics of his or her ideal self and evaluate how far from that ideal the day-to-day self is. Success in therapy, Rogers contended, was marked by a notable reduction of the distance between the real and ideal self.

Avoiding 'Undesired Self'

But in a 1987 article in the *Journal of Personality and Social Psychology,* Dr. Ogilvie cites evidence showing that, in predicting satisfaction, the closeness a person feels to his idealized self-image is not so crucial as is the distance from those aspects of himself he abhors.

"The ideal self is so abstract that we never quite know if we're there or not," Dr. Ogilvie said. "And it's a continually receding goal; whenever we feel we're getting near it, we raise the ideal a bit. It serves to motivate us, to keep us striving."

What he calls the "undesired self" consists of memories such as of being "bad," of dreads, guilts and embarrassments, as well as fears and shameful impulses—in sum, the ways one does not wish to be or feel.

"The undesired self is a much stronger influence on how satisfied we are because the ideal self is so vague, while we know exactly how we do not want to feel," said Dr. Ogilvie. "People seem to use their undesired self as a marker to judge how their life is going; it gives us a concrete navigational cue."

Dr. Ogilvie's research does not deny the role of positive strivings in life. But, he says, "there is both a push away from the undesirable, and a pull toward the ideal, with the push being more powerful than the pull" in enhancing or reducing satisfaction.

How Retirees Spend Time

In related research with people on the verge of retirement, Dr. Ogilvie has found that another powerful factor in satisfaction is how much a person can spend time doing those things that he does best, enjoys the most and finds most meaningful. While the observation may seem evident, it has been largely ignored in most of the research, as well as in much of the advice given to people about to retire.

"Much of the pre-retirement counseling going on in corporations these days has finances as the primary focus," said Dr. Ogilvie. "It is, of course, important to know about pensions and diversification of assets, Social Security benefits and the like, but it misses much of the point. People might also want to know that for middle-income groups, income accounts for a trivial degree of people's satisfaction with their lives after retirement."

Far more useful for satisfaction, Dr. Ogilvie believes, would be having people consider the various identities they have filled in life and evaluate which give them the greatest sense of meaning and allow them to express most fully who they consider themselves to be.

"Some people discover, when they take stock, that their identity at work is what has held them together and others that their jobs have been holding them back," said Dr. Ogilvie. "If their jobs have been the key, then they have to be careful about what they replace them with."

"Post-retirement depression can result when someone whose most positive identity has hinged on work leaves it behind totally," Dr. Ogilvie added. "But it is possible to transfer those abilities to something similar, and find the same kinds of satisfaction that work gave you. One of the most content people I studied was a woman who had an unexciting job at a laundry, but loved it because it allowed her to serve people, which gave her a sense of meaning. When she retired, she moved in with her 89-year-old sister, to help her. It let the woman use those skills that gave her most satisfaction."

One of the least satisfied people

Dr. Ogilvie studied, however, took pleasure in his roles as a salesman, an investor and a grandfather. But, having retired, he spent the most time, he reported, as a husband, in which role he felt "on edge"; as a son-in-law, which made him feel "put upon and angry"; as a golfer, which made him feel "competitive," and at home gardening, where he felt "difficult to live with and snappy." One of the few pleasures he gave much time to was reading; another was working as a handyman, which made him feel "confident and respected."

In research to be published in the *Journal of Personality and Social Psychology,* Dr. Ogilvie found that on average people's opportunity to spend time in meaningful activities was three to four times as powerful a predicter of satisfaction with life than health was. In the large survey studies, health had emerged as the strongest correlate of satisfaction.

In general, people report feeling the highest levels of satisfaction when they are with their friends, and the lowest when they are alone, according to research that asked people to report how they felt at random moments during the day.

"People with psychological problems tend to spend more time alone, and feel the worse for it," said Reed Larson, a psychologist at the University of Illinois, who did the study of people's mood fluctuations during the day while he was at the University of Chicago. "Bulimics, for example, are fine when they are with other people but completely fall apart when they are alone."

Some researchers believe the relationship between good health and satisfaction may work both ways; It is not just that good health makes people more content but that feeling content about life may be physically beneficial.

"Recent studies have found that on days when people are feeling good, their immune system is stronger," Dr. Diener said. "Being more satisfied with life, and so being in positive moods more often, seems to be good for your health."

Is Analysis Testable as Science, After All?

December 22, 1985

A new generation of psychoanalytic thinkers is undertaking the kind of rigorous research that critics contend has been grossly lacking in the discipline but that is essential if psychoanalysis is ever to become truly scientific.

In the process, they are discarding some long-held psychoanalytic tenets, modifying others and establishing an empirical basis for still others.

This scientific treatment of psychoanalysis, some psychoanalysts say, threatens to diminish the richness of their clinical craft by reducing a complex process to simplistic terms. However, a growing number of psychoanalysts are coming to believe that, if the discipline is to survive and flourish, it will have to be tested and refined in accordance with the canons of scientific method.

Although it is much too early for a consensus, many involved in the new effort are proposing which parts of analytic theory can be validated and which cannot. For instance, according to Jonathan Winson, a neuroscientist at the Rockefeller University, "Some concepts just don't stand up."

"For example," he said, "the idea of libido seems to make no sense in terms of the reality of the brain. Neither does Freud's idea of a death wish. On the other hand, many of the key concepts of psychoanalytic theory do hold up. These include the importance of early childhood experience, the existence of the unconscious, and transference."

Psychoanalysis, which grows out of the clinical experience of Freud and his followers, is only one of many current theories of human behavior. But it remains perhaps the most influential in the practice of psychotherapy.

Although efforts to establish its scientific validity are not new, observers argue that the bulk of past research has been grossly deficient from the standpoint of scientific method. The present research, while striving for great rigor, is still vulnerable to criticism. Indeed, some skeptics contend that tests of analysis will never prove worthwhile.

"If you have a sprawling, unparsimonious theory like psychoanalysis," asks Stephen Harnad, a cognitive psychobiologist, "are you better off trying to use the scientific method to extract the small part that is testable, or should you chuck it and test a theory that is more plausible from the outset?"

The journal Dr. Harnad edits, *Brain and Behavioral Sciences;* will devoted fall 1985 issue to the challenge raised by Adolf Grünbaum, a philosopher of science at the University of Pittsburgh, who questions the scientific testability of psychoanalysis. About 50 authorities in the field will respond to Dr. Grünbaum's critique in the journal.

"Mainstream cognitive psychology is rapidly converging on many of Freud's key insights," said Matthew Erdelyi, a psychologist who makes that case in his book, *Psychoanalysis: Freud's Cognitive Psychology,* published by W.H. Freeman. "These include the unconscious, the power of hidden meanings, symbols, and metaphors, and the vagaries of memory, including the fact that seemingly forgotten memories can be recovered."

"What Dr. Grünbaum fails to recognize," said Dr. Erdelyi, "is the problem of ecological validity. You can't reproduce in the lab the actual phenomenon you're trying to test—it's too artificial. For example, investigators have tried to study repression by shocking volunteers when they were presented with certain words, and then seeing if they had amnesia for those words later. That is just not the same as the actual failures of memory that Freud meant by repression."

"Or, consider transference, the patient's feelings toward his parents that he carries over to the psychoanalyst," Dr. Erdelyi added. "How would you possibly duplicate it in the laboratory, without recreating the clinical relationship itself? You'd have to run the subject for two years to elicit enough transference to study."

One of those doing just such long-term research is Lester Luborsky, a psychoanalyst at the University of Pennsylvania. In a 1985 article in the *Clinical Psychology Review,* he reports a scientific study of transference, done not in the laboratory, but rather on the basis of tape recordings of actual psychoanalytic sessions—a method of research also being used by others, notably Merton Gill, a psychoanalyst at the University of Illinois Medical School in Chicago, and by the Psychotherapy Research Group at Mount Zion Hospital in San Francisco.

In Dr. Luborsky's study, independent raters evaluated episodes in which the patient narrated experiences in relationships to parents, siblings, spouses, bosses or the therapist. From these narratives, the raters distilled a pattern of conflict that seemed to emerge in one form or another in each of the episodes, reflecting the patient's main wishes and needs toward others.

This research, Dr. Luborsky concludes, seems to corroborate nine of

Freud's original observations about transference, including that each person has one such distinct pattern; that it relates to "the conduct of his erotic life" and that the pattern is constantly repeated in all other important relationships, particularly with the therapist.

Using a similar technique, Dr. Luborsky has also studied momentary forgetting during psychoanalysis. For example, in an article in *Psychoanalysis and Contemporary Science,* he reports analyzing 13 spontaneous instances of momentary forgetting by a woman during 300 sessions of her psychoanalysis.

Such moments are particularly meaningful, Dr. Luborsky speculates, because they may be live instances of what Freud called repression, the forgetting of emotionally painful information. However, some critics cite studies such as this as embodying many problems of the entire effort. One difficulty is in equating momentary forgetting, which can be studied in this way, with actual repression, which is difficult to capture clinically, let alone scientifically.

The patient in the study was a thirty-one-year-old, single professional woman whose main complaint in therapy was that she had had a series of relationships with unsuitable men, by whom she invariably felt mistreated, so that she would terminate one relationship only to begin another just like it soon afterward.

Each of the thirteen instances of momentary forgetting, Dr. Luborsky found, fit into a pattern directly related to her main problem. Each time, the woman was about to tell the therapist about her expectations that he would reject her.

A different approach to testing psychoanalytic ideas about the unconscious and its role in psychological defenses is taken by Howard Shevrin, a clinical psychologist at the University of Michigan. In a paper given at the Center for the Advanced Study of Behavior Science, Dr. Shevrin reported a study in which he used the evoked potential, a measure of the speed with which the brain registers information, to investigate the unconscious.

Dr. Shevrin's research focuses on how the unconscious mind treats material that has especially potent psychological meaning. For example, in one young man with a blood phobia, Dr. Shevrin found, in clinical interviews, that the phobia was the result of deeper feelings, particularly sadistic impulses toward women—beginning with his mother—whom he both yearned for and hated because he felt she deprived him of affection.

The same patient was presented with lists of words while evoked-potential measures were taken. Some words were presented clearly, others so rapidly that he was not consciously aware he had seen them at all. The lists included especially disturbing words relating to his underlying problem, such as "tormented" and "deprived." The evoked-potential data showed that the disturbing words were actually registered by the brain more quickly when presented unconsciously than consciously.

Dr. Shevrin speculates that the upsetting words were delayed when presented consciously because it took the mind more time to defend against them by finding a nonthreatening meaning.

Another researcher whose work is pointed to by many as validating some basic precepts of psychoanalysis is Lloyd Silverman, a clinical psychologist at New York University. For several years, he has conducted studies in which he uses a tachistoscope to flash words and pictures to volunteers in his experiments at a speed so rapid that they have no conscious awareness of their content. The messages do, nevertheless, seem to have an impact on the volunteers' behavior, and so, Dr. Silverman contends, must register unconsciously.

He has tested the psychoanalytic hypothesis that some schizophrenic patients suffer from a deep, unsatisfied wish to feel psychologically fused with their mothers. In his book *The Search For Oneness* (International Universities Press), Dr. Silverman presents data showing the subliminally flashing the message "Mommy and I are one" temporarily reduced symptoms in certain types of male schizophrenics, while the message "I am losing mommy" had the opposite effect.

Although Dr. Silverman's findings have been disputed by other researchers, in a recent article in *Empirical Studies of Psychoanalytic Theory,* Dr. Silverman reviews a range of studies by investigators using his technique, which have generally confirmed his results.

Some of those involved in the new research are searching for support of analytic concepts in the biological workings of the brain.

One advocate of this approach is Dr. Winson of Rockefeller University who argues in his book *Brain and Psyche* (Double-day) that a "biological understanding leads to a new conception of the unconscious as well as of repression and the meaning of dreams."

In drawing connections between psychoanalysis and the workings of the brain, Dr. Winson is joining several others, including Morton Reiser of Yale, whose recent book *Mind, Brain and Body* covers similar territory, and Eric Kandel, a neuroscientist at Columbia University.

"We now have enough neuroscience knowledge to begin to put psychoanalysis on a scientific footing," Dr. Winson said in an interview.

Dr. Winson, for example, sees the power of childhood experience as based in the fact that there is an early critical period in brain development during which the neocortex—including the prefrontal cortex, which is a key center for decision-making and emotion—is formed.

"Once this period passes," Dr. Winson said, "that brain circuitry will not easily change. The unconscious, which stores our most basic fears and anxieties, is captured in this circuitry and its many connections to the brain's emotional center, the limbic system. The unconscious is at work when these circuits are activated. For example, in transference, analysts report that the patient acts as though the therapist were someone from that early period of his life. I think there is something about the psychoanalytic situation—perhaps the vulnerability of lying down and free associating—that evokes these early childhood responses, with all their fears."

New Scales of Intelligence Rank Talent for Living

May 5, 1988

In an effort to make up for some of the glaring limitations of I.Q. tests, researchers have begun to develop new ways to measure the kinds of emotional factors and psychological attitudes that lead to success in everyday life.

While I.Q. tests remain excellent predictors of how well one will do in school, they have little or nothing to do with who will earn the most money or prestige, or have the most satisfying social life or relationships. The new tests are intended to assess the more practical intelligence that underlies these accomplishments.

The new approach goes beyond purely mental skills to assess emotional factors and psychological attitudes that can either interfere with or facilitate the use of those skills.

The recent research has fostered new theories of what it means to be smart. The old theories focused on academic skills, such as verbal or mathematical quickness. But the new theories describe a spectrum of practical talents, such as the ability to pick up the unspoken rules that govern success in a corporate or professional career, or the habits of mind that foster productivity.

"I.Q. and success in living have little to do with each other," said Seymour Epstein, a psychologist at the University of Massachusetts. "Being intellectually gifted does not predict you will earn the most money or achieve the most recognition, even among college professors."

One factor emerging as crucial for life success is what might be called emotional intelligence.

"How well people manage their emotions determines how effectively they can use their intellectual ability," Dr. Epstein said. "For example, if someone is facile at solving problems in the quiet of her office, but falls apart in a group, then she will be ineffective in a great many situations."

Dr. Epstein has developed a test that measures "constructive thinking," the ability to respond effectively to life. The test measures how well a person manages his emotions and challenging situations, as well as habitual responses to problems such as setbacks and failures. It differs from earlier alternatives to the I.Q. scale that attempted to measure such factors as creativity.

Most of the constructive attitudes the test measures have the ring of common sense. People who think constructively, for instance, tend not to take things personally and not to fret about what others think of them. Rather than complaining about a situation, they take action.

Dr. Epstein has found that many academically bright people have self-destructive habits of mind, such as holding back from new challenges because they fear the worst possible outcome for themselves. Among these non-constructive ways of thinking were holding to private superstitions, such as that talking about a potential success would keep it from happening; a naîve, unrealistic optimism—for instance, that people can do absolutely anything if they have enough willpower—and a generally negative, pessimistic outlook.

"Typical of destructive ways of thinking is one student I recall who played a beautiful solo with a band," Dr. Epstein said. "He had been dreading it, convinced he would do terribly. When people praised him, he discounted it, saying that even if he did well that once, he'd certainly do terribly the next time."

How well people score on the test of constructive thinking, Dr. Epstein has found, predicts a great range of life success, from salaries and promotions, to happiness with friendships, families and romantic relationships, to physical and emotional health. Among people bright enough to attend college he found that I.Q., was related to none of these sorts of success; it was simply irrelevant.

"In a sense, there are two minds," Dr. Epstein said. "One, the experiential mind, has to do with how you react to the world emotionally; it makes instantaneous decisions and calls the shots day to day. It has nothing to do with I.Q. The other, the rational mind, has to do with how we explain what we do, and how well we understand a novel or know math. It has little to do with success in living."

Training in Independence

Certain childhood experiences seem to shape constructive thinking, for better or worse. Those who scored higher on the test of constructive thinking, Dr. Epstein found, reported having parents who did not overprotect them, but rather trained them in independence. The sense of having been loved or rejected by one's parents, however, did not relate to scores on the test.

"Constructive thinking depends to a large extent on having parents who teach you to be strong in the world, to learn to handle things on your own," Dr. Epstein said. "Love is not enough; it takes training in doing things yourself."

Still, many practical talents that lead to success in life are rarely taught explicitly. Rather, those who excel seem able to absorb this knowledge tacitly.

In one recent study, psychologists at Yale developed a test that measures the knack of selling. The psychologists see the art of persuasion as essential to success in much of life.

"The ability to sell is a kind of persuasion everyone needs," said Robert Sternberg, the psychologist at Yale who is doing much of the new work. "You sell yourself when you meet someone, you sell your ideas or point of view, you sell when you negotiate a deal. Sales is a skill that demands a specific kind of practical intelligence."

Factors in Talent for Sales

In research with Richard Wagner and Carol Rashotte at Florida State University, Dr. Sternberg found that the talent for sales included such things as knowing that when someone stalls in making a decision, the best approach is not to press him but rather to ask him why he's not prepared to make a decision at that moment. Another persuasion tactic used by those with sales talent was not to argue with the person one is selling to, but rather to acknowledge the validity of his position and then make one's own point.

While such rules of thumb may sometimes be taught as sales strategies, more often successful sales people seem to grasp them intuitively.

When the test was given to people who sell insurance, high scores were correlated with the number of years they had been in sales, the number of sales they made and awards they had received.

Practical Intelligence

In another study with Dr. Wagner, included in *Practical Intelligence*, pub-

lished by Cambridge University Press, Dr. Sternberg studied the kinds of tacit knowledge typical of successful business managers. The test assessed three kinds of practical intelligence. One was how well a person managed himself, dealt with procrastination, for instance. Another was the ability to manage others, such as knowing how to assign and tailor tasks to take maximum advantage of another person's abilities. The third was knowing how to manage one's career, how to enhance one's reputation, for example.

A typical question asks what should be the basis for selecting new projects to tackle; often there are more than a dozen choices, including that the project should be "fun," that it enable one to demonstrate one's talents, or that it require working directly with more senior executives. The people that are most successful tend to choose the same top priorities. Those executives who did best on the test tended to have more years of management experience and to have higher salaries than those who did less well, Dr. Wagner and Dr. Sternberg found.

One of the first techniques for assessing practical intelligence was developed by David McClelland, a psychologist at Boston University, and George O. Klemp, Jr, a consulting psychologist at Charles River Associates in Cambridge, Massachusetts. By careful comparisons of outstanding performers in a given field with mediocre ones, they were able to uncover many of the specific competencies that set the two groups apart.

In a study of managers, for instance, the problem-solving skills of the best managers included the tendency to push for concrete information when faced with ambiguity; another was the ability to seek information from as wide a range of sources as possible. They also displayed a curious knack for finding unusual analogies to explain the essence of a situation.

The best managers were adept, too, at influencing people. They consistently anticipated the impact of their actions on others in the company and did not hestitate to confront people directly when there were problems.

They also were adept at building a sense of collaboration by, for instance, involving subordinates in making decisions that would affect them, particularly controversial decisions, according to results obtained by Drs. Klemp and McClelland.

The new line of research was triggered by an influential critique of I.Q. tests Dr. McClelland published in in 1973 when he was at Harvard, and by a series of equally skeptical articles written about the same time by Ulric Neisser, a cognitive psychologist then at Cornell. They were among the first prominent psychologists to argue that academic intelligence had little or nothing to do with success in life. Until then, it was widely assumed that a central core of intelligence, which was measured by I.Q. tests, could be applied by bright people to find success in almost any field.

But as Dr. Neisser pointed out, the questions on I.Q. tests are nothing like the challenges one meets in life. I.Q. questions tend to be formulated by other people, to offer all the information one needs to answer them, and to have nothing to do with people's own experience or interests. They are also well defined, Dr. Sternberg observes, with only one correct solution, and usually just one way to arrive at the right answer. But none of that is usually true of the problems people face in their daily lives, such as how to find a mate or a better apartment, handle personal finances or get ahead in one's career.

Seven Kinds of Intelligence

Dr. Sternberg has proposed a theory of intelligence that includes such traits as how well a person plans strategies for problem-solving or handles novel situations. And a theory put forth by Howard Gardner of Harvard describes seven kinds of intelligence, including the body control displayed by athletes and dancers, musical talent, interpersonal skills such as being able to read another's feelings, as well as more academic abilities like mathematical and logical reasoning.

Much of the new work examines attitudes that allow people to make best use of whatever mental skills they may have. One such outlook is what psychologists call "self-efficacy," the belief that one has mastery over the events of one's life and can meet a given challenge.

"People's beliefs about their abilities have a profound effect on those abilities," said Albert Bandura, a psychologist at Stanford University, who has done the major research on self-efficacy. "Ability is not a fixed property; there is huge variability in how you perform. People who have a sense of self-efficacy bounce back from failure; they approach things in terms of how to handle them rather than worrying about what can go wrong."

In the study of exceptional managers by Drs. McClelland and Klemp, for instance, the best ones displayed a strong self-confidence, seeing themselves as the most capable person for their job and as being stimulated by crisis. Along similar lines, Dr. Martin Seligman, a psychologist at the University of Pennsylvania, has shown that people who are more optimistic do better than pessimists in a wide variety of endeavors, from selling insurance to achievement in school.

Self-efficacy varies from one part of a person's life to another. A self-confident manager, for instance, may feel ineffective as a father. Dr. Bandura and other researchers have found that self-efficacy acts as a powerful force in people's choices of what they will try in life and what they avoid. Many women, they have found, have a low level of self-efficacy with regard to computers or math, and so tend to shy away from careers that depend heavily on those skills.

Some of the psychologists believe that although the practical intelligence seems to come naturally to certain people, other people can be trained to be smarter in this way, to some extent. Dr. Sternberg and Dr. McClelland, for example, have worked on developing training techniques to enhance different aspects of practical intelligence.

Rethinking the Value of Intelligence Tests

November 9, 1986

Judy is a bright-eyed four-year-old who stays by herself during playtime in her class at the Eliot-Pearson Preschool on the campus of Tufts University in Medford, Massachusetts. Anyone who watched her might think Judy is a bit of a wallflower and certainly behind her more gregarious peers in social development. But when a researcher asks Judy to play the Classroom Game—which is actually a test of social perceptiveness—her apparent indifference to her classmates' social lives falls away. Judy, it turns out, has a level of social intelligence far beyond that of most of her classmates.

The Classroom Game is a dollhouse version of Judy's preschool class, a precise duplicate complete with stick figures that have photographs of a student or teacher pasted on the models. It is one of dozens of games developed by Project Spectrum, a Harvard-Tufts research project that uses Judy's preschool class as a laboratory to study how intelligence develops.

"When I asked Judy to put each child in the part of the classroom where he or she most likes to play, such as the art corner, she was able to do it with complete accuracy," says Ulla Nalkus, supervisor of a research study at the school. "Then, when I asked her to put each child with the children he or she most likes to play with, she matched best friends for the entire class."

"Such accuracy marks Judy as having exceptional social perceptiveness for a four-year-old," Ms. Nalkus says. "She has a perfect social map of the classroom. Many socially outgoing children do not have this skill, but many who hang on the periphery, like Judy, turn out to have superior social analytic abilities."

In later life, as a social perceptiveness like Judy's blossoms, it could lead to an outstanding career in any of the numerous fields where "people skills" count, from psychotherapy and social services to sales and management, or even diplomacy and politics. But critics say that social intelligence is one of many such abilities that are largely ignored by the intelligence and achievement tests that schools use to rank their students' potential.

"The time has come to redefine giftedness and broaden our notion of the spectrum of talents," says Dr. Howard Gardner, the Harvard psychologist and MacArthur Prize Fellow who directs Project Spectrum with Dr. David Feldman, a professor of developmental psychology at Tufts. Dr. Gardner and Dr. Feldman are among a growing number of educators and psychologists who are seeking alternatives to the tests long used to guide schools in pupil acceptance placement and advancement because they believe such tests are inadequate and slight such crucial gifts and talents as the social perceptiveness Judy displays.

"The single most important contribution education can make to a child's development is to help him toward a field where his talents best suit him, where he will be satisfied and competent." Dr. Gardner says. "We've completely lost sight of that. Instead we subject everyone to an education where if you succeed you will be best suited to be a college professor. And we evaluate everyone along the way according to whether they meet that narrow standard of success."

"We should spend less time ranking children and more time helping them to identify their natural competencies and gifts and cultivate those," he adds. "There are hundreds and hundreds of ways to succeed and many, many different abilities that will help you get there."

Consider the moral and ethical strengths of Dr. Martin Luther King Jr. or the sensitivity to inner nuance that distinguishes the novels of Virginia Woolf or Henry James. Such gifts and talents emerge at an early age, according to Dr. Gardner. But he and other critics of standard I.Q. tests contend that too often they are ignored or stifled by an education system that prizes only the narrow range of abilities—mainly verbal and mathematical skills—that are related to the academic life.

In particular, new views about the nature of being gifted have spawned a skepticism toward the I.Q. test score once sacrosanct among educators. The idea that a single number can summarize a person's intelligence and abilities has come under intense criticism from many psychologists, who believe that the tests are narrow and misleading and predict, at best, only a limited range of talents.

I.Q. test scores, the critics say, may reflect a student's capacities for academic work, but life requires—and rewards—a far broader range of talents than those cultivated in school. Indeed, several major studies have shown that intelligence-test scores are, at best, poor predictors of success later in life.

"No doubt the kind of intelligence measured by I.Q. tests is important in elementary and secondary school, and perhaps even in college," says Dr. Robert Sternberg, a psychologist at Yale University. "But once one leaves the academic niceties of a school setting, other aspects of intelligence that the I.Q. test ignores become much more important."

Dr. Sternberg and Dr. Gardner are at the forefront of a movement to identify those other kinds of intelligence, to develop new ways to spot a child's strengths and weaknesses and to tailor his or her education accordingly. Their efforts, which have revolutionary implications for education, are gathering momentum. The psychologists are courted by testing companies and asked by school systems to be consultants, and their theories influence the thinking of psychologists and educators everywhere.

Their work brings together many earlier threads. Some of the pioneers of intelligence testing such as Louis Thurstone and J.P. Guilford proposed that there were many aspects of intelligence; Guilford alone posited more than 120 components to intelligence. But until recently their theories were largely ignored by leading test makers.

In the early 1970's the Department of Education formulated a policy that encouraged the identification of talents other than math and verbal skills in children. Philosophers such as Ernst Cassirer and Susanne Langer had described "different ways of knowing," and psychologists like Jean Piaget and more recently Ulrich Neisser had urged measuring cognitive capacities in their natural setting rather than by paper-and-pencil tests.

The key concept in the new way of viewing intelligence is "multiple." Intelligence is not thought of as a single property of the human mind that can be measured once and for all by an instrument called the intelligence test. Rather there are many intelligences, which may be relatively independent of one another and which may not lend themselves to measurement by short-answer, paper-and-pencil tests. There is no magic number to such multiplicity.

Dr. Sternberg has proposed that there are three main aspects to intelli-

gence. Dr. Gardner, in his influential book *Frames of Mind,* published by Basic Books in 1983, enumerates seven major intelligences.

In addition to those skills commonly assessed on standard I.Q. tests—verbal and mathematical-logical abilities—Dr. Gardner's list includes the spatial abilities of good architects; the bodily grace of the superb athlete or dancer; musical gifts; the interpersonal abilities that make a great salesman or diplomat, and the inner attunement that allows someone to lead a life in keeping with his true feelings.

But even that list of intelligences is growing. On the basis of his practical experience observing children in a preschool setting, Dr. Gardner, with a Harvard graduate student, Thomas Hatch, has recently expanded his theory of seven intelligences to include twenty.

In place of a single social intelligence, for example, he believes there are four distinct abilities: leadership; caretaking (such as keeping friends); mediating conflicts; and social analysis.

Dr. Sternberg, in his theory of intelligence, describes a triad of interlocking mental abilities, the sum total of which determines a person's intellectual strengths and weaknesses. Borrowing from recent research on how the mind processes information, Dr. Sternberg's theory measures several components of cognition that, he believes, underlie what we mean by "intelligence," but that by and large have not been included in previous measures of intelligence. These underlying skills, he believes, are a truer gauge of intelligence than the tests now in use.

One of these abilities, for example, is the capacity to learn from context rather than from explicit instruction. Many I.Q. tests use vocabulary as a key test of intelligence. By contrast, Dr. Sternberg's tests assess the ability to learn the meaning of words from context rather than simply testing how large a person's vocabulary is.

"Most new words are encountered in textbooks, novels, newspapers and the like," he says. "More intelligent people are better able to use surround-

ing contexts to figure out the word's meanings. As the years go by, these people acquire the larger vocabularies. Because so much learning is from context, this is a key skill in intelligence."

Another ability Dr. Sternberg sees as crucial to intelligence is mental flexibility, or adapting to novelty. People skilled at thinking in non-entrenched ways do well, for example, at solving an analogy with a surprising premise. Insight is another capacity that Dr. Sternberg places as central to intelligence. Insight allows the solution to those problems that come to mind all at once, or not at all.

Crucial to the new theories is a conviction that intelligence alone—even multiple intelligence—is not enough to predict outstanding performance. Inspiration, as the saying has it, requires perspiration. And studies of highly gifted adults have shown that productivity depends as much on these psychological factors as it does on raw intellect.

"When you look at gifted performance in real settings, and can actually see a person struggling with day-to-day problems—in physics or art, say—you see that it requires so much more than simple intellectual abilities," says Dr. Mihalyi Csikzentmihalyi, a professor of psychology at the University of Chicago, who has been studying creative people. "With gifted people who are highly productive, there are motivational factors that can make all the difference. You find many high-I.Q. people who do nothing in life because they don't have the drive."

One of the abilities that emerges time and again as marking the high achiever has more to do with temperament than intellect, persistence. It is not enough to have a talent to excel; one must also have tenacity and determination. In a study by B.S. Bloom and L.A. Sosniak of high achievers, for example, it was found that by age twelve the highly talented group were spending as much time immersed in what was to become their field of excellence as their peers did watching television.

"Without the support of traits such as the willingness to work hard in achieving excellence, it is impossible to rise above mediocrity," says Dr. Abraham Tannenbaum, professor of education and psychology at Teachers College of Columbia University.

Because so many factors apart from those identified in I.Q. tests seem to matter in actual excellence in life, many outstanding youngsters who could benefit greatly from programs for the gifted are being excluded from them, according to some experts. Such programs typically select students who score in the top five percent on tests. But in the view of Joseph Renzulli, an educational psychologist at the University of Connecticut, that may exclude the majority of those who should be in them.

Dr. Renzulli points out that research on people who have made outstanding contributions to a variety of fields finds that most scored *below* the 95th percentile on tests. "Nor," he adds, "were they necessarily straight-A students who learned early how to play the lesson-learning game."

"In other words," Dr. Renzulli says, "if such cutoff scores are needed to determine entrance into special programs, we may be guilty of actually discriminating against persons who have the greatest potential."

The movement to identify and nurture multiple intelligences grows out of a recognition of the narrow range of abilities measured by current tests. "Generally speaking, the movement away from exclusive reliance on I.Q. and its correlates to define giftedness is not intended simply to devalue the I.Q.," Dr. Tannenbaum writes in *Conceptions of Giftedness,* a collection of views of intelligence, published by the Cambridge University Press. "Instead, the argument is that I.Q. limits giftedness to traditional academics." Instead of spotting those talents that will be most important for success in the wide range of possibilities that life holds out to the young, critics say, current tests focus on academic abilities that, as one leaves school, become increasingly trivial. "Schools train students in modes of thinking that are irrelevant or even counterproductive in later life," Dr. Sternberg argues. "The problems presented to students in schools are nothing like those confronted in life."

"Whether it's finding a mate or realizing you should look for a new job or a new house, first you have to realize you have a problem," Dr. Sternberg observes. "In life, problems are usually ill defined; no one tells you the problem is there. If you're sharp enough to know you have a problem, then you have to get the relevant information yourself. Once you've done that, there are typically multiple solutions, and many ways to get to them. And you may never know for sure if you've found the best answer."

Another fallacy of academics and the tests currently used, in Dr. Sternberg's view, is the assumption that "smart is fast." This assumption, he argues, underlies the majority of intelligence tests, virtually all of which are timed. Dr. Sternberg sees that as missing the point. What is critical, he says, is not speed per se, but knowing what to do quickly and when to act slowly.

"Snap judgments are often poor judgments," Dr. Sternberg points out. "Jumping into problems without adequate reflection is likely to lead to false starts and erroneous conclusions. Yet timed tests often force a person to solve problems impulsively. But most of us encounter few significant problems in work or personal life that demand an answer in only 5 or even 50 seconds, the typical time allotted for a solution on a standardized test."

The old tests being challenged include everything from the venerable Stanford-Binet I.Q. test, recently revised in its fourth version in 70 years of use, to such standards as the Miller Analogies Test, which is widely used as an admissions test for graduate studies.

To be sure, the 200 or so intelligence measures currently available, and particularly the half-dozen most commonly used by schools, will not soon disappear from the scene; they serve a function that society seems to find very useful.

I.Q. tests have an unquestioned utility in the eyes of many educators and psychologists. Academic abilities are of immense importance in a child's life, and the tests can help educators place him in a setting that best suits him, or spot problems that need special help.

Even critics of I.Q. tests concede the tests have proved efficient as a way to sort out capabilities among people in large groups, such as schools and the armed forces—and so help match them to their appropriate niche. Jerome Kagan, a developmental psychologist at Harvard and a longtime critic of I.Q. tests, acknowledges that "I.Q. tests solve such practical problems as placing a kid in the right reading group of classroom in school," even though he would rather see an alternative developed.

But some psychologists argue that the scores themselves have taken on an importance that far outweighs their true significance. Educators and parents can be impressed, even entranced, by a child's test scores, and yet have little idea of how those scores translate—or do not—into real-life abilities.

Dr. Sternberg recounts hearing about a teachers' college in Missouri that, like most graduate schools, required that prospective students attain a certain score on the Miller Analogies Test to gain acceptance. The test, in which a person completes a series of analogies in a fixed time, is thought by graduate-school admissions officers to be a sound predictor of a student's ability to do graduate work.

At the Missouri school, a promising student was admitted to the education program despite having a score below that usually required on the analogies test. She went through the program with distinction, but when the time came for her to get her diploma, she was told that she would have to take the analogies test again and pass it with the score required for entry into the program she had just finished.

"Consider the logic here," Dr. Sternberg says. "The test score had come to surpass in importance what it was supposed to predict, school performance."

Dr. Sternberg is working with the Psychological Corporation, one of the giants of the testing industry, to put his theories to practice by developing a test of "practical intelligence." Instead of yielding the usual I.Q.-test measures of verbal and math abilities, it will focus on assessing a person's strengths in the various components of intelligence described in Dr. Sternberg's model, such as the ability to cope with novelty and the capacity for insight.

Dr. Gardner is working with the Educational Testing Service, which developed, among others, the Scholastic Aptitude Test used in college admissions, to devise a way to identify strengths in the arts and humanities that do not show up in standard tests. And at the Harvard School of Education, he is concentrating on devising tests that will spot budding talent, even in preschoolers, on the twenty kinds of intelligence he has identified.

The new approaches to intelligence may lead not just to innovative tests but to entirely new curriculums as well. Dr. Sternberg, for example, has been preparing courses that will help people improve the skills he identifies as underlying intelligence. His primer, "Intelligence Applied," is already being used by high schools and colleges for courses in thinking skills.

Dr. Gardner envisions devising a set of activities and exercises that children can use to further develop the specific abilities for which they show a natural affinity, or to strengthen skills in which they seem weak. "One of my major goals," he says, "is to empower people by letting them know more about their intellectual abilities. It is extremely useful to know what you're good at, what you could be good at, and what you need help with."

An Emerging Theory on Blacks' I.Q. Scores

April 10, 1988

Most social scientists know—though few publicly discuss it—that there has been a puzzling gap of about fifteen points in I.Q. test scores, on average, between blacks and whites in America ever since the tests were first widely used more than seventy years ago. After long debate over why blacks score lower, and what it means, a fresh theory is putting the discussion into perspective.

That theory challenges earlier views that had laid the blame on a defect in heredity or home life, and points instead to the social and psychological toll taken by broad social inequities that stand in the way of academic success for many blacks.

To be sure, the gap does not apply to all blacks, but is based on the averages of millions of test scores. There are blacks among the brightest one percent on I.Q. tests, just as there are whites among those with the lowest scores. But on the whole, the difference in I.Q. points between the groups is quite significant. It means that the top sixth of blacks score only as well on I.Q. tests as do the top half of whites.

That gap exists not only between blacks and whites, but also, to a lesser degree, between whites and certain other underprivileged minorities, notably Mexican-Americans, native Hawaiians and American Indians.

The question why children in these minorities, but not others, so often fall below their peers in I.Q. scores and school achievement is as much political as academic. While hotly debated in the 1960's and 1970's, the issue is rarely discussed in public by social scientists these days. In private, many of them tacitly seemed to cede the argument to those who claimed that the disparity was traceable to some deficiency, such as in genetic endowment or in the home.

One of the more startling new theories holds that most blacks in America are in a social position strikingly similar to other "castelike" minorities around the world, such as the Harijans, or untouchables, of India, the Maoris of New Zealand and the Burakumi in Japan. The gap between blacks' and whites' I.Q. scores is similar to that between the privileged and deprived groups in each of these other cultures, education experts say. Where tests have been given, the children of these underprivileged groups score an average 10 to 15 points below children in their country's dominant group. (On the other hand, one study shows that Burakumi children in America, where they are treated as any other Japanese, they do as well on I.Q. tests and in school as other Japanese.)

This "caste" point of view is receiving an increasingly wider and more influential hearing since John Ogbu, a Nigerian anthropologist at the University of California, first proposed it close to a decade ago. And the newspaper *Education Week* surveyed black educators on their opinions of Dr. Ogbu's theory, particularly his conclusion that one effect of the "lower caste" view of themselves on many young blacks is to see working hard in school as an actual betrayal of their roots. A large number of the educators were put off by the theory, seeing it as overly pessimistic.

"There is a general agreement among anthropologists and sociologists of education that social status is so highly correlated with I.Q. that it casts suspicion on I.Q. scores as reflecting intelligence rather than socioeconomic status," Frederick Erickson, professor of education at the University of Pennsylvania, said in an interview. "It suggests there's something wrong with our society, not our poor people."

Dr. Ogbu is one of many to note that the black-white I.Q. debate is not a uniquely American issue. The same gap prevails, Dr. Ogbu contends, wherever castelike divisions exist in society. And according to Ulric Neisser, a cognitive psychologist at Emory University, "All over the world, lower-caste children do less well in school than upper-caste children, have lower test scores, and don't stay in school as long." Dr. Neisser is editor of *The School Achievement of Minority Children,* published by Lawrence Erlbaum Associates, in which Dr. Ogbu makes his case.

But the experience of castelike minorities is far different. Their status in American society is a quirk of history, not their choice. The first blacks, of course, were brought here against their will; American Indians and native Hawaiians are descendants of groups who were conquered by a white majority. And later immigrants from Mexico have been treated as as those early Mexicans who were displaced from power by whites.

The distinctive social marks of belonging to a castelike minority include prejudice—for example, being regarded as less desirable neighbors, employees and schoolmates by the dominant group—and a lack of political and economic power.

Being born into a castelike minority, Dr. Ogbu observes, too often leads one to grow up with the conviction that life will be restricted to a small and unrewarding set of options. The consequences for I.Q. test scores and school performance are the same worldwide, children in the lower "caste" suffer.

The lower I.Q. scores of children in these minorities, Dr. Ogbu and others propose, spring from factors such as prejudice, either blatant or subtle. In one pernicious form, it becomes a self-fulfilling prophecy growing out of teachers' expecting less of black children, and so tacitly treating them in ways that make that expectation come true. "Too many educators underestimate the potential and ability of poor kids generally, and castelike minorities in particular," said Dr. Erickson of the University of Pennsylvania, "One of the most powerful influences on a black child is the beliefs of his teachers about his academic potential."

Another factor is the grinding poverty in the lives of many blacks and other minority children. The poor child is vulnerable to many stresses from which his better-off classmates are protected; when something goes wrong in the family, the poor child is more likely to carry such problems into his school life.

Perhaps most demoralizing—and with greatest consequences for I.Q. and school achievement—is that blacks and other minority members face a job ceiling. Consistent pressures and obstacles relegate them to jobs of low status and income, while whites compete far more successfully for jobs above that ceiling. They see that others in their group hold menial jobs, that relatively few attain outstanding career success, and that even those who do attain middle-class jobs still often feel discrimination.

The net result for many black children, Dr. Ogbu believes, is that they become convinced that it is difficult if not impossible for them to advance in the mainstream by doing well in school.

One consequence is that many black children turn their backs entirely on school as an avenue to a brighter future. In *The Urban Review,* Dr. Ogbu reported on a study of two groups of equally bright black high school students, one doing well and one failing in school. Those who fared poorly, he found, saw being studious as betraying their racial identity—by "acting white," in the students' words.

"It's not that the black children can't do the work, but that they don't make the effort," Dr. Ogbu said in an interview. "The underlying issue for them is one of racial identity. They see doing well in school and getting a high-status job as selling out. You see the same dynamic among Mexican-American children, they identify achievement with betraying their roots."

Another major blow to the argument that the difference between black and white I.Q. scores points to a deficit in the racial gene pool is a series of recent findings by a New Zealander, James R. Flynn, a political scientist at the University of Otago in New Zealand. In *The Psychological Bulletin* Dr. Flynn reports data from fourteen nations revealing large I.Q. gains—from 5 to 25 points—in a single generation. In the Netherlands, for instance, I.Q. scores between 1952 and 1982 rose twenty-one points as measured by a test given by the Dutch Army to virtually all Dutch men when they reached eighteen. Dr. Flynn found similar gains in every country for which he could obtain data, from France and Norway to Australia and Japan.

The data from the United States are most telling in terms of the current difference between black and white I.Q. scores. In an earlier study in *The Psychological Bulletin,* Dr. Flynn reported that a comparison of the scores on I.Q. tests of Americans between 1932 and 1978 revealed a steady rise in performance over the half-century.

His research examined results of more than 73 studies involving close to 7,500 people ranging in age from 2 to 48. The comparison was made possible because I.Q. tests are regularly updated. As part of the process of finding norms for interpreting test scores on the new form of the test, psychologists give both the old and new versions to the same group of people. Thus, for example, the same children's scores were obtained both on the Wechsler Intelligence Scale for Children from 1948 and the new form introduced in 1972.

While "caste" conjures up images of India, similar social divisions prevail in many countries, from Britain and Israel to Japan and New Zealand. Such distinctions are not necessarily based on race. In many nations they are based on tribe or sect, such as Shiite Moslems in pre-civil-war Lebanon.

In Israel, the Jews of North Africa fall heir to the role of undesirable caste; in Britain, the most downtrodden group is West Indians. In Japan the Burakumi, who were emancipated only in 1871 from pariah status that resulted from their work as tanners, are still largely treated as outcasts.

Not all American minorities have a castelike social status. Mormons and Jews, for instance, are numerical minorities, and may be victims of prejudice, but by and large they are not subordinated politically or economically.

Recent immigrant groups, too, are free of such status. While Southeast Asians, Chinese or Filipinos who have come to America may hold menial jobs, they have immigrated to upgrade their status. And, Dr. Ogbu observes, they tend to compare themselves not with dominant groups in America so much as their peers back home. Thus, even in their menial jobs they tend to feel better off than those back home.

From such studies, Dr. Flynn got a surprising result, without exception, those taking the I.Q. tests get higher scores on the earlier forms of the test. Tests made up in the 1950's yield higher I.Q.'s than those from the 1960's, and so forth.

Put differently, someone who got an I.Q. score of 100 in a test from the 1970's would likely get an I.Q. score several points higher on the same test in its 1950 form. Thus, in general, children today scored higher than their grandparents did on those same tests. (The downward trend, until recently, of S.A.T. scores over the previous couple of decades, Dr. Flynn argues, reflects a worsening of high school education—the I.Q. assessments reflecting basic cognitive abilities, while the S.A.T.'s measure advanced academic skills.)

Indeed, Dr. Flynn found that by the 1980's the children taking the tests outperformed the 1930 groups by about 15 I.Q. points—precisely the same difference found currently between black and white children on the same sorts of tests.

Since the whites taking the test over the years were from the same gene pool, the results evidently represent some environmental force at work rather than a genetic upgrading, Mr. Flynn argues. Indeed, the identical upward drift has occurred among black I.Q. scores. Comparisons of the scores of black United States Army draftees in World War I with black draftees during the Vietnam War shows a gain in I.Q. of about 15 points.

"There seems to be an environmental gap between blacks and whites just like that between whites today and their parents," Dr. Flynn said in a telephone interview from New Zealand. "No sane person can think we're that much innately smarter than our parents or grandparents. Also, the environmental advantages whites enjoy over blacks, particularly if you throw in the impact of racism, are enough to explain the difference in I.Q. scores."

The upward drift in I.Q. scores seems to indicate changes in environment because no genetic influence is possible in so short a time, Dr. Flynn observes. He thus discounts the argument that deficits in I.Q. scores of groups like blacks in America or Maoris in New Zealand show they are "inherently inferior." "Statements that this group or that group cannot maintain or develop a modern industrial civilization because they have a mean I.Q. of only 85 are suspect," Dr. Flynn wrote in *The New Scientist*, a

British journal. "American whites circa 1930 had a mean I.Q. of 85 scored against current norms and yet they developed the industrial civilization we have today."

What, then, do I.Q. tests measure? They were designed to measure one thing, a child's ability to perform in school. That, education experts will agree, they do well. (I.Q. tests, however, are notoriously poor predictors of job success or of how well one does financially as an adult, for example.)

Thus the fact that school children in Japan-score between four and eleven I.Q. points higher than their American peers does not mean that Japanese are that much "smarter" than Americans, but rather that they have a range of academic advantages, from intense parental pressure for achievement to long hours of homework, that most American children do not.

By the same token, the disparity between black and white scores, Dr. Flynn and others argue, is because of similar disadvantages. The current worldwide disparity between privileged and deprived groups in I.Q. and school performance, they argue, is mainly a product of environmental influences—notably prejudice, low expectations, inferior schools and bad teaching.

When those factors are eliminated, new data show, the test scores of underprivileged minorities approximate those of whites. Research by George Chambers, professor of education at the University of Iowa, compared scores of Hispanic and white high school students on the American College Test, or A.C.T. The national average A.C.T. scores for Mexican-Americans is 15.2, for whites 19.6.

But when Dr. Chambers compared Hispanic and white students who were carefully matched in pairs for family income, courses taken and

eleven other background factors, the differences between the groups' scores largely vanished. Among the most advantaged pairs (for instance, those with family incomes over $36,000 and who had taken advanced math and science courses) the Hispanic students scored an average 21.8, and the whites 23.4.

Perhaps the most telling bit of evidence comes from the I.Q. scores of castelike minorities who emigrate. Once they arrive in a country where they are free of any particular social discrimination, their children's I.Q. scores and school performance tend to match those of other children in the new country.

For instance, research by George DeVos, an anthropologist at the University of California at Berkeley, shows that in Japan the I.Q. gap between Burakumi and other Japanese is about as large as that between blacks and whites in America. But when the Burakumi come to this country, where they are treated as are any other Japanese, their children do as well on I.Q. tests and in school as do other Japanese.

Dr. Flynn sees his data as a direct challenge to the theories of Arthur Jensen, an educational psychologist at the University of California at Berkeley, who has calculated that 80 percent of I.Q. is traceable to genetic differences, while only 20 percent is traceable to environment. The great malleability of I.Q. scores in a single generation, however, points to environment, rather than genes, as having a much larger influence.

Dr. Neisser of Emory agrees. In his view, the low I.Q. scores and poor academic achievement of black children "has little to do with their race or their genes, it is a consequence of the structure of society as a whole."

Child Development

How do the childhood years shape emotional, cognitive, and social development? The research covered in these articles refines—and sometimes challenges—psychology's answers to this question.

The influences that shape a child's growth and development begin in the womb. One danger during the prenatal period is "fetal alcohol syndrome," in which a pregnant mother's heavy drinking produces drastic abnormalities, such as mental retardation, in the child. "Lasting Costs for Child Are Found from a Few Early Drinks" describes new data showing that lower levels of alcohol can also impair intellectual function. By the early school years there was a five-point drop in the IQ scores of children born to mothers who had three drinks or more a day in the first two months of pregnancy, even when the mothers stopped drinking after the second month.

It has long been considered a mark of healthy development for infants at around nine months of age to show distress at the presence of a stranger. But now researchers are challenging the notion that "stranger anxiety" is a major milestone in an infant's emotional growth, saying whether a baby cries in the presence of a stranger is more a sign of temperament than of bonding to its caretaker. Ready why in "New Research Overturns a Milestone of Infancy."

Since Freud, a child's emotional development has been seen as shaped by a series of distinct critical phases. That view is challenged now in research detailed in "Child Develop-ment Theory Stresses Small Moments." Instead, some developmental psychologists now say, a child's emotional development and personality are shaped more by the countless smaller exchanges of daily life between parents and child, rather than by events during critical phases.

"What Do Children Fear Most? Their Answers Are Surprising." While adults tend to think that children's greatest fears are of major traumas such as the birth of a sibling or having an operation, children say otherwise. Their worst fears revolve around school life and peers—a sign of the importance of friends in a child's developing self-image. The research also points up the difference between how children experience their world, and their parents' perceptions.

The toll of a traumatic childhood is not always emotional trouble in adulthood, according to the research reviewed in "Thriving Despite Hardship: Key Childhood Traits Identified." While some people are emotionally disabled later in life by painful childhood experiences, others are surprisingly resilient, growing up to thrive despite the difficulties of their early years. This research pinpoints the traits that help a child thrive in the face of hardship.

Are you the first-born? Does it make any difference in life? While some data show links between the order in which children are born and their success late in life, the research in "Spacing of Siblings Strongly Linked to Success in Life" looks at the number of years between the birth of children rather than their birth order. It finds that the spacing of siblings has as much to do with later life success as does birth order.

One of the main influences in children's development is how their parents treat them. But what if your parents have problems themselves, like alcoholism or depression? The research in "Depressed Parents Put Children at a Greater Risk of Depression" shows just that, the child of a depressed parent is more likely than other children to grow up being prone to depression. This research points to the kinds of interactions that depressed mothers have with their children as being likely to cultivate depressive tendencies in the child, passing on the problem to the next generation.

Lasting Costs for Child Are Found from a Few Early Drinks

March 9, 1989

Even moderate drinking by women in the first month or two of pregnancy, often before they realize they are pregnant, can impair the child's intellectual ability upon reaching school age, a new study indicates.

The researchers found significant effects for women who consume a daily average of one to three drinks each containing half an ounce of pure alcohol. That is equivalent to one to three daily cocktails, bottles of beer or glasses of wine.

The scientists interviewed 491 Seattle women in the fifth month of pregnancy and followed up with assessments of their children, measuring intelligence, reaction time and attentiveness.

The study took into account factors such as parents' incomes and educations, which are known to effect a child's intelligence, and found that drinking had an effect apart from these influences. The impairment was noticed even when the pregnant woman cut back her drinking in the first or second month of pregnancy.

Lower I.Q. Scores

The most recently published finding from the research involved fifty-three mothers who had on average three drinks or more a day in the first month or so of pregnancy. Their children were found at age four to score substantially lower on intelligence tests than the other children in the study. Specifically, the average score on I.Q. tests for these children was 105, five points below the average for all children in the study.

Separately, the researchers have reported that children born to mothers who had as little as one or two drinks a day in the first months of pregnancy were found by their early school years to have a slower reaction time and to have difficulty paying attention. These conclusions were also based on the 491 women and their children.

While previous studies have indicated that very heavy drinking by a pregnant woman can cause mental retardation in her children, the Seattle research is the first to show serious effects to the intellectual capacities of children at school age whose mothers drank at moderate levels while pregnant. It is also the first to distinguished the effects of alcohol from that of other factors such as smoking or caffeine use.

"We recommended that women who are trying to become pregnant or might become so do not drink alcohol at all," said Dr. Ann Streissguth, a psychologist in the department of psychiatry and behavioral sciences at the University of Washington School of Medicine, who directed the Seattle study. "The effects on children occur even at the social drinking level. The women in our study did not see themselves as having alcohol problems."

'First Good Study'

Experts in the field see the two reports from the Seattle study as particularly significant.

"This is the first good study of the relationship between normal drinking levels in pregnant women and intellectual effects in their children," said Dr. Claire D. Coles, a psychologist at the Human Behavior Genetic Research Laboratory at the Emory University Medical School in Atlanta. Dr. Coles is conducting similar research but is not involved in the Seattle study.

The Seattle researchers asked the 491 pregnant women in their study about drinking, smoking, the use of marijuana; as well as the use of aspirin, caffeine and other substances. Their children have been assessed regularly since the initial interviews.

The latest findings, which detected the differences on intelligence tests, were reported in the February 1989 issue of *Developmental Psychology*. The findings on attention levels were published in 1987 in the journal *Neurobehavioral Toxicology and Teratology*. (Teratology is the study of substances that can harm the development of a fetus.)

Individual Effects

Not all children whose mothers drank had problems. The study found that while there is a strong relationship on average between a mother's drinking while pregnant and deleterious effects on a child's intellectual development, there is no certainty that a given child will show the effects.

"The effects vary greatly in individual cases," Dr. Streissguth said. "There are many children who were exposed to alcohol who were not affected at all."

But of all the substances thought to have ill effects on children, the studies indicated that alcohol had a more severe impact than tobacco, caffeine, aspirin or marijuana.

"The worst effects by far were from alcohol," said Helen Barr, a statistician in the Department of Psychiatry and Behavioral Science at the Medical School of the University of Washington, and one of the study's co-authors.

Question of Smoking

The findings call into question earlier studies that seemed to show impaired cognitive development in children born to mothers who smoked. The researchers said those studies failed to take into account the effects of the mother's drinking, which they said was a serious mistake, since mothers who smoke also tended to drink.

The report noted that some of the heaviest drinkers in the study, and thus the mothers of the children most at risk, were the most highly educated professionals.

"Many career women seem to assume the drinking habits of professional men—a few glasses of wine at dinner, some drinks over lunch or at a cocktail party," Dr. Streissguth said.

The least educated women in the study were among the heaviest drinkers, the researchers said.

Studies with animals have shown that alcohol crosses the placenta and can interfere with the normal development of the embryo's nervous system. Still, the effects detected in the study were relatively subtle in comparison with the effects of fetal alcohol syndrome, in which flawed physical growth accompanies mental impairment. In the study, ten children had the syndrome which occurs in some children of alcoholic mothers. On the Intelligence tests, their scores were more than 15 points lower, on average, than the other children in the study, but their results were excluded from the final sample.

Stopping at Four Weeks

Average alcohol consumption for all women in the Seattle study was one drink a day until they knew they were pregnant, and half a drink a day afterward.

Many of the mothers in the study stopped drinking when they found out they were pregnant, but that was typically not until four to six weeks into the pregnancy, Dr. Barr said.

The negative effects of alcohol on the children still prevailed when the women stopped or sharply reduced their level of drinking after learning they were pregnant. The effects were stronger for alcohol use in the first month or two of pregnancy, than for drinking afterward, a result supported by other research.

New Research Overturns a Milestone of Infancy

June 6, 1989

For years it was considered a mark of healthy development for infants at around nine months of age to show distress at the presence of a stranger. Indeed, the dogma that "stranger anxiety" is a major milestone in an infant's emotional growth is still espoused in most books of advice for parents, and in many textbooks on child psychology.

But now developmental psychologists have concluded from recent research that whether an infant cries or not when a parent leaves or a stranger appears is determined by its temperament, not its level of emotional security. Some babies who cry in that situation may be emotionally healthy, while others may not.

The best measure of emotional health in an infant, many experts now say, is the day-to-day rapport between baby and parents, not the degree of anxiety when meeting strangers.

"Many infants who are quite healthy emotionally don't have stranger anxiety at all," said Stanley Greenspan, a psychiatrist who specializes in treating infants, and a clinical professor at George Washington University Medical School in Washington. "Indeed, stranger anxiety, if extreme enough, can be a sign of problems, not healthy adaptation."

Jay Belsky, a developmental psychologist at Pennsylvania State University, said that only in the last five years have a majority of experts "begun to acknowledge that it's totally misguided to see such anxiety as a sign of security."

The widely held if paradoxical belief that a baby's anxiety over strangers or separation from parents is a sign of emotional security followed from the pioneering work in the 1950's of John Bowlby, a British psychoanalyst, and others who studied the bonds between infants and their parents. It was thought that at around seven to ten months of age stranger anxiety was a positive developmental step, a first indication that the infant could distinguish familiar from unfamiliar people. Such anxiety was also taken as an indirect sign of the depth of attachment the infant had formed with his or her parents.

Studies in orphanages had shown that infants raised there, who were presumed to be emotionally insecure because of lack of caring attention from an adult, often reached out to be held by any stranger, while children who were brought up in secure homes were more likely to show fear of strangers.

The most recent, and strongest, evidence against that view was published in the May issue of *The Journal of Abnormal Psychology*. The small but illuminating study was conducted by Richard Davidson, a psychologist at the University of Wisconsin, and Nathan A. Fox, a developmental psychologist at the Institute for Child Study at the University of Maryland.

They analyzed the brain-wave patterns of thirteen infants, ten months of age, and found marked differences between those who later cried when their mothers left the room and those who did not. Those who cried tended to have far more brain-wave activity on the right front side of their brain than on the left even before their mothers left the room. Those who did not cry tended to have the reverse pattern.

Negative and Positive Emotions

In other studies, Dr. Davidson has determined that activity in the right frontal area of the brain is associated with negative emotions like fear, while activity in the left frontal area is found during positive emotions like joy. They have observed these effects in infants as young as three days old.

In the new study, the brain activity was measured by a special cap, containing electronic sensors, that the infants wore while they sat at a feeding table. Their mothers then left the room. All but one of the infants who cried when their mothers went out of the room had much stronger activity on the right side, the seat of negative emotions, than the left. And every one of those who did not cry had stronger activity on the left side. The results strongly suggest that whether or not a baby cries in this situation is largely a matter of the baby's temperament.

In unpublished research done with Jerome Kagan, a psychologist at Harvard University, Dr. Davidson found that three-year-olds who are inhibited and fearful had the same pattern of higher brain activation in the right frontal region as did the younger infants who cried when their mothers left the room. The research suggested that the pattern of brain activity was a sign of temperament, which shows up in different ways at different ages.

Experts on child development now say that security in infants is not measured by whether they get upset when confronted with a stranger but rather by whether they are able to find solace and be soothed after becoming upset. The baby's capacity to be consoled has been studied in a test called the "strange situation," developed by Mary Ainsworth, a developmental psychologist at the University of Virginia.

Managing the Temperament

The test involves observations of an infant as a stranger enters the room and as the baby's mother leaves for three minutes and then returns. Of particular significance is what the infant does when the mother returns, whether or not the infant cried in her absence.

"The secure babies are able to find solace in their mother's arms when she returns if they were upset when she left, or give her a greeting that shows they're glad she's back if they weren't distressed," Dr. Belsky said. "The insecure ones, though, either stay upset and resist comforting if they were upset by her leaving, or avoid or ignore her if they didn't get upset."

He added, "It's babies' innate level of emotionality that dictates whether a child cries or not. A kid with an emotional temperament may still be secure. Security has to do with how well they manage that predisposition."

Infants who are insecure are un-able to find solace, even in their mother's arms, Dr. Belsky's research has found.

The key to emotional security lies in the rapport between parents and their infants, experts say. In a study published in the April issue of *Developmental Psychology,* conducted with Russell A. Isabella of Utah State University, Dr. Belsky found that certain kinds of interactions between mothers and infants were more likely to make the infants insecure, while others built a sense of security.

The researchers observed infants interacting with their mothers at home when the infants were one month, three months, and nine months of age. Then, at one year, the infants and mothers were observed during the "strange situation" test.

Overstimulating and Intrusive

Mothers of infants who were secure in the strange situation test at one year were found to have been highly responsive to their infants in the earlier home observations. For instance, if the infant made some sound, the mother would make a similar sound back; if the infant cried the mother would soothe it.

But mothers of infants who ig-nored attempts to console them had behaved differently during the observations at home. Many of these mothers seemed to overwhelm their infants; they were overstimulating and intrusive. They would talk incessantly to their babies, no matter what the baby was doing, crying, looking around, or even sleeping. Oddly, the one thing these mothers responded to the least was the sounds the baby actually made.

Anger or resistance to a mother's attempts to console the infant was associated with interactions at home in which the mothers were relatively indifferent to their baby's needs. These mothers, for instance, tended to make minimal responses to their baby's cries, or to ignore them. Though the studies were done with mothers, experts say the results could equally apply to fathers or other care takers.

"The establishment of a sense of security begins in the first months of life, in the baby's ability to use its parents to calm down," Dr. Greenspan said. "The best sign that a baby is developing security is that the baby and its parents have well-attuned interactions, no matter what the emotion, whether it's fear, anger, curiosity, or joy. The baby does something and the parent responds accordingly, and the baby closes the circle by responding to that."

Child Development Theory Stresses Small Moments

October 21, 1986

Children's personalities are shaped more by everyday interactions with parents than by dramatic events or major developmental stages, according to a new theory that has gained widespread adherence but has also stirred bitter debate.

Assailing some of the most revered ideas in behavioral science, the theory asserts that there are no critical phases in a child's life—the oral and anal periods of psychoanalysis, for example—but rather a long continuum of important moments.

An infant discovers the first inkling of autonomy, according to the new thinking, from small acts of assertion. At four months of age it averts its eyes; at about twelve months it can walk away and at eighteen months it says, "No."

All of these are acts of will, each given a different flavor by the natural development of the central nervous system. As this evolution goes on, there is a drumbeat of self affirmation that creates the sense in a child's mind that he or she is an individual with a will.

It is a development that can be stymied or skewed, however, by parents or other adults whose own needs thwart a child's normal urge for independence. It will happen continually, quickly and in ways so small that it is not realized. The mother who always insists on meeting her child's gaze even when he turns away, for instance, is engaged in a subtle battle of wills.

That kind of battle has been witnessed in rigorous scientific studies by Daniel Stern, a psychiatrist at Cornell Medical School, and by other psychoanalytic researchers. But Dr. Stern draws the most far-reaching conclu-

sions and poses the deepest challenge to established psychoanalytic thought and practice.

Dr. Stern has videotaped newborn infants and their mothers during their normal activities, filming them periodically for about two years. While Dr. Stern's work has focused on mothers and their infants, he said he believed it applies as well to fathers and infants or anyone else who spends prolonged periods caring for a small child.

There is a danger that Dr. Stern's work will unduly alarm mothers. "What matters most about a baby's caretakers, whether the mother or someone else, is that they love the baby, are reasonably relaxed, and generally sensitive," said Paula Caplan, director of the Centre for Women's Studies in Education at the University of Toronto. Dr. Caplan has studied the tendency of some psychological theories to blame mothers for problems of their children.

Dr. Stern's results show the importance of the countless small exchanges of daily life between mother and child for shaping the child's pattern of interaction in later relationships in life. For instance, in a typical study, Dr. Stern videotaped all the activity between a twenty-five-year-old mother and her twin sons, Mark and Fred, in periodic three-hour sessions until they were fifteen months. The films of the mother and her twins were exhaustively analyzed.

The results were telling. At three-and-a-half months there were repeated exchanges in which the mother and Fred would gaze at each other. Fred would avert his face, his mother would respond by trying to engage eye contact again and Fred

would respond with a more exaggerated aversion of his face. As soon as the mother looked away, though, Fred would look back at her, and the cycle would begin all over, until Fred was in tears.

With Mark, the other twin, the mother virtually never tried to forced continued eye contact. Mark could end contact with his mother when he wanted. According to Dr. Stern, when the infants were seen at twelve to fifteen months, Fred seemed notably more fearful and dependent than Mark, and often used the same aversion of his face he had used with his mother to break off contact with other people. Mark, on the other hand, greeted people openly, looked them straight in the eye; to break eye contact, instead of turning his face down and away, Mark would turn his head slightly to the side and up, with a winning smile still visible.

Cases such as these, in Dr. Stern's view, raise the question of whether a temperamental mismatch between infant and mother may lead to problems such as Fred's. He has also found that a mother's hidden beliefs and fantasies about her children can shape her relationship with the infant; in this case, the mother felt Mark was "more like herself" and Fred "more like father."

Dr. Stern believes infants learn extremely powerful lessons from these continually repeated interactions. "These small moments, rather than the traumatic or dramatic moments of a baby's life, make up the bulk of the expectations that adults bring to their relationships," he said.

Of special importance, Dr. Stern believes, is a sort of attunement in which mothers somehow let their infants know they have a sense of the infants' feelings. If a baby squeals in delight, for instance, the mother might give the baby a gentle shake. In that interaction—which mothers and infants go through about once a minute while actively engaged with each other—the main message is in the mother's more or less matching the baby's level of excitement.

"If you just imitate a baby, that only shows you know what he did, not how he felt," said Dr. Stern. "To let him know you sense how he feels, you have to play back his inner feelings in another way. Then the baby knows he is understood."

The pattern of an infant's lifelong social relationships begins with such simple encounters, though that pattern can change later in life. Dr. Stern's theory holds that it is from these attunements that an infant begins to develop its "subjective self," a sense that other people can and will share in its feelings. This aspect of the personality begins to emerge at around eight months, and will continue to develop throughout life, according to Dr. Stern. In the same way, other aspects of the sense of self—such as the sense of having a personal history, and of being independent—first emerge in the earliest months of life and grow through the lifespan.

Attunements can be as subtle as a mother matching the pitch of her voice to her baby's squeal, or as obvious as her giving a quick shimmy in response to his shaking a rattle. In Dr. Stern's view, they give an infant the deeply reassuring sense of being emotionally connected to someone else.

An infant will not overtly acknowledge that feeling of being connected, Dr. Stern says, but will often respond to its absence. In one experiment, he had mothers purposely over- or under-respond to their infants, rather than matching them in an attuned way. When they did, the baby's reacted with surprise or dismay. "The infants would stop and look around as though to ask, what was that about?" Dr. Stern said.

When parents consistently fail to match the child in this way, it affects the child's development, Dr. Stern finds. With one mother who continu-

ally undermatched her baby's level of activity, he found, the baby eventually learned to be passive. "An infant treated that way learns, when I get excited, I can't get my mother to be equally excited, so I may as well not try at all," said Dr. Stern.

The psychological imprints of these early encounters, Dr. Stern believes, are not irrevocably set. "Relationships throughout life—with friends or relatives, for example—or in psychotherapy continually reshape your working model of relationships," he said. "An imbalance at one point can be corrected later, there is no crucial period early in life—it's an on-going, life-long process."

"There is no data yet that shows any grave effects for a child who has a non-attuned mother," said Jerome Cagan, a developmental psychologist at Harvard. "Many mothers are away from their infants and toddlers much of the day, and the children seem to turn out just fine."

Dr. Stern's work is part of a broad effort by psychoanalytic researchers to study infants and children directly. Unlike other researchers, Dr. Stern has used his findings to mount a vigorous challenge to basic tenets of psychoanalytic thought.

"Our findings, like Dr. Stern's, put some psychoanalytic theories in question," said Robert Emde, a psychoanalyst who is studying infants at the University of Colorado School of Medicine in Denver. "But Dr. Stern goes much further in the implications he draws."

"My research questions more clinical assumptions than it confirms," Dr. Stern said. One of the main psychoanalytic views challenged by his research is that psychological growth, as Dr. Stern puts it, "is a parade of specific epochs, in which each of the most basic clinical issues of life passes by in its own separate turn. They do not."

One of the direct implications for psychotherapy from Dr. Stern's work is that there need be no single event in childhood that is the source of a psychological problem in adulthood. "One beauty of psychoanalytic theory was that when you saw a specific symptom in a patient, you had an idea of where in his development the prob-

lem began, and so knew more or less where psychoanalytic enquiry should move back to," Dr. Stern said. "I'm saying you do not know; the problem could have developed right along, from day one, as an accretion of small episodes not from some critical incident."

Even though Dr. Stern rejects the stages assumed in psychoanalytic theories, he does find that there are discrete phase in development. "There is no question that a baby goes through leaps in development," he said. "With some variation in exact timing, you see a striking change at about six to eight weeks, another at five to six months, one at the end of the first year, another around eighteen months." But these changes, Dr. Stern believes, are signs of dramatic shifts in the child's nervous system, which continues to develop throughout childhood, rather than markers of the psychological phases that have often been linked to them.

The predominance of a specific psychological issue—such as trust or autonomy—at a particular phase in an infant's life "is in the eye of the beholder, not in the infant's experience," Dr. Stern writes in *The Interpersonal World of the Infant* (Basic Books). The book Dr. Stern's first full statement of his findings and their implications, has caused a major controversy among psychoanalysts and developmental psychologists. The journal *Contemporary Psychoanalysis* will devote an issue to comments by Dr. Stern's detractors and defenders alike.

Among those whose objections to Dr. Stern's views will be printed in the journal are Louise Kaplan, a psychologist and a follower of the late Margaret Mahler, an influential pioneer in pyschoanalytic research on infants. Dr. Stern has contested parts of Dr. Mahler's theory, particularly her notion that young infants go through an "autistic" stage, and that they begin life psychologically merged with their mothers and need to separate from her.

In Dr. Kaplan's view, the alternate theories proposed by Dr. Stern are "unverified hypotheses" that "when scrutinized turn out to be unsupported by the research."

Among those psychoanalysts who

have been more receptive to Dr. Stern's views are adherents of the theories of Heinz Kohut, who emphasized the importance of the self and Harry Stack Sullivan, who emphasized interpersonal relationships. Followers of these theorists see some confirmation of their views in Dr. Stern's work.

Stanley Spiegel, a psychologist at the William Alanson White Institute in New York, said that Dr. Stern's book "will clearly be the book of the decade in its influence on psychoanalytic theory."

What Do Children Fear Most? Their Answers Are Surprising

March 17, 1988

Children have a more finely tuned sense of pride than most adults realize, recent studies indicate.

For children fear of being humiliated far outranks many concerns that adults assume they are most troubled by, like the birth of a sibling or having an operation. Children also say they are disturbed by incidents that would make them seem "bad." Among their biggest concerns are being caught stealing or being sent to the school principal's office.

This glimpse into the children's world serves notice to adults to be more aware of how easily a child is mortified. And it may give pause to parents who, failing to respect or understand children's feelings, may drag them into painful situations.

Adults, recalling their own childhoods as well as the received wisdom from experts, presume to know what troubles a child. But rarely has anyone systematically asked children just what they think is most troubling about their lives.

'We Don't Really See or Hear'

"We all think we know our own children, but all too often we don't really see or hear, nor understand, what is really troubling them," said Kaoru Yamamoto, a psychologist at the University of Colorado School of Education, who has done the main research on child perceptions of stress.

The latest study, published in the current issue of the *Journal of Child Psychology and Psychiatry*, involved surveys of 1,814 children in grades three through nine in six countries: the United States, Australia, Canada, Egypt, Japan and the Philippines. Children were asked to rate the stressfulness of common experiences.

One surprising finding, researchers said, is that children share similar fears and concerns, even across national boundaries. The researchers had not expected these concerns to transcend cultural differences.

In an earlier study, Dr. Yamamoto provided experimental evidence for the gap in adult and children's views. The survey asked adults and children to rank twenty events and to assess the stressfulness of each on a scale of one to seven. Not only did the adults' rankings differ sharply from the children's, but also the intensity of stress varied sharply for many of the events.

School Life and Peers

In general, the children's ratings pointed to the emotional prominence of school life and peer opinions in their world. While family life offers a child a basic sense of security, experts say, school and peer life also shape a child's perception of accomplishment and personal worth.

One of the sharpest differences between adults and children was in how traumatic they felt it was for a child to have a new sibling. Both clinical wisdom and most children's therapists rate a new baby in the family as one of the most stressful events in a child's life. The children, however, rated having a new brother or sister as the least troubling of the twenty events.

It is quite probable that a child asked about a hypothetical sibling would not realize the mix of emotions the actual birth of a baby might evoke. But the study points to the child's sense of what is troubling, rather than how events may actually affect him.

From the children's point of view, the possibility most haunting them, after a parent's death, was going blind. Other particularly troubling events in their view included being kept back a grade, wetting their pants in class and seeing their parents fight.

Emerging Sense of Worth

The survey results underscore how an embarrassment or humiliation can be an especially stinging blow to a child's emerging sense of worth.

"One of the most common triggers of suicide in children and teens in a humiliating experience, like getting caught stealing," said Ann Epstein, a child psychiatrist at Harvard Medical School.

"A child's self-image is forming continually, and is very shaky," Dr. Epstein added. "They tend to blow some things up out of all proportion. And their sense of guilt is much stronger and more moralistic than in adults. So the idea of getting caught doing something bad, in the child's mind, may mean to them that they will always be seen as bad, or if they're embarrassed, that they'll never attain their dignity again."

"These injuries to self-esteem, in their minds, can come to define their whole identity," she observed.

Dr. Yamamoto's findings suggest that many seemingly trivial moments in a child's life, such as being sent to the principal, may loom among the more daunting, and that parents, teachers and even child counselors, are likely to miss their emotional importance for the child.

Fears and Perceptions of Fears

For his research on a child's fears and adult perception of those fears, Dr. Yamamoto asked 39 child experts, 97 teachers and 61 college students to rate the stressfulness for a child of the same events the children had rated. The experts included social workers, school psychologists, and special education teachers. The research, conducted in the United States, was published in *Psychological Reports*.

The adults, like the children, showed a strong unanimity in their judgments. But while adults tended to agree, there were major discrepancies between their views of what events would most trouble children and what the children said. Indeed, the experts were no better than the college students in gauging children's reactions.

The adults were accurate about the impact of some things, such as the death of a parent. But there was a major difference between the adults and children on the impact of sixteen of the twenty items. The events that adults took too lightly included receiving a bad report card and witnessing parents quarrel. On the other hand, the adults exaggerated the trauma for children of such things as going to a dentist.

"Through the school years, many children don't have the ability to make many of their true feelings known to parents, or they are too reluctant," Dr. Yamamoto said. "And the younger they are, the harder it is to present their case."

For the parent who wants to understand better what might be troubling a child, researchers recommend making a specific effort to let the child be heard, something many parents do not take the time to do.

"Parents too quickly impose what they think is going on in the child's mind, and make a snap decision about what's best for them," said Dr. Robert Coles, a child psychiatrist at Harvard University, whose research involves interviewing children at length. "You've got to pause to hear what the child really is seeing and feeling."

"Kids will tell you how they're bearing up, if you make the effort to pay attention," Dr. Coles added. "But you've got to be patient with the fact that there is a difference between grown-ups and kids in frame of reference, how they use language, and the way the mind works. You've got to suspend your interpretive zeal for a few moments."

Thriving Despite Hardship: Key Childhood Traits Identified

October 13, 1987

A woman, a paranoid schizophrenic, ate all her meals in restaurants because she was convinced someone was poisoning her food at home. Her twelve-year-old daughter developed the same fears and likewise ate in restaurants. Her ten-year-old daughter would eat at home if her father was there, but otherwise went along with her mother.

But the woman's seven-year-old son always ate at home.

When a psychiatrist asked the boy why, he said with a shrug, "Well, I'm not dead yet."

After several years, the older daughter developed paranoid schizophrenia like her mother. The younger daughter, while sharing some of her mother's fears, managed to go to college and adjust fairly well to life. But the son went on to perform brilliantly in college and in his adult life.

The young boy is one of a group of children who are holding an increasing fascination for experts on child development; brought up under the most chaotic, abusive or impoverished circumstances, they go on to thrive. The data on how they thrive have been growing, becoming more specific and offering a cohesive picture of children who had been the most baffling of enigmas.

There is no single set of qualities or circumstances that charactizes all such resilient children. But psychologists are finding that they stand apart from their more vulnerable siblings, almost from birth. They seem to be endowed with innate characteristics that insulate them from the turmoil and pain of their families and allow them to reach out to some adult—a grandparent, teacher or family friend—who can lend crucial emotional support.

Grinding hardship will leave even these children with psychological scars. But by and large they are able to thrive in circumstances that leave other children emotionally disabled.

"Such children flourish despite horrendous conditions," said E. James Anthony, a psychiatrist at Chestnut Lodge Hospital in Rockville, Maryland, who interviewed the self-confident young boy.

Research by Dr. Anthony and other scientists is creating a composite view of trajectories resilient and vulnerable children seem to follow.

Some of the most recent findings on the lifelong attributes of resilient children are from a study of nearly 700 children born in 1955 on the Hawaiian island of Kauai. All the children were born to impoverished families whose parents worked on sugar and pineapple plantations. One parent, and sometimes both, was alcoholic or mentally ill, and, to add to the difficulties, the children themselves suffered a trauma at birth, such as oxygen deprivation or forceps delivery.

Each of these factors increases the odds against a child's emotional adjustment. And, over the years, many of the children have shown signs of psychological disturbance. But about one in ten not only could withstand the difficulties, but also developed exceptionally well.

Substitute Parent

In findings reported last July in Tokyo at the International Society for the Study of Behavioral Development, data from the first thirty years of the children's life highlighted the impor-

tance of their ability to find someone who could help them face the world with trust.

"Without exception, all the children who thrived had at least one person that provided them consistent emotional support—a grandmother, an older sister, a teacher or neighbor," said Emmy Werner, a psychologist at the University of California at Davis, who directs the study. "These are kids who are good at recruiting a substitute parent who is a good model for them."

In interviews when they were thirty years old, many of the resilient children could recall a teacher from as early as the first grade who acted as a mentor, giving them a sense that they could achieve despite the difficulties of their childhood.

"The absence of a supporting adult in a child's life is seen over and over in a range of problems, from delinquency and drug abuse to teen suicide," said Norman Garmezy, a psychologist at the University of Minnesota, who has been at the forefront of the new research. Dr. Garmezy leads a network of research projects at different universities, financed by the MacArthur Foundation, which are studying the factors that project children or put them at risk.

Special Interests or Talents

In addition to a winning sociability that drew people to them, most of the resilient children in the Hawaii study also had a talent or special interest that absorbed them and gave them a feeling of confidence.

"They were able to use whatever skills they had well, even if they were not terribly bright," Dr. Werner said. "For some it was simply being good at swimming or dance, for others being able to raise prize-winning animals. But these activities offered them solace when things got tough."

By age thirty, the resilient children had gotten more education and reached higher economic levels than others in the study, Dr Werner said. Among them were an architect, a district attorney and a composer.

Another study of children from deprived and troubled homes, by J. Kirk Felsman and George E. Vaillant, psychiatrists at the Dartmouth Medical School, tracked 456 men from early adolescence into middle age. It found that the more successful adults were set apart by industriousness and organization in early adolescence. Sometimes this meant working in a part-time job, taking on major chores at home or being intensely involved with a school club or team.

'Ability to Bounce Back'

As younger children, they showed a dogged persistence in the face of failure. "You can see their ability to bounce back in simple tasks, like building a tower with blocks," Dr. Anthony said "A less resilient child will stop when the tower falls, or not try to build it very high. But the resilient child keeps going each time it falls."

Some children have protective traits virtually from the beginning of life, according to Ellen Farber, a psychologist at the State University of New York at Buffalo, and Byron Egeland, a psychologist at the University of Minnesota. Their findings appear in *The Invulnerable Child,* published last month by Guilford Press.

At birth, they found, the resilient children were more alert and interested in their surroundings than the others. At the age of one, the children had a secure and warm relationship with their mothers, an experience researchers believe may be particularly important in helping them recover from abuse in later life, even when that abuse comes from the mother.

Independence and Enthusiasm

By the age of two, the more resilient toddlers—most of whom were suffering abuse or neglect—were nevertheless marked by a comparatively high degree of independence, an easygoing compliance, enthusiasm and a high tolerance for frustration. And by three and one-half, these children were more cheerful, flexible and persistent than the others.

Perhaps most significantly, they also showed a clear ability to seek help from adults.

A major difference between abused children who, as parents, abuse their own children and those who do not is that those who do not perpetuate the cycle of abuse had a supportive relationship with the nonabusing parent, according to Joan Kaufman and Edward Zigler, psychologists at Yale who published their findings in an article in the *American Journal of Orthopsychiatry.*

One of the first efforts to identify the qualities that set resilient children apart was begun at the Menninger Foundation in Topeka in the 1950's. The project focused on examining the ways children handled stresses—a divorce, a move, the illness of a parent—as they grew. Among the key traits of the more resilient children identified in that study was the ability to recover quickly from upsets, said Lois Barclay Murphy, a psychologist at the Menninger Foundation.

Being easygoing, which makes children less likely to become upset, may also protect some children because it keeps them from being a target of their parent's anger. Michael Rutter, a psychiatrist at the Institute of Psychiatry in London, writing in a recent issue of the *American Journal of Orthopsychiatry,* notes that children with difficult temperaments are more likely to become a parent's scapegoat than their more cheerful and malleable siblings.

Dr. Rutter, one of the pioneers of research on resilient children, also reports data suggesting that, in late adolescence, the more successful children tend to plan rather than make snap decisions.

One trait that seems to buffer chil-

dren from their parents' troubles is the ability to create an emotional distance. "A parent's stresses can be transmitted to the children," said Lawrence Fisher, a psychologist at the University of California at San Francisco.

"Those children who are closest emotionally to a distressed parent are the most likely to show signs of distress themselves. They will be more self-derogatory, anxious or depressed, or have physical symptoms" than their siblings who are more distant from the disturbed parent.

A similar finding emerged from a study by Dr. Anthony of the Chestnut Lodge Hospital of "superadjusted" children of psychotic parents. These children were able to maintain an emotional distance from their parents, while finding another adult—often a teacher—to provide emotional support.

Still, even resilient children may pay a subtle psychological cost for their deprived or abusive family life. In a study of children of psychiatric patients, researchers at the University of Rochester found that by late adolescence one group of children who ostensibly had adjusted well seemed to cling to a moralistic outlook.

"From a distance these kids look good, but up close, in their intimate relations, you find they are disagreeable and judgmental," said Lyman Wynne, a psychiatrist at the University of Rochester. "They put down their siblings who are not doing as well, but they themselves are constricted and overcontrolled. Their normality is based on being uptight straightshooters."

Another kind of psychological price for thriving was found by Dr. Anthony. As young adults, the resilient children of psychotic parents—particularly when the disturbed parent was of the opposite sex—often brought an emotional distance into their intimate relationships. Many had a history of breaking off relationships at the first hint of closeness. Others sought partners with problems and then dedicated themselves to helping them. Still others threw themselves into consuming projects that required cooperation, but at a comfortable emotional distance.

Spacing of Siblings Strongly Linked to Success in Life

May 28, 1985

Scientific interest in the effects of birth order on later development, an interest that has fallen in and out of vogue several times in the last few decades, seems to be coming back again with a rush.

Early findings showed that firstborns and only children had a higher proportion of successes in later life and that they tended to have higher I.Q.'s than later-born children have. Firstborns and only children were also shown to be overrepresented in such groups as those listed in "Who's Who," astronauts and students in graduate and professional schools. Critics have maintained that the birth-order effect has been exaggerated and is more ephemeral than its supporters suggest.

The new inquiries tend to affirm much of the earlier work, but they also significantly modify those findings. For instance, some data show that the amount of time between births in a family has perhaps as much to do with the development of a child as does that child's place in the order of births.

Testifying to the new ferment in this field were the papers presented at the annual of meeting of the American Association for the Advancement of Science in Los Angeles, each addressing a small piece of this large area of inquiry.

One report was delivered by Judith Blake, a professor of population in the department of public health and sociology at the University of California at Los Angeles. She found that an only child is likely to get three years more schooling than a child from a family of six, and thus was likely to find greater success in later life. She said that this was only partly due to

financial factors. She found that many of the later-borns drop out of high school without finishing. Families with two children, for example, have a proportion of high school graduates about twice that of families with seven or more children.

In a related paper given at the meeting it was predicted that American children's performance on such tests of intellectual achievement as the Scholastic Aptitude Test should rise significantly for the rest of this century, and then gradually decline again. The theory, put forward by Robert Zajonc, a psychologist at the University of Michigan, holds, in brief, that the greater the number of children in a family and the shorter the time between their births, the lower will be the intelligence of the children, particularly those born later.

Because of the trend toward smaller American families in the 1960's and 1970's, Dr. Zajonc predicts that the rise in S.A.T. scores that began in 1980 will continue for about 18 more years. But a more recent trend toward larger families would begin to lower the scores around the turn of the century, Dr. Zajonc said.

But Dr. Zajonc added, "The rise and fall may follow the curve of family size, but how much they rise and fall depends on how much better we educate our youth. There are many factors which affect the S.A.T. This is one that can be measured." Dr. Zajonc's report pointed to an area of investigation that has been given increasing weight in recent years. It focuses on the lifelong consequences of the spacing between children in a family. The research suggests that there are advantages to spacing chil-

dren within a year or so of each other on the one hand, or five years or more apart on the other, instead of the more popular two- to three-year gap.

There were marked differences, however, in the interpretations of data. Dr. Blake said, "The advantages of coming from a small family are gigantic—by that I mean two or three children."

Dr. Zajonc said, "I would not advocate any pattern of spacing of children because many other factors are completely unknown."

"Parents just don't have good information on how the spacing of births and numbers of children are likely to affect their children in the long run," said David Heer, a sociologist at the Population Research Laboratory at the University of Southern California.

Although most studies have failed to take it into account, the spacing between the births of children can override many psychological effects from the child's birth order, according to research by Jeannie Kidwell, a psychologist at the University of Tennessee.

In a national survey of more than 1,700 teen-age boys, for example, Dr. Kidwell found that children had a more negative view of themselves and their parents when their closest siblings were around two years apart. However, if the space between siblings is under one year or over four years, the negativity disappeared.

For children born within about a year of each other, the older child does not seem to experience a "dethronement" from being the parents' sole focus, according to Dr. Kidwell. Such children seem to feel that they have always had to share their parents' time with a sibling with almost identical needs, and so they do not feel the intense resentment toward the younger sibling that firstborns often display. However, if the firstborn has reached the age of two by the time the younger child is born, those feelings of resentment are more likely to emerge.

Research at Colorado State University, for example, has found that for firstborns, having a younger sibling born two or more years later dealt the older child a blow to its self-esteem, while having a sibling born less than two years later did not have that effect.

The Colorado group proposes that this may be so because a child raised alone is privy to all his parents nurturance and affection. The longer a child has to get used to this relationship, the more negatively he will experience the birth of a younger sibling. However, if the child has reached the beginnings of independence at the age of 5 or 6, the birth of a younger sibling no longer seems to have the same psycholgocal impact.

Moreover, observational studies of mothers and infants have found that if four years or more have passed since the birth of the last child, a mother is more likely to treat a new infant with the special care and attention she lavished on her firstborn.

Children born about two years apart, Dr. Kidwell points out, are likely to have the most intense competition for parental attention, throughout their lives.

"A spacing of about five years is apparently optimal," Dr. Kidwell said. "It frees the parent from having to meet the demands and pressures of two children close together in age, thus allowing parents and children more time in one-to-one interaction for a more supportive and relaxed relationship."

The importance of spacing can be seen in findings on the self-esteem of middle-borns, a group that has also been neglected in the research on birth order. Dr. Kidwell has found that, at least in adolescence, children who fall in the middle ranks of three or more siblings tend to have poorer self-esteem than do both their older and younger siblings.

In addition, Dr. Kidwell said, "The middle-born believes his parents are more punitive and less loving toward him than to his older and younger siblings."

It is not that parents actually behave that way toward their middle children, in Dr. Kidwell's view, but that circumstances—particularly the intensity of competition between siblings and the strain on parents to meet the demands of several children—tend to make those children perceive that to be the case.

These feelings in middle-borns are strongest, she finds, when the spacing between siblings is about two or three years. When the spacing is greater than four years or less than two the effect is minimal, often disappearing altogether.

The middle-born's feelings of self-esteem also vary with the sex of the sibling. For boys, having a brother makes the lowered self-esteem worse, while having sisters seems to have a positive effect. Dr. Kidwell proposes that this is because the feeling of being special enhances self-esteem in children, and so being the only male qualifies the child as being unique and valued.

How similar are only children and firstborns? The new research focuses on some significant ways in which they differ.

The idea that there should be such a difference dates back to the ideas of the psychiatrist Alfred Adler in the early decades of the century. According to Adlerian theory, the firstborn, as an only child, feels in a privileged position by virtue of being the sole focus of parental attention. With the birth of a younger sibling, however, the older child is deprived of that attention.

Direct observations of mothers and their children, have found that the small drama of "dethronement" of the firstborn is, perhaps inevitably, the case. With the birth of the second child, there is a drop in the amount of time the mother talks with and plays with the firstborn, and an increase in the frequency of her setting limits and disciplining him.

The firstborn child, in turn, becomes more demanding and negative toward the mother, and has more problems, such as in eating and sleeping.

Since an only child does not experience this dethronement or the other experiences that having a sibling brings there are clear psychological differences between them and children who have a sibling, according to findings reported in *The Single Child Family* (Guilford Press). "There is no real evidence that only children are at a psychological disadvantage, despite the stereotypes to the contrary," according to Toni Falbo, a psychologist at the University of Texas, who edited the volume.

In a review of more than 200 studies Dr. Falbo found that the evidence strongly suggests that only children, in comparison to those raised with one or more sibling, tend to be more intelligent in childhood, show more autonomy and psychological maturity by college age, and attain higher incomes and more occupational prestige in adulthood.

Other research, however, is revealing some less positive commonalities between only children and the youngest in large famiies. One theory that such children are reared in a more permissive fashion than others has been indirectly supported by a study of alcoholics by James Conley, a psychologist at Wesleyan University.

In a study of close to 5,000 adult alcoholics and nonalcoholics Dr. Conley found that there were disproportionate numbers of only children and last-borns from large families among the alcoholics, and that their upbringing seemed particularly permissive. In Dr. Conley's view, the increased susceptibility to alcoholism among these groups may be due to the traits of dependence and impulsivity that a permissive upbringing fosters.

Dr. Conley, who has done several large studies of the effects of birth order, has also proposed an original, though highly speculative, explanation for the superiorior achievement of firstborns and only children. In his view, it is related to a biological difference found in primates and other mammals, which suggests that the firstborn is prepared by nature for a more difficultl birth and a less experienced mother than are subsequent siblings.

"The uterus puts much greater pressure on a firstborn's head than it does on later-borns," according to Dr. Conley. "And first deliveries are, on average, almost twice as long as later ones. There is evidence that the firstborn develops in a different biochemical environment than do later-borns. And after they are born, the firstborns of most primate species scream louder and more often than do later-borns. And there's a good reason. Even among rodents and primates, mothers take longer to respond to their firstborn than to their later offspring."

Depressed Parents Put Children at a Greater Risk of Depression

March 30, 1989

The first careful observations of normal encounters between seriously depressed parents and their children are leading researchers to conclude that the parents may treat their children in a way that will make them more susceptible to depression themselves as they grow up.

These parental attitudes, which include being highly critical or withdrawn, may lead to depression in the children apart from any genetic factors, the researchers believe. While some studies suggest that a tendency toward certain kinds of depression is inherited, researchers so far have been unable to distinguish how much of that is caused by family environment and how much by genes.

"The rates of depression in children of depressed parents are very high," said Myrna Weissman, a professor of epidemiology and psychiatry at Columbia University's Medical School. "There's about a threefold increase in risk."

Justin D. Call, chief of child and adolescent psychiatry at the Medical School of the University of California at Irvine, said, "A seriously depressed mother or father is not able to have an emotionally attuned, reciprocal engagement with anyone. That can have devastating effects on their children."

Ways to Cushion Children

By identifying difficulties in the way depressed parents treat their children, researchers hope to design ways to intervene that could cushion children from the impact of a parent's depression.

Typically, there are several specific problems with the interactions between depressed parents and children, said Marian Radke-Yarrow, chief of the Laboratory of Developmental Psychology at the National Institute of Mental Health, who has conducted much of the research on depressed parents and their children.

For the research, depressed parents and children are invited in pairs to a comfortable apartment designed so they can be observed unobtrusively. The parents and children spend half a day there, going through such normal activities as playing, making and eating lunch, and napping.

At the Society for Research in Child and Adolescent Psychopathology last month, Dr. Radke-Yarrow reported on one such study, which involved depressed mothers and their small children. She identified the main differences between life for a child in families where a parent is seriously depressed and those where there are no such problems. Among the differences were these:

- *Depressed mothers are more likely to back off when they meet resistance from children while trying to control them. The mothers seem uncertain and helpless, typical signs of depression.*

- *Depressed mothers were less able to compromise in disagreements with their children, and they often confused their children's normal attempts at independence as breaking rules.*

- *While making and eating lunch, the depressed mothers spoke to their children far less than did other mothers. The children of the depressed mothers also spoke infrequently.*

- *When the depressed mothers did speak to their children, they made more negative comments than did other mothers.*

While the research involved mothers and their children, the findings are thought to apply as well to depressed fathers.

Each of the patterns can have harmful effects on a child's emotional development.

Among the children who become depressed, those with depressed parents become so at an earlier age, on average, than the children whose parents are not depressed, according to a study by Dr. Weissman. They also have more frequent recurrence of episodes of depression, and are more impaired by their depression in school and in their social life.

Some of the most recent clues in the search to help the sons and daughters of depressed parents come from those children who seem to thrive against the odds. In a study to be published in the book *Risk and Protective Factors in the Development of Psychopathology* (Cambridge University Press), Dr. Radke-Yarrow reported on several children of depressed parents who were doing well despite their troubled family life.

One child was the daughter of a severely depressed mother who often reacted to the day's crises by staying in bed, and of a depressed, alcoholic father. The daughter herself was diagnosed as diabetic when she was six years old. By the age of nine, however, she was caring for her diabetes virtually on her own, said she was happy and was well-liked at school, where she excelled.

Traits of Resilient Children

Her secret? Apparently the daughter's resilience sprang from her seeking neighbors and other children to fill her social and emotional needs Dr. Radke-Yarrow said.

This girl, like other children of depressed parents, who nevertheless did well, shared certain traits. All of these resilient children "have winning smiles and are attractive charming and very socially engaging," Dr. Radke-Yarrow found.

The children's happy temperament in infancy often made them special favorites of their mothers, who were otherwise harried and depressed. Many of these children became confidants of their depressed parents early in life, which seems to have given them a social confidence and a feeling that there was something "good" or "special" about them.

By meeting their parents' emotional needs, Dr. Radke-Yarrow concludes that these children have "received as much of the family's scant social and emotional resources as the family can muster."

Empathy's Roots Traced to Infancy

March 28, 1989

On seeing another child fall and hurt himself, Hope, just nine months old, stared, tears welling up in her eyes, and crawled to her mother to be comforted—as though she had been hurt, not her friend. When fifteen-month-old Michael saw his friend Paul crying, Michael fetched his own teddy bear and offered it to Paul; when that didn't stop Paul's tears, Michael brought Paul's security blanket from another room.

Such small acts of sympathy and caring, observed in scientific studies, are leading researchers to trace the roots of empathy—the ability to share another's emotions—to infancy, contradicting a longstanding assumption that infants and toddlers were incapable of these feelings.

And in some of the most recent and surprising findings, researchers have identified individual neurons in primates that respond primarily to specific emotional expressions—a response that could be a neural basis for empathy. These findings are opening a new research area in which scientists are searching for the specific brain circuitry that underlies the empathic impulse.

The scientific interest is spurred, too, by the critical role of empathy in many facets of life, from management and sales to friendship and parenting, to compassion and moral awareness.

The absence of empathy is also telling. Its lack is seen not just in criminal sociopaths, who have no concern for their victims. A deficiency in empathy also marks disorders like autism and chronic schizophrenia, "where the impoverishment of skills like empathy is a major deficit," said Leslie Brothers, a psychiatrist at the California Institute of Technology, who is conducting brain studies on empathy.

Among the strongest spurs for research on the neurology of empathy have been experiments showing that newborn babies will cry in response to the cries of another infant. In the studies, newborn babies cried more loudly to the sounds of other babies crying than they did to a computer simulation of infants' cries and to other sounds that were equally loud and startling.

"Virtually from the day they are born, there is something particularly disturbing to infants about the sound of another infant's cry," said Martin Hoffman, a psychologist at New York University. "The innate predisposition to cry to that sound seems to be the earliest precursor of empathy."

Researchers cannot know for sure, of course, that the newborn's cries reflect empathy rather than, say, a reflexive tendency to respond upon hearing's another cry of alarm. Still the responses of infants like Hope clearly go far beyond a reflex, scientists say.

Pain of Others

These and other findings on infants and toddlers contradict an influential view offered several decades ago by Jean Piaget, the Swiss developmental psychologist, who contended that children could not feel empathy until they had achieved cognitive abilities that allow seeing things from another person's perspective. These abilities, he believed, developed around age seven or eight.

However, researchers are finding that the sympathetic distress of infants occurs long before they acquire the sense that they exist apart from other people, late in the first year.

From a few months after birth through the first year of life, studies have shown, infants react to the pain of others as though it were happening to themselves. On seeing another child get hurt and start to cry, they themselves begin to cry, especially if the other child cries for more than a minute or two.

But around one year of age, infants begin to realize that the distress is being felt by someone else. "They realize it's the other kid's problem, but they're often confused over what to do about it," Dr. Hoffman said. For instance, one boy of that age brought his mother over to comfort a crying friend, even though the other child's mother was also in the room.

During this phase, toddlers often imitate the distress of someone else—apparently, researchers say, in an effort to better understand what the other person is feeling. This kind of imitation, called "motor mimicry," was the original meaning of the word "empathy," which was coined by a psychologist early in this century.

The theory was that empathy was based on physically imitating the distress of another, in order to better understand what that person was feeling. The word was coined to distinguish it from "sympathy," a feeling of concern for another person that may not necessarily be based on sharing what that person himself feels.

"From around fourteen months to two or two and one-half years, you see children feel their own fingers to see if they hurt when someone else hurts their fingers," said Marion Radke-Yarrow, chief of the Laboratory of Developmental Psychology at the National Institute of Mental Health, where much of the work on altruism in children has been done.

"By two and one-half, though, toddlers clearly realize that someone else's pain is different from their own, and know how to comfort them appropriately."

Overall Life Situation

The next major landmark in the evolution of empathy occurs around age eight, according to Dr. Hoffman. "At that age you can empathize with a person's overall life situation, not just their immediate circumstances," he said. "For instance, you could be sad for someone with a life-threatening disease, even if she seemed happy at the moment."

Beginning in early childhood, differences emerged in the degree to which people are empathic. "From around two or three, you begin to see children develop their own style of empathy, with some showing increasing awareness of other people's plight, while others seem to turn away from such concerns," said Dr. Radke-Yarrow.

In studies with Carolyn Zahn-Waxler, Dr. Radke-Yarrow found that children were more empathic when their mothers disciplined them for the distress their "being bad" had on another child, saying, for example, "Look how sad you've made her feel."

Differences in empathy, in Dr. Brothers' view, reflect both how children are raised and, to some degree, biological differences in the brain.

By adulthood, the differences in empathy affect people's moral awareness, Dr. Hoffman said. For instance, people who are highly egoistic and presumably lacking in empathy keep their own welfare paramount in making moral decisions like how or whether to help the poor. For those who are highly empathic, on the other hand, the welfare of others is paramount in their moral judgments.

Empathy plays different roles in various realms of life, though. "When you encounter someone else in need, empathy triggers the urge to help," Dr. Hoffman said. "But empathy can also be a tool of manipulation in, for instance, trying to make a sale, particularly when the salesman has convinced himself about the worth of what he's selling."

The developmental changes in empathy through childhood seem to reflect, in part, the growth of the central nervous system in those years. "Empathy matures with the growing brain," Dr. Brothers said.

It is data from infants and from observations of empathy in other species that has led Dr. Brothers to seek the brain circuits that are essential to the emotional response, a research effort she described in the January issue of the *American Journal of Psychiatry*.

For many years scientists were skeptical that animals could display empathy. But Dr. Brothers, in her article, points to one classic study conducted in the 1950's which showed they could.

In the study, monkeys were trained to avoid an electrical shock by pressing a lever after they heard a certain sound. Once trained, the monkeys were separated, but connected through closed-circuit video. Only one could hear the sound, while only the other could pull the protective lever.

Whenever the one monkey heard the sound, the other monkey saw its distressed face and promptly pulled the lever.

"The monkey that controlled the shock prevented the other monkey from getting it on the very first trial, the moment it saw the distressed face," Dr. Brothers said.

Neurological data from brain damage in humans has helped focus the brain research on certain neural areas. For instance, injury to certain areas of the parietal lobes, at the back of the brain, produces an inability to understand the emotions expressed through tone of voice. And patients with injuries in some parts of the brain's right hemisphere complain that, although they feel emotions, they cannot convey them in their tone of voice or gestures.

Response to Facial Expressions

Dr. Brothers's research has focused on the visual cortex, the area of the brain that registers the meaning of what is seen, and its connections to the amygdala, part of the brain's limbic system, which responds to emotions.

Studies by several groups of researchers, including one led by Edmund Rolls, a neuroscientist at Oxford University, have discovered that specific neurons in that area of the brain respond mainly to facial expressions or to movements that have social meaning in the world of primates, such as crouching.

In research to be published in the journal *Experimental Brain Research*, Dr. Brothers, with her colleague Michael Hasselmo, a neurophysiologist, report finding specific neurons in macacque monkeys that respond to certain emotional expressions. In their study some of the neurons became active only when the monkeys saw another open its mouth without showing its teeth, a threatening gesture; other neurons activated only in response to a grimace indicating fear.

"The evidence seems to suggest that there are specific brain circuits for social response to emotional signals," Dr. Brothers said. "This is the type of neural activity that should lie at the base of empathy."

The Life Span: Continuity and Change

Is the child father to the man? How much can you predict from childhood observations about a person's development over the course of life? The articles in this section all use long-term follow-up to seek answers to these questions.

Do you remember your school having a bully? The research in "The Bully: New Research Depicts a Paranoid, Lifelong Loser" suggests that he (almost all bullies are boys) did not turn out happily. Their way of seeing the world puts them at odds against imagined enemies, a way of perceiving that leads to troubles at every age.

Whether or not it takes the form of being a bully, a child's inability to control aggression is the single trait that most strongly predicts later emotional problems, according to data reviewed in "Aggression in Children Can Mean Problems Later." But the article also describes interventions that can head off problems later in life for the aggressive child.

If you look into the past of parents who abuse their children, more often than not those parents were them-selves abused in childhood. But the vicious cycle does not always perpetuate itself. The research in "Sad Legacy of Abuse: The Search For Remedies" identifies what can help an abused child grow into a caring parent, while others go on to repeat that pattern with their own children.

What is the aftermath for a child of growing up in a war zone, such as Beirut, or in an atmosphere of political terror, as in Cambodia under the Khmer Rouge or some Central American countries? The particular emotional problems such a childhood breeds—as well as the ways such children can be helped—are covered in "Terror's Children: Healing Mental Wounds."

Most everybody lies from time to time. But did you know that a child's first lie is seen by some psychologists as a developmental milestone? Children who lie the most, though, seem to be at risk for growing into pathological liars or criminals, according research in "Lies Can Point to Mental Disorders or Signal Normal Growth."

The Bully: New Research Depicts a Paranoid, Lifelong Loser

April 7, 1987

It is as if the young bully's life were destined to leave his victims laughing last.

The bully, conspicuous in his tormenting of others, victimizes himself through a lifelong pattern of self-defeating aggression and the failures that grow out of it, new studies reveal.

Rapidly accumulating research on the psychology of bullies also shows that the belligerence of these youngsters arises not just from nastiness, but also from a perceptual bias that leads them to see—and retaliate against—threats where none exist.

"Bullies see the world with a paranoid's eye," said Kenneth Dodge, a psychologist at Vanderbilt University. "They feel justified in retaliating for what are actually imaginary harms."

With the growing understanding of what makes a bully, and the realization that bullying may blight a child's entire life, psychologists are trying new tactics to help youthful tyrants change their ways before it is too late.

Of course, rough-and-tumble aggression is typical of normal children, particularly boys. The bully is set apart by his quickness to start fights, to use force to get his way and his general belligerence. Only a small fraction of boys, those who are extremely aggressive, are thought to fall into this category.

Because girls by and large are less physically aggressive than boys, they do not seem to be at risk for the long-term problems that befall bullies. But some of the most aggressive girls, as adults become the mothers of bullies. Researchers do not yet know whether that is a result of inherited factors or of such things as the severity with which they punish their children.

The recent work adds a new twist to older theories about the roots of human aggression. While Freud saw aggression as a basic human drive that had to be channeled by the controls of the ego and superego, many psychologists now feel aggression stems from faulty thinking and a penchant for retaliation that verges on the paranoid.

Some current findings are consistent with such older views as the idea, inspired by the work of Alfred Adler, that the bully is compensating for deep feelings of inferiority.

"We find that bullies have a strong need to control others," said John Lochman, a psychologist at Duke University Medical School. "Their need to be dominant masks an underlying fear that they are not in control, and they mask the sense of inadequacy by being a bully."

Treatment does not challenge those underlying feelings but rather tries to use them constructively.

"We tell the boys that if another kid gets them so mad they blow up, then the kid is controlling them," said Dr. Lochman. "We tell them they can win by not getting mad."

Even though this approach may not deal with the child's deeper troubles, it seems to work, at least in improving relationships at school according to Dr. Lochman. Some psychologists believe that such problems as the bully's troubles with others can often be remedied with minor intervention, while by adulthood those same patterns require intensive therapy.

The new intervention programs focus on younger children, from four years of age to ten. "It's harder and harder for kids to change once the pattern is set and time goes on," said Leonard Eron, a psychologist at the University of Illinois at Chicago. Dr. Eron published an article on the lifelong patterns of bullies in the January 1987 issue of the *The Journal of Personality and Social Psychology*.

The bully's aggression is his undoing, Dr. Eron has found. It not only makes him a social outcast, but also interferes with learning; teachers tend to loathe such troublemakers.

In a twenty-two-year-study, done with Rowell Huesmann and other colleagues, Dr. Eron tracked 870 children from Columbia County, New York, from the time they were eight until they were thirty.

The study found that though bullies do not seem to have lower intelligence than other children, as adults they score less well on tests of intellectual achievement, evidently reflecting the difficulties they had in school. They also have more run-ins with the law and less desirable jobs than do their more peaceable peers.

Problems as Adults

Of the 427 children who could be tracked down at the age of nineteen, those who had been most aggressive as children were more likely to have dropped out of school and to have a criminal record. And of the 409 who were found at the age of thirty, data from eighty-two who had children between the ages of six and ten showed that parents who were bullies tend to have children who are bullies.

In addition, the study found that, compared with those who were not troublemakers in childhood, the grownup bullies are far more likely to abuse their spouses, punish their children more severely and have more convictions for crimes of violence.

To be sure, not every aggressive child will end up doing poorly; there are several kinds of bullies. "Some children are bad at school but not at home, and some children are aggressive but not social outcasts," said Karen Bierman, a psychologist at Pennsylvania State University. "Those who are aggressive across the board, and who have no friends, are at the most risk in life."

The bully's traits can be traced over three generations, Dr. Eron's research shows. The bullies had parents who disciplined them severely, and those who had been bullies as children tended to have children who themselves were troublemakers at elementary school age.

Although boys are, in general, more aggressive than girls, the meaner girls also tended to raise mean children.

"One way women manifest their aggression is by punishing their children," Dr. Eron said. "The more aggressive little girls grew into mothers who punished their children harshly."

Although the bullies were punished more severely, their parents did not seem to take much interest in them, the study found. "These are kids who are often ignored by their parents," said Dr. Eron. "It's not just a lack of nurturance; these parents don't notice what's going on or know much about them."

Such lack of interest typically creates in a child a diminished sense of worth, but with the aggressive children the problem seems to be compounded by the intensity of punishment, which adds its effects to the child's sense of worthlessness. More over, the parent presents the child with the vivid model of aggressiveness, a model the child seems to use in dealing with other children.

To make things worse, there is a quality of capriciousness about the punishment meted out by the parents of bullies, so that the bully's world seems to be particularly threatening and unpredictable.

Dr. Gerald Patterson, a psychologist at the Oregon Social Learning Center in Eugene, found that the parents of aggressive school children typically punish according to their mood rather than according to what the child has actually done. When the parent is angry, the child is punished; if the parent is in a good mood, the child can commit mayhem with impunity.

This home life could be a major factor in another hallmark of the bully, a sense that threats are all about and might strike at any time. Research by Dr. Dodge shows bullies tend to interpret an neutral encounter—an innocent bump, say—as an intentional attack.

"Bullies see threats where none exist," said Dr. Dodge. "And they take these imagined threats as provocations to strike back."

The bullies tend to attribute hostile intentions to other children who actually mean them no harm, Dr. Dodge found. This habitual misinterpretation seems to emerge as a fixture of personality by around the age of seven or eight, according to his report, published in the April, 1987 issue of *Child Development*. Dr. Dodge is now beginning a study of 500 four-year-old children to see how and when these thinking patterns develop.

In addition to finding threats everywhere, bullies do not seem to realize just how aggressive they are, according to research by Dr. Lochman published in *The Journal of Clinical and Consulting Psychology*. In the study, bullies were paired with a less aggressive boy and shown videotapes of boys in conflict. In one, for instance, one boy knocks into another, causing him to drop his books; when other children laugh, the boy becomes enraged and hits the other.

The pairs of boys discussed the tapes and what each boy in the videotape felt; they had to defend their positions in a way designed to assess how aggressive they felt during the discussions. The most telling discrepancy, Dr. Lochman feels, is that the bullies saw the other child they discussed the film with as more aggressive during their disagreements, while they did not see themselves as combative at all.

"Bullies see their anger as justified," Dr. Lochman said. "They see the other kid as having started the trouble," Lochman said.

Such perceptual distortions seem to lie behind the bully's belligerence and set him apart from his classmates beginning in the early grades.

While most four-year-olds are rambunctious, they generally become more self-controlled as they go through kindergarten and first grade. The bullies, however, get worse. By second grade, while other children have learned negotiation and compromise, the bully comes to rely more and more on bluster and force.

Experts now favor attempts to change the ways of bullies as soon as the problem can be identified, or to head it off altogether, if possible. The new intervention programs typically do not focus on the marks on personality left by family life, an approach followed by child and family therapists. Instead, they use the school to take a more immediate focus on teaching bullies—or those who are likely to become bullies—more peaceable ways of getting their way with other children.

At Duke University, Dr. Lochman's program involves small groups of four or five children who have been identified by their teachers as troublemakers. "We tell the boys that this is a group that will teach them how to better handle situations that get them frustrated and angry," Dr. Lochman said.

"These kids are thin-skinned," Dr. Lochman said. "When you ask them what makes them mad, it's usually things like being teased, put down or taken advantage of by other kids. We give them new ways to respond, instead of getting angry, for instance, they can try out coming back at a kid in a playful way."

Most of the children are unhappy about losing their temper so easily. The groups also teach the children to control their anger before responding, by counting to ten, for example, or walking away from the situation.

Another technique used is role-playing, which gives the children a chance to practice such things as starting a conversation with another child, or getting on a school bus when other children are taunting them.

"One large problem for these children is that they can't think of a friendly response that preserves their own dignity and self-image," said Dr. Dodge. "Being teased or insulted is an afront that they can only respond to by hitting, crying or running away. They need to learn other approaches, to say they don't like kids doing that, or ask them to stop it."

Aggression in Children Can Mean Problems Later

October 6, 1988

It is the extremely aggressive child, rather than the anxious or depressed one, who is most likely to have emotional troubles later in life, new studies are showing. The findings contradict prevailing wisdom in child development, which holds that anxiety is the most basic source of emotional difficulties.

The findings underscore the importance of identifying children who are highly aggressive and teaching them how to control their anger while they are still young. Recent data from programs at Duke University that teach such children how to better handle their anger showthat they were better adjusted emotionally by the time they reached adolescence than were other aggressive youngsters who did not receive the training.

"To our surprise, aggression in childhood is the emotional trait that is the strongest predictor of later maladjustment," said Alexander Thomas, a psychiatrist at the New York University Medical School, who directed the study along with his wife, Stella Chess, who is also a psychiatrist there. Results were reported in the October, 1988, issue of *Child Development*.

Study Began in 1956

The study used data from 75 children who had been assessed since they were infants in 1956 as part of the New York Longitudinal Study under the direction of Dr. Thomas and Dr. Chess. The individuals, now in their thirty's, have repeatedly been interviewed and given psychological assessments over the years; their teachers and parents have also been interviewed.

The new data from the study show that children who were rated as aggressive when they were seven to twelve years old were most likely to be among those who had difficulties adjusting in adolescence. But few such problems in adolescence were found in children who, while in grade school, had been identified as anxious, depressed, disobedient, unable to get along with their peers, or having academic trouble.

Aggressiveness in the children included not only getting into fights but also belittling or being hostile to other children, their families, teachers or schoolmates. In adolescence, these same children were found to have the greatest difficulties in school, with their peers, and, particularly, in getting along with their own families.

Analyses have not yet been done that would show whether the problems of the aggressive children continued through adolescence to early adulthood, although evidence from other studies suggests that it probably does, Dr. Thomas said.

A study of children who had been brought to a child guidance clinic in St. Louis, for instance, found that when they were later contacted in adulthood, the children who had problems with aggression were the most likely to have difficulties later in life, ranging from trouble with the law to depression and neuroses.

Early Treatment Recommended

The report in *Child Development* recommends that such children be treated while they are still young, so that they can learn to control their aggressiveness before it leads to more serious troubles. The more aggressive children are about twice as likely to be boys as girls, Dr. Thomas said. "My general advice to the parents of highly aggressive kids is that they need to be shown other ways to get what they are seeking," Dr. Chess said. "It rarely helps to simply tell them just to stop what they are doing; it's far more helpful to offer them an alternative for getting what they want, to show them another way to obtain their goal without getting angry."

Sad Legacy of Abuse: The Search for Remedies

January 24, 1989

Children and adults who were victims of child abuse are coming under intensified study by researchers who hope to learn what distinguishes those who go on to become abusers themselves from those who grow up to be good parents.

In the hope of finding ways to break the tragic cycle, the new research is identifying particular experiences in childhood and later in life that allow a great many abused children to overcome their sad legacy.

Studies also now indicate that about one-third of people who are abused in childhood will become abusers themselves. This is a lower percentage than many experts had expected, but obviously poses a major social challenge. The research also confirms that abuse in childhood increases the likelihood in adulthood of problems ranging from depression and alcoholism to sexual maladjustment and multiple personality.

The studies are also uncovering specific factors that help many victims grow into a well-adjusted adulthood, and factors that push others toward perpetuating the pattern of violence. The findings should help therapists improve treatment of abused children or for merly abused adults, helping them recover from their trauma.

"Studies showing that a high proportion of troubled adults were abused in childhood tell only part of the story," said Dr. Richard Krugman, a professor of pediatrics at the University of Colorado Medical School and director of the C. Henry Kempe Center for Prevention and Treatment of Child Abuse and Neglect. "There are substantial numbers of men and women who were abused as children, but who are not themselves child abusers, drug abusers, criminals or mentally disturbed."

Key factors found to worsen the long-term impact of abuse are: abuse that started early, abuse that lasted for a long time, abuse in which the perpetrator had a close relationship to the victim, abuse that the child perceived as particularly harmful, and abuse that occurred within a cold emotional atmosphere in the family. These factors, researchers say, help identify which children need treatment most urgently.

Victims of abuse frequently respond to the trauma by denying that any abuse occurred or by blaming themselves for the abuse, which they often view as justified discipline from adults, the studies show. But many victims can overcome the trauma with the emotional support of a friend or relative or through therapy that makes them aware that they were not to blame for abuse inflicted by their parents. Victims of abuse can almost always benefit from therapy to deal with the psychological effects of being so terribly treated, such as a damaged sense of self-worth and conflicts between wanting to love their parents while recognizing the abuse that happened.

"Child abuse" refers to a range of maltreatment. In addition to physical harm and sexual abuse, researchers also include serious neglect of a child's emotional and physical needs and forms of emotional abuse such as incessant berating of a child. They are finding that the longlasting effects of all these kinds of abuse share much in common.

In any given year, from 1 percent to 1.5 percent of American children are subject to abuse of some kind, according to Dr. Krugman. By the time they reach adulthood, about one in four men and women will have experienced at least one episode of abuse at some point during childhood.

Numerous studies have found those who were victims of child abuse to be more troubled as adults than those who were not. There are disproportionate numbers of victims of abuse among prostitutes, violent criminals, alcoholic and drug abusers, and patients in psychiatric hospitals.

The more severe the abuse, the more extreme the later psychiatric symptoms. For instance, a study by Judith Herman, a psychiatrist in Somerville, Massachusetts, found that among women who had been victims of incest, although half seemed to have recovered well by adulthood, those who suffered forceful, prolonged, intrusive abuse, or who were abused by fathers or step-fathers, had the most serious problems later in life.

Virtually all those who suffer from multiple personality, a rare but severe psychiatric disorder, have a history of being severely abused; the disorder is thought to stem from ways some children try to mentally isolate themselves against the horror of unremitting abuse.

A 1985 study of all fifteen adolescents in the United States who were condemned murderers found that thirteen had been victims of extreme physical or sexual abuse. In nine cases the abuse was so severe—characterized as "murderous" by the researchers—that it led to neurological damage. Similarly, a study of nine women imprisoned for fatal child abuse found that all of them had experienced severe maltreatment themselves.

While all these studies depict an alarming pattern, researchers point out that the statistics do not reflect the large numbers of abused children who do not suffer from these problems.

That abused children need not go on to abuse their own children was shown in a study of more than 1,000 pregnant women, 95 of whom had been abused as children. The report, by William Altemeier, a pediatrician at Vanderbilt University Medical School, and his colleagues, was published in 1986 in the journal *Child Abuse and Neglect*.

Strongest Predictive Factor

The study found that the strongest predicter from childhood of becoming an abusive parent was not having been abused, but rather having felt as a child that one was unloved and unwanted by one's parents—an attitude common, of course, among abused children, but also found in families in which there is no overt abuse.

However, studies in which there have been more careful observations of mothers and their children have found a stronger link between having been abused in childhood and being an abusive parent. In a survey of such studies, Joan Kaufman and Edward Zigler, psychologists at Yale, concluded that 30 percent is the best estimate of the rate at which abuse of one generation is repeated in the next.

Denial that one has been abused is emerging as a source of trouble later in life. Researchers find that many adults who were abused as children do not think of themselves as having been victimized. For instance, three-quarters of men in one study who described punishments that, by objective standards, constitute abuse—such as being burned for an infraction of a minor household rule—denied that they had been abused.

That phenomenon is common among those who go on to become child abusers, according to Dr. Krugman, and is part of the cycle by which abused children become abusive parents.

"When you ask them if they were ever abused, they tell you, 'No,'" Dr. Krugman said. "But if you ask them to describe what would happen if they broke a rule, they'll say something like, 'I was locked in a closet for a day, then beaten with a belt until I was black and blue.' Then you ask them, was that abuse? and their answer is, 'No, I was a bad kid and my parents had to beat me to make me turn out okay.'"

While there has been much attention by psychotherapists in recent years on women who were sexually abused in childhood, a more recent focus is on men who suffered sexual abuse. Such men are much more reticent than women about admitting what happened to them and dealing with the trauma, according to Mike Lew, co-director of The Next Step Counseling Centre in Newton, Massachusetts, and author of *Victims No Longer*, (Nevraumont) about the problem.

Children fare better after abuse, researchers have found, when they have someone in their life—a relative, teacher, minister, friend—who is emotionally nurturing.

In helping a child recover from abuse, "you need to counteract the child's expectations that adults will be deeply uncaring," explained Martha Erickson, a psychologist at the University of Minnesota.

Among adult victims of childhood abuse who are in therapy, a common refrain from patients is that "it just wasn't that bad," said Terry Hunt, a psychologist in Cambridge, Massachusetts, who specializes in their problem. "The key to their treatment is facing the fact that their parents were so cruel to them; they've bought the parent's word that they were bad and deserved it. The damage shows up in their intimate relationships, they're waiting to get hit or used again."

One of the crucial differences between those abused children who go on to become abusers and those who do not, he said, is whether they have the insight that their parents were wrong to abuse them.

Often, Dr. Hunt finds, the most troubled among his patients are those who were told as children, by adults other than their abusing parents, that the abuse was justified.

"If an abused child thinks, 'that was wrong, they shouldn't have done that to me—I'm not that bad,' then he can still love his parents, but decide not to repeat the abuse when he becomes a parent," said Dr. Krugman. "The child somehow gets the message that what happened is not his fault, that he is not to blame."

When parents are not the abusers, how they react to its discovery is crucial. In a study of children who had been involved in sex rings, those who had fewest lasting problems in later years were the children whose parents had been understanding of the child, according to Ann Burgess, a professor of nursing at the University of Pennsylvania Medical School.

"These kids recovered with no symptoms, while those whose parents blamed them had the worst outcome," Dr. Burgess said.

The factors that lead some children to become abusers while others become excellent parents is being revealed in research at the University of Minnesota. Psychologists there are currently studying a group of children born to parents with a high probability of becoming abusers. Not all those in the study were abused as children; they were selected instead because they were poor, single, got pregnant at an early age, and had chaotic households—all factors that correlate highly with child abuse.

In addition to physical and sexual abuse—the two varieties most often studied—the researchers are also studying children whose physical care is neglected, those whose parents constantly berate and criticize them and those whose parents are completely unresponsive to their emotional needs.

Followed from Birth

The study, one of the few that has followed children from birth, is finding that there are different emotional effects from each of the different kinds of abuse, and that these effects change from age to age. For instance, children whose mothers were emotionally cold during infancy had emotional and learning problems at the age of six that were as severe as—and sometimes more severe—than those found in children whose mothers had been physically abusive but emotionally responsive during their infancy.

When the same children were

studied between the ages of four and six, the most serious problems were found in those whose mothers neglected their physical care.

The study is also finding general effects that come from maltreatment of any kind.

"The earlier the maltreatment occurs, the more severe the consequences," said Martha F. Erickson, a psychologist at the University of Minnesota, who is one of those conducting the study. Dr. Erickson, with Byron Egeland and Robert Pianta, two colleagues, will publish early findings from the study in a chapter in *Child Maltreatment,* a published by Cambridge University Press.

Many of the lifelong psychological effects of abuse stem from a lack of nurturance, they conclude, a lack that lies behind all the kinds of maltreatment.

The Minnesota researchers report that among those abused children who go on to become abusing parents, there is little repetition of a specific type of abuse.

For instance, of thirteen women who had been sexually abused, six were physically abusing their children; of forty-seven who had been physically abused, eight were physical abusers by the time their children reached six years, while eight neglected their children, and six had homes where children were being sexually abused, often by a boyfriend of the mother.

Terror's Children: Mending Mental Wounds

February 24, 1987

Recent efforts to treat and study young survivors of civil war and terrorism have yielded important new insights into the special emotional needs of violence-scarred children.

Scientists working with children caught in the civil strife of Cambodia and other countries as well as children who have suffered from family violence, have developed a new understanding of their long-term psychological wounds and how best to mend them.

The researchers are finding that, with time and the right care, most children show a great capacity for emotional renewal after even the most nightmarish experiences. But the psychological scars of terror and turbulence in childhood can impair emotional and intellectual growth. Symptoms, often disguised, can emerge years later.

The research has also found that children terrorized in radically different ways—from wartime atrocities to family violence—share certain remarkably similar symptoms of lasting emotional pain, some subtle, some blatant. The new evidence that trauma, even a single brush with it, can lead to serious, long-lasting problems has led to a plan to extend the psychiatric diagnosis of "post traumatic stress disorder" to children.

"The body and mind handle terror in the same way, whether you were beaten by your father or by Pol Pot's soldiers," said Bessel van der Kolk, a psychiatrist at Harvard Medical School who directs the Trauma Clinic at the Massachusetts Mental Health Center in Boston.

The new studies, most of them completed within the last five years, greatly extend older findings in a research area that has largely been dormant since World War II, when Anna Freud, John Bowlby and a handful of others studied children who were evacuated during the London blitz, those who survived concentration camps as well as war orphans.

Although earlier work found that a child's reaction to trauma might be alleviated by the presence of a comforting adult, the new work has uncovered long-term effects regardless of how adults behaved in the crisis itself.

One of the major new studies described forty Cambodian teen-agers held in Khmer Rouge camps between 1975 and 1979, when they were twelve or younger. Many suffered near-starvation and beatings and witnessed the torture and murder of family members. The children, who now live in Oregon, were examined in 1984 by a team of psychiatrists from the Oregon Health Sciences University in Portland. The research, led by Dr. David Kinzie, was reported in the *Journal of the American Academy of Child Psychiatry* in 1986.

The children, by then fourteen to twenty years old still suffered a range of psychological problems, including recurrent nightmares, difficulty in concentrating and in sleeping, and being easily startled. About half showed symptoms of depression, lack of energy or interest in life, brooding and feelings of self-pity, and a pessimistic outlook. "Despite their great inner distress, many said they never told anyone about these feelings," said William Sack, one of the psychiatrists who studied the Cambodian teenagers.

About two-thirds seemed to be suffering from "survivor's guilt," the deep sense of remorse at having lived while other family members died—a phenomenon found among Holocaust survivors.

There was no direct relationship between the severity of the hardships the children endured and the severity of their symptoms years later. There was, however, a strong relationship between their current living situation and their psychological problems.

Role of the Family

While all the children had been separated from their families in the camps, those who were later able to reunite with family members fared better than the others. Of the twenty-six teenagers living with relatives, only twelve had—serious psychiatric problems, whereas of the fourteen living in foster homes thirteen had such problems.

"If children feel there is someone they can cling to, someone to count on, they survive the brutality far better than those who have no one to turn to," said Dr. van der Kolk of Harvard.

Other aspects of the social environment, too, alter the effect of war on children. In Northern Ireland, Catholic children appear to show more signs of psychological damage than their Protestant counterparts do, according to Terry Tibbetts, a clinical psychologist at the State Diagnostic Center in Los Angeles, who has studied children in Belfast.

"The Protestant kids don't show as many signs of the stress; they perceive their world as well-protected, with the police and British troops on their side," said Dr. Tibbetts. "But the Catholic children grow up believing the police, the troops and the Protestant paramilitary are all out to get them. They experience a more dangerous, threatening and unpredictable universe."

'Outlet for Anger'

Rona Fields, a psychologist who has studied children in Northern Ireland as well as in Beirut and other war-torn areas, has found that many who felt terrorized by war as children became easy recruits for the war itself as they approached adolescence. Similarly, said Dr. Tibbetts, when children in Northern Ireland who felt chronic fear and anxiety reach adolescence they translate those feelings into aggression; many join groups like Irish Republican Army. "The I.R.A. offers a Catholic kid a legitimate outlet for his anger," he said.

Children as young as eight or nine are being recruited and trained as soldiers in Central America, Africa and the Middle East, according to a report in *Cultural Survival Quarterly*, published by a private anthropological group in Cambridge. The long-term effects for these children, some evidence suggests, may be more grim than for those who were passive victims of war.

"In the Cambodian refugee camps, some of the children who had the roughest time were those who had been soldiers for the Khmer Rouge," said Neil Boothby, a Duke University psychologist who has studied and treated Cambodian refugees both at camps in Thailand and after they were resettled in New England.

"They had done a lot of killing when they were as young as eight years old and continued to assassinate people until they were around fourteen," he said. "They were psychologically intact as long as they stayed with the Khmer Rouge. But when they finally came to a refugee camp filled with Pol Pot's victims, they fell apart."

On the basis of their experience with Cambodian and other children Dr. Boothby and his colleagues have written, *Unaccompanied Children: Care and Protection in Wars, Natural Disasters and Refugee Movements,* published by Oxford University Press. The book offers guidelines for those who run relief operations on how to minimize the psychological impact of such catastrophes.

A study of children who have come to Los Angeles as refugees from war in Central America shows that psychological problems vary with age, according to William Arroyo, a pscyhiatrist at the University of Southern California. His research was published in the book *Post-Traumatic Stress Disorders in Children* (American Psychiatric Press).

Adolescents generally react to violent trauma with misbehavior: truancy, promiscuity, drug abuse and delinquency, said Spencer Eth, a child psychiatrist at the U.C.L.A. Medical School who did the research with Dr. Arroyo. This was not the case with the Cambodian teen-agers, perhaps, the researchers suggest, because of cultural differences.

On the other hand, children under five, who feel the most defenseless in the face of threat, often respond to trauma, by regressing, showing such symptoms as a return to bed-wetting or loss of toilet training, extreme anxiety about strangers or a parent's leaving, and the loss of recently mastered skills like speech.

Sometimes preschoolers who witness terrible violence react by becoming mute or stunned. Dr. Eth tells of a three-year-old girl who sat next to her slain mother for eight hours before being found by a returning housemate. The little girl did not speak of the murder until a week later, telling her great-grandmother that her father had been the killer.

Very young traumatized children are also prone to sleep disturbances.

School-age children often use play or daydreams to deny what actually happened, creating a happier outcome in which they save the victim by calling the police, giving first aid or capturing an assailant.

They can also react to trauma by obsessively repeating joyless games that reenact the event, rather than deny it. A seven-year-old girl whose father strangled her mother and then carried the body into the bedroom, for instance, insisted that her friends play the "mommy game," repeating the scene.

Paradoxically, reenactment plays a part in a treatment technique being developed. In this "incident-specific" treatment, children with severe symptoms learn to master the trauma by reliving the event in great detail— but in the company of a specially trained therapist who seeks to help the child face what happened and then move beyond it.

"Merely talking about it will not suffice in undoing serious psychic trauma in children," said Calvin Frederick, a psychologist at U.C.L.A.

However, there is, as yet, no single best treatment for trauma effects in children, according to Lenore Terr, a child psychiatrist at the University of California Medical School in San Francisco. At the same time, by learning as much as they can about the effects of trauma, the researchers are finding avenues of treatment.

For instance, one of the most frequent effects of extreme trauma on school-age children is problems in school. These problems, according to Dr. Eth, are caused by intrusive memories that distract the child from schoolwork. And the child's effort to forget the trauma can impair memory generally.

But not all school abilities suffer, "and many of these children do well in expressive arts, like painting and acting; these may be the best way to approach them in therapy," said Nina Murray, a clinical psychologist at Harvard who works with Dr. van der Kolk.

Although symptoms of trauma in children can persist for years—particularly in the absence of therapy—the long-term outlook is not all bleak. Dr. Murray cites a recent follow-up study of children who survived the Holocaust. Although they suffered greatly in childhood, "they are well-adjusted" as adults, said Dr. Murray. "They do have occasional symptoms, such as flashbacks and nightmares, but they are generally stable, productive, and compassionate people, who are not cynical or pessimistic, but optimistic, despite what they have lived through."

Lies Can Point to Mental Disorders or Signal Normal Growth

May 17, 1988

While recognizing that lying is a universal lubricant of social life, psychiatrists are seeking to determine when it becomes destructive and just which kinds of mental problems it can typify.

An article in 1988 in the *American Journal of Psychiatry* calls attention to the general neglect of lying as a topic for psychiatric research and marks the first systematic attempt to understand the role lying plays in normal everyday life as well as in specific psychiatric problems.

Psychologists who are studying how and why children learn to lie are finding that certain lies play positive roles in a child's emotional development. A child's first successsful lie, for instance, is seen by some researchers as a positive milestone in mental growth.

While the recent research sees lying that does damage as a matter for concern, it is pragmatic in taking the occurrence of lying in social life for granted. One study, for instance, found that, on average, adults lie—or admit to doing so—thirteen times a week.

"Lying is as much a part of normal growth and development as telling the truth," said Arnold Goldberg, a professor of psychiatry at Rush Medical College in Chicago. "The ability to lie is a human achievement, one of those abilities that tends to set them apart from all other species."

Psychiatrists see lying as pathological when it is so persistent as to be destructive to the liar's life, or to those to whom he lies.

The most blatant lying is found in the condition called "pseudologia fantastica," in which a person concocts a stream of fictitious tales about his past, many with a small kernel of truth, all self-aggrandizing.

"One patient blithely told me that he spoke his first complete sentence at three months, at three years gave sermons to crowds at his church work, and had a job at a news magazine where he made $8 million a week," said Bryan King, a psychiatrist at the U.C.L.A. School of Medicine. Dr. King wrote the article on pathological lying in the *American Journal of Psychiatry* with Charles Ford, a psychiatrist at the University of Arkansas Medical School, and Marc Hollender, a psychiatrist at Vanderbilt University School of Medicine.

"Pathological liars seem utterly sincere about their lies, but if confronted with facts to the contrary, will often just as sincerely reverse their story," Dr. King said. "Their stories have a believable consistency, but they just do not seem able to monitor whether they are telling the truth or not."

Research suggests that this most extreme form of lying is associated with a specific neurological pattern: a minor memory deficit combined with impairment in the frontal lobes, which critically evaluate information, according to Dr. King. In such cases, the person suffers from the inability to assess the accuracy of what he says, and so can tell lies as though there were true.

Not all pathological lying stems from such neurological difficulties. Psychiatrists are also grappling with lies that typify certain emotional disorders, and are told by people who know they are lying. Dr. King's article describes five varieties of lies, each of which comes more naturally to those who suffer from one or another of five common personality problems.

While such lies could be told by anyone, they are far more likely in those with the following personality problems, according to Dr. King, because each kind of lie springs from the pressing psychological needs at the core of the disorders:

● *Manipulative lies are the hallmark of the sociopath, or "antisocial personality," who is driven by utterly selfish motives. Such people are not necessarily criminals; they may gravitate toward the fringes of trades like sales, where their bent toward lying may serve them well. Since sociopaths feel no remorse or empathy for their victims, they are capable of the most cold-hearted of lies.*

● *Melodramatic lies which make them the center of attention are natural to the hysteric, or "hystrionic personality." Such people are searching desperately for love. They are also more taken with emotional truths than the facts of a situation. "Casual lies are to the hysteric what license is the poet," according to Dr. King.*

● *Grandiose lies typify the narcissist, whose deep need to win the constant approval of others impels him to present himself in the most favorable light. They are prone to exaggerate their abilities or accomplisments in order to seem more impressive. Because narcissists feel entitled to special treatment—for instance, believing that ordinary rules do not apply to them—they can be reckless in their lies.*

● *Evasive lies are typical of the borderline personality, whose wildly vacillating moods and impulsive actions constantly get him into trouble. Many of the borderline person's lies are told to avoid blame or shift responsibility for his problems to others.*

• *Guilty secrets account for many lies of the compulsive person, a type who generally is scrupulously honest. Compulsives pride themselves on following the rule and attention to facts and details. But they also suffer from a fear of being shamed, and so lie to prevent other people from finding out about things they feel would meet with disapproval. Their lies are often mild, about things most others would find no cause for lying; one man, for instance, lied to his wife to keep her from finding out about his being in therapy.*

Studying the Normal Lie

Along with the new focus on lying in psychiatric problems, there is intense research on the role lying in normal development. Researchers feel they must first understand what is normal about lying before they can know what leads to pathological lying.

Oddly, the research has resulted in an appreciation of the positive role lying plays in psychological growth, with some child experts seeing great significance in a child's first lie.

In this view, which is part of psychoanalytic "self" theory, the child's first lie, if successful, marks the initial experience that his parents are not all-knowing. And that realization, which usually occurs in the second year of life, is crucial to the child's development of the sense that he is a separate person with a will of his own, "that he can get away with things," Dr. Goldberg said.

But that lie also is the beginning of the end of the idealization of one's parents that all infants feel, he added. "The first time you see a limit to your parents' powers is a developmental step forward, towards a more realistic view of others," he said.

The ability to lie, in the view of other researchers, is a natural by-product of a child's psychological growth. "The crucial human skills

are among those that equip children to lie: independence, intellectual talents, the abilities to plan ahead and take the other person's perspective and the capacity to control your emotions," said Paul Ekman, a psychologist at the University of California at San Francisco, whose book, *Why Kids Lie* was published in 1988 by Scribners.

The years from two to four seem to mark a crucial period for children in mastering the art of the lie, according to studies by Michael Lewis, a psychologist at Rutgers Medical School.

Peeking at Toys

"In one study we've just completed with three-year-olds, we set up an attractive toy behind the child's back and tell him not to look at it while we leave the room," Dr. Lewis said. "About 10 percent don't peek while we're gone. Of the rest, a third will admit they peeked, a third will lie and say they did not peek and a third will refuse to say."

"Those who won't answer seem to represent a transition group, who are in the process of learning to lie, but don't do it well yet," said Dr. Lewis. "They are visibly the most nervous. Those who say they did not look—who lie—looked the most relaxed. They've learned to lie well. There seems to be a certain relief in knowing how to lie effectively."

By and large, children lie for the same reasons adults do: to avoid punishment, get something they want or make excuses for themselves. However, preteenagers usually have not yet learned to tell the white lies of adults, which work as social lubricants or to soothe another's feelings, researchers say.

One of the more common kinds of lies for preteenagers is the boast, inventing or embellishing on one's deeds, which is meant to win the approval and admiration of one's peers. Grandiosity is frequent in children of this age, such as boasts that one is able to do things like ski or speak a foreign language, when it is simply not true.

'Fine-Tuning Their Superego'

"Children at that age are fine-tuning their superego, or conscience," said Dr. Goldberg. "The first evidence of pathological lying shows up during these years, in children who have a faulty superego and think they can get away with anything."

Sometime between the ages of ten and fourteen, most children become as capable as adults in their lies, according to Dr. Ekman. "If a child did not develop the abilities that allow him to lie, he would remain immature," he said. "The question is, will they lie, and if so, why?"

Adolescence marks another point in development where lying takes on a special psychological significance. "Adolescence is a time of a renewed search for ideals, when the child's ideals undergo a major transformation," said Dr. Goldberg. "The adolescent is seeking a model, a perfect person to emulate. It's much like the moment in infancy before they realized their parents' imperfections."

This reassessment of values can lead the teen-ager to "a sense of that he can do whatever he wants," Dr. Goldberg added. "They start to test limits all over again, to see what they can get away with—and lying to parents can be a large part of that."

Although there are obvious problems in finding out exactly how common lying is, studies based on reports by parents and teachers put the frequency of children who lie more than occasionally as about one in six. But more than that—up to one in four adults—will admit to having lied fairly frequently as children.

Serious Lies, Serious Trouble

In only about 3 percent of children, though, is lying so constant that it is a serious problem, according to Magda Stouthamer-Loeber, a psychologist at the Western Psychiatric Institute and Clinic in Pittsburgh.

Understandably, children who get into trouble frequently are also those who tend to lie the most. Thus children who are brought to clinics for mental health problems—mainly problems in conduct like aggressiveness—are two and a half times as likely as other children to be chronic liars, according to a review of findings in the *Clinical Psychology Review* by Dr. Stouthamer-Loeber.

Children who are chronic liars, studies have found, tend to get into more serious trouble as they grow older. For example, a British study found that 34 percent of boys who were rated by their parents or teachers as lying had criminal offenses fifteen years later. And in an American study of 466 men from the Cambridge, Massachusetts, area, those labeled as "liars" while they were in elementary school were significantly more likely than other boys to have had a conviction for a crime such as stealing by the time they reached their twenties.

Still, researchers are uncertain just how much lying is a cause, and how much a symptom, of the problem. "We don't know if lying is a stepping stone that leads to maladjustment, a warning sign of later trouble, or is just one feature of a larger problem," said Dr. Ekman.

Children who are chronic liars tend to come from families where they were poorly supervised or felt rejected by their parents, according to research with more than 300 boys from nine to sixteen by Dr. Stouthamer-Loeber, published in the *Journal of Abnormal Child Psychology*.

"Happy married mothers supervised their boys more than did mothers who were not happy in their marriages or who were single," said Dr. Stouthamer-Loeber. "It is easy to imagine that parents under pressure have less time and inclination to keep an eye on their children. And when there is less supervision, lying is less risky."

Some children may become chronic liars by observing their parents. According to Dr. Ekman, some studies have found that parents who are more "Machiavellian," who themselves do not hesitate to lie in order to get their way, are more likely than others to have children who do likewise.

Adolescence, Adulthood, and Aging

Each phase of life has its own emotional focus and psychological needs. These articles investigate new findings about adolescence, adulthood, and the processes of aging.

The leading cause of death in teenagers is accidents, and teenagers are the only group in which the death rate has been rising since 1960. Beneath this statistic is a psychological fact: teenagers are drawn to risks. Just why this is, and what might be done to minimize the dangers, are explored in "Teenage Risk-Taking Rise in Deaths Prompt New Research Effort."

We assume that adolescence ends with the teen years. But in a psychological sense, adolescence continues into the twenties, particularly in terms of how much people lean on their parents for help and decision-making. The bounds of adolescence, and the processes that draw it to an end, are described in "a Last Outpost of Adolescence in Adulthood."

While much research has focused on the "mid-life crisis" of people in their forties, more recent work is looking at the psychological turmoil that comes to may people in their fifties—a decade that has been largely overlooked by researchers investigating the psychology of aging. Once thought a rather placid epoch of life, new studies now find that the fifties are often a period of search for meaning in life and a first realization of the inevitability of death. The new research is described in "For Many Turmoil of Aging Erupts in the 50s Studies Find."

While there is a common stereotype of the elderly person slowly growing senile, old age need not be a time of declining intellectual ability. "The Aging Mind Proves Capable of Lifelong Growth" tells of evidence that certain kinds of intelligence continue to increase throughout the life span, into old age.

But the illnesses that become more common as people reach old age can mask cases of depression, as the research shows in "Depression Among Elderly Patients Is Often Undetected Studies Find." Such symptoms as loss of appetite, fatigue, or insomnia, common symptoms of depression, are often misinterpreted by physicians as symptoms of illness when reported by elderly people. That means they are mistakenly treated for medical problems instead of the depression that underlies the symptoms.

The most influential theory of adult development is that of Erik Erikson. Now himself in his eighties, Erikson has continued to revise that theory, as described in "In Old Age, Erikson Expands His View of Life." From the vantage point of his ninth decade, he is amplifying the description of old age, pointing out the lessons from earlier decades that culminate in a final sense of integrity and wisdom.

Teenage Risk-Taking: Rise in Deaths Prompts New Research Effort

October 24, 1987

Alarmed by the rising toll of accidents and violence among teenagers, the Federal Government and private foundations have embarked on a major new program of research on why teenagers take so many foolish risks—and how such dangerous behavior can be curbed.

From acrobatics on skateboards to sex without contraceptives, teenagers are notoriously reckless. Research suggests a combination of hormonal factors, an inability to perceive risks accurately and the need to impress peers help explain this. All of these influences seem to peak in the years between ten and the mid-twenties.

Driving the new research effort is a chilling fact, adolescents are the only age group in which mortality has risen since 1960. Three-quarters of adolescent deaths are caused by accidents, homicide and suicide, all of which indicate a lethal propensity for risk-taking. Accidents alone account for 60 percent of those deaths.

"The three biggest killers of young people are essentially psychological," said Lewis Lipsitt, a developmental psychologist at Brown University. "They are dying of their own reckless behavior."

Dr. Lipsitt organized a meeting of scientists at the National Institute of Mental Health to draw up a research agenda on risk-taking by teenagers and what to do about it. A follow-up meeting is planned for this spring. The meetings are part of efforts by the government and foundations to identify teenagers most likely to take dangerous risks and to find ways to head off the peril.

In seeking the causes of the risk-taking, researchers are confronted with a fact known to every parent: teen-agers can seem to live in an orbit all their own, in which the reasonable imperatives of the adult world have little, if any, relevance. What seems a clear danger in the eyes of an adult, the researchers say, may seem safe, or safe enough, to the teenagers.

The ability to evaluate risk seems to be skewed in many teenagers. For instance, when they were asked to anticipate what risks become more or less dangerous over time, they saw addiction from drug use and pregnancy from unprotected intercourse as becoming less rather than more likely, according to Charles Irwin, a pediatrician at the University of California at San Francisco.

Further, perception of some risks may fade in the face of peer pressure. For example, when it comes to using condoms, the major concerns of adolescents are not the risks of pregnancy, but rather such matters as whether they think their peers use condoms and whether condoms are inconvenient or might make them look "silly," according to Nancy Adler, a health psychologist at the University of California at San Francisco, and a colleague of Dr. Irwin.

"The immediate experience is what matters to them, not worries about long-term consequences," Dr. Adler said.

Psychological Growth

Risk-taking is part of the natural exploration and assertion of independence that every healthy teenager goes through to one extent or another. The pursuit of new activities and taking of initiative are crucial for the psychological growth that young people undergo through adolescence. That natural tendency makes risk-taking all the more likely.

"Part of adolescence is trying on new roles and seeking new experiences," said Beatrix A. Hamburg, a child psychiatrist at Mount Sinai Hospital in New York City. "But by age ten or so, they enter a risky period when they do lots of exploring at a time when their cognitive development has not yet reached the point where they can make judgments that will keep them out of trouble. They cannot really comprehend laws of probability. And they also have ideas of invulnerability that persuade them that they can safely take a known risk."

One of the major deficits in the thinking of teenagers, particularly in early adolescence, is in evaluating the probabilities of a risk. "Often, if a teenager does something several times—like not breaking his neck when he does something stupid, or not getting his partner pregnant after sex without contraceptives—he will assume it becomes less risky each time, not more so," Dr. Hamburg said.

Teenagers are also prone to exaggeration, Dr. Hamburg said. "Adolescents tend to grossly over- or underestimate based on their immediate experience," she said. "When they say, 'Everyone's doing it—why shouldn't I?' they wildly overestimate the actual numbers. And, by the same token, they wildly underestimate the safety of the dangerous things they do."

For instance, Dr. Hamburg cited a study of smoking among youths ten to fourteen years old. About 15 percent of them said they sometimes smoked. But when asked about smoking in their age group, they put the figure at nearly 80 percent. Those who had the most exposure to smoking by family members of friends overestimated the rates of smoking most.

College students in another study overestimated the reliability of condoms by close to three times, according to Baruch Fischhoff, a psychologist at Carnegie Mellon University.

'Bad Girls,' 'Macho Boys'

Some of the new research focuses on identifying exactly which risks teenagers are likely to take. For example, Dr. Adler has developed profiles of "bad girls" and "macho boys," those most likely to take risks, and the risks they are likely to take.

Dr. Adler studied girls aged eleven to fourteen in San Francisco inner-city schools to see which risks those who were most reckless took.

She found that such girls had already started smoking and experimenting with drugs and were exposed to other risks—such as riding in cars going too fast—far more than other girls their age. Other risks that these "bad girls" took included drinking, fighting, hitchhiking, arguing with strangers, seeking entertainment in high-crime areas and carrying a knife.

A hallmark of the most reckless girls, Dr. Adler found, was their intent to become sexually active in the next year. This intention was far less common among girls who engaged in few risky behaviors.

For boys in the same age group, a cluster of activities set the most risk-prone youths apart from their peers, but no single marker emerged. The activities included drinking, smoking cigarettes and marijuana, riding on motorcycles and getting knocked unconscious.

Biology, too, seems to push some adolescents to take more risks than others, according to studies of sensation-seeking by Dr. Marvin Zuckerman, a psychologist at the University of Delaware.

4 Sensation-seeking is a personality trait that includes the desire for thrills and adventure, the enjoyment of physically risky activities and the need for sensory and social stimulation such as loud music or parties.

According to Dr. Zuckerman, there is a direct relationship between how people score on a personality test for sensation-seeking and how fast they say they drive on an open highway. People who have the lowest sensation-seeking scores drive, on average at 55 miles an hour. As the scores rise, so does the average driving speed; in the highest range it is over 75 miles an hour.

Death in Auto Accidents

That relationship between sensation-seeking and speed is of great concern because the leading cause of death for people up to the age of thirty-nine is auto accidents. "Adolescence is, statistically, the most dangerous age period for accidents," according to Herschel Leibowitz, a psychologist at Penn State University, who studies psychological factors in auto accidents.

The urge for sensation-seeking, in general, reaches a peak during the late teen years and then declines gradually throughout life. Those who are highest in sensation-seeking, Dr. Zuckerman has found, tend to have higher levels than others of the sex hormones, particularly testosterone, a male hormone.

Another biological factor in sensation-seeking may be monoamine oxidase, or MAO, an enzyme that regulates levels of some brain chemicals such as serotonin, which regulates mood. People with low levels of MAO can have very high or very low levels of serotonin, among other chemicals.

Sensation-seekers tend to have low levels of MAO, according to research by Dr. Monte Buchsbaum, a psychologist at the University of California at Irvine. People with low MAO levels, Dr. Buchsbaum found, tend to smoke and drink more than others and are more likely to have a criminal record. Although MAO levels have not been tested in younger teenagers. Dr. Buchsbaum found that among those he tested the lowest levels were in college-age people and that levels tended to rise with age.

"People in their late teens are at double biological risk, because of the combination of high hormone and low MAO levels," Dr. Zuckerman said.

Researchers say adults should handle dangerous activities by teenagers not by squashing the tendency to take risks but rather by understanding what lies behind the most foolish and dangerous activities. In reaching teenagers, adults particularly need to understand that adolescents see their world in far different terms than they do.

"The meaning of drinking to a teenager is entirely different from how their parents see it," said Dr. Irwin. "Teens don't see drinking in terms of its negative effects, the risk of drunk driving, for example. Instead, they think something good will happen if they drink: it will improve their self-confidence or help their social life."

As children progress from childhood to adolescence, their new social role is ambiguous, leaving even the most stable feeling like outsiders, unusually susceptible to social influence and insecure about their own judgments and values.

"Not all risk-taking is really adventurous," Dr. Hamburg said. "Sometimes it is risk-avoidant to take a drink, smoke a joint or have sex rather than be ridiculed, shunned or deprecated by peers."

Dr. Fischhoff agreed. For teenagers, he said, "the risk is in social rejection from not doing what other kids do."

Educational programs about the health risks of smoking, for instance, were not as effective among adolescents as approaches that incorporated the teenager's social world. In some of the more successful programs, student leaders were used in a role-playing exercise on how to refuse a cigarette.

Any approach to risk-taking must take into account the social realities of young people, Dr. Fischhoff said.

"Adults don't know enough about the realities of kids' lives and how they think," said Dr. Fischhoff. "Teens haven't seen as much of the adverse consequences of something like drunk driving or sex without contraceptives. And their lives are far more chaotic. It's easy enough to say have safe sex if you're in the same bedroom with the same partner all the time. But it's much different if you're petting in the back of a Chevy."

Therapists Find Last Outpost of Adolescence in Adulthood

November 8, 1988

While adolescence by common reckoning ends with the teen years, it continues psychologically until the end of the twenties, when young people are finally able to establish a fully mature relationship with their parents, psychologists are finding.

Although clinical lore has long suggested that adolescence lingered into the twenties, only now are scientific studies showing just how true that is. One new study has discovered a dramatic shift in psychological maturity that seems to occur in most young adults between twenty-four and twenty-eight.

Before the shift, the men and women studied said they usually relied on their parents to make important choices in life and felt unable to cope with life's difficulties without some help from them. After the change, they felt comfortable making choices based on their own values and confident in their abilities to live on their own.

Such findings are leading developmental psychologists to revise their views of emotional growth in adolescence and early adulthood and to set back the timetable for the end of adolescence. This phenomenon may be a product of this century when, for the first time, most young people remained dependent on their parents for their support through the teen years and beyond.

"Adolescence doesn't really end until the late twenties," said Susan J. Frank, a psychologist at Michigan State University. "The emotional ties that bind children to their parents continue well after they leave home and enter the adult world. There's an astonishing difference between those in their early and late twenties in doing things without leaning on their parents."

Kathleen White, a psychologist at Boston University who has conducted much of the research on maturation in young adults, said this shift also entails a changing view of parents. "By their mid-twenties," she said, "most young people are not ready to appreciate their parents as separate individuals, as having needs and strengths and weaknesses in their own right, apart from being parents.

"They still see their parents in egocentric fashion, were they good or bad parents, did they love me or not, were they too restrictive or demanding, and so on."

In a study of 84 adults between the ages of 22 and 29, Dr. White assessed several aspects of maturity, particularly their ability to form intimate relationships and to see their parents independent of their role as parents.

Those in their later twenties had "far more perspective on their parents" than those in their early twenties, Dr. White said.

A similar finding was reported by Dr. Frank and her colleagues in the November, 1988, issue of *Developmental Psychology*.

Rage or Dependency

During their twenties, people go through gradual shifts in their sense of independence from parents and in their relationships with them, according to the work of Dr. Frank and other researchers. Emotional maturation in the third decade of life can be charted by these shifts, following general theories of adult development.

For instance, in terms of autonomy, less mature young adults not only tend to rely on their parents to help with decisions, but they also are often overwhelmed by intense feelings of rage or dependency. At its worst, these feelings can lead them to lash out at their parents, even when the parents are trying to be helpful.

Often the less mature adults are emotionally estranged from their parents or have only superficial exchanges with them. They also tend to have little interest in their parents' welfare and little understanding of the complexities of their parents' lives and personalities.

In Control of Emotions

By contrast, more mature young adults tend to have strong confidence in their abilities to make decisions on their own and feel in control of their emotions toward their parents. They also see themselves, rather than their parents, as the best judges of their own worth and so can risk parental disapproval by expressing values that may clash with those of their parents.

They tend to have strong emotional ties to their parents and are able to talk with their parents about feelings and concerns of importance to them, while feeling free to disagree. They also are concerned about their parents' well-being and are able to understand the complexities of their parents' lives, rather than painting them in black-and-white terms. The more mature tend to acknowledge or feel proud of their parents as role models.

"In the twenties, it's not just that you achieve separateness from your parents, but also that you feel connected to them as an adult," Dr. White said. "That includes empathy for them, and seeing things from their points of view. Most young adults don't have this perspective until their late twenties.

Using scales that measure these changes, Dr. Frank and her colleagues assessed the development of 150 men and women in their twenties on their relationships with their parents. All those studied were from middle-class suburbs and lived within a two-hour drive from their parents.

Patterns of Maturation

While Dr. Frank's results bore out the general theories, she found the reality to be more complex, the real-life patterns not fitting a continuum of maturity. There were, she said, several major patterns of maturation among the young adults she studied, with significant differences between men and women.

Women most often fell into a pattern of "competent and connected" relationships with their parents. These people—the pattern fit 40 percent of women and 6 percent of men—had a strong sense of independence and often held views that differed radically from their parents. But even so, they felt more empathy for them, particularly for their mothers for whom they were often confidantes. Among the women, mothers were often seen as demanding and critical, but since they understood their mothers' shortcomings, they were able to keep conflicts from getting out of hand.

Another pattern more common among the women than the men was to be dependent or emotionally enmeshed, most often with their mothers. Although troubled by their inability to handle life without their parents' help, these young people felt trapped by the relationship. Some saw their parents as overbearing and judgmental, others as emotionally detached. Childish power struggles with parents were common in this group.

The largest number of men, however, had "individuated" relationships in which they felt respected by their parents and prepared to meet the challenges of life on their own. Thirty-six percent of the men and 6 percent of the women fell into this group. While they felt a clear boundary between their own lives and those of their parents, they also felt free to seek advice and assistance. Although they enjoyed their parents' company, there was an emotional distance. Their relationships generally were lacking both in discussions of very personal matters and conflicts.

Another pattern more common in men than women was a false autonomy, in which the young adults feigned an indifference to clear conflicts with their parents, which they handled by avoiding confrontations. With their fathers, the main complaint was of mutual disinterest; with their mothers it was the need to hold an intrusive parent at bay. These people resented their parents' offers of help and often held them in contempt. They also harbored resentment at their parents' inability to accept them as they were.

Reconnecting with Parents

Dr. Frank's findings are consistent with the work of Bertram Cohler, a psychologist at the University of Chicago. Dr. Cohler has proposed that when youths make the transition into adulthood, they become more interdependent with rather than more independent of their parents.

Dr. Frank found that over the course of their twenties, those in her study tended to move in the more mature direction. Although most had made the shift by twenty-nine, some still remained in an emotional adolescence.

Dr. Gould said, "There are some eternal adolescents, who never achieve a sense of their own maturity in these ways."

The Question of Marriage

While many influential theories of adult development hold that marriage is a key turning point in emotional maturation, Dr. Frank did not find this to be the case. She found that apart from age, it made no difference in people's psychological growth.

"The clinical literature says that the degree to which you've worked through your emotional relationship with your parents determines your ability to develop a close relationship with your spouse," Dr. White said.

"But that's not what I've found," she added. "People tend to be more mature in their relationships with their spouses than with their parents, if they are mature in either. People are more compelled to work out their marital conflicts than they are to work out their relationships with their parents. Your parents are your parents forever."

For Many, Turmoil of Aging Erupts in the 50's, Studies Find

February 7, 1987

While any number of people anguish over their 30th birthday and try to hide their 40th, it is with the 50th that most start to actually see themselves as beginning to be old, researchers are finding.

It is in their fifties, for example, that most people first think of their lives in terms of how much time is left rather than how much has passed. This decade more than any other brings a major reappraisal of the direction one's life has taken, of priorities, and, most particularly, how best to use the years that remain.

"The fifties is a kind of fulcrum decade, a turning point in the aging process during which people, more sharply than before, are made to feel their age," David Karp, a sociologist at Boston College, wrote in the February, 1987 issue of *The Gerontologist.*

Yet despite its significance, the fifties are a relatively unknown decade, little discussed, and even less studied. "There may be more taboo about looking at your life during the fifties than any other decade," said Daniel Levinson, a psychologist at Yale Medical School. "For many there is a silent despair, a pressing fear of becoming irrelevant in work or marriage, with no real alternative in sight. And for others, who are able to make vital choices during their fifties, there is a hard time of personal struggle early in the decade."

That struggle centers on questions like the value of a marriage or career, or what changes will allow a more meaningful life, said said Dr. Levinson, the author of *The Seasons of a Man's Life.* In that book, published in 1978, Dr. Levinson found that the years of the mid-forties were a crucial transition point for most people. He now believes that inner struggles occur with renewed intensity in the mid-fifties.

To be sure, researchers say, there is no exact age at which these psychological changes occur; their timing depends more on the benchmarks of work and family life than chronological age. "The struggle or despair are not universal, but they are particularly common during the fifties," Dr. Levinson said.

Studies have found that men and women in their fifties react to aging differently. For instance, men, often reaching the peaks of their careers, may be looking at how many years they have left at work, while women, at the end of their child-rearing roles, are often eager to plunge into work outside the home.

Despite the shock of aging, the fifties are by no means grim, Dr. Karp found. Along with the rise in reflectiveness, people described a feeling of wisdom that they had not had before. Many said they felt freer to enjoy life—that they were less irritated by things, spent less time worrying and fought less often.

For the men and women Dr. Karp studied, the fifties are "a time of liberation in their lives, a time during which they are able to view their lives in a broader way," he said.

The psychological crises that typify the fifties are triggered by the quickened pace of reminders about aging, the new research is showing.

While some of the reminders are subtle, others are dramatic and many come from other people. Dr. Karp believes that "we are as young or old as other people make us feel." He tells of one man, for instance, who suddenly felt old when one of his younger teammates in an informal basketball game turned to him afterward and said, "Nice game, sir."

Perhaps the starkest reminders come from the obituaries page. "During the fifties people find that others their age die with some regularity," Dr. Karp said.

The result is that people begin to "personalize death, to see it as something that can happen to them, because it's happening to friends," said Bernice Neugarten, a psychologist at the University of Chicago. "A focus on fear of heart attacks begins around fifty in many people as men start to die from them in noticeable numbers."

Women, Dr. Neugarten has found, do not focus so much on their own health during the fifties as they do on that of their husbands. Many fear being widowed.

Confronting Time Limits

"In their fifties, as never before, people confront the fact there are time limits to their lives," Dr. Karp said, and begin to look at projects they take on in terms of whether they can reasonably be completed at this point in life, or even whether they want to spend the remaining years working on them.

Dr. Karp's findings are based on indepth interviews of 72 men and women between the ages fifty and sixty. The interviews, reported in the November 1987 issue of *The Gerontologist,* were designed to learn how people see themselves, their careers, and aging.

While those interviewed were all professionals, mainly academics, doctors and lawyers, researchers see their responses as typical of most men and women. However, working class people, who leave school earlier and marry earlier, tend to go through the stages of psychological development about five years earlier, on average, than do professionals, said David Gutmann, a psychologist at Northwestern University who is also studying psychological changes during mid-life.

The new focus on the fifties highlights the subjective nature of aging itself, a process that allows people to perceive themselves as either much younger or much older than their actual chronological age.

For almost all the men and women Dr. Karp studied, the idea that they were aging as they reached their fifties seemed strange. "They knew they were no longer young, but still could not quite believe it," Dr. Karp said. Even so, they do not think of themselves as old.

Some of the strongest reminders of aging were physical changes.

Onset of Physical Problems

The shock was not just that they were noticeably less agile or had less endurance during sports—signs that begin in the thirties and forties—but that they had suffered serious illnesses or knew people their age who had become seriously ill.

Several of those studied had had heart attacks, others had undergone major surgery, and others had problems, like arthritis and prostate trouble, that they saw as "diseases of the old," or went through changes like menopause.

Although they saw old age as distant—most thought it began somewhere around seventy—they saw their physical disabilities as the first undeniable harbinger of old age. The psychological impact of their physical problems was particularly strong, according to Dr. Karp, because most saw the true mark of old age not as reaching some specific year of life, but as the onset of physical impairment.

Other signals of aging come from the workplace. The peak of a work career—particularly for professionals—has typically been achieved by the early fifties and sometimes in the forties, recent research has shown.

"Most men reach the highest rung they will on the organizational ladder by their fifties," Dr. Karp said. "Many feel topped out. They know where they'll be for the rest of their occupational life."

For many women, though, the experience is quite different. For those who took time out of careers to raise children, and then started or resumed a career as their children had grown, the fifties are a time when the pace of their careers are accelerating.

"Many of the women had followed what they call the 'standard version,' being helpmates to their husbands, mothers to their children, and putting their careers on hold," Dr. Karp said. "Many didn't enter the work force until their forties."

The result is that during their fifties, men and women often have opposite attitudes toward their careers. "The men are developing an exit mentality, calculating how many years are left at work. But the women of the same age are thinking about making their mark," said Dr. Karp.

Most people with children become grandparents during their fifties, studies have shown, yet another signal to people that they are aging, Dr. Karp said.

Another powerful reminder was the symbolic meaning of the number fifty. Reaching fifty is, in terms of the actual average life span, about two-thirds of the way through life. But because fifty marks half of century, the birthday carries a strong symbolic connotation of being the midpoint, Dr. Karp found, marking the entry into the last half of life. Even though birthdays at each decade are usually marked by a special celebration, those for fifty are often unusually large.

With that symbolic moment comes a change in the meaning of time. "Even though people in their fifties don't see themselves as old, there's a reversal of the direction of time," Dr. Neugarten said. "You count the number of birthdays left instead of how many you've reached."

The net result of the shifts that go on during the fifties are to make people more introspective. "It is a time of taking stock and increased reflection," said Dr. Neugarten.

Repressing and Venting Emotion

Men and women tend to differ in what that introspection leads to, however. One of the greatest differences between the sexes is in the psychological consequence of no longer having children to care for, said David Gutmann, a psychologist at Northwestern University Medical School and head of the program there in the clinical psychology of aging.

"The period of life when we are raising children tends to be something of a chronic emergency, a time of watchfulness over our children, protecting their welfare and our own," he said. "During that period, women tend to suppress their anger instead of giving it full vent, while men tend to suppress the qualities—like emotionality, tenderness, sensuality—that might interfere with their breadwinner role."

But once children reach the point where they can care for themselves, those suppressed qualities come to the fore, Dr. Gutmann said. During their fifties, "women take on more aggressive qualities, while men are freer to express their more tender and nurturant side," he said.

The result can be a very different focus for men and women during the fifties, Dr. Karp said. Men, feeling a new freedom to pursue things that their careers have kept them from, often become more interested recapturing the intimacy in their marriage. Women, on the other hand, often want to plunge into their careers now that they are liberated from the demands of child-rearing.

For men, especially, the forties were looked back on as a golden period, Dr. Karp found. In those years many men "were pretty much at the top of their occupational game, had their family life under control, and still enjoyed good health," he wrote in the report of his study in *The Gerontologist.*

One of the heartening experiences for many in their fifties was going to reunions. Being with large groups of men and women their own age allows most people to find some basis for comparisons that justify the feeling that they themselves are aging better than most.

The Aging Mind Proves Capable of Lifelong Growth

February 21, 1984

Researchers can now demonstrate that certain crucial areas of human intelligence do not decline in old age among people who are generally healthy.

Moreover, although some other aspects of intelligence do diminish, the decline is relatively inconsequential and has been exaggerated in the past, the experts assert.

The new research challenges beliefs long held by scientists and the public and suggests that, among people who remain physically and emotionally healthy, some of the most important forms of intellectual growth can continue well into the 80's. It also suggests that declines in intelligence can be reversed in some instances and that earlier notions about the loss of brain cells as a person ages were in error.

This more optimistic view of the mental capacities of the aged emerges from a broad range of current studies, from recent literature in the field and from interviews with gerontologists, psychologists and experts in related health sciences.

Some of these experts suggest the old ideas about aging and intelligence may have had tragic consequences. Countless intellectually vigorous lives may have atrophied on the mistaken assumption that old age brings an unavoidable mental deterioration.

"The expectation of a decline is a self-fulfilling prophecy," said Warner Schaie, an eminent researcher on aging. "Those who don't accept the stereotype of a helpless old age, but instead feel they can do as well in old age as they have at other times in their lives, don't become ineffective before their time."

In recent years, accumulating data have firmly shown that one key mental faculty, called crystallized intelligence, continues to rise over the life span in healthy, active people. Healthy in this context means an absence of diseases that affect the brain, such as a stroke.

Crystallized intelligence is a person's ability to use an accumulated body of general information to make judgments and solve problems. In practical terms, crystallized intelligence comes into play, for example, in understanding the arguments made in newspaper editorials, or dealing with problems for which there are no clear answers, but only better and worse options.

John Horn, a psychologist at the University of Denver who has done the main research, said crystallized intelligence continues to increase steadily throughout life, although in old age the increments become smaller.

"As for the intelligence that may be lost," said Dr. Jerry Avorn of the Division on Aging at Harvard Medical School, "the deficits found in the healthy aged are in a minor range, not at all clinically impairing.

"At worst they're a nuisance," he said, "like not being able to remember names or phone numbers as well. They present no real problem for daily living."

History offers ample instances of brilliance in life's later years from Michelangelo to Martha Graham.

The new research provides a better understanding of what, apart from a lucky genetic endowment, might allow such people to maintain their mental capabilities through old age.

The key factors included these:

- *Staying socially involved. Among those who decline, deterioration is most rapid in old people who withdraw from life.*

- *Being mentally active. Well-educated people who continue their intellectual interests actually tend to increase their verbal intelligence through old age.*

- *Having a flexible personality. A longitudinal study found that those people most able to tolerate ambiguity and enjoy new experiences in middle age maintained their mental alertness best through old age.*

"The ability to bring to mind and entertain many different facets of information improves in many people over their vital years," Dr. Horn said. "One way this shows up is in the ability of older people to wax eloquently. They have a rich, evocative fluency; they can say the same thing in five different ways. In our research, they're better in this sort of knowledge than the young people we see."

This increase occurs despite the simultaneous decline from early adulthood onward of "fluid intelligence," a set of abilities involved in seeing and using abstract relationships and patterns, such as in playing chess. Fluid intelligence, Dr. Horn believes, may be more vulnerable to changes in the nervous system as a person ages than is crystallized intelligence.

According to Martha Storandt, a psychologist at Washington University in St. Louis, "The fluid intelligence drop has some impact, but people learn to compensate, even in later life. You can still learn what you want to; it just takes a little longer."

Researchers also report finding mental abilities closely related to crystallized intelligence that improve throughout old age. Roy and Jane

Lachman at the University of Houston measured age differences in "world knowledge," the information people acquire in both their formal education and day-to-day experience. This knowledge ranges from facts like the name of Britain's Prime Minister to knowing signs of danger in the street. The total store of such information, they found, increased with age through the seventies. What's more, the oldest group tested was more efficient in recalling these facts than groups in middle age or in their twenties.

Memory loss that does occur in old age appears, in some measure, to be exaggerated because it is awaited with such dread. Marion Perlmutter, in *New Directions in Memory and Aging* (Lawrence Erlbaurn Associates) observes that a decline in some memory ability appears in early adulthood, too, but it is not so alarming then. It is possible, she writes, that "age merely increases sensitivity or awareness and disturbance about memory problems."

"When people say 'Old Granny's lost her memory,' " Dr. Horn added, "there's generally a little truth in it, but not as much as people make out."

In the forefront of the current research has been Dr. Schaie, who for several years directed a study of aging in Seattle. That project was one of the first to show how various mental capacities changed as people aged. Begun in the mid-1950's, the study has had more than 3,000 participants, some retested every seven years for as long as twenty-one years, and has followed some into their late eighties.

Dr. Schaie, writing in *Longitudinal Studies of Psychological Development* (Guilford Press), reports that, on average, the declines in such mental abilities as fluency and spatial relations, while clear from test results, have little practical significance until the mid-seventies or early eighties.

"For some mental capacities," he said in an interview, "there begin to be slight declines in the sixties, and, for most people there are meaningful declines by the eighties. But some mental capacities decline very little, or can even improve in old age."

As people reach their seventies, the Seattle study shows, there is increasingly great variability in mental capacities, some people faring quite poorly, while others retain their abilities well.

"Some of our people have shown no declines that interfere with daily living into their eighties," he said.

One of the major factors in maintaining or improving mental capacities was social involvement. Elderly people who lived with their families and were actively engaged with life actually showed an increase in mental abilities over a fourteen-year-period, while those who lived on their own and were withdrawn from life had a decline. The greatest decline was among widowed housewives who had never had a career of their own and led restricted lives.

The study found, too, people who in midlife had more flexible personalities and were able to see life from differing points of view performed at higher intellectual levels in old age. Declines in such abilities as spatial orientation can be reversed in the elderly with simple tutoring. "The use-it-or-lose-it principle applies not only to the maintenance of muscular flexibility, but to the maintenance of a high level of intellectual performance as well," Dr. Schaie said.

Others agree the faculties people use most are likely to hold up best in old age. Nancy Denney, a psychologist consulting at the Institute on Aging at the University of Wisconsin, said, "What one does during one's life makes all the difference." The reason verbal abilities can increase over the lifetime is that people exercise that capacity all the time.

Gerontology texts in the past contained a litany of studies showing a relentless decline in mental abilities of the aged. It now appears much of that research may have been inadvertently biased against the elderly.

"Many tests that were used to assess the cognitive abilities of the elderly are biased in favor of younger people with whom they are compared," said Leonard Poon, a psychologist at Harvard Medical School. "One test involved remembering pairs of nonsense words. College students are motivated to try their best on such tests. But older people just don't care much about nonsense words. What looks like a diminished ability in the elderly may partly be lack of interest."

Writing in *The Journal of the American Geriatrics Society*, Dr. Avorn of Harvard criticized much of the scientific literature comparing mental abilities of aged and young groups. While nearly all college students are free of major illness, Dr. Avorn noted, the same assumption cannot be made about people in their seventies. Nonetheless, researchers have often asked the aged only if they were in good health, thus failing to weed out people whose conditions could impair mental performance. Such performance lags may be erroneously attributed to aging rather than to disease. Another hidden bias, Dr. Avorn said, is that many elderly people take medications that can diminish mental function.

Still another cause of distortion is the practice of comparing people in their seventies who have had little education with college students. The older group is thus at a disadvantage both by virtue of educational status and unfamiliarity with test-taking.

In studies in which researchers used such incentives as Green Stamps to motivate elderly subjects, there were significant gains in scores on abilities like reaction time, which are typically listed among the faculties that undergo inevitable decline with age. Such studies are among those suggesting that many cognitive deficits in the aged are largely a result of social or psychological factors. The new view is accompanied by data attacking the notion that the brain degenerates precipitously with aging. The widespread belief that there is devastating cell loss in the elderly brain—and the related claim that each drink of liquor destroys a large amount of brain cells—seem now to be unfounded. Marian Diamond, a neuroanatomist at the University of California at Berkeley, tried to track down the source of the belief and could find no definitive study proving it.

Dr. Diamond's own research was one of the few studies ever done to directly assess cell loss rates as the brain ages. Her results indicate that, while there is some cell loss, the greatest decrease is early in life and subsequent losses are not significant, even into late life.

A study of brain chemistry at the National Institute of Aging, using a brain scan to study men whose ages ranged from twenty-one to eighty-three, found that "the healthy aged brain is as active and efficient as the healthy young brain," based on the direct assessment of metabolic activity in various parts of the brain.

The researchers also propose that declines in vision or hearing may account for changes in the level of brain activity that some investigators have attributed to brain aging.

It might also mean, they suggest, that the developing human brain acquires more brain cells than it will ever need, and that whatever brain cell loss there might be, there are still more than enough surviving cells to support efficient functioning.

"The belief that if you live long enough you will become senile is just wrong," said Robert Butler, a psychiatrist who was the founding director of the National Institute on Aging and is now head of the program in geriatric-medicine at Mount Sinai Hospital. "Senility is a sign of disease, not part of the normal aging process."

The widespread belief in an inevitable mental decline in old age, though, has sometimes led people to mistake a reversible mental deterioration in an older person for the beginnings of senility.

"What can happen," Dr. Avorn said, "is that an older person who is admitted to a hospital for something like a broken hip or heart attack can become confused as a side effect of drugs or simply from the strangeness of the hospital routine. The condition is reversible, but the family, or even the physician, doesn't recognize that fact. They assume this is the beginning of senile dementia, and pack the person off to a nursing home."

"No one knows what exact proportion of people in nursing homes needn't be there," he said, "but we have ample evidence that the numbers are large."

Depression Among Elderly Patients Is Often Undetected, Study Finds

December 22, 1988

As many as one in seven elderly medical patients suffers from severe depression in addition to physical illness, a new study has found. And in many cases, or perhaps most, the depression goes undiagnosed and untreated, frequently worsening or complicating the physical disorder.

"Our research and that of others shows that when depression accompanies a medical problem, patients are sicker, need more medication and spend more days in the hospital," said Stephen R. Rapp, a psychologist at the Veterans Administration Hospital in Jackson, Mississippi, who conducted the study.

The difficulty of detection is most severe among the elderly, according to the study, published in the December 1988 issue of *The Journal of Consulting and Clinical Psychology*.

The study dealt with 150 aged patients who were admitted to an unidentified hospital for physical problems and who were interviewed and given tests to determine whether they suffered from any psychiatric disorders as well. The examining physicians failed to detect a single case of depression, even though 15 percent of the patients were severely depressed, as determined in reexamination by Dr. Rapp and his colleagues.

Varying Rates

Rates of undetected depression are lower in younger patients, other studies have found. The higher rate among the elderly is due partly to their tendency to have more complicated medical conditions than younger patients, and to be taking more medications. That makes a physician more likely to pursue medical diagnoses for what are actually symptoms of depression.

Further, Dr. Rapp said, the elderly tend to be more taciturn about psychological problems.

"Older people seem to be reluctant to open up about their psychological distress to anyone, even their physicians," he said. "They are very unlikely to go into a doctor's office and say, 'I'm depressed; let me tell you what's on my mind.' They complain of their physical problems instead."

Among all age groups, depression is the most difficult psychological problem to detect in medical patients.

"The signs of depression are particularly easy to mistake for any of a wide range of medical problems," said Dr. Rapp. "In general the rate of detection of depression in their medical patients by physicians is under 20 percent."

Four of the nine main signs of depression can also be symptoms of many other illnesses or side effects of medication, according to Dr. Rapp. These signs are appetite loss or weight change, insomnia or a sudden need for more sleep than usual, agitation or extreme slowness in movement or speech, and constant fatigue.

Five other signs of depression are more obvious. In addition to sadness or irritability, depressed people commonly undergo a marked loss of interest in formerly pleasurable activities, feel worthless or guilty, are unable to concentrate or make decisions, and can have recurrent thoughts of suicide or death.

The problem for physicians comes when a patient who is depressed mentions only the symptoms that can mimic those of physical problems and fails to mention any of those that would more clearly point to a diagnosis of depression. Many doctors then assume that what are actually signs of depression are indicators of some other, purely physical disorder.

Ten percent of the patients in Dr. Rapp's study suffered from other severe psychiatric problems, like schizophrenia. But symptoms of these problems were more obvious to physicians.

Depression among elderly medical patients is about seven times as common as among their healthy peers, according to Dr. Rapp's study. Often, the depression is a reaction to the illness it accompanies.

But depression is considered one of the most treatable of serious psychological problems. The treatment, whether drugs or psychotherapy, can often have a salutary effect on the medical problem or at least reduce psychological suffering, Dr. Rapp said. It may also improve a patients's willingness to carry out doctor's instructions.

"Studies have shown that when patients with both depression and a medical problem are treated for both conditions," Dr. Rapp said, "it improves their physical health and sense of overall well-being, as compared to similar patients who are treated for the medical problem alone."

Because of this importance in

treating depression in medical patients, the National Institute of Mental Health has begun a program, Depression/Awareness, Recognition, Treatment, that attempts to alert physicians who are not psychiatrists to signs of depression and to make them aware of the treatment available for it.

In Old Age, Erikson Expands His View of Life

June 14, 1988

In his ninth decade of life, Erik H. Erikson has expanded the psychological model of the life cycle that he put forward with his wife, Joan, almost forty years ago.

Their original work profoundly changed psychology's view of human development. Now, breaking new ground, they have spelled out the way the lessons of each major stage of life can ripen into wisdom in old age. They depict an old age in which one has enough conviction in one's own completeness to ward off the despair that gradual physical disintegration can too easily bring.

"You've got to learn to accept the law of life, and face the fact that we disintegrate slowly," Mr. Erikson said.

On a recent afternoon, in a rare interview, they sat in their favorite nook in a bay window of Mrs. Erikson's study on the second floor of their Victorian house near Harvard Square in Cambridge, Massachusetts. "The light is good here and it's cozy at night," Mrs. Erikson told a visitor.

Although Mr. Erikson has a comfortable study downstairs, and Mrs. Erikson, an artist and author in her own right, has a separate workroom, they prefer to spend their time together in this quiet corner, in the spirit of their lifelong collaboration.

Mr. Erikson, who never earned an academic degree (he is usually called Professor Erikson), deeply affected the study of psychology. Many believe that his widely read books made Freud pertinent to the struggles of adult life and shaped the way people today think about their own emotional growth. He gave psychology the term "identity crisis."

When Mr. Erikson came to this country in 1933 from Vienna, he spoke little English. Mrs. Erikson, a Canadian, has always lent her editorial hand to those writings of her husband on which she did not act as co-author.

As Mr. Erikson approaches 87 years of age and Mrs. Erikson 86, old age is one topic very much on their minds.

Their original chart of the life cycle was prepared in 1950 for a White House conference on childhood and youth. In it, each stage of life, from infancy and early childhood on, is associated with a specific psychological struggle that contributes to a major aspect of personality.

In infancy, for instance, the tension is between trust and mistrust; if an infant feels trusting, the result is a sense of hope.

In old age, according to the new addition to the stages, the struggle is between a sense of one's own integrity and a feeling of defeat, of despair about one's life in the phase of normal physical disintegration. The fruit of that struggle is wisdom.

"When we looked at the cycle in our forties, we looked to old people for wisdom," Mrs. Erikson said. "At eighty, though, we look at other eighty-year-olds to see who got wise and who not. Lots of old people don't get wise, but you don't get wise unless you age."

Originally, the Eriksons defined wisdom in the elderly as a more objective concern with life itself in the face of death. Now that they are at that stage of life, they have been developing a more detailed description of just what the lessons of each part of life lend to wisdom in old age. For each earlier stage of development they see a parallel development toward the end of life's journey.

For instance, the sense of trust that begins to develop from the infant's experience of a loving and supportive environment becomes, in old age, an appreciation of human interdependence, according to the Eriksons.

"Life doesn't make any sense without interdependence," Mrs. Erikson said. "We need each other and the sooner we learn that the better for us all."

The second stage of life, which begins in early childhood with learning control-over one's own body, builds the sense of will on the one hand, or shame and doubt on the other. In old age, one's experience is almost a mirror image of what it was earlier as the body deteriorates and one needs to learn to accept it.

In "play age" or preschool children, what is being learned is a sense of initiative and purpose in life, as well as a sense of playfulness and creativity, the theory holds.

Two lessons for old age from that stage of life are empathy and resilience, as the Eriksons see it.

"The more you know yourself, the more patience you have for what you see in others." Mrs. Erikson said. "You don't have to accept what people do, but understand what leads them to do it. The stance this leads to is to forgive even though you still oppose."

The child's playfulness becomes, too, a sense of humor about life. "I can't imagine a wise old person who can't laugh," said Mr. Erikson. "The world is full of ridiculous dichotomies."

At school age, the Erikson's next stage, the child strives to become effective and industrious, and so develops a sense of competence; if he or she does not, the outcome is feelings of inferiority.

Humility in Old Age

In old age, as one's physical and sensory abilities wane, a lifelong sense of effectiveness is a critical resource. Reflections in old age on the course one's life has taken—especially comparing one's early hopes and dreams with the life one actually lived—foster humility. Thus, humility in old age is a realistic appreciation of one's limits and competencies.

The adolescent's struggle to overcome confusion and find a lifelong identity results in the capacity for commitment and fidelity, the Eriksons hold. Reflections in old age on the complexity of living go hand in hand with a new way of perceiving, one that merges sensory, logical and esthetic perception, they say. Too often, they say, people overemphasize logic and ignore other modes of knowing.

"If you leave out what your senses tell you, your thinking is not so good," Mrs. Erikson said.

In young adulthood, the conflict is between finding a balance between lasting intimacy and the need for isolation. At the last stage of life, this takes the form of coming to terms with love expressed and unexpressed during one's entire life; the understanding of the complexity of relationships is a facet of wisdom.

"You have to live intimacy out over many years, with all the complications of a long-range relationship, really to understand it," Mrs. Erikson said. "Anyone can flirt around with many relationships, but commitment is crucial to intimacy. Loving better is what comes from understanding the complications of a long-term intimate bond."

She added, "You put such a stress on passion when you're young. You learn about the value of tenderness when you grow old. You also learn in late life not to hold, to give without hanging on; to love freely, in the sense of wanting nothing in return."

In the adult years, the psychological tension is between what the Eriksons call generativity and caring on the one hand and self-absorption and stagnation on the other. Generativity expresses itself, as Mrs. Erikson put it, in "taking care to pass on to the next generation what you've contributed to life."

Mr. Erikson sees a widespread failing in modern life.

"The only thing that can save us as a species is seeing how we're not thinking about future generations in the way we live," he said. "What's lacking is generativity, a generativity that will promote positive values in the lives of the next generation. Unfortunately, we set the example of greed, wanting a bigger and better everything, with no thought of what will make it a better world for our great-grandchildren. That's why we go on depleting the earth; we're not thinking of the next generations."

Understanding Generativity

As an attribute of wisdom in old age, generativity has two faces. One is "caritas," a Greek word for charity, which the Eriksons take in the broad sense of caring for others. The other is "agape," a Greek word for love, which they define as a kind of empathy.

The final phase of life, in which integrity battles despair, culminates in a full wisdom to the degree each earlier phase of life has had a positive resolution, the Eriksons believe. If everything has gone well, one achieves a sense of integrity, a sense of completeness, of personal wholeness that is strong enough to offset the downward psychological pull of the inevitable physical disintegration.

Despair seems quite far from the Eriksons in their own lives. Both continue to exemplify what they described in the title of a 1986 book, *Vital Involvement in Old Age.* Mr. Erikson is writing about, among others things, the sayings of Jesus. Mrs. Erikson's most recent book, *Wisdom and the Senses,* published in 1988 by W. W. Norton & Company. In it, she sets out evidence that the liveliness of the senses throughout life, and the

creativity and playfulness that this brings, is the keystone of wisdom in old age.

"The importance of the senses came to us in old age," said Mr. Erikson, who now wears a hearing aid and walks with a slow, measured dignity.

In her book, Mrs. Erikson argues that modern life allows too little time for the pleasures of the senses. She says, "We start to lose touch with the senses in school: we call play, which stimulates the senses and makes them acute, a waste of time or laziness. The schools relegate play to sports. We call that play, but it isn't; it's competitive, not in the spirit of a game."

The Eriksons contend that wisdom has little to do with formal learning. "What is real wisdom?" Mrs. Erikson asked. "It comes from life experience, well digested. It's not what comes from reading great books. When it comes to understanding life, experiential learning is the only worthwhile kind; everything else is hearsay."

Mr. Erikson has been continuing a line of thought he set out in a *Yale Review* article in 1981 on the sayings of Jesus and their implications for the sense of "I," an argument that takes on the concept of the "ego" in Freudian thought.

"The trouble with the word 'ego' is its technical connotations," Mr. Erikson said. "It has bothered me that 'ego' was used as the translation of the German word 'Ich.' That's wrong. Freud was referring to the simple sense of "I."

Another continuing concern for the Eriksons has been the ethics of survival, and what they see as the urgent need to overcome the human tendency to define other groups, as an enemy, an outgrowth of the line of thinking Mr. Erikson began in his biography of Gandhi.

Mr. Erikson was trained in psychoanalysis in Vienna while Freud was still there, and worked closely with Freud's daughter Anna in exploring ways to apply psychoanalytic methods to children. That expertise made him welcome at Harvard, where he had his first academic post.

There he began the expansion of Freud's thinking that was to make him world famous. By describing in his books *Childhood and Society* and *Identity and the Life Cycle* how psychological growth is shaped throughout life, not just during the formative early years that Freud focused on, Mr. Erikson made a quantum leap in Freudian thought.

Over the years since first coming to Harvard, Mr. Erikson has spent time at other universities and hospitals, including Yale in the late 1930's, the University of California at Berkeley in the 40's, the Austen Riggs Center in Stockbridge, Massachusetts, in the 50's, and again at Harvard through the 60's. Until last year, the Eriksons lived in Marin County near San Francisco, but it is to Cambridge that they returned.

One lure was grandchildren near by. Their son Kai, with two children, is a professor of sociology at Yale, and their daughter Sue, with one child, also lives nearby.

Informally, Mr. Erikson still continues to supervise therapists. "The students tell me it's the most powerful clinical supervision they've ever had," said Margaret Brenman-Gibson, a professor of psychology in the psychiatry department at Cambridge City Hospital, a part of Harvard Medical School.

In Cambridge, the Eriksons share a rambling three-story Victorian with three other people: a graduate student, a professor of comparative religion and a psychologist. The housemates often take meals together.

"Living communally," said Mrs. Erikson, "is an adventure at our age."

Health

The growing scientific evidence for links between the brain and the immune system—the body's first line of defense against viruses, bacteria, and cancer—has made health psychology an important field. When this body of knowledge is applied to clinical interventions, it is known as "behavioral medicine." The field has grown beyond just helping people cope with stress, to include unveiling the connections between emotions, health, and diseases of every kind.

While psychologists have long taught people to relax in order to counter the psychological costs of stress, there is a new reason, to help maintain physical health. "Relaxation: Surprising Benefits Detected" tells of research showing that becoming deeply relaxed can have beneficial effects on the immune system, as well as a host of other medically valuable physiological changes.

Confession, whatever it may do for the soul, appears to be good for the body. "Confiding in Others Improves Health" describes studies that show that confiding in someone about feelings that have been troubling has positive effects for physical health. The act of confiding a long-held emotional burden, it seems, can have long-term health benefits.

On the other hand, people who habitually repress troubling feelings seem to put their health at risk by doing so. "New Studies Report Health Dangers of Repressing Emotional Turmoil" describes research on people who keep a stiff upper lip no matter what. Such people, called "repressers," appear to be out of touch with the symptoms of stress in their own bodies—a fact that may be based on brain function.

Another link between personality and health is made by data showing that people who are neurotic—who tend to be chronically anxious, pessimistic, tense, sad, or hostile—are at a greater risk for diseases of all kinds. While past research has made links between some diseases and specific emotions—such as hostility and heart disease—the research in "Study Affirms Link of Personality to Illness" shows that a broad range of negative emotions seems to heighten the risk of disease in general.

Another health risk is social isolation. While psychologists have long had evidence of an association between being lonely and illness, they did not know which was cause and which effect. The data in "Researchers Add Sound of Silence to the Growing List of Health Risk" shows that being cut off from friends and family can heighten the risk of falling ill.

People who go through surgery are, understandably, often frightened and apprehensive. But a program of emotional preparation for surgery can not only calm those fears—it can aid in medical recovery afterward. Just why is reviewed in "Emotional Preparation Aids Surgical Recovery."

The idea that one's emotional state can affect physical health is new to medicine and has met some resistance. There is an ongoing debate pro and con regarding the connections between emotions and disease. Read the views of both sides in "Debate Intensifies on Attitude and Health."

Despite the scientific controversy over links between psychological factors and disease, there has been steady growth in the field of behavioral medicine. The psychologists who practice behavioral medicine use psychological techniques to help people resist or recover from disease. The field, and its scientific basis, is described in "The Mind Over the Body."

Relaxation: Surprising Benefits Detected

May 13, 1986

The simple act of becoming relaxed can have surprising health benefits, new research is showing. In addition to the obvious psychological effects of relieving stress and mental tension, the new findings indicate, deep relaxation, if practiced regularly, can strengthen the immune system and produce a host of other medically valuable physiological changes.

In asthmatics, for example, relaxation training has been found to widen restricted respiratory passages. In some diabetics, relaxation can reduce the need for insulin. In many patients with chronic, unbearable pain, the training has brought about significant relief.

Moreover, the research shows, relaxation may help ward off disease by making people less susceptible to viruses, and by lowering blood pressure and cholesterol levels.

Intensive Techniques Are Used

Although such benefits have long been associated with meditation, a particular form of relaxation, the experimental evidence available now is much stronger than it was for mediation a few years ago. In addition, any form of deep relaxation seems to bring these benefits.

The medical advantages are not from ordinary relaxing activities, such as catnaps or gardening, but from intensive techniques that allow people to evoke a specific physiological state. "Just sitting quietly or, say, watching television, is not enough to produce the physiological changes," said Herbert Benson, director of the Division of Behavioral Medicine at Beth Israel Hospital, a part of Harvard Medical School in Boston. "You need to use a relaxation technique that will break the train of everyday thought, and decrease the activity of the sympathetic nervous system."

Ancient and Modern Methods

Like meditation and yoga, some of the relaxation techniques being used are quite ancient. Others, like biofeedback or progressive muscle relaxation, are relatively new. And some, like repetitive prayer, may seem worlds away from medicine. All of the techniques, though, seem to evoke a single physiological state that Dr. Benson some years ago called the "relaxation response."

The findings have led many hospitals to teach their patients ways to relax as part of their medical treatment. In some hospitals physicians can now prescribe a relaxation program that is broadcast on televisions in hospital rooms, so that patients can learn the techniques from their hospital beds.

"More and more doctors are seeing the value of these techniques as a way to tap the inner capacity of patients to help with their own healing," said Jon Kabat-Zinn, director of the Stress Reduction and Relaxation Program at the University of Massachusetts Medical School in Worcester. A fifty-seven-minute relaxation videotape made by Dr. Kabat-Zinn is in use at about a hundred hospitals. On that videotape, for example, patients are taught to meditate on their breathing, and are led in scanning the sensations throughout their bodies.

Fight-or-Flight Syndrome

The sympathetic nervous system reacts to stress by secreting hormones that mobilize the body's muscles and organs to face a threat. Sometimes called the "fight-or-flight response," this mobilization includes a variety of biological responses, including shifting blood flow from the limbs to the organs and increased blood pressure. The stress response does not require an emergency; it can be triggered merely by everyday worries and pressures.

In contrast, the relaxation response releases muscle tension, lowers blood pressure and slows the heart and breath rates.

The new work is showing that along with these changes come shifts in hormone levels that seem to produce beneficial effects on the immune system. For example, relaxation training in medical students during exams was found to increase their levels of helper cells that defend against infectious disease, according to a report in the current issue of the *Journal of Behavioral Medicine*.

The degree of benefits depends on the rigor with which people use the relaxation techniques. Those medical students who used the techniques just a few times showed little or no changes in the immune measure. Those who did the exercises most faithfully had the strongest immune effects, according to the report by Janice Kiecolt-Glaser and Ronald Glaser of the Ohio State University College of Medicine at Columbus.

In another study, the Ohio State researchers taught relaxation techniques to residents of a retirement home, whose average age was seventy-four years. After a month of training their levels of natural killer cells and antibody titers—indicators of resistance to tumors and viruses—had improved significantly, according to a report in Health Psychology.

"These improvements are particularly important for the elderly, since the immune system weakens with aging," Dr. Kiecolt-Glaser said.

Cardiovascular Problems Abate

Much interest in the medical use of relaxation has been for patients suffering from cardiovascular problems. A report in the *British Medical Journal,* for example, said that patients who had been trained to relax significantly lowered their blood pressure, and had maintained that reduction four years later.

In research at the Harvard Medical School, associates of Dr. Benson found that regular sessions of a simple meditation technique decreased the body's response to norepenephrine, a hormone released in reaction to stress. Although the endocrine system continued to emit the hormones, they did not seem to have their usual effects.

"Ordinarily, norepenephrine stimulates the cardiovascular system," Dr. Benson said. "But regular relaxation training resulted in less blood pressure increase to norepenephrine than is usually seen. Relaxation seems to mimic the action of the beta-blocking drugs used to control blood pressure."

Research by Dean Ornish, director of the Preventive Medicine Research Institute in San Francisco, has shown that relaxation training improves blood flow to the heart. Silent ischemia, which chokes off that blood flow, can damage the heart without causing noticeable pain. He also found that relaxation lowered cholesterol levels and lessened the severity of angina attacks.

In 1984, a National Institutes of Health report recommended the use of relaxation, along with salt restriction and weight loss, as the first therapy for mild hypertension, before resorting to drug treatments. Never-theless, many cardiologists have been slow to use the relaxation techniques.

"Most cardiologists still can't believe that stress has much to do with heart disease, or that relaxation can help in more than a minor way," Dr. Ornish said. "They don't learn about relaxation techniques in medical school, so they ignore them. But, slowly, relaxation is making more sense to them."

Diabetes and Chronic Pain

Diabetics can benefit from relaxation, according to research by Richard Surwit, a psychologist at the Duke University Medical Center. In a series of studies, Dr. Surwit found that relaxation improved the body's ability to regulate glucose in patients with the most common type of diabetes, which has its onset in adulthood. It is the body's inability to control glucose, or blood sugar, that ultimately leads to the damage done by the disease.

Relaxation seems to offer relief to many asthmatics by diminishing both the emotional upsets that can trigger attacks and the constriction of air passages that chokes breathing, according to a report by Paul Lehrer of Rutgers Medical School in the current issue of the *Journal of Psychosomatic Research.* The effects have been more pronounced for those who suffer chronic asthma, rather than those whose asthma is seasonal.

One of the major boons of relaxation training has been in lessening or alleviating chronic, severe pain. Such pain can arise from many different causes, including backache and chronic migraine or tension headaches, diseases such as cancer, and even as the unintended outcome of operations to control pain.

In a 1986 article in the *Journal of Behavioral Medicine,* Dr. Kabat-Zinn reported a sharp decrease in pain and related symptoms in patients trained in relaxation at the University of Massachusetts Medical Center in Worcester. The patients in the study, who included the full range of those typically seen in pain clinics, were able to lessen or, in some cases, stop altogether their use of pain drugs.

Four years after their training ended, the majority of patients were still faithful in their use of the relaxation practice, and still reported a decrease in pain and less reliance on drugs to control it, Dr. Kabat-Zinn said.

Relaxation is being used clinically in a much larger range of medical problems than the research so far has been able to assess. These include the management of the side effects of such medical procedures as kidney dialysis and cancer chemotherapy, gastrointestinal problems like irritable bowel syndrome, and insomnia, emphysema and skin disorders.

Evaluating Overall Effectiveness

Although clinical successes have been reported in individual cases with these disorders, research is now under way at Harvard and other centers to evaluate the overall effectiveness of relaxation in their treatment.

"It's not yet clear that relaxation will help with every kind of stress reactivity," Dr. Kabat-Zinn said. "And we've just begun to sort out which relaxation techniques work best with which medical problems. Most may be interchangeable, because of their general neuroendocrine effects, but we do not know yet for sure."

In research at Harvard, students who were identified as being easily engrossed in thoughts and images were trained in muscle relaxation and then asked to visualize certain specific images. Relaxation alone increased defenses against upper respiratory infections. The added imagery, however, enhanced the effect. The research was done by Mary Jasnoski, a psychologist who reported the findings at a meeting of the Society of Behavioral Medicine in San Francisco.

Although their biological effects are essentially similar, the relaxation techniques are very different. In Dr. Kabat-Zinn's "mindfulness" training, for example, patients pay careful attention to the sensations in their bodies, sweeping slowly from head to foot. They do not try to change those sensations, but note them precisely, with a neutral awareness. They are also taught a set of gentle yoga movements and stretches, which they do with the same careful attentiveness. Patients are encouraged to extend a relaxed mindfulness into the rest of their daily lives, especially when stressed.

In progressive relaxation, Dr. Lehrer's patients learn to recognize the often-subtle signals of tension in the major muscles of the body, and to systematically release that tension, leaving their whole body in a state of deep relaxation.

And Dr. Benson has found that for many of his patients the relaxation response can be evoked by their sitting quietly with eyes closed for fifteen minutes twice daily, and mentally repeating a simple word or sound. "Eighty percent of patients choose a simple prayer to repeat," Dr. Benson said.

The experts caution that intensive training, followed by regular use of the techniques, may be required before many medical benefits appear. Most training programs last several weeks. And, according to Dr. Lehrer, relaxation may be better when it is taught in person rather than learned from a tape.

The benefits seem to come from the physiology of relaxation rather than from mere suggestion, according to Dr. Lehrer. In a recent study, he found that asthmatic patients who were highly open to suggestions and hypnosis actually benefited the least from his relaxation training.

"Just feeling relaxed may not be the same as being truly relaxed physically," Dr. Lehrer said.

Not everyone is helped by the relaxation training, said Joan Borysenko, who directs the relaxation program for outpatients at Beth Israel Hospital in Boston. "Some people don't change much, some do a little, some a lot. And there are a few whose lives turn around totally."

Confiding in Others Improves Health

September 10, 1987

Confession, whatever it may do for the soul, appears to be good for the body.

New studies show that people who are able to confide in others about their troubled feelings or some traumatic event, rather than bear the turmoil in silence, are less vulnerable to illnesses.

The belief in the value of sharing one's deepest sense of guilt and turmoil with others has always been a basic tenet of some aspects of religion, psychotherapy and folk wisdom. But like so many attractive beliefs its value has been assumed largely in the absence of rigorous scientific scrutiny. This is changing, as a handful of behavioral scientists start to report their findings.

The findings about health are emerging especially rapidly now because of the work of James Pennebaker, a Southern Methodist University psychologist who is well-known for his contributions to behavioral medicine. In a series of studies soon to be widely reported, he has demonstrated that confiding in others, while often painful, seems to have long-term health benefits.

Dr. Pennebaker's research appears to show that the act of confiding in someone else protects the body against damaging internal stresses that are the penalty for carrying around an onerous emotional burden, such as unspoken remorse. Bereavement, for instance, when it is a sense of pain borne alone, seems to be linked to physical ailments, but when it is shared it seems to do far less damage.

Along similar lines, psychologists at Harvard University have pointed to a possible physical mechanism that accounts for the better health of those who can confide in others. They found that people whose approach to life made them less able to share intimacies also had less effective immune systems.

None of the new research is meant as an argument for any and all self-revelations. "It does not mean that it's always good to say whatever is on one's mind, indiscriminately," said Robert Wallerstein, chairman of the department of psychiatry at the University of California Medical School at San Francisco. Confiding, when done for the wrong reasons, such as an effort to make the listener feel guilty, "can be mischievous or even antagonistic," he said. Also, people who confide too freely sometimes betray a self-centeredness that can antagonize the sympathetic listener, who comes to feel used.

Nevertheless, there is now clear evidence for the health benefits of confiding. In a study published in *The Journal of Abnormal Psychology,* Dr. Pennebaker used coroner's records to contact the surviving spouses of men and women who had committed suicide or died in auto accidents in a large Southern city.

A year or more after the accident, those widows and widowers who kept their grief to themselves tended to have many more health problems than those who talked over their troubles with someone else.

In fact, the group that was open about the grief, showed no increase in health problems at all after the death of a spouse.

Similar to Suppression

Not confiding one's troubles, Dr. Pennebaker said, requires a physiological effort that combines with the normal upheavals of the trauma itself to produce the most stress, and over time, he proposes, that combined stress can lead to disease.

This process, he said, is similar to the psychological defense mechanism called suppression, in which a person actively tries to put disturbing thoughts out of his mind. As Freud proposed, Dr. Pennebaker said that such psychological inhibition requires an active mental effort. That effort, he writes, "is the central feature in the connection between life trauma and illness."

Supporting evidence for this has come from a series of studies at Harvard University on the reactions to stress of people who, as part of an overall personality pattern, keep their feelings to themselves. According to David McClelland, a psychologist who was one of those conducting the research, such people when under stress have been found to release hormones that tend to lower their immune system's resistance to disease.

However, the interaction between emotions and health seems ever more complex as an increasing number of researchers look at it. Thus Dr. McClelland noted cautiously that the poor results in his study may be due to other aspects of personality than specifically to the failure to confide.

Relaxation Amid Stress

Nevertheless, Dr. Pennebaker's conviction is that the act of confiding can be singled out for an important role in physical health. This belief led him to a series of experiments. In one, he had volunteers tell an experimenter, who was hidden by a curtain, about a traumatic event in their lives, a situation much like a confessional. Others talked into a tape recorder.

The volunteers had been prepared to talk about important upsetting events that had been preying on their minds. As part of the experiment, some were first asked to describe a trivial event. During the description of the insignificant event, physiological measures revealed, their bodies were tense and agitated.

"They were in the position of someone who is preoccupied by troubling thoughts he doesn't divulge," Dr. Pennebaker said in an interview.

When these volunteers talked about their genuine turmoil, though, their bodies showed a marked relaxation, even though many were visibly upset as they spoke, some crying, others speaking in quaking voices.

Writing Is Found Effective

Confiding can be effective, it seems, even when it is not spoken. When Dr. Pennebaker had volunteers merely write about personal traumas for four fifteen-minute periods over consecutive nights, he found that they made fewer visits to physicians for the next six months than did volunteers who wrote only about trivial matters.

One woman told of her longstanding remorse about leaving a toy where her grandmother tripped over it, breaking her hip; the grandmother died of complications during surgery for the break. One man recounted the moment in his childhood when his father, while divorcing his mother, said it was the boy's birth that had ruined the marriage. Another woman confessed her turmoil about having recently become a lesbian.

One of the volunteers later said, "Although I have not talked with anyone about what I wrote, I was finally able to deal with it, work through the pain."

Looking at long-term suppression of the major traumas of a person's life, Dr. Pennebaker surveyed more than 700 undergraduates who were women. He found that about one in twelve acknowledged having had a traumatic sexual experiences in childhood.

In general, women who had experienced such sexual traumas reported more health problems like headaches, tension and stomach ailments than did other women, including a group of women who as children had gone through nonsexual traumas such as the death of a parent or divorce.

But Dr. Pennebaker found that a failure to talk about the sexual trauma seemed to compound the problem, and those who kept their secrets to themselves suffered the most from poor health.

This line of evidence can be used to explain why talking over one's psychological troubles with a therapist may be physically beneficial. Studies of several thousand patients in national health plans in Europe and of users of Blue Cross in the United States have found that people in psychotherapy tend to consult physicians for medical problems less often than those not in therapy.

Dr. Pennebaker said these beneficial effects may extend to any act of confiding, including religious confession, talking to friends or even keeping a diary. For creative artists, he said, the act of writing or painting may serve the same function.

Not All Confidants Are Helpful

But not all confidants can serve equally, in the view of some experts. "There is a major difference between confiding in a spouse or friend, and confiding in a therapist," according to Jerome Frank, a psychiatrist emeritus at Johns Hopkins School of Medicine who is the author of several books on the relationship between healing and therapy.

"With a spouse or friend, you have to be thinking of the other person's feelings," Dr. Frank said in an interview. "And there may be things you don't want to reveal, because they might be held against you." In many instances, a therapist may be more helpful. "With a therapist you have the understanding that he will keep your best interests at heart," Dr. Frank said, "and that he will stick by you no matter what you have to say."

"Friends you can trust that completely are rare but they, too, are especially valuable," he added.

New Studies Report Health Dangers of Repressing Emotional Turmoil

March 3, 1988

New studies are drawing a portrait of one of the most mystifying personality types: those people who maintain a stiff upper lip under all circumstances.

Behavioral scientists report that these people are not simply successful at masking emotion or staying cool under pressure; often they are not even aware of their own inner stress, even as the body registers it with higher blood pressure or more rapid heartbeat. As a result, studies are showing these "represser" personality types are more prone than others to some diseases. And when they do get sick they are more likely to wait too long to seek help.

The ability to tune out feelings like anger and anxiety is reflected in brain function. A recent study of stiff-upper-lip types found they had a lag in the time it took certain information to get from one hemisphere of the brain to the other. The lag was only for disturbing messages, not for neutral ones, according to the study by Richard Davidson of the University of Wisconsin.

Although experts believe that the represser personality is rooted in psychological experiences of childhood, the findings on brain function provide a tangible marker of the syndrome. In effect, the brain hampers the conscious registering of negative emotions.

'They Are Very Dependable'

"As adults, repressers tend to be overly concerned with meeting other people's needs," said Gary E. Schwartz, a professor of psychology and psychiatry at Yale Medical School. "They are very dependable and often very successful. But their marriages do poorly because they are unable to engage emotionally in intimate relationships." Mr. Schwartz is also director of the Yale Psychophysiology Center, where much of the original work on repressers was done.

Decades ago Freud postulated that important feelings could be stifled before they entered consciousness. And in the years since, others have asserted that repressed feelings could emerge as illness. The new work is documenting those observations for the first time and expanding on them.

About one in six people tends to fall into the represser category, according to Daniel Weinberger, a psychologist at Stanford University. Researchers distinguish between repressers, or those whose physiological responses show that beneath the conscious surface they are actually quite prone to anxiety, and people who genuinely tend to feel little anxiety or stress.

"Repressers tend to be rational and in control of their emotions," Dr. Weinberger said. "They see themselves as people who don't get upset about things, who are cool and collected under stress. You see it in the competent surgeon or lawyer who values not letting his emotions shade his judgment."

The represser's calm is bought at a great price. Recent reports have linked a repressing personality to a higher risk for asthma, high blood pressure and overall ill health.

"Over time, the represser's style of stifling reactions tends to take its toll on health," Dr. Weinberger said.

In a study of 120 managers and engineers at an aerospace company, researchers at the Stanford University School of Medicine found that the repressers had higher blood pressure and reacted with an even greater rise in blood pressure to a simple stress test than did non-repressers.

"Despite their calm exterior, under a mental challenge the repressers had a higher blood pressure rise than even highly anxious people," said Abby King, a psychologist at the Center for Research in Disease Prevention at Stanford, who did the study.

More generally, the represser's style has been associated with a reduced resistance to infectious diseases. Researchers at the Yale School of Medicine found that in 312 patients treated at an outpatient clinic there, the repressers tended to have lower levels of certain disease-fighting cells of the immune system, and higher levels of cells that multiply at the time of allergic reactions.

Research by Dr. Weinberger and others suggests that repressers invest heavily in a self-image of themselves as imperturbable. When they are disturbed, as gauged by their physiological reactions, the repressers tend to ignore the physical manifestations of their agitation.

The repressers' tendency to ignore distressing information, some experts believe, can come from a family situation in which the child learned to survive a risk, such as an abusive parent, by being well-behaved and suppressing their own anger and anxiety. Or, in families where the parents themselves are repressers, the child learns that the expression of emotions is to be avoided.

They Are Reluctant to Seek Help

Because repressers avoid facing the reality of the troubled side of their life, they are typically reluctant to seek psychotherapy. However, some therapeutic approaches have been found effective. At the Yale Behavioral Medicine Clinic, Dr. Schwartz has been treating repressers with biofeedback, in which electrodes are used to detect subtle physiological responses, helping a person learn to control responses.

"With the biofeedback," Dr. Schwartz said, "we can show them the difference between their experience and how their body actually behaves.

Study Affirms Link of Personality to Illness

January 19, 1988

A major new study links personality traits with illness on such a broad scale that some psychologists depict being neurotic as a key factor in susceptibility to disease.

The study found that traits that typify the neurotic person—chronic anxiety, long periods of sadness and pessimism, unremitting tension, incessant hostility—were associated with asthma, headaches, peptic ulcers and heart disease.

In the past, specific traits were often tied to one or another of these diseases. But that point of view had largely fallen into disrepute because the studies were so contradictory.

No sooner would one study show a relationship than another would come along and fail to confirm the link of specific traits to specific diseases. Even in heart disease, where a large number of studies have shown an association with hostility, many other studies have shown no link.

But now the effort to tie personality to disease has been reinvigorated with the work of Howard Friedman and Stephanie Booth-Kewley, psychologists at the University of California at Riverside. Researchers say the new study bolsters the view that, for some people, psychotherapy may foster physical as well emotional well-being.

Dr. Friedman and Dr. Booth-Kewley believe that their research, which pulls together and interprets many smaller studies, strongly re-establishes the tie between illness and personality and that other researchers had erred by trying to make the thesis too specific. The two psychologists' data suggest that being neurotic makes a person twice as likely as someone not neurotic to contract to some kind of illness—that constant hostility is as dangerous as high cholesterol or smoking is in heart disease, for example.

The new findings have inspired intense debate. No one doubts that there appears to be an association between personality and disease, but critics argue vigorously that much of the correlation can be explained by the complaining nature of neurotics and their tendency to be sensitive to every discomfort.

"Neurotics' complaints are best viewed as exaggerations of bodily concerns rather than as signs of organic disease," according to an article in *The American Psychologist* by Paul T. Costa and Robert R. McCrae of the National Institute on Aging.

Still, many experts believe that the effect of neuroticism on disease is real. Joan Rittenhouse, executive secretary of the behavior medicine study section at the National Institutes of Health, acknowledges that neurotics complain more than other people do but she says hard medical evidence shows that the complaints often have a genuine foundation.

"The weight of research, including many studies that used objective tests and diagnoses instead of people's reports of symptoms, supports Dr. Friedman's conclusion that there is a link between neuroticism and disease," she said.

Dr. Friedman's research, published in a 1988 issue of *The American Psychologist,* was an analysis of data from 101 previous studies that had investigated links between personality traits and particular illnesses. Many of those studies had not found significant links.

Dr. Friedman used a recently developed statistical method, called "meta-analysis," which allows all 101 studies to be combined as though they were one huge research project focusing on thousands of research subjects. This simulation of a large study allows the researchers to detect important but subtle links that would not emerge in studies that use only dozens or even hundreds of people.

Standard Method of Review

The method has become increasingly popular in the social sciences in the last few years. It has become the standard technique used to review any major field where there are a multitude of studies that used differing measures of the same broad topic.

In his meta-analysis, Dr. Friedman found a previously undetected link between some or all of the neurotic traits and susceptibility to five diseases that were being studied: asthma, headaches, peptic ulcers, arthritis and heart disease.

Previous studies, by and large, had examined the association between a single trait and a single disease. But Dr. Friedman found instead a broad association between neuroticism and illness in general.

In a new study that supports Dr. Friedman's finding, researchers have found that people's psychological outlook during their twenties predicts their robustness or their vulnerability to disease as they enter midlife. "People who are pessimistic in their twenties are more likely to be ill or to have died twenty to thirty years later," said

Cristopher Peterson, the University of Michigan psychologist who did the study.

Turning Point in Early Forties

The study was based on intensive interviews of members of the Harvard classes of 1939 through 1944 who were deemed "fittest" among their classmates. Those who were most pessimistic or fatalistic as students, the study found, were more susceptible to diseases of all kinds in later life.

"There was little difference in health among these men for more than two decades; the turning point came during their early forties when the more pessimistic ones began to fall ill," said Dr. Peterson. His study was published in the summer 1988 issue of *The Journal of Personality and Social Psychology*.

Other supporting evidence can be found in research showing that psychotherapy seems to be associated with improved physical health. In addition, one trait usually considered to be part of the neurotic personality, depression, has been linked in studies with an impaired response by the immune system to disease.

"It's not just that being sick makes you more neurotic or that being neurotic makes you complain more," said Dr. Rittenhouse of the National Institutes of Health. "Studies that use hard diagnostic measures substantiate the conclusion that neurotics are at greater risk for disease because of their personalities."

However, Dr. Costa and Dr. McCrae of the National Institute on Aging are adamantly unpersuaded. They point to their study of 347 adult men who were given medical and psychological tests several times over two decades.

Those with the highest scores on tests of neuroticism consistently reported more medical complaints of all kinds, from respiratory problems to skin disease. But on the basis of findings from 294 men who died during the study, the neurotics had as long a lifespan as those who were not neurotic.

The study was published in the January, 1988 issue of *The Journal of Personality*.

Researchers Add Sounds of Silence to the Growing List of Health Risks

October 7, 1987

Being cut off from friendships and one's family doubles a person's chances of sickness or death, a new report indicates.

Although social scientists have long known there was a strong association between loneliness and illness, it was unclear until recent studies which was the cause and which the effect.

But the new studies, summarized in a 1988 issue of *Science* magazine, show that a lack of social relationships in and of itself heightens people's susceptibility to illness.

"The data shows that people who are isolated but healthy are twice as likely to die over the period of a decade or so as are others in the same health," said James House, a sociologist at the Institute of Social Research at University of Michigan, a co-author of the report.

Effect Found at Extremes

The report, co-written by two other researchers, Karl Landis and Debra Umberson, summarizes studies in the United States, Finland and Sweden on the effects isolation has on health that have been done over the last two decades. In the studies, more than 37,000 people were assessed over periods of up to twelve years.

Of course, many people who live on their own or see few friends are content and healthy, Dr. House said. Living alone or being somewhat reclusive is not enough by itself to make a person so isolated that his or her health is likely to suffer.

"It's the 10 to 20 percent of people who say they have nobody with whom they can share their private feelings, or who have close contact with others less than once a week, who are at most risk," Dr. House said.

The finding comes at a time when the trend toward social isolation is strengthening. Americans are increasingly less likely to live with others, to be married, to belong to social clubs or to visit with friends than they were twenty or thirty years ago, the report said Federal statistics show.

"It is ironic that just as we are beginning to understand the importance of social relationships for health," they are on the decline, the report said.

More Risky Than Smoking

In adding to the list of factors that put people at an increased risk for disease, the report said social isolation "is as significant to mortality rates as smoking, high blood pressure, high cholesterol, obesity and lack of physical exercise."

"In fact, when age is adjusted for, social isolation is as great or greater a mortality risk than smoking," it added.

While smoking makes a person about 1.6 times more likely to develop illnesses of all kinds, social isolation makes a person twice as likely to become sick, the researchers said.

"After controlling for the effects of physical health, socioeconomic status, smoking, alcohol, exercise, obesity, race, life satisfaction and health care, the studies found that those with few or weak social ties were twice as likely to die as were those with strong ties," Dr. House said. "Until now, skeptics could argue that people who are sick, crazy, or have bad health habits were just more likely to alienate people or just lacked the energy to get together with friends."

Greater Effect on Men

Isolation is more devastating to men than to women, the research shows. In a study by University of Michigan researchers of 2,754 men and women, isolated men were two to three times more likely to die as were men with close social ties. For isolated women, the risk was only one and a half times as great as for women with close ties.

The difference between men and women may be due to women having a higher quality of relationships than men, the Science report suggested. Because social isolation was evaluated by the number of social contacts rather than their quality, it may be a poorer measure of social isolation for women than for men.

The Science report also cited recent laboratory experiments with rats, mice and goats showing that the mere presence of a familiar member of the same species can lessen the physiological impact of stress in producing ulcers, hypertension and "neurosis." One study showed that rabbits who were fed a high-fat diet developed less arteriosclerosis if they were petted regularly by a human.

Effect in Brain Theorized

Other studies cited in the report have shown that the presence of another person can reduce anxiety and lessen unhealthy physiological activity in people in intensive care units. The comforting effect of another person's presence has been shown to lower not just heart rate and blood pressure but also the secretion of fatty acids that can block arteries.

One theory of why the presence of another person might help suggests that there is an effect in the brain from social contact. The theory holds that social contact inhibits activity in the posterior hypothalmic zone of the brain, lowering the rate of secretion of acetylcholine, cortisol and catecholamines, chemicals that trigger more rapid breathing, a quickened heartbeat and other physiological signs of stress.

The risks from social isolation are not just for physical illness. It also makes people more likely to suffer an accident or commit suicide, the report said.

This harks back to the first suggestion of a link between isolation and mortality, by Emil Durkheim, the French sociologist. In 1897, Mr. Durkheim found that people who were alienated, or cut off from social ties, were far more likely than others to commit suicide.

While some people are socially isolated for unavoidable reasons, such as severe disability, many people find themselves alone for psychological reasons. Thinking patterns that encourage isolation are particularly common, psychologists say.

One is a sense of social incompetence, which results in shrinking from contact with others. The deep belief that one is unattractive, socially inept, or otherwise undesirable is often at the root of this attitude.

Another is fear of intimate emotional contact, based on the belief that one is fundamentally unlovable.

Some people "feel they are basically defective, that if someone got to know them well, they would dislike them," said Jeffrey Young, a psychologist in New York City who has written on the psychological causes of social isolation. "These people have social contacts, but keep everyone at a distance."

Those who feel others cannot be trusted also tend to isolate themselves. "They think that people will use them, put them down or abandon them, that its dangerous to be close to others," Dr. Young said.

But he said people can often take steps to overcome self-imposed isolation. For instance, those who fear closeness can push themselves to open up about themselves a bit once they know and trust someone. And although it will undoubtedly be difficult, those who feel unlovable should attempt find someone, either a friend or a relative, who can offer a candid evaluation in areas where they feel inadequate.

"People are usually far more harsh on themselves than reality justifies," Dr. Young said.

Often people who hold such self-defeating beliefs resist doing the things that would allow them to be less isolated. David Burns, a psychiatrist at the University of Pennsylvania who has written about loneliness, tells of a patient who desparately wants to have a girlfriend, but who dresses in an unappealing manner.

When Dr. Burns gently suggestted that he might have more luck with women if he improved how he dressed, the man threatened to quit therapy, saying, "How I dress reflects my true self. I can't compromise on that!"

Emotional Preparation Aids Surgical Recovery

December 10, 1987

The trauma of surgery, part biological and part psychological, can be greatly eased by psychologically preparing patients for surgery, studies are finding. The techniques are proving to aid physical recovery and lessen the pain and anxiety that surgery brings.

A variety of preparations, ranging from hypnosis and relaxation training to educational videotapes, seem to help. The benefits, though, seem due to a psychological factor that underlies them all: heightening the patient's feelings that he has some control over his recovery, and that he is not just a passive victim.

Nevertheless, surgeons and anesthesiologists seem slow to take steps to help patients prepare psychologically, according to researchers, some of whom view the delays as tragic.

"From the surgeon's point of view, these psychological preparations matter little, while from the patient's they matter tremendously," Henry Bennett, a psychologist who works with patients undergoing spinal surgery at the University of California Medical School at Davis, said in a telephone interview.

Linked to Earlier Release

A review of thirty-four studies involving more than 3,000 patients, published in *The American Journal of Public Health,* found that patients who received psychological preparation were released from the hospital an average of two days earlier than those who received the usual presurgical treatment. The preparations ranged from brief psychotherapy or

classes with a nurse two weeks before surgery, to listening to a tape.

"Psychological preparation can lessen medical complications, can soothe pain and fear and feelings of helplessness and anger, and can give the patient the sense that he has some small say in a matter so vital in his life," Dr. Bennett said.

Writing in the journal *Advances,* Dr. Bennett argued that surgeons and anesthesiologists too often see the patient as "only a body."

One recent study was conducted by Erling Anderson, a psychologist in the Department of Anesthesiology at the University of Iowa Medical Center. He reported in the *Journal of Consulting and Clinical Psychology* that sixty men undergoing coronary bypass grafts at the medical center were divided into three groups. One group received the hospital's standard preparation, a brochure on the procedures and a short visit from a nurse to answer questions.

The other groups watched a videotape called "Living Proof" that followed a patient through the operation and recovery. In addition, one group received advanced instructions in the physical therapy exercises—such as deep breathing to expand their lung capacity—they would be doing to help recovery.

Tension Can Be Deadly

While 75 percent of those with the standard preparation suffered after the surgery from acute hypertension—a condition that can endanger coronary bypass patients in the first twelve hours after surgery—less than

45 percent of those who saw the tape had the problem.

The patients who viewed the tape also had less anxiety as they waited in the hospital before the surgery, and reported less stress and seemed more relaxed to nurses in the week after the surgery. The group that received extra instruction in the physical therapy went into surgery feeling less anxious than the other groups.

But Dr. Anderson added that information alone is not enough for patients. "They need time to mull it over and ask questions," he said.

Patients having elective surgery often are briefed by a nurse or the anesthesiologist the day before. This may give patients too little time to absorb the information and to ask crucial questions, the experts say.

"When people gather information to handle stress, at first it raises their anxiety," Dr. Anderson said. "But as they think it over and find ways to deal with it, they end up with a reassuring sense of control."

Dr. Anderson suggested that patients begin to ask for information about their surgery as soon as it is scheduled. He also advised that they seek ways to ease their recovery, learning physical therapy exercises or relaxation techniques. He also suggested that patients learn as precisely as they can what they will experience.

Of course, not all surgeons have been slow to adopt the new techniques. Dr. Nilima Patwardhan, a general surgeon at the University of Massachusetts Medical School in Worcester, prescribes an instructional relaxation videotape that is available on the hospital's closed-circuit television system for patients who are anxious. In fact, when she had surgery for a cervical disc that had paralyzed her arm, she used the videotape herself.

Not all patients are open to such preparations, Dr. Patwardhan added. Dr. Malcolm Rogers, a psychiatrist at Harvard Medical School, writing in *Advances in Psychosomatic Medicine,* has proposed that the information and training given patients before surgery should fit their personality, some people naturally wanting as much information as possible, others preferring to deny the threat.

"There's nothing in the training of surgeons or anesthesiologists about psychological preparation for surgery," said Dr. William Hawke, a surgeon at the University of Michigan Medical School. "What each surgeon or anesthesiologist does depends on his personal preference. Some spend a great deal of time with patients, or have a nurse do so, while others see the patient as just another gall bladder to remove, not a person with feelings."

Debate Intensifies on Attitude and Health

October 29, 1985

In an editorial in June, 1985, the influential *New England Journal of Medicine* concluded that "our belief in disease as a direct reflection of mental state is largely folklore." That statement touched off a furor.

The American Psychological Association responded with a resolution denouncing the editorial as "inaccurate and unfortunate," asserting that it ignored a substantial body of research findings linking psychological factors and health.

"No one argues that you can get cancer just because you're feeling depressed, or hypertension just by being hostile," said Jerome L. Singer, a psychologist at Yale who was one of those issuing the psychologists' statement. "But emotions clearly contribute to the onset and course of the disease; it's dead wrong to call it folklore." point to a major article that appeared in July, 1985, in an equally respected publication, *The Lancet,* the British medical journal. The article reviewed studies linking psychological factors and disease and concluded, in contrast to *The New England Journal's* editorial, that counseling and psychological support may be as important as many medical measures.

Indeed, there is a rapidly growing movement to complement medical treatment with psychological intervention, and a wide range of treatments are already in use. The supporters of this approach argue that evidence linking the brain, the immune system and the course of disease is strong and that psychological treatment can often enhance the effectiveness of biological measures. For example, a recent study has suggested that cancer patients who received psychotherapy along with chemotherapy lived longer than did those who received chemotherapy alone.

According to Marcia Angell, the Journal editor who wrote the editorial, people have been led to believe that the links between emotions and disease are well-founded when, in her view, the evidence is not convincing. "I'm not saying that there's no point in pursuing this research," Dr. Angell said in an interview. "But I'm saying the conclusions don't follow from the findings. I'm still waiting for proof that the way we think has a major clinical impact on the immune system. The studies so far are inadequate."

Some clinicians object that the editorial's widely publicized conclusion—that psychological factors have no meaningful effects on disease—can have a negative effect on patients, particularly those facing severe illness such as cancer. Such patients, they fear, may fall into feelings of helplessness, an attitude that, according to some studies, may be associated with a poor survival rate and that at any rate could add more mental suffering to the patient's burden.

Dr. Angell, on the other hand, believes there is greater danger in raising the hopes of patients that their attitudes can save them from disease. "The dark side of assuming there is a connection between emotions and health," she said, "is that people who fall ill may blame themselves, and feel even guiltier if they get worse."

'Astonished' by the Response

"I've been astonished by the intensity of the debate," she added. "It's as though I had attacked motherhood and happiness. People seem to want to believe that how we think matters for our health—that we have the power to control things that are powerful and frightening—but it's like doing a rain dance."

The editorial, Dr. Angell said, elicited as much mail, most of it critical, as *The Journal* has received on almost any article. The publication plans to print some of the letters, with her replies, next month.

Many researchers in the field object to what they see as the cavalier dismissal by Dr. Angell of a significant scientific literature establishing relationships between psychological factors and health.

"There's been a strong feeling among those doing the research that the editorial was just bad science," said Barry Flint, director of the New York-based Institute for the Advancement of Health, a clearinghouse for research on links between the mind and disease. "It ignores the thousands of studies showing connections between mental factors and disease."

The Institute, in cooperation with Steven Locke of Harvard Medical School, recently published *Mind and Immunity,* an annotated bibliography summarizing 1,400 scientific reports on the topic, and is now publishing a four-volume bibliography of more than a thousand reports on the psychological treatment of medical disorders.

Some Conclusions 'Simplistic'

Many researchers concede that the specific links between mental factors and disease are complicated and that some of the findings, a few dating back a century, are contradictory and tenuous.

In other words, many experts now believe that there is an important relationship between emotions and illness, but that what to do about it remains far less clear. "Some people are drawing conclusions that are too simplistic," said Lydia Temoshok, a psychologist at the University of California at San Francisco. "The immune system is incredibly complex. In a study of emotions and acquired immune deficiency syndrome, for example, we are taking twenty-seven different immune measures and finding that some go up while others go down. It's not at all clear which of these will be crucial to the medical outcome."

Dr. Temoshok is directing one of several research projects that seek to evaluate exactly how helpful psychological treatment may be in supplementing medical treatment of serious disease. These projects are intended not only to enhance the patient's immune resistance to disease, but also, more generally, to improve the quality of their lives while under medical care.

Typical of the new projects is one directed by Jon Kabat-Zinn at the University of Massachusetts Medical Center at Worcester. "We are sent patients with a wide range of disorders, including people with coronary bypasses, hypertension, cancer, chronic headaches or pain, and gastrointestinal disorders," Dr. Kabat-Zinn said in an interview. "The idea is to complement their medical care with self-regulatory techniques, such as a relaxing mental scan of the body and yoga exercises that help reverse muscle atrophy."

'Mindfulness' About Emotions

"We feel it's important to give patients methods they can use throughout the day, especially when they find themselves in a stressful or painful situation," Dr. Kabat-Zinn added.

"One such technique is mindfulness, paying careful attention to one's sensations and thoughts. This can give patients that moment it takes to reframe difficulties so that they are less stressful. For example, if your boss criticizes you, instead of letting it trigger all your insecurities and defenses, with mindfulness you watch your initial reactions go by before you speak."

Neal Flore, a psychologist at the University of California at Berkeley who was treated in 1974 for cancer of the testicles, said, "When I went into the hospital, I couldn't believe how primitive it was in handling the emotional side of my treatment." He described his feelings of helplessness and depression in a 1979 article in *The New England Journal of Medicine,* and told of the steps he took to become more actively involved in his treatment. Further, he proposed methods for marshaling the patient's own psychological resources, ranging from stress management to having more control over chemotherapy, such as helping decide the pace of the treatment.

Dr. Flore now applies those techniques in counseling medical patients. "The passivity and loss of control the patient feels can create a sense of helplessness which compounds their problem," he said in an interview. "Giving patients some sense of more active participation in treatment seems to have a positive effect on their bodies' ability to combat disease."

The theory that psychological help can buttress medical care has been supported by several recent studies, such as one by German researchers of 100 women with breast cancer that had begun to spread to other parts of the body. The study is reported in the book *Health Care and Human Behavior* (Academic Press). Women who received a combination of chemotherapy and psychotherapy survived longer, on average, than did

those who received chemotherapy alone, the study found.

Another study, reported in October, 1985, in *Health Psychology,* found that training in muscle relaxation enhanced levels of natural killer cells in a group of men and women sixty to eighty-eight years old. Such killer cells, part of the immune system, can attack malignant cells. The study, by Janice Kiecolt-Glaser and Ronald Glaser of the Ohio State University College of Medicine, concluded that relaxation training may be of particular importance as a preventive measure in the elderly, since the efficiency of their immune system decreases markedly.

An Emerging Consensus

Many experts welcomed the debate prompted by *The New England Journal's* editorial and the consensus that seems to be emerging in its wake.

This emerging view is evident in a joint statement by two whose work was mentioned in the editorial—Norman Cousins, who has popularized the effects of the mind on disease and who now teaches at the medical school at the University of California at Los Angeles, and Barrie Cassileth, the University of Pennsylvania sociologist whose study of advanced cancer patients prompted the editorial.

The statement said, "Few things are more important in the care of seriously ill patients than their mental state." Even so, it said, patients "should not be encouraged to believe that positive attitudes are a substitute for competent medical attention."

Nor is anyone prepared to suggest at this point that all the answers are yet at hand; more research remains to be done on just how emotions work on disease and how to make positive use of them. But the general belief does seem to be growing that emotions can be an important additional medical weapon.

The Mind Over the Body

September 27, 1987

When John Morgan first came to the behavioral-medicine program of Cambridge Hospital, he couldn't speak. He wrote notes to the doctors. The pain in his back was so intense and so constant that all he could do was sob. Mr. Morgan, a name used to protect the patient's privacy, had twisted his back in an automobile accident that had sent him smashing through the windshield, and he had since endured, in vain, six rounds of surgery for the pain. He was in despair.

At the hospital, he attended a weekly group session for those who, like himself, suffer pain so intractable that it becomes a continuous presence, a constant psychic companion. Chronic pain of this sort is a medical enigma—there is no specific site that accounts for it, and sometimes, as in Mr. Morgan's case, there is simply no medical procedure that can offer surcease.

As observed by closed-circuit television during a therapy session with Daniel P. Brown, the psychologist who directs the Cambridge program, Mr. Morgan, dressed in a black T-shirt, jeans and workboots, sits hunched in his chair, gazing at the floor like a shy child. The session continues for forty-five minutes, with Mr. Morgan practicing focusing attention on his breathing to put himself in a soothing trance—a technique he is learning to employ whenever and wherever his pain becomes intolerable. At the session's end, somewhat bewildered, he says "I don't understand what my body does to stop the pain, but it has stopped."

Mr. Morgan's physical problems remain the same as when he came to the hospital a few months previous. What is different is his state of mind. Treatments of the sort he is undergoing are part of a burgeoning, controversial medical field that for the last eight years has officially been termed behavioral medicine. Its techniques use the minds of patients to help heal their bodies.

The efficacy of behavioral medicine is increasingly supported by research evidence, the extent of which may surprise some detractors. And the degree to which the field is now accepted by health professionals would have been undreamed of as recently as fifteen years ago. When I did my doctoral research on relaxation and stress at Harvard in 1973, for instance, many of the techniques now used in behavioral medicine were just beginning to find acceptance among psychotherapists for treating anxiety, but very few professionals saw them as having more than minimal use in medicine.

Although acceptance has widened markedly since then, the notion that psychological techniques may have healing biological effects is, in many medical circles, still dismissed outright. *The New England Medical Journal* has called it "folklore." Nevertheless, the field is growing rapidly—for reasons that have to do with scientific discoveries, with clinical results and with economics.

The pioneering work in biofeedback of Neal E. Miller, an emeritus professor of psychology at Rockefeller University, now a research affiliate at Yale, gave behavioral medicine its first clinical credibility, in the late 1960's. That credibility was enhanced ten years ago, when Robert Ader, now director of the division of behavioral and psychosocial medicine at the University of Rochester's Medical School, demonstrated that, just as a dog can be conditioned to salivate when a bell rings, the immune system in rats could be conditioned to the taste of saccharine so as to suppress an antibody response. Mr. Ader's work launched the study of the links between the mind, the brain and the immune system.

Today, experts on the field estimate, there are approximately 400 universities that offer some level of training in behavioral medicine. Thousands of hospitals, clinics and individual practitioners offer the treatments in one form or another.

There has been a growing number of academic and popular books on the field by professionals with solid scientific credentials. In *Hypnosis and Behavioral Medicine,* Daniel Brown of Cambridge Hospital and Erika Fromm of the University of Chicago review recent research showing that a host of largely interchangeable methods—including muscle relaxation, hypnosis, meditation, controlled breathing and biofeedback—has helped in the treatment of some types of allergies, asthma, hypertension, migraine and tension headache, herpes lesions, irritable-bowel syndrome and peptic ulcer. *Love, Medicine & Miracles,* by Dr. Bernie S. Siegel, a Yale surgeon, points to the role of the patient's mind and emotions in healing. And *Minding the Body, Mending the Mind,* describes the behavioral-medicine program used by Joan Borysenko, a cell biologist and psychologist at Harvard Medical School, in "Mind/Body" clinics.

One weekend, a group of a dozen or so leaders of behavioral medicine gathered for a closed meeting in an unlikely setting: the Playhouse at Pocantico Hills, the Tarrytown, N.Y., estate built by John D. Rockefeller. The Playhouse is a long, rambling building in which, at one time, John D. Jr.'s five sons and his daughter could play in a tiled indoor pool, indoor tennis or squash courts, a bowling alley and a billiard room.

It was John D. Jr.'s granddaughter, Eileen Rockefeller Growald, who convened the meeting. Those gathered for dinner in what had been the card room were all members of the scientific advisory council and board of trustees of the Institute for the Advancement of Health, an organization, based in New York City, that Mrs. Growald has founded and which is at the vanguard of this medical movement.

"Our goal is empowerment of the patient," says Mrs. Growald. "You can't feel empowered when you just sit in the doctor's office and passively accept his prescription. You start to feel it when you ask about side-effects, or about alternatives. But empowerment means something more: not just being an informed medical consumer, but also using the new mind-body techniques to help in your own healing."

The institute came about because of the contrast between the deaths of two of Mrs. Growald's mentors. One was a former teacher, Walter Clark, founder of the North Country School in upstate New York, which she attended. His personal philosophy had been one of "ruggedness, resiliency and resourcefulness," but after he underwent successful bypass surgery at seventy-six, he suffered medical complications and a deep depression, according to Mrs. Growald. He went into a decline and died within five months.

"He was rendered helpless," says Mrs. Growald. "He had been self-reliant all his life; it was the helplessness that did him in."

About the same time, another mentor, Harold K. Hochschild, then eighty-eight, was dying of leukemia. A week before his death, Mrs. Growald visited him and found him re-markably cheerful and alert. "Eileen," he told her, "I've lived a long good life, and if I can only live 50 percent, I don't want to go on."

"Here was Harold, so at peace and ready to go, and Walter, so bewildered and depressed," recalls Mrs. Growald. "I wondered about the difference between their deaths, wondered if there were differences in their attitudes, the medical advice they got and its effects."

And, at just about the same time, Norman Cousins, another mentor of Mrs. Growald, was returning to a full work schedule after refusing bypass surgery following a heart attack and restoring himself to health, as he has reported, by a program of exercise, diet and lifting his spirits. "The contrast between Walter on the one hand and Harold and Norman on the other moved me to explore more deeply how attitudes and emotions are connected to health and illness," she says.

The result of that exploration was the founding, in 1983, of the institute, an organization that occupies a middle ground between the public and health professionals.

Realizing that the public may often be confused by the rapid developments in behavioral medicine and what can be outlandish claims for treatments from less-than-scrupulous practitioners, the institute has begun a newsletter, *Mind-Body-Health Digest.* The publication aims to offer responsible advice, distinguishing for the lay reader between the proven and the puffery on such topics as psychological factors in cancer and the efficacy of relaxation techniques.

For professionals, the Institute for the Advancement of Health has brought out three ponderous volumes that methodically summarize the published studies on the mind's effect on disease—a compilation that did not exist anywhere before. The work was done principally by Dr. Steven E. Locke, a psychiatrist at Harvard Medical School, who, though impressed by the quantity of research, is careful to point out the limitations of much of the scientific efforts so far. He says, "With the exception of a few areas, like hypertension and headache, there are very few studies in behavioral medicine that have true randomized, well-controlled clinical trials, of the sort that are standard in medical research. There are many studies that show improvement after treatment, but the problem is that some patients may come when their condition is at its worst. Some of the improvements you see may be due to the normal oscillation in the condition, not the treatment itself."

Through its journal, *Advances,* the institute welcomes from researchers papers more speculative than they could publish in regular scientific journals. For instance, in a recent issue, Candace B. Pert, chief of the section on brain biochemistry in the clinical neuroscience branch of the National Institute of Mental Health, puts forth an idea that, she concedes, some scientists might describe as "outrageous." She says that, because of newly discovered biochemical links between hormones in the body and cells in the immune system and brain, "I can no longer make a strong distinction between the brain and the body."

Specifically, she and her colleague Michael Ruff have found that monocytes—cells in the immune system that act to heal wounds, repair tissue and ingest bacteria and other foreign bodies—are shaped in such a way that they invite chemical interaction with a family of biochemicals called the neuropeptides. These serve as chemical messengers between brain cells, and they also regulate organs such as the kidneys. There is, the team found, a particularly strong concentration of cells shaped to interact with neuropeptides in the limbic system, the network of brain structures that controls emotion. Moreover, the immune system itself, research suggests, is one source of the chemicals that, in the brain, control mood.

One implication of all this, Candace Pert observes, is that emotions can play a key role in disease. But she goes much further in the paper she published in *Advances,* taking a speculative leap that could never appear in an academic journal. Referring to the "bias built into the Western idea that consciousness is totally in the head," she writes, "I believe the research findings I have described indicate that we need to start thinking about how consciousness can project into the body."

Some professionals who attended the Playhouse meeting employ what many in the medical establishment might consider to be unorthodox techniques. Among them is Dr. Martin L. Rossman, a general practitioner whose medical practice in Marin County, California, includes teaching patients to "dialogue" with their symptoms "to find what it is they are trying to tell you," a method closer to psychotherapy than to medicine. Similar to Dr. Rossman in outlook is Dr. R. Naomi Remen, who was for many years a professor at Stanford University Medical School but who now devotes her time to counseling people with life-threatening and chronic illnesses. Dr. Remen's perspective springs from her own health history, she has had a serious gastro-intestinal disease for thirty-five years; nine bouts of major surgery have left her with about one-third of her intestinal tract.

"Without conventional medicine, I would have died," she says. "And without alternative approaches, I would have been an invalid. Conventional medicine just did not help me live with what I had."

Commonweal, a nonprofit health center where Dr. Remen acts as medical director of the cancer-help program, is situated in a cluster of buildings on 1,000 acres of land at the entrance to Point Reyes National Seashore near Bolinas, Calif. Cancer patients, all of them under the care of traditional physicians, come for a one-week group-support program directed at their perceptions, emotions and understanding of their diseases. Eight to twelve people at a time go through a regimen that includes relaxation yoga and massage—as well as touches such as walks in the garden and sandplay, a therapy technique in which the patient, playing like a child creates landscapes in sand and people the scenes with toy figures.

In group-therapy sessions led by Dr. Remen, patients discuss their deep feelings about cancer, their fears of separation, loss and death. The goal is acceptance of whatever happens. "Without acceptance there is no way to take charge of your life," Dr. Remen tells the group. "Without acceptance you just react out of fear. If you can accept even the fact of death, then you can use it to tell you what's important, to cut through the bull, to love better."

Michael A. Lerner, Commonweal's founder and president and a MacArthur Foundation "genius award" winner, goes further; the point, as he sees it, is not just to feel better about what you've got, but to help heal yourself. "Attitudes themselves have a very potent effect on the immune system," he says. "You become different from the person who developed the cancer. Becoming a different personality may change the environment the cancer grew in; it may become so inhospitable that the cancer shrinks."

Words like that, applauded by many in behavioral medicine, rankle most physicians and appall most oncologists, and they draw objections even from the ranks of the advisory board of the Institute for the Advancement of Health, who watched a videotape of the Commonweal program at the Playhouse meeting.

Robert Ader, a University of Rochester researcher and an institute board member, takes a tolerant but guarded view of the new techniques. "The mind always mattered in medicine," he says. "If I accept the data showing that the mind affects susceptibility to one disease, I have to consider that it probably affects all diseases to some extent. But it is going to be a hell of a long time before the techniques being used can be tested by good clinical studies."

Others who are knowledgeable researchers have similar reservations. "The numbers of people offering behavioral medicine make me uncomfortable," says Dr. Sandra M. Levy, associate professor of psychiatry and medicine at the University of Pittsburgh School of Medicine. "I have a feeling that many in the field promise cures although they don't really know

what they're talking about. It gives behavioral medicine a fringy, illegitimate taint in the eyes of some physicians and researchers." Dr. Levy headed a behavioral-medicine research program at the National Cancer Institute until the effort was discontinued in 1983. Now, though, Dr. Levy has been asked back to the National Cancer Institute to participate in a conference investigating the evidence that psychological factors may play a role in the progression of cancer.

The skepticism of some physicians toward the field was, no doubt, confirmed by an editorial that ran in the influential *New England Journal of Medicine* in 1985. The editorial branded the belief that disease reflects mental states as "folklore," on the grounds that the research findings had failed to show a strong link between people's thoughts and feelings and the immune system. But even some researchers who themselves harbor reservations about claims made for the medical efficacy of psychological techniques feel the New England editorial went too far in dismissing the mind-disease connection. Dr. Levy, for instance, has recently finished a study, not yet published, suggesting an important role for emotion in the progression of some cancers.

After researchers at Johns Hopkins reported that cancer patients who showed angry defiance, a "fighting spirit," tended to live longer than did those who were passive and "good," Dr. Levy began to follow a group of thirty-six women who had been diagnosed as having advanced breast cancer. After seven years, twenty-four of the thirty-six women had died. To her surprise, Dr. Levy found that, after the first year, anger made no difference in survival. The only psychological factor that mattered for survival within seven years seemed to be a sense of joy with life.

The primary factor that predicted survival, she found, was already well established in oncology: the length of time the patients remained disease-free after first being treated, and before having a relapse. But the second-strongest factor was having a high score on "joy" on a standard paper-and-pencil test measuring mood. Test evidence of joy was statistically more significant as a predictor of survival than was the number of sites of metastesis once the cancer spread. That a joyous state of mind should be so powerful a predictor of survival was completely unexpected.

"Perhaps the sense of joy is a reflection of the body's resilience and stamina," Dr. Levy conjectures.

It is research findings such as these that justify the proliferation of behavioral medicine to those working in the field. And there are, literally, hundreds of such studies, though they vary greatly in their scientific rigor. The weight of evidence suggests the treatments work at least sometimes, for some people. That is not to say that psychology overwhelms biology, but that, within bounds, it can have a telling impact on the course of many diseases.

Still, what the field has lacked is a unifying theory. There is no overarching statement of precisely why becoming deeply relaxed, say, should seem to relieve symptoms for so many patients with medical disorders. Therapists are at a loss to explain the precise biological mechanisms that produce beneficial effects.

One of the more promising theories, put forth by George S. Everly Jr., a clinical psychologist at Harvard University, and Dr. Herbert Benson, director of a behavioral-medicine program at the Deaconess Hospital at Harvard Medical School, is that medical problems that can be helped by relaxation treatments are all, to some extent, "disorders of arousal," in which the limbic circuitry in the brain has become hypersensitive. Training oneself to become deeply relaxed, the two authors argue, retunes the nervous system. More specifically, their hypothesis holds, repeated relaxation dampens the activity of certain brain chemicals, the adrenergic catecholamines, which stimulate the limbic system. Research has shown that excessive activity within the limbic system may serve to inhibit immune function and lead to other problems.

Quite apart from scientific arguments for and against behavioral medicine, one of the reasons the new approaches are spreading is money. The treatments, in an age of ascending medical costs, are profitable, both for hospitals and for medical plans such as health-maintenance organizations.

According to Dr. Neil Smithline, president of Current Health Concepts, a health-care consulting concern in Sausalito, Calif., a behavioral-medicine treatment group, which meets for two hours every week for ten sessions at a private hospital, can cost each patient in the group $500 to $900 for the full program. Each group can have twenty to forty members. Gross take, by Dr. Smithline's calculations, $10,000 to $36,000. The direct costs to the hospital, apart from overhead, are negligible, a room and the salary of the group leader.

In today's competitive environment, many hospitals, hurt by empty beds, are now in search of new profit centers. They need all the patients they can find. Many are advertising their behavioral-medicine programs to draw in patients with relatively minor problems who, they hope, will be loyal when one day they choose a hospital for, say, elective surgery.

The prepaid medical plans, on the other hand, put a premium on cutting down the number of visits a patient makes to a doctor. Psychological treatments appear, on average, to decrease the visits. In a study of patients at the Harvard Community Health Plan, for instance, those who went through six-week behavioral medicine groups for a variety of medical disorders paid far fewer visits to physicians during the six months after their sessions than they had for the six months previous. The savings to the health plan would be an estimated $171 for each of the fifty patients for each six-month period, according to Caroline J. C. Hellman, a graduate psychology student at Harvard, who did the study with Dr. Matthew A. Budd, an internist at the plan.

In an age in which the individual feels ever less able to control his destiny in the face of economic, political and social tides, the methods of behavioral medicine may offer a sense of redress. To control, at least, one's own body may, in itself, be curative.

A body of data is emerging showing that enhancing the feeling of being in control of one's life has positive health benefits. In a series of experiments at the University of Pennsylvania, for instance, laboratory rats implanted with tumors and then subjected to electric shocks rejected the tumors more frequently if they were themselves able to end the shocks. And, at Yale, a study of elderly men and women in convalescent homes showed that, among other things, changes increasing their control over their lives—allowing them to decide what to have for meals, or letting them turn their telephones off or on—lowered their mortality rate over a period of eighteen months by 50 percent, compared to residents in the same homes for whom things did not change.

The feeling of empowerment, of being able to do something for oneself, no matter how small, seems to be an important psychological ingredient in whatever successes the behavioral-medicine methods are having. All the techniques now being used give patients skills, such as the ability to relax, that are their own personal tools in the fight against illness.

"Most of what we do to patients as doctors in the name of helping them has the effect of making them dependent," said Dr. Dean Ornish, president and director of the Preventive Medicine Research Institute in San Francisco. "But if you give people something they can do for themselves it gives them a sense of mastery, and that has benefits over and above what you do medically."

Psychological Disorders

The list of disorders in the offical psychiatric diagnostic manual has changed over the years. The changes are brought about both by new research findings and a shifting consensus in the psychotherapy community. When new categories for diagnosis are proposed, there is often controversy, as is described in "New Psychiatric Syndromes Spur Protest."

Perhaps the single most common psychological problem is social anxiety—shyness so extreme it becomes almost paralyzing. At a party, for instance, as many as three-quarters of the people there may feel anxiety about meeting strangers, according to some of the findings in "Social Anxiety: Focus Leads to Insights and Therapy." The search is on for an understanding of why the problem is so widespread.

The fears a child holds change with age. In trying to sort out which fears are normal and which amount to phobias that might require treatment, researchers are paying attention to the specific fears most common at a given age. The results are shown in "Little Fears That Grow with Age of Child."

Any catastrophe can bring about the symptoms of post-traumatic stress disorder. Earthquakes, fires, traffic accidents, muggings—any disaster that shakes one's sense in a safe and predictable world—can have lasting psychological effects. "Emotional Impact of Disaster: Sense of Benign World is Lost" details the range of ways one's emotional world can be shaken.

The world of the obsessive-compulsive is filled with odd, private rituals and urgent worries. Once thought to be relatively rare, the disorder turns out to be far more common than experts had thought, according to findings in "Obsessive Disorder: Secret Toll Is Found." But often people keep their obsessions secret.

Psychopaths are people who can commit cruelty without a tinge of remorse; many serial murderers are psychopaths. "Brain Defect Tied to Utter Amorality of the Psychopath" tells of findings suggesting that this lack of a conscience may be due to a difference in brain function.

Multiple personality disorder is one of the more fascinating psychological disorders; the movies *The Three Faces of Eve* and *Sybil* were based on actual cases. "Probing the Enigma of Multiple Personality" shows a new fascination for researchers: the various sub-personalities seem to differ in their physiological profiles, even to the extent of having different allergies and eyeglass prescriptions.

Schizophrenia, one of the most serious psychological disorders, begins in small ways for some people as early as childhood. "Schizophrenia: Early Signs Found" describes data suggesting what some telltale hints during childhood might be that a person is at risk for schizophrenia in adulthood.

Many of the homeless people who live on the streets of the nation's towns and cities are suffering from schizophrenia, not poverty. "To Expert Eyes, City Streets Are Open Mental Wards" describes the expertise being developed by a new breed of workers who minister to their needs.

New Psychiatric Syndromes Spur Protest

November 19, 1985

The proposed addition of three new psychiatric disorders—for those with a masochistic personality, for men who rape and for women with premenstrual syndrome—to the official diagnostic manual aroused vigorous opposition at a meeting of psychiatrists today.

Opponents charged that the diagnoses would offer a legal defense to rapists and wife beaters and stigmatize women with menstrual problems. Supporters argued that the new diagnoses would alert clinicians to psychological problems that have often gone unrecognized, and so provide relief to patients who would not otherwise receive treatment.

The meeting, called to air all points of view on the proposal, ended with the threat of a lawsuit by a group of women who predicted adverse consequences if the diagnoses were approved. The opposing views were presented at a closed meeting at the Columbia-Presbyterian Hospital here. According to Robert Spitzer, the psychiatrist in charge of the revisions to the diagnostic manual, the meeting was called in response to a campaign by women's groups among psychiatrists and psychologists.

"Although the psychiatrists listened to our arguments," said Lenore Walker, a psychologist who attended the meeting, "it was obvious they are unwilling to change their views and that they are guided not by research, but by psychoanalytic anecdotes."

In an interview after the meeting, Dr. Spitzer said, "We didn't anticipate the strong objections of many, both in psychiatry and psychology, to this proposal. The discussion was very heated." During the meeting, he said, the committee in charge of the manual revision decided to change the name of one proposed category from "masochistic" to "self-defeating" personality disorder, and to exclude its application if its symptoms appeared only in an abusive situation. That category was the focus of the meeting today.

Discussions are planned next month on the two other disputed diagnoses, but Dr. Spitzer said, "We probably will withdraw the diagnosis of rapism because of the legal implications." The Committee on Women of the American Psychological Association argued that the diagnosis, which would apply to men who are sexually aroused by fantasies of rape, would "provide an instant insanity plea for anyone charged with rape."

The women's committee also objects to the proposed diagnosis of "premenstrual dysphoric disorder" on the ground that it would stigmatize as psychiatrically disturbed women who were reacting to such biological discomforts as painful bloating. They also noted that there is no clear psychiatric treatment for the problem.

Some legal experts have objected that the premenstrual diagnosis could be used as a legal defense against, for example, charges of child abuse.

Feelings of Martyrdom

The "masochistic personality disorder" discussed today is characterized, according to the originally proposal, by feelings of martyrdom and self-defeating habits. The key signs of the disorder were to include staying in an abusive or exploitive relationship despite chances to leave or change it, rejecting help, sabotaging one's own efforts, and feeling underserving of success.

By the end of the meeting, the criteria for the diagnosis had been changed, so that, for example, staying in an abusive relationship had been dropped. Such criteria as feeling depressed by one's success were added.

"Clinicians agree that there are people who feel martyred, unhappy and complain, yet remain in abusive relationships," said Renee Garfinkel, a psychologist who has led much of the opposition. "Despite substantial research to the contrary, however, psychoanalysts view these as flaws in the person. But much research indicates that this so-called masochism is the result of abusive relationships."

"It is clear from research that people who are exploited or abused over a long period of time show all these so-called masochistic symptoms," Dr. Garfinkel said. "If the problem is thought to be located within the patient we have merely blamed the victim once again."

The concept of masochism has been a controversial one since Freud proposed in 1924 that the feminine personality predisposed women to masochism, a concept developed in more detail by his discipline Helene Deutsch.

Psychoanlysts distinguish between sexual masochism, in which a person takes sexual pleasure in pain or humiliation, and masochistic personality, in which a person finds psychological, rather than sexual, gratification in self-defeat. Sexual masochism is already an accepted diagnostic category.

Defending the personality diagn

sis, Richard Simmons, a psychiatrist at the University of Colorado Medical School, notes that the disorder is likely to be as common among men as among women, although more frequently diagnosed in women. Dr. Simmons contends that it is important to recognize masochistic personality among psychiatric patients since, if unrecognized, it can sabotage therapy as well as other relationships in the patient's life.

"I am convinced that masochistic phenomena are among the most common that we encounter in our psychiatric practices—and are among the most commonly overlooked and misdiagnosed," Dr. Simmons wrote in a paper supporting the new diagnosis. This kind of masochism, he said, leads a person to a repeated chain of self-defeats, without being conscious of what he or she is doing. It can take the form, for example, of a woman who repeatedly chooses boyfriends who beat her up, or a man who provokes employer after employer to dismiss him.

The Diagnostic and Statistical Manual of Mental Disorders, now in its third edition, is the official standard by which psychiatric diagnoses are made. Diagnoses listed in the manual are generally recognized by courts in making legal decisions, by hospitals and psychotherapists in keeping records and by insurance companies in reimbursing for treatments.

New diagnoses are periodically added when there is a consensus among psychiatrists that the syndrome can be clearly defined and that it is an important mental disorder, according to Dr. Spitzer.

Social Anxiety: New Focus Leads to Insights and Therapy

December 18, 1984

Social anxiety, in its many forms, is epidemic.

About 40 percent of Americans think of themselves as shy, while only 20 percent say they have never suffered from shyness at some point in their lives. Nearly one in four men and one in eight women report high anxiety when going out on a date, while a third of men and almost a half of women report such feelings at dances and discothèques. And the most frequent fear in one survey of 3,000 adults was found to be speaking before a group.

"Social anxiety can be the surface sign of much deeper psychological conflicts, such as hidden hostility or guilt," said Seymour Epstein, a clinical psychologist at the University of Massachusetts, who has written extensively on anxiety and personality.

While there have long been people who complained of social anxiety, as well as those who have sought to cure the problem, of late there has been a mushrooming of serious research by social psychologists on the topic, and new clinical treatments offered for those who view ordinary social contacts as dangerous and threatening.

Much of the new work, rather than dwelling on deep, hidden causes, has focused on the social triggers that lead to anxiety and relatively straight-forward ways to alleviate the fear.

Shyness, the most common form of social-anxiety, occurs when a person's apprehensions are so great that they inhibit his making an expected or desired social response. Symptoms of shyness can be as minor as failing to make eye contact when speaking to someone, or as major as avoiding conversations whenever possible.

"Shy people tend to be too preoccupied with themselves," said Jonathan Cheek, a psychologist at Wellesley College who is one of those at the forefront of current research on the topic. "For example, for a smooth conversation, you need to pay attention to the other person's cues—what he is saying and doing. But the shy person is full of worries about how he seems to the other person, and so he often misses cues he should pick up. The result is an awkward lag in the conversation. Shy people need to stop focusing on themselves and switch their attention to the other person."

Nevertheless, shy people by and large have better social abilities than they think they do. When Dr. Cheek videotaped shy people talking to strangers, and then had raters evaluate how socially skilled the people were, he found that, in the eyes of other people, the shy group had few obvious problems. But when he asked the shy people themselves how they had done, they were unanimous in saying that they had been social flops. "Shy people are their own worst critics," Dr. Cheek said. In general, he added, shy people feel they are being judged more negatively than they actually are, and overestimate how obvious their social anxiety is to others.

Signs of Social Anxiety

A large body of research on the nature of social anxiety has pinpointed its most common signs, including these:

• *Negative and debilitating thoughts, such as "I'm going to make a fool of myself." Such thoughts are especially frequent as an anticipated social interaction looms.*

• *A poor evaluation of one's social performance, despite one's actual social competence.*

• *Exaggerating the extent to which others see one in a negative light in social situations, and having a better memory for embarrassing events than for those social moments that went well.*

• *Blaming oneself for social failures, while seeing social successes as resulting from some external factor.*

Root of Problem

Not all self-consciousness leads to social anxiety, in the view of Arnold Buss, one of the first psychologists to study the phenomenon. The garden variety of self-consciousness, Dr. Buss has written, is simply an introspective awareness of one's thoughts and feelings. What he calls "public self-consciousness," on the other hand, is a powerful perception of oneself as the object of social scrutiny. The latter is the root of social anxiety.

People with this sort of self-consciousness, studies have found, are more sensitive than others to rejection, and are preoccupied with how they appear in others' eyes. This preoccupation leads to anxiety when such people are in doubt about their ability to make a good impression; for example, when they believe something might happen that will undermine their public image.

Social anxiety generally creates three different kinds of problems, which can occur separately or in tandem, according to Dr. Cheek. For some people, their social anxiety is primarily cognitive; they suffer from repetitive thoughts expressing their fear of making a poor impression, such as "He must think I'm an idiot," or "I can't think of anything to say."

Other people, though, experience their social anxiety almost entirely through physiological symptoms, such as blushing, a pounding heart or sweating in social situations.

In either case, these symptoms lead to a set of behavioral ones; for example, not being able to speak although one wants to, or a general social awkwardness.

According to data collected by Dr. Cheek, the physiological variety is more likely to occur from early life onward, while the cognitive variety more often first shows up in late childhood and early adolescence, mainly in girls in the fifth through eighth grades.

This suggests, according to Dr. Cheek, that some shyness has a physiological basis, while another variety is, in the main, learned.

Data collected by Jerome Kagan, a developmental psychologist at Harvard University, seems to corroborate the idea that some shyness results from a temperamental trait present in infancy, and possibly even at birth.

Dr. Kagan observed twenty-one-month-old infants in a free play situation with other infants and experimenters. Some were bubbly and spontaneous, playing with the other infants without the least hesitation. Others, though, were obviously uncertain, staying close to their mothers, drawing back from the other children, and being very quiet and reticent. Other measures showed these same timid infants to have a heightened physiological response to the situation, their hearts racing.

Almost four years later, when these same children were in kindergarten, Dr. Kagan studied them again, comparing the children who had been the most timid with those he had found the most outgoing. Over the intervening years, none of the outgoing children had become timid, while only one-third of the timid, mainly among the boys, had become less so. Further, the timid children still had the same physiological response to mild stress that they had shown as infants.

"Some children seem to begin life with a neural circuitry that makes them more reactive to stress," Dr. Kagan said in an interview. "This reactivity manifests, to some degree as inhibition—they're more timid in general."

"Those children who had become less timid by kindergarten seem to have had parents who put gentle pressure on them to be more outgoing," Dr. Kagan added. "Although this temperamental trait seems slightly harder to change—probably because of its physiological basis—no human quality is beyond change."

Different Schools of Thought

Many theorists link social anxiety to psychological causes, not to temperament. While behaviorists see the symptoms as simply a learned fear associated with social interactions, other schools of thought look to sources deep within the personality.

"What appears on the surface as social anxiety may often trace back to early psychological issues," said Dr. Epstein, the Massachusetts psychologist who specializes in personality theory. "For example, Karen Horney proposed that we all suffer a basic anxiety stemming from our early helpless dependence on our parents. This leads to the sense of being a helpless, isolated person in a hostile world. Freud suggested something similar when he traced anxiety back to the Oedipal situation."

"Horney pointed out that people cope with this basic anxiety in different ways," Dr. Epstein said in an interview. "Some turn against others, becoming aggressive. Others turn toward them, becoming overly compliant. And some people handle the insecurity by withdrawing. These are the people who develop what we see as shyness and social anxiety."

In 1980 the new edition of the *Official Psychiatric Diagnostic Manual* added the category of "social phobia," the clinical extreme of social anxiety. About two percent of Americans are thought to suffer from social phobia so severe that they need treatment.

Social phobia is characterized by a persistent fear of situations in which one might be scrutinized by other people, and apprehension that one will be humiliated or embarrassed. These fears are so great that the person tries to avoid such situations, whether it be public speaking, using public lavatories or even eating or writing when a stranger is present.

Often the specific fear is that others will detect one's anxiety—in a sense, the fear is of fear itself. Thus a person who is fearful of writing in front of others may focus on the thought that others will see his hand shake. But that fear itself can amplify his anxiety, thus creating the very hand tremor the person feared. In this way, a self-confirming cycle begins in which fear generates the awkwardness that justifies the fear.

Range of Social Phobia

Social phobia ranges along a continuum. At the mild end of the spectrum are people who experience distress in specific, isolated situations, but who can still function adequately in them despite their anxiety.

Somewhat more severe is a social phobia that causes the person to feel extreme anxiety in the feared situation that he does whatever he can to avoid it. Often such people rearrange their entire daily routine, or even avoid careers they would otherwise prefer, in order to minimize the chances that the feared situation will arise.

At the clinical extreme are those with social phobias so intense that swing between panic and paralysis, their lives stifled by incapacitating fear.

While social phobias focus anxiety on a particular situation, such as talking on the telephone or asking for a date, they often are the obvious signs of a more fundamental, hidden fear. Richard Heimberg, a clinical psychologist at the Phobia and Anxiety Disorders Clinic at the State University of New York at Albany, gives the example of a woman with a phobia regarding speaking to attractive men her own age, and who consequently cut short any such contacts. In therapy, she revealed that her actual fear was that the men might see she was nervous and find her flawed, so that she would end up without a mate for the rest of her life.

Aaron Beck, a psychiatrist at the University of Pennsylvania Medical School, classifies social anxiety as one of a range of "evaluation anxieties," fears having to do with being judged negatively. Test anxiety, in his view is another such fear.

Dr. Beck, who is one of those who has pioneered in the treatment of these problems, posits that the thoughts that race through the mind of a person feeling social anxiety have at their root the deep belief that one will be found inadequate by others. A constellation of faulty beliefs seem to accompany this accompany this basic one, Dr. Beck has found. These include the idea that it is shameful to appear anxious in front of other people; that others are aware of one's social fears, and that they will be put off by observing that fearfulness.

In the treatment program Dr. Beck has developed, these erroneous beliefs are challenged in the actual situations in which they arise. In *Anxiety Disorders and Phobias,* a book to be published Basic Books, Dr. Beck outlines his view of the causes and treatment for social anxiety.

"We actually reproduce the situation that makes the patient anxious," Dr. Beck said in an interview. "For example, if it's a man who can't bring himself to strike up a conversation with a woman, we'll send a therapist along with him to a singles bar. She'll sit at a table with him, and suggest that he go over to a woman and start talking to her. Typically, at first he'll freeze up and say, 'Let's leave—I'll just make a fool of myself.' "

"The therapist will challenge him on the spot, asking him for the evidence that supports that belief," Dr. Beck added. "How can he know unless he tries? These people are filled with irrational thoughts like, 'If I fall at this, I won't ever be able to do it with anybody.' The initial hurdle in therapy is that people like this freeze when they think about doing the thing they fear. But if we can get them to try it, the more they do it, the easier it becomes."

Little Fears That Grow with Age of Child

April 21, 1988

Most fears in a child's world are only natural for those who are small and helpless in a large and sometimes dangerous place.

But for some children, the fears are so pronounced that they may presage a lifelong vulnerability to chronic anxiety, according to new research reported in the current issue of *Psychiatric Annals*. And because these extreme fears can be debilitating, other experts say, more children should be treated for anxiety problems than currently receive such care, not only to provide immediate relief for the child but also because the problem can sometimes persist into adulthood if untreated.

Most children pass through periods of intense fearfulness at different ages, but these episodes typically end in a few weeks or months. The children in whom the fearfulness becomes a perpetual part of their lives, preventing them from normal play or school attendance, are in need of treatment.

Such therapy frequently involves counseling to reinforce the proper behavior or to help a child learn to deal with the fear. Drug therapies commonly used with adults have been used experimentally but are rarely prescribed.

"The first question to ask is if the fears a child has are normal for his age," said Kathy Sheehan, a psychologist at the University of South Florida College of Medicine, and one of the authors of the article in *Psychiatric Annals*. "Most children between nine and twelve may have fears about school exams, getting hurt or how they look, for instance. But if the fears are so intense they keep the child from doing the things others his age do, then it is a serious emotional problem."

Small Portion Need Help

A random survey in Ontario, Canada, found that among children living in cities, about 6 percent of those from four to eleven years old were so fearful or anxious that they might need treatment. Among those twelve to sixteen, the figure was 2.5 percent. The survey involved 2,621 children. Of the troubled children, however, only one in five had ever received professional help, said Paul Links, a psychiatrist at McMasters University in Hamilton, Ontario, who did the survey.

In a study at the Harvard Medical School, 25 percent of adults with the pervasive fear agoraphobia reported that the problem began by age twenty, most often with a fear of going to school or of being separated from their families. In addition, 4 percent of those with this fear of being in public places recalled having the problem before age ten and some said they had it to some extent all their lives. The study was published in *Comprehensive Psychiatry*.

Citing this and other studies, Dr. Sheehan proposed that severe anxiety problems in children be seen as the early stirrings of the same disorders in adults, rather than as unique problems of childhood. Dr. Sheehan wrote the article in *Psychiatric Annals* with David Sheehan, her husband, and Kailie Shaw of the department of Psychiatry at the South Florida Medical School.

The current *Psychiatric Manual for Diagnosis* lists several varieties of anxiety problems in children, including anxiety about being apart from parents, fearfulness of strangers and being overly worried about potential calamities. But Dr. Sheehan argues that the many varieties are actually all part of a single syndrome.

The important distinction, she argues, is between levels of severity. In the more severe form, the child falls victim to several fears so intense they are disabling. The symptoms a child experiences are akin to aspects of panic attacks in adults, including a racing heart, dizzy spells, nausea or diarrhea attacks and trembling. These symptoms can occur suddenly, with little or no apparent reason.

In the less severe form, the child has a specific phobia, such as a dread of going to nursery school or to camp for the first time. The fear is related to a specific situation, rather than being pervasive, and it generally fades as time goes on.

"There's no need for a parent to worry if the fears last for just a few weeks," Dr. Sheehan said. "But if they persist for more than a month, and they keep the child from leading a normal life, then the child may benefit from therapy."

One of the most common forms of treatment for extreme fearfulness in children is cognitive-behavioral treatment, therapy that involves relaxation and changing self-defeating thoughts, which helps the child learn to master the feelings of fear.

"For children older than nine or so, relaxation training with self-coaching works well," said Thomas Ollendick, a psychologist at the Virginia Polytechnic Institute in Blacksburg, Virginia, who has been studying the treatment of anxiety in children. "For those between six and nine, direct reward for doing what they're afraid of is the better approach."

He added, "Both approaches give the child a better sense of control over the situation."

In the self-coaching treatment used by Dr. Ollendick, children learn to talk themselves through anxiety-provoking situations by thinking about what they can do to make it less threatening. They might, for instance, take a deep breath or tell themselves that they will perform properly.

In the reward treatment, younger children are encouraged to be brave, and they are rewarded for staying in the situation they dread. If a child is afraid of staying in bed at night, for instance, he might track his nights of braveness on a calendar and earn a reward, like a model car, after attaining a certain number.

Other child therapists differ in their view of the childhood fears, seeing deeper issues at work and urging consideration of such possibilities when treating a child.

"A child who is afraid of going to school may be responding to more than a fear of separating from his mother," said Richard Gardner, a clinical professor of child psychiatry at Columbia University Medical School. "His fear may cover a deeper hostility, which comes from anger at an overprotective or emotionally depriving parent. As a psychoanalyst, I assess such underlying factors when I see an anxious child."

Emotional Impact of Disaster: Sense of Benign World is Lost

November 26, 1985

In a major catastrophe like the Mexican earthquake and the mud slides in Colombia, experts say, the psychological world collapses just as resoundingly as the physical one.

The most prominent psychological casualty is the sense of invulnerability with which most people manage to face the risks of daily life. Also shattered, psychologists are finding, are a person's sense that his or her world is comprehensible and has meaning, and for many years after the trauma a person's very sense of worth may be damaged.

"The common belief that people recover after a few weeks from disaster is based on mistaking denial for recovery," said Dr. Mardi Horowitz, a psychiatrist at the University of California Medical School at San Francisco.

Delayed Psychological Reactions

Dr. Horowitz's research has shown that many psychological symptoms do not appear until long after the victim seems to have fully recovered from the disaster, and when the problems do arise—such as difficulty concentrating, depression or sleeplessness—their causes may go unrecognized.

The study of the psychological impact of trauma of all sorts has become a major topic for researchers. While psychoanalytic theories have dealt in the main with the devastating effects of emotional trauma in early childhood, the new work examines the emotional aftershocks of disasters of every sort.

As psychologists and psychiatrists assess the impact of catastrophes large and small, they are finding that the worst natural disaster holds something in common in its psychic impact with what may seem a minor crisis, such as a witnessing a brutal crime. And they find, for example, that children come to grips with disaster in ways that are very different from those of adults. Moreover, the evidence is that rescuers and even bystanders also can be vulnerable to psychological costs.

Basic Assumptions Crumble

"Whenever someone becomes victimized by a disaster, whatever its nature," said Ronnie Janoff-Bulman, a psychologist at the University of Massachusetts, "their most basic assumptions about themselves and the world are undermined. Psychological recovery, to a large extent, requires rebuilding those assumptions."

The key assumption that crumbles in a disaster, according to Dr. Janoff-Bulman, is that of invulnerability, the sense that the world is benevolent, controllable and fair, and that so long as one acts as one should, nothing untoward will happen. "The assumption of invulnerability begins very early life, as early as the first two or three years of age," Dr. Janoff-Bulman said in an interview. "That is when the child forms a sense of basic trust, the feeling that the world is a predictable place in which good things will come to you. And from that the child comes to see himself as worthy of that kind of care. These beliefs are at the core of a person's most basic sense of himself and the world."

s "A catastrophe attacks those deeply held beliefs," Dr. Janoff-Bulman said. "Suddenly all the world seems malevolent. And because the two beliefs are so intimately linked, you lose not only your sense that the world is safe for you, but that you are worthy of that safety."

People who have suffered catastrophes afterward may undergo a diminished sense of self-worth for ten or fifteen years, or even longer, Dr. Janoff-Bulman has found in her research. "When you've been victimized," she said, "it leads you to ask, 'Why me?' You may start looking at yourself to find something in you to blame it on, to justify and make some sense out of such a horrible fate. That leads you to highlight the negative aspects of yourself, which lowers your self-esteem."

Some research suggests that the more benevolent a person had assumed the setting of a disaster to be, the worse its psychological impact can be. A study at the University of Illinois found that women who had been raped in settings they once thought were safe were more fearful in general afterward that were women who had been raped in dangerous settings.

Children vary in their reactions depending on their age, according to research by two psychiatrists, Dr. Robert Pynoos of the University of California at Los Angeles and Dr. Spencer Eth of the University of Southern California, who have studied children who witnessed brutal crimes. The severest impact is on the youngest children, those of preschool age. "They feel the most helpless and passive when confronted by overwhelming danger, and require the most assistance to reestablish psychic equilibrium," Dr. Pynoos and Dr. Eth wrote in an article in *Trauma and Its Wake* (Bruner/Mazel).

Young children in severe danger often react by a mute, stunned withdrawal; one three-year-old sat next to her murdered mother for eight hours until a roommate discovered them. After the disaster has passed, preschool age children often regress, acting like an anxious younger child, whining, clinging or throwing tantrums. Children at this age are most likely to dwell on the fantasy that the tragedy has not occurred, and that everything is magically all right.

Children of school age, on the other hand, have a much broader repertory of responses. Some children at this age will spend an inordinate time retelling the traumatic incident in detail, but with a lack of emotion. Others will become fixated in a state of constant guardedness, as though braced for danger at any moment.

Aware of the irreversibility of death, they are less prone than the younger child to dwell incessantly on the fantasy that a dead loved one will return. But children of this age will often reenact the tragedy in fantasy, imagining themselves as having rescued the victim, according to Dr. Pynoos and Dr. Eth.

Teenagers, they write, tend to resemble adults in reacting to disaster. One common reaction is a premature entrance to adulthood, a false sense of readiness to take on adult responsibilities. Teenagers are also prone to respond with rebelliousness, such as truancy and sexual adventures, all out of keeping with their personality before the trauma. Dr. Pynoos and Dr. Eth note that teenagers are much more realistic in their understanding of the event itself than are the younger children, who sometimes blame themselves for the disaster. Teenagers, on the other hand, while they can accurately assess how little their own acts may have figured into the chain of events, may still inflate their guilt feelings at having survived, as many adults do.

Such variations in the impact of disaster must be seen against the broader background of the normal progression of psychological re-sponses, which have been recognized for centuries. When the diarist Samuel Pepys described his reactions to the Great Fire of London, which destroyed much of the city in 1666, his account followed what psychologists have come to see as a classic pattern: disbelief followed by a forgetfulness of the disaster, insomnia, disturbing dreams and extreme anxiety.

Similar symptoms are commonly observed among the "shell shock" victims of the wars. The pattern, now called the "post-traumatic stress syndrome," includes recurrent dreams of the traumatic event, the numbing of emotions, and guilt about having survived when others have not.

While there is no prescribed sequence for psychological recovery from disaster, experts recognize specific stages that oscillate in ways that can differ from person to person. Some of the most detailed research on the emotional aftermath of disaster is described by Dr. Horowitz in his book *Stress Response Syndromes,* published by Jason Aronson.

Normal Recovery Process

The normal immediate response to a severe trauma, Dr. Horowitz says, is an outcry of fear, rage or sadness at the terrible impact on one's life, which is often followed closely by a state of dazed shock. That shock is the beginning of a psychological denial of the tragedy, a denial that seems to serve a positive purpose in allowing the person to come to grips with his shattered world at a rate he can manage. For weeks or even years after the event, denial—blocking the facts from awareness—oscillates with intrusive thoughts of the tragedy, as the person slowly comes to face its full emotional truth.

When that process of adjustment goes awry, though, a variety of more severe problems can arise, according to Dr. Horowitz. For example, the immediate impact of the disaster may be overwhelming, leaving the person emotionally swamped. If the initial reaction of, say, distress and fear is not relieved, the person may sink into a state of total exhaustion or the feel-ings may escalate into outright panic.

During the longer course of recovery, Dr. Horowitz has found, people may either fall prey to extremes of denial or to being emotionally flooded by thoughts of the event. Extreme denial can take many forms, including a general numbing of emotions, serious loss of the ability to concentrate or to follow a train of thought, or an avoidance of topics even vaguely associated with the event. On the other hand, when memories of the event intrude too much, it can take such forms as an excessive alertness of dangers that do not exist, sudden waves of uncontrollable emotion, bad dreams or constant rumination on the event that cannot be put out of mind.

When the psychological process of coming to grips with the event goes uncompleted, Dr. Horowitz notes, the dangers can be more subtle, sometimes taking the form of psychosomatic complaints like stomach problems, headaches or inability to work or to love. When the recovery process goes awry in these ways, Dr. Horowitz notes, psychotherapy that deals with the original trauma is called for, even years later.

"The sudden emergence of fears or nightmares long after the tragedy has passed usually surprises everyone else, who thought the person had already recovered," Dr. Horowitz said. A recent report in *The American Journal of Psychiatry* tells of a World War II veteran who had no post-war problems until, forty years later, he became haunted by a repeated nightmare of an incident from the last days of the war. In that encounter, he had shot German soldiers who turned out to be teenage boys in uniforms with imitation rifles; in the dream they appeared as his own grandson.

Witnesses Affected as Well

Witnesses to a disaster can be as profoundly affected as the victims. One risk to bystanders or unseasoned rescue workers at the scene of a disaster is from encountering a dead and mangled body, according to Dr. Horowitz, who said, "The sight can leave a person with a profound death fright, feeling that life has no meaning, or severly depressed if they are prone to it."

To be sure, disasters can bring out the best in people, who put aside fear and self-concern to rally to the needs of the moment. "Even though people may be dazed," Dr. Horowitz said, "most function enormously well during the emergency itself, especially in direct response to seeing someone in pain or need."

Obsessive Disorder: Secret Toll Is Found

December 13, 1988

When James was three years old, he began a strange habit, whenever he crossed the street, he would walk in circles around the manhole covers. In kindergarten, he would sit for hours drawing circles on pieces of paper. At the age of eight, he would stand up and sit down seventeen times before finally sitting in a chair, and would go back and forth through a door seventeen times before finally exiting.

James suffered from obsessive-compulsive disorder. Scientists have assumed that the problem is extremely rare. But a new national survey of households has found that the disorder is 25 to 60 times more common than had been thought, afflicting perhaps one in 40 Americans at some point in their lives.

The disorder is vastly underreported, researchers say, because many who suffer from it keep their symptoms secret. While their symptoms are seldom as severe or obvious as those of James, millions of people find their lives dominated by desperate attempts to fight off strange impulses and bizarre thoughts.

The most widely accepted previous estimates put the prevalence of obsessive-compulsive disorder at about one person in every 2,000. The new study, to be published in the December 1988 issue of the *Archives of General Psychiatry,* estimates that from 1.9 to 3.3 percent of Americans will have the disorder during their lives.

"The obsessive-compulsive is at the extreme end of a continuum that begins with the person who, for instance, is scrupulously neat about his desk," said Blanche Freund, a psychologist at the Program for the Clinical Study of Anxiety Disorders at the Medical College of Pennsylvania, in Philadelphia. The program is one of several across the country that specialize in treating the disorder.

"Being especially neat is not a problem; a compulsive style like that can be a distinct asset in some ways," Dr. Freund said. "More serious is the compulsive personality, someone who gets completely lost fussing over details, and who, for example, needs everyone to be equally neat in order to make him feel comfortable. And at the extreme are people who spend most of their day obsessing or performing compulsive rituals."

Obsession and compulsions are symptoms of the same disorder. Obsessions are thoughts that completely preoccupy a person, while compulsions are actions that people feel they must perform. Although obsessive-compulsive disorder has long been regarded by psychotherapists as one of the most difficult problems to treat, new techniques using medication or behavioral therapy have proven highly effective in recent years.

Treating Disorder With Drugs

"Between drugs and behavior therapy, about 70 to 80 percent of those with the most extreme symptoms can have significant improvement or be cured," said Dr. Judith L. Rapoport chief of child psychiatry at the National Institute of Mental Health.

Dr. Rapoport, who has been studying obsessive-compulsive disorder for fifteen years, reported on progress in drug treatment of the disorder in the November 18, 1988, issue of the *Journal of the American Medical Association.* James is a pseudonym Dr. Rapopor gave for one of the children who have been successfully treated for the disorder at her facility.

The most promising new treatments for obsessive-compulsive disorder are three drugs developed as antidepressants: clomipramine, fluoxetine, and fluvoxamine, all of which are undergoing testing. In the most effective behavioral techniques, the patient is methodically exposed to things he dreads while being forbidden to indulge in his compulsions.

The world of the obsessive-compulsive is often nightmarish and bizarre. One form it may take is the compulsion to pluck one's hair out strand by strand. Young women often pluck their hair to baldness.

Some obsessive-compulsive people will take hours to leave their homes because they check and recheck every appliance in the house to be sure that it is off. Others feel compelled to perform private rituals, such as the man who spent hours circling the same route in his car, fearing he had struck a pedestrian.

"If you ask someone with extreme obsessions how much of the day their thoughts are free of the obsession, they will say almost never," Dr. Freund said.

Though people with obsessions realize that their thoughts are strange or unwanted, they feel unable to stop them. Similarly, people with compulsions say that although they often do not want to perform the act, anxiety builds until they give in.

Often, though, the disorder is less debilitating, confining itself to compulsive rituals done in secret, or those that interfere little with a normal life.

Another of Dr. Rapoport's patients, a sixteen-year-old girl, every Sunday spent hours removing everything from her room, then washed the walls and floors. In other respects, her life was not unusual, she did well in school and led a normal social life.

Symptoms Often Concealed

Researchers believe that such circumscribed symptoms are one reason that estimates for the prevalence of obsessive-compulsive disorder have been low, symptoms are often concealed from family or friends.

The new, higher estimates come from part of a national survey of 18,572 men and women conducted door-to-door in New Haven, Baltimore, St. Louis, the Piedmont region of North Carolina and Los Angeles.

One question to detect people with obsessive-compulsive disorder concerned common obsessions. These included persistent, unpleasant thoughts, such as that they might harm someone they love, that their hands were dirty no matter how much they are washed, or that relatives may have been hurt or killed.

In trying to detect compulsions, the interviewers asked if the people felt they had to "do something over and over again," even if they considered it foolish or tried to resist it.

Respondents were also asked whether they felt they had to do something in a particular order, like dressing, and whether they felt they had to repeat the entire sequence if something was done improperly.

Combination of Disorders

Some people suffer mainly from obsession, others from compulsions, and still others from a combination. While the vast majority of those people who come for treatment often suffer from both problems, only 9 percent of those surveyed had both obsessions and compulsions.

To qualify as a symptom for the survey, the obsessions or compulsions must have been present for at least three weeks, have persisted despite all attempts to get rid of them, and have interfered to some extent with aspects of the person's life.

In the survey, 468 people were identified as qualifying for the diagnosis. Although the national average was 2.5 percent, it varied from 1.9 to 3.3 percent among the five areas.

The results were reported by Marvin Karno, a psychiatrist at the University of California at Los Angeles, and colleagues at other institutions.

It is not necessarily abnormal for children to develop an obsession or compulsion, such as counting cars that pass by. But when these become such strong forces in their lives that they interfere with normal play or school, they are considered symptoms that should be treated.

Following a Brain Circuit

Evidence from brain studies of people with severe obsessive-compulsive disorder, done by teams led by Dr. Rapoport and by Lewis Baxter, a psychiatrist at U.C.L.A., suggest the involvement of a brain circuit that runs between the frontal lobes and the basal ganglia, a series of structures at the base of the brain.

Those brain areas are involved in coordinating what the senses register with how the body responds to it. Dr. Rapoport believes they may have a role, for instance, in patients who doubt the evidence of their senses.

"These patients will turn a knob to check that a door is locked, then start to doubt it as they are going down the steps, and go back again and again to recheck," Dr. Rapoport said.

The medications that have been particularly effective for people who suffer from obsessions seem to act on the basal ganglia, Dr. Rapoport said. Clomipramine, fluvoxamine and fluoxetine all block the uptake in the brain of serotonin, a brain chemical for which the basal ganglia have particularly dense receptors.

All the medications for obsessive-compulsive disorder are still under investigation; psychiatrists who want to prescribe them can obtain them only from the manufacturers. While the drugs seem to be effective in reducing symptoms in 70 percent of patients, their side-effects, such as difficulty with ejaculation in males, lead some patients to stop them.

On the other hand, behavior therapy techniques that work best with obsessive-compulsive patients are so demanding that about a quarter of those who seek help decline to go through the process, according to report by Gail Steketee, a clinical social worker, and Edna Foa, a psychologist at the Eastern Pennsylvania Psychiatric Institute in Philadelphia.

"We recommend that patients try behavior therapy first, and then if that does not work for them, try medications," Dr. Rapoport said. "Some people respond best to drugs, some to behavior therapy. If people are motivated enough to stick with the treatments, the odds are excellent that they can be helped."

For patients who go through a three-week program of behavior therapy, about 80 percent experience a significant decrease in symptoms, their report said. Of these, only about 20 percent have a serious return of symptoms.

One technique used in behavior therapy consists of exposing patients to the object of their fears. A patient who feared getting cancer was taken to a cancer ward.

In another technique, patients who feel compelled to engage in specific rituals are forbidden to do so. A man who dreaded touching cigarette ashes and "low-class" people felt compelled to scrub his hands for three minutes as often as thirty times a day.

But during the treatment, he was kept from washing his hands, and was also exposed to the things he dreaded, ashes and "low-class" people. At the end of treatment, he washed his hands just six times a day, and then only for twenty seconds.

While those who undergo treatment typically retain vestiges of their obsessions or compulsions, treatment is considered successful if symptoms no longer interfere with the person's life.

"They might still check the door an extra time or two to be sure it's locked," Dr. Freund said. "But they don't do it for hours on end, like they used to."

Brain Defect Tied to Utter Amorality of the Psychopath

July 7, 1987

Psychological researchers are finding evidence of fundamental differences in the brain that may lie behind the inhuman behavior of the psychopath.

Although the term psychopath is popularly applied to an especially brutal criminal, in psychology the term refers to someone with one of the most perplexing of emotional defects, the apparent incapacity to feel compassion or the pangs of conscience. The new research indicates that the slippery ease with which psychopaths lie, twist language and manipulate and destroy people in the pursuit of their own ends is associated with brain function that differs from that of normal people.

The psychopath confronts danger or the threat of danger without the rise in bodily responses to anxiety that normal people would show. Moreover, psychopaths, about 80 percent of whom are men, seem to have an unusual pattern of brain organization, with the center that controls language showing signs of irregular development.

Although these insights suggest a neurological defect, therapists are reporting success in treating the disorder with behavioral methods. The new treatments, which are coming amid signs that psychopathy may be on the rise, force the psychopath to confront a deep despair born of his inability to make emotional connections with others.

"Despite his cool exterior, inside he is like a poor child on a cold night looking through a window at the warmth of a family gathered by the fire," said William H. Reid, a psychiatrist at the University of Texas Medical School at San Antonio.

The detachment may be partly due to problems in moral and intellectual development that can be dealt with through behavioral treatment. But it also seems to be associated with the irregularity that psychologists have found in the psychopath's language control center.

The psychopath shows a facile use of language, but the defect leaves him oblivious to the emotional meaning of the words he speaks and hears.

"The con man understands what he's saying at the intellectual level, but when he uses words they don't carry the same emotional baggage for him as they do for other people," said Robert Hare, a psychologist at the University of British Columbia, who has done research on psychopaths for more than twenty years. "Ask a psychopath what love is, and he'll go on and on, but he has never felt it himself. He can use words any way he wants. If you catch him lying, he'll just shift gears and go on as though nothing had happened."

Dr. Hare has developed a scale to assess whether a person is a psychopath. Among the key traits the scale tests are glibness and superficial charm, grandiosity, lack of guilt and shallow feelings, impulsiveness and lack of realistic long-term plans. Dr. Hare says these traits have typified many killers, including Ted Bundy now on Florida's death row; Gary Gilmore, executed in Utah for killing a clerk during a holdup, and Angelo Buono Jr., the "Hillside Strangler" in Los Angeles.

The scale seems to predict which prison inmates will violate parole terms better than parole boards do, according to research published in the *Journal of Clinical and Consulting Psychology.* In the study, more than 75 percent of parolees shown by the scale to be high in psychopathy violated parole within a year of release from prison, while only 20 percent of those who scored low violated parole.

"The psychopath smooth-talks the parole board—he knows just what to tell them," Dr. Hare said. "But he screws up quickly once he's out."

But he noted that the traits of the psychopath were by no means unique to criminals. "You find psychopaths in all professions," Dr. Hare said. "He's the shyster lawyer, the physician always on the verge of losing his license, the businessman with a string of deals where his partners always lose out."

Behind the Glibness

The psychopath's glibness hides a defect in his emotional understanding of what he is saying, according to Dr. Hare's findings. For instance, when words are flashed very quickly—for about a tenth of a second—normal people react differently to neutral words like tree than they do to emotional words like death. If the word is emotional, most people can tell more quickly if its letters have been scrambled. And, as they decide, their brains show a distinctive wave pattern.

Psychopaths, though, do not respond more quickly to the emotional words, nor do they have the distinctive brain wave pattern. Dr. Hare interprets these results to mean that the psychopaths have a more shallow understanding of the meanings of words, particularly emotional terms.

"There is something odd about the psychopath's language to the clinical ear," Dr. Hare said. "Face-to-face most people do not notice the oddness because of the psychopath's charm and the sureness with which he speaks. He will blithely talk to a physician in medical terms with utter reassurance, though he knows he is using them incorrectly."

The psychopath's impaired understanding of feelings may be related to an unusual neurological pattern that Dr. Hare has found, in research to be reported in *Personality and Individual Differences.* The language center of right-handed people is almost always in the left hemisphere of the brain. But, Dr. Hare discovered, in many right-handed psychopaths language is controlled as much by the right hemisphere as by the left—a highly unusual pattern that he interprets as possibly signifying a failure of neurological development.

Measuring Body Signs of Anxiety

It is this sort of evidence that persuades Dr. Hare that the behavior of many psychopaths can be attributed at least in part to physiology.

On the surface this appears to put him in a long line of theorists who have tried to define the "criminal mind." But Dr. Hare points out that only one-quarter of convinced criminals appear to be psychopaths and that many psychopaths are not criminals.

Other indications of unusual physiological patterns in psychopaths that may account for their callousness have come from earlier work by Dr. Hare, recently confirmed by Stephen Wong, a psychologist in Saskatoon, Saskatchewan. In measuring the sweat response of psychopaths about to receive a mild electric shock, Dr. Hare discovered that they did not show the surge of anxiety that normal people exhibit. This could explain the psychopath's lack of concern for the future, including the threat of punishment.

In contrast, psychopaths expecting an electric shock do have an exaggerated increase in heart rate. Other researchers have found that this can occur when people tune out their immediate environment. Dr. Hare proposes that tuning out danger physiologically may be the mechanism that allows hardened criminals to remain devoid of the fear—or compassion—that others would feel.

The Psychology of a Ten-Year-Old

Along with these unusual physiological patterns, psychopaths tend to lag in their moral and intellectual development so that their psychology resembles that of a pre-adolescent, according to Robert Kegan, a psychologist at Harvard University.

The psychopath, Dr. Kegan points out, is said to be a con-man, manipulative, a facile and convincing liar, selfish, callous, charming, naîve, irresponsible at home and work, and prone to break the rules. It is no accident that the same is true of many a ten-year-olds, Dr. Kegan argues, since both share the same developmental stage. The psychopath is not so much amoral, then, as morally retarded—a notion that echoes 19th-century theories of criminality.

Although the psychopath is capable of intricate plots, at the same time he sets off with no clear goal in mind. This kind of rudderless intelligence, in Dr. Kegan's view, is typical of the stage of cognitive development that Jean Piaget calls the stage of "concrete operations," in which a child can hold many pieces of information in his mind, but cannot construct long-range plans or abstract generalizations from them.

Effective therapy for the psychopath, Dr. Kegan argues, would help him reach the next stage of psychological development, in which he would acquire an adult sense of responsibility. Such a treatment would more or less duplicate the tightly structured protective environment of a home, with clear rules.

Rigid Rules in Treatment

Similar recommendations for the treatment of psychopaths are made by other experts, notably Dr. Reid of the University of Texas Medical School. In *Unmasking the Psychopath,* published by W. W. Norton & Company, Dr. Reid writes that within recent years several treatment centers have begun to report success with psychopaths. The new treatments mark a turn away from the hopelessness of earlier generations of psychotherapists, who generally believed psychopaths were untreatable because they could not form the bonds essential for therapy.

According to Dr. Reid, the more effective treatment centers force psychopaths to stay for months or years in a program where the rules are firm and rigidly interpreted, so that the psychopath cannot talk his way around them. "When the psychopath is around people he can't con, and in treatment he can't escape from, his first reaction is depression as he becomes aware of his inner emptiness and hopelessness," said Dr. Reid.

In such an environment the psychopath can gain essential psychological abilities he has lacked; the ability to feel, to learn from experience, and to fantasize about and plan for the future, Dr. Reid said. One of the more successful programs, according to Dr. Reid and others, is the Patuxent treatment center in Jessup, Maryland, a facility to which criminals are paroled.

Whether or not they receive treatment, psychopaths tend to become tamer as life goes on. In a study by Dr. Hare of psychopaths over thirty years, from sixteen to forty-five years of age, almost all became more social as they aged, though their basic personality did not seem to change.

"Something dramatic happens at around thirty-five to forty, where there is a sharp drop in the psychopath's overt criminality," Dr. Hare said.

Problem May Be Increasing

The new research on the psychopath, whose basic traits have been studied since the pioneering psychiatric work of Hervey Cleckley in the 1940's, has a greater air of urgency because of data suggesting their ranks may be on the rise. In general, about 2 to 3 percent of people are estimated to be psychopaths, with the rate twice as high among those who live in the fragmented families and brutal poverty of the inner cities, according to a recent national study.

But some experts say the true rate of psychopathy is greater than those numbers suggest, and is increasing. Among the evidence experts cite are recent Federal statistics showing that crimes of violence are being committed by younger and more brutal criminals.

"The young criminal you see today is more detached from his victim, more ready to hurt or kill," said Jose Sanchez, a criminologist at Kean State College in Union, New Jersey. "The lack of empathy for their victims among young criminals is just one symptom of a problem that afflicts the whole society. The general stance of the psychopath is more common these days; the sense that I am responsible for the well-being of others is on the wane."

Objections to Diagnostic Criteria

The psychopath is likely to get into trouble with the law early in life, and to be in and out of trouble as an adult.

If the official psychiatric diagnosis for the psychopath, or "antisocial personality," is used, about 50 percent of inmates fit, according to Dr. Hare. But he and other experts argue that the figure is overstated; they say the diagnostic criteria focus too much on criminal misbehavior—because they were developed through the study of psychopaths who got caught—and too little on the underlying personality problems.

This also means, the experts say, that there are many more psychopaths at large than is generally realized.

"I wonder about those in business, say, who are just as unscrupulous, though they many never get caught breaking a law," said Remi Cadoret, a psychiatrist at the University of Iowa School of Medicine. "Their lack of remorse and empathy may be just as great as the most callous criminal, but we just do not see them in our prisons or clinics to study."

Probing the Enigma of Multiple Personality

June 28, 1988

When Timmy drinks orange juice he has no problem. But Timmy is just one of close to a dozen personalities who alternate control over a patient with multiple personality disorder. And if those other personalities drink orange juice, the result is a case of hives.

The hives will occur even if Timmy drinks orange juice and another personality appears while the juice is still being digested. What's more, if Timmy comes back while the allergic reaction is present, the itching of the hives will cease immediately, and the water-filled blisters will begin to subside.

Such remarkable differences in the same body are leading scientists to study the physiology of patients with multiple personalities to assess how much psychological states can affect the body's biology, for better or worse. The researchers are discovering that such patients offer a unique window on how the mind and body can interact.

Researchers feel that the study of these patients may also have significant implications for people with the medical disorders that are found to differ from one sub-personality to another. If the mechanisms through which these differences occur can be discovered, it may be possible to teach people some similar degree of control over these problems.

"We're finding the most graphic demonstrations to date of the power of the mind to affect the body," said Dr. Bennet Braun, a psychiatrist at Rush-Presbyterian-St. Luke's Medical Center in Chicago, and a leading pioneer in the research.

"If the mind can do this in tearing down body tissue, I think it suggests the same potential for healing," said

Dr. Braun, who directs a ten-bed psychiatric unit that uses psychotherapy, hypnosis and drugs to treat people with multiple personalities. He said he believed that the drastic physical changes seen in patients going from personality to personality could be duplicated for emotionally normal people under hypnosis.

In people with multiple personalities, there is a strong psychological separation between each sub-personality; each will have his own name and age, and often some specific memories and abilities. Frequently, for example, personalities will differ in handwriting, artistic talent or even in knowledge of foreign languages.

Multiple personalities typically develop in people who were severely and repeatedly abused as children, apparently as a means to protect themselves against the pain of the abuse. Often only one or two of the sub-personalities will be conscious of the abuse, while others will have no memory of experience of the pain. It is unclear why some abused children develop the syndrome while others do not.

For more than a century clinicians have occasionally reported isolated cases of dramatic biological changes in people with multiple personalities as they switched from one to another. These include the abrupt appearance and disappearance of rashes, welts, scars and other tissue wounds; switches in handwriting and handedness; epilepsy, allergies and color blindness that strike only when a given personality is in control of the body.

Today, using refined research techniques, scientists are bringing greater rigor to the study of multiple personalities and focusing on a search for the

mechanisms that produce the varying physiological differences in each personality.

Reaction to Medication

One of the problems for psychiatrists trying to treat patients with multiple personalities is that, depending which personality is in control, a patient can have drastically different reactions to a given psychiatric medication. For instance, it is almost always the case that one or several of the personalities of a given patient will be that of a child. And the differences in responses to drugs among the sub-personalities often parallel those ordinarily found when the same drug at the same dose is given to a child, rather than an adult.

In *The Treatment of Multiple Personality Disorder,* published by the American Psychiatric Press, Dr. Braun describes several instances in which different personalities in the same body responded differently to a given dose of the same medication. A tranquilizer, for instance, made a childish personality of one patient sleepy and relaxed, but gave adult personalities confusion and racing thoughts. An anti-convulsant prescribed for epilepsy that was given another patient had no effect on the personalities except those under the age of twelve.

In another patient, 5 milligrams of diazepam, a tranquilizer, sedated one personality, while 100 milligrams had little effect on another personality.

Some of the recent findings on such changes will be reported at an international conference on multiple personalities that Dr. Braun will convene in Chicago. The reports will include other physical differences from personality to personality, such as seizures, eating disorders, and different neurological and sensory profiles.

Optical Differences

One of those reports will be on a study by Scott Miller, a psychologist at the University of Utah, of optical differences in people with multiple personality. Dr. Miller had an opthalmologist give a battery of standard optical tests to ten patients and a control group of nonpatients. After each battery, the opthalmologist would leave the room while the patient switched personalities, sometimes at will and sometimes with prompting, then return and repeat the test.

Method First Used in '61

The approach being followed in the current studies was first employed in Copenhagen in 1961, where researchers undertook to follow the children of 207 women diagnosed as schizophrenic. Early findings from that study prompted a spate of researchers at other centers to follow suit in the early 1970's.

Today the High Risk Consortium comprises fifteen major research centers around the world. All told, the research groups have studied about 3,000 children, 1,200 of them with schizophrenic parents. Of these, thirty-five to forty have already shown clinical signs of the disorder, a higher portion than would be expected in a normal population.

The children of schizophrenics were made a focus of study because it has long been known that a larger than average proportion of these children would fall prey to the disorder. While it is believed that only 15 to 20 percent of schizophrenics have a parent with the disorder, having a schizophrenic parent greatly increases a child's chance of becoming a victim.

The child of a schizophrenic parent is at least three to six times more likely than other children to develop the disorder; some experts estimate the risk may be as high as fourteen times nor-

mal. A person with two schizophrenic parents is estimated to be at least thirty-five times more likely than others to become schizophrenic.

Challenge to Researchers

Even so, most children of schizophrenic parents do not develop the disease. That is the challenge to researchers, to sort out the events and characteristics that distinguish between those who develop schizophrenia and those who do not.

The method the researchers have adopted, matches children who have a schizophrenic parent with children having a parent who has had psychiatric problems other than schizophrenia. In this way the researchers hope to isolate such effects as the stigma or chaos that having a mentally ill parent can cause. These two groups of children, plus another whose parents have no known psychiatric problems, are then followed over the course of their development to see which will become schizophrenic.

That has recently begun to happen. Most of the projects are ten to fifteen years old, tracking children who are now approaching their twenties. The majority of people who become schizophrenic do so between the ages of fifteen and forty-five with the most frequent onset in the early twenties.

While close to forty of the children studied have already shown signs of schizophrenia, more than three times that number can be expected to do so over the next decade or two.

"Some significant leads are emerging from several research projects," said Dr. Norman Watt, a psychologist at the University of Denver who is one of the major investigators. Dr. Watt is the main editor of *Children at Risk for Schizophrenia,* a major collection of research papers published by Cambridge University Press.

Key Findings Are Cited

Among the key differences found between children who have become schizophrenic and those who have not at this point, are these:

Their mothers' schizophrenia was more chronic and severe than that of others with schizophrenia, had an earlier onset, lasted longer and involved more pronounced symptoms. The mothers also displayed poor social and personal adjustment.

These children were more likely than others to have had complications in delivery, such as abnormal birth positions.

They had more often been separated from their parents and raised in institutions or by foster parents.

In school they often created disturbances, being anxious, easily angered and aggressive.

Communications Within Families

However, researchers are not able to discount entirely the possibility that characteristics such as these may be preclinical signs of schizophrenia itself rather than precursors.

One of the more promising lines of research focuses on the way families communicate among themselves. A team of investigators at the University of California at Los Angeles has been studying communications in the families of sixty-five adolescents who showed signs of maladjustment. The adolescents were followed for ten years, and close to a dozen were eventually classified as showing symptoms of schizophrenia, though not all were hospitalized for the problem.

"The parents of these kids engaged in character assassinations," said to Dr. Michael J. Goldstein, the director of the study. "Instead of criticizing what the child had done, they would make a personal attack, saying, 'You're no good,' which damages the child's self-esteem."

"The parents also were highly intrusive, telling the kid what he thinks or feels without regard to what the kid says, things like, 'You know, you really don't like that kid you go around with.' The kid can easily become unsure of what he really does think.

"These parents also spoke in a way that leaves the child feeling confused or uncertain. They'd use words inappropriately, or undercut what they'd said by denying it or making it ambiguous. The result is to leave the child feeling that he doesn't know what to believe, with a shaken sense of reality. Further, the child learns a peculiar style of reasoning, and a chaotic way of thinking."

While such communications would not put most children at risk for schizophrenia, those with an inherited susceptibility to the disorder seem vulnerable. The combination of bizarre communication style and negative, intrusive messages from parents, Dr. Goldstein believes, leaves such a child particularly susceptible to a break with reality.

"Under stress," he said, "these children's thought processes are more easily derailed." Similar differences were found in other patients. "One patient had had his left eye injured in a fight, so that it turned out," said Dr. Miller. "But the condition only appeared in one of his personalities. It disappeared in the others, nor was there any evidence of muscle imbalance."

The study corroborates an observation of vision differences that had often been made by those treating multiple-personality cases. "Many patients have told me they have a drawer full of eyeglasses at home, and they never are quite sure which to bring when they go out," Dr. Braun said.

How Mind Regulates Biology

The medical phenomena beings discovered in multiple personalities stretch the imagination, but researchers believe that they represent only the extreme end of a normal continuum. The effects found in these patients, they say, are graphic examples of the power of states of mind to regulate the body's biology. By studying them, researchers hope to find clues to links between mind and body that can help people with other psychiatric problems, as well as point the way to powers of healing that may one day be of use in treating normal medical patients.

The lesson for psychophysiology from multiple personalities is that a given personality has as its biological underpinning a specific pattern of mental and biological states, according to Dr. Frank Putnam, a psychiatrist at the Laboratory of Developmental Psychology at the National Institute of Health. In a sense, Dr. Putnam said, there is a "biological self" that corresponds to the psychological self; as the psychological one shifts, so does the biological.

"We have a work self and a play self, for instance, but we are the same person," said Dr. Putnam. "But each of those selves has its own repertoire of emotional states, memories and, to some extent, an underlying biological pattern. Those minor differences are seen in their extremes in the patients with multiple personality."

The biological differences found in the patients, Dr. Putnam believes, reflect the range of states of mind that each sub-personality typically manifests. Many of them are extreme, the terror of a frightened child, the hatred of an avenger.

"A given state of consciousness has its biological reality," said Dr. Putnam. "By keeping these states separate and distinct, the patients create biologically separate selves."

Mechanisms of Change

Dr. Putnam, who has done extensive research on patients with multiple personalities, is now focusing his interest on how they switch from one personality to another. During the switch, there is typically a period of seconds or even minutes when heart rate, breath rate and other physiological markers show a disorganization, which is followed by a new pattern typical of the personality that is emerging.

Some of the most striking changes occur in the tension levels of the person's facial muscles. It is almost as though the person were donning a new face, according to Dr. Putnam.

The changes also include blood flow patterns in the brain, according to findings by Dr. Putnam and other researchers. The blood flow changes were observed while different personalities performed the same mental tasks.

"The transitions in children from one extreme state to another is every bit as abrupt as in the patients," said Dr. Putnam. "You see it in the child who switches from crying to laughing, or who cries himself to sleep. Normally, adults don't switch that abruptly; one of the tasks of growing is learning to keep the switching under control. Children have to make an effort so that their school self doesn't behave like their home self, for instance."

In the children who respond to severe abuse by developing multiple personalities, Dr. Putnam believes, the usual integration of various "selves" did not occur. Such children seem to make use of two psychological capacities to protect themselves against the pain of abuse. One is the ability to enter an altered state of consciousness, such as a hypnotic trance, an ability that peaks at around the age of nine. Another is the capacity to dissociate, to separate one aspect of experience from another.

"It's adaptive for the children to keep the states separate, so that they can keep the awareness of the abuse from their other selves," said Dr. Putnam. "That way the feelings and memories don't flood them while they are at school, for instance."

Universal Phenomenon

The switches that patients with multiple personality go through are a special case of a universal phenomenon, according to an article by Dr. Putnam in the current issue of *Dissociation,* a journal devoted to multiple personality and related disorders. Anyone who goes from one extreme emotional state to another undergoes major biological shifts akin to those observed in those with multiple personality, according to Dr. Putnam. They are no different from the plunges into extreme emotion seen, for instance, in patients who go from depression to a manic state, or in someone having a panic attack, he said.

"But the switches are harder to catch in other disorders; they're more random," said Dr. Putnam. "But some multiples can switch six times in an hour. They're a better laboratory for study."

Through studying such patients, Dr. Braun believes, wider medical applications may be discovered. He points, for instance, to one patient who had a blood pressure of 150/110 when one personality was in control, and a pressure of only 90/60 when another personality took over.

"They can teach us much about the mechanisms by which we shift from one state of consciousness to another," Dr. Putnam said. "Most of psychiatry deals with helping people shift from one unpleasant state to another, more pleasant one."

Schizophrenia: Early Signs Found

December 11, 1984

Through a major new approach to fighting the disorder, an international research group has begun to identify signs in children that may predict which of them will eventually fall victim to schizophrenia, the most severe form of mental illness.

The findings are the work of behavioral scientists in the United States and abroad as part of a project called the High Risk Consortium. The project, designed to continue for many years, has already yielded new data on the social and psychological precursors of schizophrenia, a disorder characterized by a loss of contact with reality.

The ultimate goal is to help prevent people at risk from becoming schizophrenic.

Earlier decades have seen researchers point to "schizophrenia-causing" mothers and "double-bind" messages as leading to the disorder. A more current focus has been to seek genetic factors that lead to biochemical causes. The current approach integrates both perspectives: it rests on the assumption that some people inherit a susceptibility to schizophrenia, but that how they weather the stresses of life determines whether they will develop the disorder. The researchers are looking for those experiences that sharply increase the likelihood a susceptible child will become a schizophrenic adult.

Many of the children had schizophrenic parents and were thus deemed to be more genetically susceptible to schizophrenia themselves. One of the most powerful recent findings, however, was among children whose parents were not considered mentally ill, although there were other suggestions that the children might be susceptible.

What characterized their parents was that they habitually gave children confusing and negative messages. This disordered communication was a strong predictor of which children in the study eventually showed signs of schizophrenia. Twelve of sixty-five children in the study developed the illness.

Specifically, when showing disapproval such parents tended to attack the child himself rather than to criticize things he had done; they habitually told the child what the child's feelings and thoughts were rather than listening to what the child had to say; and the parents would often speak ambiguously, saying one thing and then partly denying what they had said, leaving the child confused.

While such disordered patterns of communication have been noted before in the families of schizophrenic patients, this is the first time those patterns have been identified as playing some role as precursors of the disorder.

Other precursors, all of which were found in the children of schizophrenics who later developed the disorder themselves, seem to include decreased verbal intelligence and having such social problems in school as being either withdrawn or abrasive. These problems, like most of the others, are not thought to lead to schizophrenia unless the child has a genetic predisposition to the disorder, such as that suggested by a family history of the illness.

The urgency of this effort to learn what distinguishes one child who matures into healthy adulthood from another who succumbs to schizophrenia is a reflection of the dimensions of the problem. Some researchers estimate that as many as 3 percent of

Americans will develop schizophrenia at some point in their lives, though many will not have symptoms severe enough to lead to treatment and many will apparently recover.

Symptoms of Disorder

The symptoms of schizophrenia include confused thinking, disturbed perceptions such as hearing voices and a preoccupation with illogical ideas and fantasies.

More than two million Americans are thought to suffer from the disorder, and on any given day about 100,000 of them are in hospitals for treatment of the problem. The economic burden to the nation is estimated by the National Institute of Mental Health to be more than $20 billion a year, mostly from the loss of the victims' productivity rather than from direct medical costs.

Decades of scientific studies of schizophrenia have had discouraging results. While science has succeeded in reducing the prevalence of almost every other major disease, schizophrenia has proven resistant to all efforts. While medications mute the symptoms, none cure the disorder. Twenty years ago about one in 100 people suffered from schizophrenia at any given time. Today that figure remains unchanged.

How to Intervene

Is there any way to intervene? Some investigators believe that teaching social skills to children at risk may help, the more so because many of those who develop schizophrenia have a history of social problems, particularly in high school.

"There may be critical periods in a child's life when he is especially vulnerable to risk factors, and long plateaus when he is not," said John Strauss, a professor of psychiatry at Yale Medical School who formerly directed the schizophrenia risk study under way in Rochester.

"One of the critical points seems to be when a child learns to socialize with other children," Dr. Strauss said in an interview. "Of course, most kids with social troubles don't become schizophrenic. But those children with a genetic predisposition who also develop poor social relations are particularly high risks for schizophrenia. Social skills can be taught. That could become a point of leverage for intervention."

Researchers have also been looking at such cognitive symptoms as distractibility and poor short-term memory. Certain children in a New York City study who later developed symptoms of schizophrenia had showed these deficits in attention earlier, according to L. Erlenmeyer-Kimling, director of the high-risk project at the New York State Psychiatric Institute.

The great variability in the behavior patterns found among the high-risk children has been a problem for investigators. One boy who became schizophrenic at the age of eighteen was described as nervous and erratic in elementary school, and by one eighth-grade teacher as "despicable." In high school he was prone to temper tantrums and fights. Yet in ninth grade he had been elected class president.

Some investigators suspect that such striking variability may itself be a sign of risk, or perhaps an early symptom of schizophrenia. But such variability makes the statistical search for risk factors elusive.

"Everyone looks for a monolithic pattern in the development of schizophrenia: a single, identifiable group of youngsters who show a distinguishing pattern and undergo common stresses on their way to becoming ill," said Dr. Watt. "Unfortunately, the evidence so far does not show that to be the case; the actual patterns turn out to be more complex and erratic, with only a few distinctive features standing out among the handful who have become schizophrenic."

The project raises difficult ethical questions. For example, identifying a child as at high risk to develop schizophrenia might itself do damage to his life. To safeguard the children involved, researchers did not reveal which were in the high-risk group and which were the offspring of normal parents in asking schoolteachers to evaluate the children.

To Expert Eyes, City Streets Are Open Mental Wards

November 4, 1986

Broadway from Columbus Circle through the West Side is filled with new condominiums and well-dressed shoppers come to sample the sparkling pleasures of gourmet delicatessens and designer boutiques.

But seen through the eyes of a mental health worker, Broadway is a very different street. The swank and style recede, and a bent old woman in filthy coat, fishing a slice of bread from the garbage can by Zabar's, and a man wrapped in a grimy blanket, huddled on the sidewalk by Lincoln Center talking earnestly with no one, come into focus.

These are the clientele of a team of health workers who cruise the Upper West Side, searching out those whose confusion, delusions and despair have driven them to a life on the streets.

This is the Broadway polite eyes avoid, an open psychiatric ward where those with severe mental illness find asylum of sorts in a bench or doorway. Broadway, with its busy traffic and mall-like traffic islands with benches, seems to be one of those public spaces that invites the mentally ill to set up housekeeping. And what is happening there is typical of many other streets and parks in cities throughout the country.

To look upon this Broadway is to see the city with new eyes. The images that leaped out block after block were revelations to me—even though as a psychologist I had worked long hours in mental hospitals and had seen every sort of schizophrenic—as I traveled with some of the workers the city depends on to lure the deranged in for treatment.

There were disabilities more florid than I had seen before; people lost in the utter apathy that schizophrenia can breed and others fighting through a paranoid world of delusional villains out to ensnare them. These disorders are found in abundance in mental hospitals, but there medications blunt their full force. On Broadway the diseased mind is free to torment its victim relentlessly.

My guides through this netherworld were the staff of Project Reachout, a group whose responsibility is the mentally disturbed on the streets of the Upper West Side and in Central Park. The group is one of a handful working in the city.

Project Reachout, a service of the Goddard-Riverside Community Center, a nonprofit charitable organization, is widely viewed as a leader in what might be called street psychiatry, a specialty that hardly existed five years ago, before the mentally ill became homeless in such numbers. Today, of the estimated 45,000 homeless in New York City, at least a third are thought to suffer mental illness.

The mentally ill on the city streets are people that the system has failed. They cannot, by law, be forced into treatment unless they are so dangerous that life is at risk—and very few are ever that dangerous. Many have been in and out of mental hospitals for years, in a revolving door that gives them care until their symptoms subside, then releases them to drift back to the streets.

An increasing number have never had any help at all for their mental problems. And, in ever-growing numbers, they have thoroughly insinuated themselves into the major boulevards, a silent witness to the heartlessness and befuddlement that has created no better alternative for them.

There is much that the mental health workers can offer: Government stipends for the mentally disabled, medical care, psychiatric help, a place to live. But the people in the streets are so disorganized, so frightened and wary, so isolated from human contact, that they are worlds away from these benefits.

The workers' challenge is to engage them in some way and then, very slowly, to build a bond of trust strong enough that they will come in for help. The effort is akin to coaxing a wary fawn to come near for food; force, or too aggressive an approach, will fail here.

Success depends on gentle patience and the instincts of the heart.

Indeed, more often that not, the first time the workers approach a potential client, they are rebuffed. "We use sandwiches as bait," Anne McGrath explained as the van for Project Reachout began it morning round. The sandwich is in a brown paper bag, along with juice, a Famous Amos cookie—donated to the project—and a slip of paper with the address and telephone number of the office, and an offer of help.

The paranoid may see the sandwich as part of a plot; the regressed and withdrawn psychotic may be too timid or out of touch to take help. The woman who had retrieved bread from the garbage can by Zabar's, for instance, pulled herself into a dignified huff and marched across the street. There, she found the remains of a pizza in another garbage can.

It often takes weeks before the offer of a sandwich is accepted, weeks more before there is conversation and months before an actual visit to the office.

479 Street Clients Monthly

Project Reachout has recently averaged each month 479 street people it is in contact with regularly—people who day after day, unless they wander elsewhere for a time, are on a bench or sidewalk, or perched on a rock in the park. An additional 120 or so people are approached just once, never to be seen again. And, in any given month, according to Diane Sondes, the project's director, about 25 percent of the street clients will finally accept the invitation to come into the project office, where they receive anything from a cup of coffee and a shower to a room, financial aid and psychiatric care.

The van's first stop on this particular morning is a Jamaican woman in her thirties who has spent the better part of a year on a bench in the mall that divides Broadway near 98th Street. The woman, Ms. McGrath tells me, is so confused and apathetic that last winter, when she lost several toes to frostbite, she did not even know she needed medical help. The Reachout workers called in Project HELP, a roving mental health team with a psychiatrist who can commit people whose mental illness endangers their life. The woman was committed, spent three months in city and state psychiatric wards and then, as often happens with the homeless, was released to a shelter. Instead of going there, though, she came straight back to the bench. She considers it a safe refuge.

As we approach her, the woman barely turns to look; when she speaks her face is expressionless. From Ms. McGrath she gets another sandwich and makes another promise to come in, a promise she will not keep—at least not yet.

Pernicious Negative Symptoms

Her apathy is a common hallmark of, schizophrenics who are not plagued by vivid hallucinations but are too confused to do much for themselves, and so overwhelmed by apathy that they do nothing anyway. Recent research on schizophrenia has emphasized the pernicious nature of these so-called "negative" symptoms, including the loss of all motivation and the muting of feeling. From a psychiatric viewpoint she might be diagnosed as a schizophrenic of the "disorganized" type, because of the absence of systematic delusions and the blunted emotions she displays even when she tells, in a monotone, of being evicted from her tiny apartment.

Traveling with the Reachout team as it searches out its clients makes clear just how destructive those negative symptoms are to the schizophrenics on the street. The woman's pattern is repeated time and again in others, their apathy and lethargy shrinking their lives to ever smaller orbits, with ever fewer efforts to care for themselves.

To the public, such people may seem perennial eyesores, somehow to blame for their pathetic circumstances; through the psychiatric lens it is clear they are victims of the subtler symptoms of schizophrenia.

In the traffic island between 82d and 83d Streets we find a woman who wears a plastic garbage bag for a skirt, a large wool pullover and a flashy green knit hat. She is talkative, mostly complaining about the frustrations of trying to get her Social Security checks. She has been camped on that island on and off for almost eighteen months, from the day she was evicted from her small room in the hotel just across the street. She is determined to get her revenge, and until then nothing will move her from that spot.

Too Wary to Go in Office

At times, the woman has angrily threatened people who dared to cross Broadway over "her" island. On this day, in a different mood, she asks Ms. McGrath for a pair of pants and some socks, and Ms. McGrath brings them later. Although the Reachout team has worked with the woman since she appeared on the island, the woman came by the office just once, and then was too wary to come in the door.

Her argumentativeness and her angry fixation on revenge, along with the apparent absence of hallucinations, mark her as a paranoid. The paranoids on the streets are among the most difficult to help, their suspicion making them steer well clear of everyone. They are most wary of those who dare approach them, even with help.

At 72d Street, sitting on the sidewalk leaning against a bank, is a woman in her fifties, whose elegant, though filthy, clothes bespeak a better past. She says almost nothing, but as she takes her sandwich, an insect touches on it and flies away, prompting her to tear off that part of bread and throw it away. Her hand remains frozen in midair for a full half-minute.

In the past, the worker tells me, the same woman has been seen inside the bank, agitatedly tearing up the deposit slips and literally tearing her hair out. At other times, she stares at a tree, unmoving, for hours. The alternation between stupor and excitement marks the woman as a catatonic, a type of schizophrenic whose most extreme symptoms are rare among hospital patients because medications suppress them. Because she lives on the streets, her symptoms run rampant.

Further down the street in front of Lincoln Center we encounter a man in his early thirties, with matted hair and beard, who lies on a bench on a small traffic island, watching the cars stream by. His is an isolated spot, the perfect place. No one comes there, and, judging by his demeanor and tone, he wants no contact.

The man takes a sandwich with a suspicious glare and responds to the offer of help if he will come into the office with an "O.K." that says "leave me alone."

"You've got to know when to back off," says Mike Mastrogiovanni, the worker, who explains that it took weeks of offering before the man would even accept a sandwich.

That is part of the art of those who work trying to build trust with the deranged of the streets. Through daily contacts with these people, the Reachout workers and others like them are building an expertise that was virtually unknown four or five years ago. Although their patients have severe mental illness, the psychiatric workers of the streets have none of the luxuries of hospital psychiatry—medications, large staffs, even a building to work in.

Movement for Asylums Recalled

They rely instead on patience, flexibility and intuition. If things continue as they are, this is a craft that will be needed more and more, as psychiatric services are redesigned to meet what amounts to a crisis. This is a moment in the history of psychiatry parallel to the 18th-century emergence of the first asylums for the mad, a movement that sought a humane for the mentally ill who then roamed the streets. Now, as then, they are in need of a more protected haven, of psychiatric care, and of someone trustworthy who can help them manage the small details of daily living that are now just too overwhelming.

On any given day on this strip of Broadway, there are an estimated eighty to one-hundred mentally ill homeless people, about thirty of whom will have contact with the Reachout workers. In the days I traveled with the workers, the most prevalent problem seen, by far, was schizophrenia in all its varieties—including the catatonic, the disorganized, the paranoid.

But the most common sort of schizophrenia that I saw seemed to fall in the "undifferentiated" category. The victims suffer a mix of delusions, hallucinations—in the form of voices in their minds—and incoherence, and are, in general, so disorganized they can barely care for themselves.

A large number of the schizophrenics seen on the streets are in a phase of the illness in which their more obvious and bizarre symptoms are less noticeable. The negative symptoms dominate: social withdrawal, a gross deterioration in personal hygiene and grooming, indifference even to their own plight, apathy.

Studies have found that there are as many deteriorated alcoholics on the streets as schizophrenics, and to the untutored eye the two groups may seem the same. Indeed, some schizophrenics will take to drinking to quiet the voices that plague them, in a desperate "self-medication." The Reachout workers will, on first sighting, check to see if an alcoholic is not actually mentally ill; the pattern of alcohol and drug abuse among the schizophrenics on the street is increasingly common. Alcoholics, though, have their own programs, centering around detoxification treatment.

There are, of course, other mental disorders that bring people to the streets, notably acute depression, which sometimes can mix with psychosis. A handful of the mentally ill seen on the streets were people for whom the sudden onset of such a depression led to their precipitous fall to homelessness.

Those who work with the homeless mentally ill say the city law that allows people to be taken forcibly to city shelters when the temperatures fall to freezing will be of little help beyond offering sheer survival. The large city shelters are, for the mentally ill, no refuge. "Being told you have to go to a city shelter is terrifying to someone who believes the streets offer a safe home," said Judy Pritchett, assistant director of Project Reachout.

"Fort Washington armory has 900 men on a good day," she said. "It's the mentally ill there who are most vulnerable, who get robbed or beaten, or even raped."

Before I embarked on this journey, the homeless seemed more or less to be all of a kind. Now, though, I see the stark difference between those who roam the streets out of poverty and those who suffer an affliction of the mind that denies them a better choice.

Waiting for a Rescue

I am thinking, for instance, of that nameless woman in her twenties who even now is undoubtedly still sitting on that bench in Central Park where she first appeared ten weeks ago. Stylishly dressed, her long black hair always neatly combed, her well-packed suitcase by her side, the woman only recently held a job in the city as a secretary, had an apartment with roommates. But now she sits waiting for a rescuer—a television announcer she believes to be her "real" mother—to come to the park and take her home. The woman with the suitcase will not move, nor will she accept any help; she clings stubbornly to her fantasy of rescue.

But, then, there is the man who had sat in the middle of a baseball field since last May, so depressed and listless he would not move out of the rain. Then, one day just last week, the Outreach workers found him crying, for the first time.

"Why are you crying?" Margarita Lopez, the worker, asked him. "I don't know," he said. And, at that, Ms. Lopez started crying, too.

The next morning, the man showed up at the door of the Reachout office and accepted, for the first time, an offer of help.

Lost in a Private World

"I was sure the world had ended and started over, that it was the Year Two, and people were being held prisoner in all the buildings and subways," said Robert, recalling the eighteen months he spent roaming New York City streets, plagued by voices in his head and bedeviled by wild delusions. Although he is under psychiatric treatment and is calm now, Robert's memories of those months are vivid still.

"I was nervous all the time and walked from Canal Street up Broadway to 116th Street, almost running like an animal; while I walked I heard people's voices—Ho Chi Minh, Genghis Khan, and a Chinese Hen," said Robert.

"I would chant as I walked. In my mind I was 'running the gauntlet,' being persecuted by Islam. For a while I worshipped the Standard Oil Building as a symbol of jealousy; I thought it was a space center—it sort of looks like a space ship."

For those months, Robert was lost to the world. He spoke to no one and never asked for help or money. Occasionally people would give him a dollar or two, which he immediately spent on cigarettes and coffee.

"I was psychotic then, but I'm on medication now," he said. "When I think about it now, it doesn't seem real, but the delusions were all very real to me then. I suffered a lot."

At forty-two, Robert seems bright and personable today. But when he was first spotted striding along Broadway by the workers for Project Reachout, "he was a wildman," in the words of Judy Pritchett, Assistant Director of the project. "He was scary-looking, with matted, wild hair and beard, and filthy clothing."

Robert remembers that, in those days, he wore two pairs of pants, several sweaters, and two overcoats, no matter the weather. He never took a shower; he felt "sealed" in his clothes.

Robert ate whatever he could find in garbage cans, food he thought was left there for him "by the deities." A big problem was where to go to the bathroom; twice he defecated in the street, but, he says, "Ho Chi Minh made fun of me."

Robert's mental map of the city combined his delusions such as a "lake of fire," with more practical landmarks, including public rest rooms and drinking fountains. Wherever he went, he carried a sleeping bag he found in the garbage; he slept in several favorite spots, particularly near the Carousel in Central Park, a place near both drinking fountains and public bathrooms. "I never worried about whether it was safe," he says.

Those eighteen months of madness on the streets were one of many such episodes in Robert's life. His first hospitalization was in Glen Oaks Hospital on Long Island, when he was seventeen, and he has gone from mental hospital to the streets many times since.

In Robert's mind, the Goddard-Riverside Reachout worker who approached him to offer a sandwich and juice was a wealthy industrialist who owned a chemical factory. Robert thought that the man was Mr. Goddard, and that he had come to recruit him for a medical research project at his factory, which was named Goddard-Riverside. The first time Robert came to the Project office and got medication from a psychiatrist, he thought it was all part of the research, which he was willing to assist.

"When I was on the streets, I was more interested in my delusions than in what was actually going on," says Robert. "They were much more interesting."

Psychotherapy

Psychotherapy has become increasingly split into factions over the years. At a historic congress held in Phoenix in 1985, leaders of the major schools of thought met, many for the first time. As is told in "Psychotherapy, at 100, Is Marked by Deep Divisions on Approaches," after a century there are many rifts when it comes to agreeing on just what therapy is, how it should proceed, and what it should accomplish.

When do people first need psychotherapy? Some do in infancy. "Infants in Need of Psychotherapy? A Fledgling Field Is Growing Fast" tells of this application of the maxim that an ounce of prevention is worth a pound of cure. The needs are greatest, of course, for infants who have been the victims of neglect or abuse. But some otherwise healthy infants and their parents may benefit from fine-tuning their interactions.

Of all the issues that a patient in psychotherapy faces, one of the most difficult is raising the question, Is this working? "When to Challenge the Therapist—and Why" discusses research that suggests guidelines for what to look for in gauging the progress of psychotherapy, and how to know when to raise questions about its effectiveness.

If you've ever tried to give up smoking or stay on a diet, you know that giving up a habit is in some ways far easier than keeping your resolve afterward. "Breaking Bad Habits: New Therapy Focuses on the Relapse" describes a new approach that makes use of slips and relapses, turning them into chances to learn how to avoid repeats.

One of the most serious of psychological disorders is autism, a developmental abnormality marked by such symptoms as indifference to other people. Autism has long baffled psychotherapists who have tried to treat it. But "Researcher Reports Progress Against Autism" tells of one program that seems to be working.

Schizophrenia is often a lifetime problem. While the more flamboyant symptoms—hallucinations and the like—can often be controlled with medication, there are other, less obvious symptoms, such as lethargy, that are also troubling but which drugs do not help. "Aid in Day-to-Day Life Seen as Hope for Schizophrenics" describes a new approach that focuses on managing the challenges of daily life.

Many psychological disorders can be treated with either medications or psychotherapy. One of these is panic attacks, in which a person feels disabling anxiety. "Nondrug Therapy Eases Panic Attacks" describes research showing that new psychotherapies can be as effective as medication.

Psychotherapy, at 100, Is Marked by Deep Divisions on Approaches

December 17, 1985

Psychotherapy, after century of existence, is splintered into factions so diverse that there is little agreement on exactly what psychotherapy is, how it should proceed or what it should accomplish. And despite the best of ecumenical efforts, the deep divisions seem to be getting even deeper.

Those rifts were apparent at a landmark conference held in December 1985, in Phoenix at which most of the great living therapists gathered to discuss their craft.

Salvador Minuchin, one of the major figures in family therapy said, "We each have our fiefdoms, the boundaries determined by the beliefs we share. Information does not cross those boundaries very easily. We almost never get together so many therapists of differing views."

It will be 100 years this spring since Sigmund Freud set up his private practice in Vienna, thus founding the field of psychotherapy. To mark that anniversary, most of the stars of the field gathered, including Carl Rogers, Rollo May and Bruno Bettelheim. All told, participants represented fifteen major varieties of therapy, some with roots in psychoanalysis but many, such as behavior therapy, owing little or nothing to Freud.

Despite serious differences of opinion over how therapy should be done, the masters were, for the most part civil with each other—even displaying those marks of the good therapist, warmth and empathy. But off the podium, and occasionally on it, they were more open about the serious fault lines that have developed in their field over the last century.

The picture that emerged from interviews was of a field divided by irreconcilable views. The issues that separate the various schools of thought are as basic as whether the therapist should actively direct the patient toward change or should simply guide him to insight; whether therapy should delve into the past or focus on the present; whether it should be long or short; whether it is science, art or religion.

The conference was the brainchild of Jeffrey Zeig, a psychologist who heads the Milton H. Erickson Foundation, which sponsored the event. Dr. Zeig is a leading proponent of the techniques of the late Dr. Erickson, who was a pioneer in both hypnosis and his own brand of therapy, and from whom many early family therapists and those who do brief therapy borrowed key techniques.

"There has never been a forum quite like this in psychotherapy," Dr. Zeig said. "Many of these therapists, leaders of the field, are meeting each other for the first time ever. Our hope is that by bringing together all the schools at one time and place, there will be a cross-fertilization, and that a common ground will emerge."

If the 7,200 psychotherapists at the conference tended to one or another loyalty, it was not clear from their pattern of attendance. Halls built for 1,500 or more people held standing-room only audiences for speakers as diverse as Aaron Beck, a psychiatrist from Philadelphia, teaching "cognitive therapy," his method of treating depression and anxiety; Virginia Satir doing family therapy; and Dr. May discussing the importance of myths in psychotherapy.

One of the main attractions was the chance to see the great therapists of the day at work, and there were some impressive demonstrations. But even these seemed at times to raise more questions than they answered.

Technique Is Demonstrated

R. D. Laing, the British psychiatrist whose methods owe much to such existential philosophers as Sartre, interviewed a paranoid woman from a Phoenix shelter for the homeless. The interview seemed to be no more than mere conversation. It began with the woman stiffly telling Dr. Laing of a grand conspiracy against her while their conversation was broadcast by closed-circuit television to a nearby audience of more than 1,000 therapists.

By the end of the interview, Dr. Laing and the woman had achieved such a rapport that she seemed much less troubled and spontaneously offered to join him on the podium in the nearby lecture hall, where she answered questions with lucidity from the assembled therapists.

The elusive nature of the therapeutic exchange was highlighted by the fact that some people in the audience maintained that nothing much had happened in the interview, while Dr. Minuchin, the family therapist, rose from the audience to praise the interview as an example of the highest clinical art. Still others objected to Dr. Laing's explanation that it is as important just to be with someone in deep rapport as it is to try to change them. That event seemed emblematic of the vast differences in perspective that plague the field.

The most heated confrontations revolved around basic philosophies of treatment. James Masterson, a psychoanalyst in New York who specializes in the long-term treatment of troubled adolescents, was attacked by Jay Haley, director of the Family Therapy Institute of Washington, who treats similar adolescents.

Mr. Haley criticized Dr. Masterson for taking the adolescents out of their families into a special residential treatment center, asserting that doing so itself created more problems for the patients, such as stigmatizing them. Dr. Masterson, though, contended that problems embedded in a person's character require just such an intensive treatment as he offers.

Two Schools of Thought

Whether therapy should focus on what is happening now, or should delve into the past, was also debated. While methods such as psychoanalysis depend on probing into the past to unravel the present, most of the newer therapies do not.

In his confrontation with Dr. Masterson, Mr. Haley said, "When you say an adolescent had such-and-such a developmental history, that's just your dream, based on fantasy or hearsay. You'll never really know what happened in his past."

Those therapies, such as psychoanalysis, that seek to help patients gain insights into their problems, also came under attack by Mr. Haley. "It's the therapist's job to change the patient, not to help him understand himself," he said.

Mr. Haley is the proponent of a type of therapy, first developed by Dr. Erickson, in which the therapist directs the patient through specific changes designed to solve his problem. "Those who do long-term therapy say it is shallow just to focus on change," he said, "but at least the patients get over their symptoms."

The idea that it is the therapist's job to tell his patient what to do in his life was challenged by both Carl Rogers, the founder of client-centered therapy in which the client is encouraged to find his own truths, and Rollo May, the existential therapist.

"I disagree with those who assume they should change another person's life," Dr. Rogers said. "It's dangerous philosophy to assume the right to be a self-appointed authority on what is best for someone else."

"Therapies that are manipulative are wrong," Dr. May said. "Who are you, the therapist, to know what is going on at my deepest level?"

While the family therapists argue that treatment is pointless unless it takes into account the patient's whole situation, especially his family, others disagree. "Family therapists ignore the whole inner world of the patient," said Dr. Masterson. "You can't get anywhere without paying attention to what is happening inside the patient."

Patterns in Families

On the other hand, Murray Bowen, a family therapist, argued that psychological patterns occur over several generations within a family and that the therapist gets the best picture of what is happening by interviewing not only a patient's siblings and parents, but also grandparents.

One of those who made the point that most therapies have little scientific evidence to show that they are effective was Joseph Wolpe, a pioneer in behavior therapy, which uses behaviorist principles. He marshaled a large number of studies to show that behavior therapy was scientifically proven, but he bemoaned the fact that, despite the studies, many therapists—particularly his colleagues in psychiatry—paid too little attention to the method.

While many new therapies emphasize brevity in treatment and a sharp focus on solving particular problems, others use a long-term treatment that, according to proponents, is slower but deeper. Bruno Bettelheim, the eminent psychoanalyst, said, "People settle for less therapy than they need in their quest for a solution that is easy, painless and fast."

Some therapists argue that a therapy that does not ask the patient to make a strong commitment can produce only trivial changes. James Bugenthal, a leader of the existential therapy movement, said, "If people won't disrupt their lives by making a serious commitment to therapy, how can they remake them?"

Issue of Involuntary Therapy

Still another issue raised was whether therapy should be given to those, such as people committed to mental hospitals against their will, who do not seek it. "The question is not whether therapy is effective," said Thomas Szasz, the psychiatrist best known for his critiques of the basic assumptions of his own profession. "The issue is whether the patient wants it or not. Therapy is like religion, there should be a free choice. The important thing is that it should not be involuntary."

One question that polarized the speakers was whether a therapist ought to offer only one method or a range of them. "There's not a single therapy which, at some point, I have not drawn on," said Virginia Satir, a leader in family therapy. "A good therapist uses all the techniques—and invents the ones that don't exist yet."

Lewis Wolberg, a psychoanalyst, criticized those in his own discipline who are rigidly tied to their approach and will not experiment with other treatments. "There are those analysts who say, 'If you put a revolver to my head I wouldn't try family therapy,'" Dr. Wolberg said. "Psychoanalysis has been bogged down by that kind of resistance to change."

One of the few voices of reconciliation was that of Judd Marmor, a psychoanalyst from Los Angeles. "There is no single best way for helping everybody," said Dr. Marmor. "Someday I hope to see an end to the claims of superiority by any one technique over all the others."

Dr. Marmor described research of his own showing that, despite the surface differences between the kinds of therapy, there is an underlying process that is common to them all. Among the universal features of therapy is that all offer emotional support from the therapist and the chance to identify with him; all use suggestion and persuasion, whether obvious or not; and each somehow guides the patient toward a healthier way of life. In Dr. Marmor's view, such common denominators may be far more important than the seeming differences.

But some speakers were troubled by their failure to find much common ground among the various therapies. "What you have among us speakers is parallel monologues, not dialogue," said Dr. Minuchin. "We are each pris-oners of our dogma. The integration will be made by the 7,000 therapists in our audience. They are, I hope, flexible enough to see that each of these approaches has something to offer."

Infants in Need of Psychotherapy? A Fledgling Field Is Growing Fast

March 23, 1989

Baby blocks are the latest accessories in some psychiatrists' offices, as a new idea is gaining popularity: psychotherapy for infants.

The fledgling field, virtually non-existent a dozen years ago, is growing rapidly. No one knows how many children have been treated or need treatment because the Government does not keep statistics on it, but as many as 10,000 professionals are now offering such therapy. In addition to psychiatrists and psychologists, the practitioners include pediatricians, social workers and nurses.

For parents, this means that there is somewhere to turn for expert advice on the emotional ups and downs of babies, and to lay to rest fears, often ungrounded, that something is awry. And, if a baby is found to have an emotional problem, a psychotherapist stands ready to help.

'Window of Opportunity'

The field's fundamental assumption is, in essence, that an ounce of prevention is worth a pound of cure.

"Therapy for minor problems in infancy can prevent major problems later in life," said Dr. Robert Emde, a psychiatrist at the University of Colorado Medical School. "This is a prime window of opportunity." Dr. Emde is also president of the World Association for Infant Psychiatry, the main professional group in the field.

In extreme cases, when the parent is inadequate or absent, therapy involves a team of caretakers who substitute for the parents. For children who are less disturbed, therapy focuses on evaluating what is wrong in the relationship between the parent and child and then coaching the parent to better respond to the child's needs.

In part, the rise of infant psychiatry is traced to recent research into emotional development in infants. While the benchmarks of biological growth have long been known, those of emotional growth have only recently been charted, allowing clear guidelines for spotting troubled infants for the first time.

"We now know much more than ever before about the emotional, social and behavioral development of normal infants," said Dr. Justin D. Call, chief of Child and Adolescent Psychiatry at the University of California at Irvine, a founder of the field. "It makes the recognition of problems clearer much earlier in life than had been possible.

Putting Infancy on the Map

"It put infancy on the psychiatric map," he said. "We saw that we should be intervening before the age of three." Infancy is reckoned to end at that age.

Dr. Eleanor Szanton, director of the National Center for Clinical Infant Programs in Washington, said twenty times more infants were being seen for emotional difficulties and related problems than were seen ten years ago because professionals now knew what to look for. Most parents, though, do not yet know to ask for help, she said.

A separate trend has also contributed to the interest in infant psychotherapy. In the last two decades, Dr. Call noted, there has been a steady increase in the number of infants born to mothers who take drugs or mothers in their early teens. Rates of infant abuse and neglect have also gone up. All these factors are tied to the likelihood of serious emotional problems in infants.

For some parents, the mere list of troubles the field treats is likely to stir concern. Much of it is unwarranted, therapists say, noting that parents have muddled through for ages without the help of infant psychiatry.

Still, various studies are showing there is a genuine need for infant psychiatry. Surveys of infants brought to pediatricians' offices in various cities have found that from 10 percent to 15 percent have a severe emotional problem, such as depression or an inability to respond to people, Dr. Call said.

Ten to 15 percent more have mild problems, like being withdrawn, that would benefit from short-term treatment, said Dr. Call.

Dr. Szanton said, "Perhaps the saddest problem of all in infants is failure to thrive, where a baby gains no weight, becomes indifferent to the world, and withers."

For practioners of infant psychotherapy, there are only a few formal training programs in departments of psychiatry or pediatrics. Some social work and nursing programs also offer courses.

The majority of those now working in the field have attended short-term training programs. The first of these postgraduate training institutes was held in 1978 with 400 participants; the most recent was held two years ago and attendance jumped to 1,200.

For a child needing psychotherapy, insurance policies that pay for psychiatric care will usually cover the costs of treating an infant. But therapists say the policies often require formal diagnosis of a specific psychological problem, which can alarm parents when expressed clinically.

The most serious psychological disturbances in infants are usually attributed to parental abuse or neglect of a baby's basic needs, like warmth or regular meals. Doctors say neglect, including of an infant's emotional needs, can slow intellectual growth.

Variety of Symptoms

Doctors who treat infants with severe problems say they display a variety of symptoms, including continuous inconsolable crying and frantic shaking, a tendency to shrink from touch, extreme sadness, lethargy, and indiscriminate rage.

Much of the work in infant psychiatry is with milder problems. Among the more common varieties are "at-tachment disorders," in which infants have difficulty forming a trusting bond with parents. The child, for instance, may shrink from parents or not respond. While the attachment problems can sometimes be severe, they are often mild reflecting minor idiosyncracies in how parents treat an infant.

One such baby was treated by Dr. Stanley Greenspan, a professor of child health and development at George Washington University Medical Center.

"He was just nine months," Dr. Greenspan said. "He was highly irritable and would cry for an hour at the slightest irritant. Whenever his mother would leave the room, he'd throw a tantrum. But while she was with him, he'd just lie there passively."

In evaluating the infant, Dr. Greenspan discovered he was hypersensitive to touch, so that a normally enjoyable cuddle would irritate him. His mother had responded to his extreme irritability by becoming overprotective. If he began to reach for something, she would get it for him before he could complete the motion.

"She was making him passive by hovering and anticipating his every move," Dr. Greenspan said. In a few sessions, Dr. Greenspan got her to delay her impulse to intervene. At the same time, he encouraged the parents to handle their baby more gingerly, so as not to irritate his skin.

"A new focus of therapy in infant psychiatry is on treating disturbances in relations between parents and infant," Dr. Call said,

Typical of these problems are lonely parents who become excessively dependent on their infants, and who keep the infant from developing the normal independence of a two-year-old. Another common pattern is seen when parents discipline an infant with stiff corporal punishment.

"Corporal punishment, especially when the child is too young to understand it, can lead the child to become defiant, even start provoking punishment, and finally, estranged from his parents," Dr. Call said.

Then there are the problems that worry parents, but are only part of the normal travails of infancy. "There are a fair number of kids who by temperament are hypersensitive to stimulation, irritable and sleep poorly," said Dr. Emde. "It's one of the most common complaints from parents. When we evaluate the child, we let the parents know it's common and doesn't go on forever."

He added, "There are some practical steps parents can take, such as keeping things quiet and calm around the infant. But when parents are far more anxious than they need to be, it just makes matters worse."

When to Challenge the Therapist—and Why

October 9, 1988

For anyone undergoing psychotherapy, the question is inevitable. Is it working? When symptoms linger, or problems that seemed gone reappear, or doubts arise about the therapist, it's natural to wonder. Is it time to switch therapists? Or is the treatment, in fact, working to the extent it can? And is the pain that persists essentially what everyone must suffer from time to time?

Until recently, there have been no sure standards by which patients could assess the effectiveness of therapy. But new research has shed light on what actually happens in the course of treatment and has spelled out what progress patients can expect.

Moreover, psychotherapy researchers are now encouraging patients who have doubts about their treatment or their progress to take up those doubts forthrightly with their therapists. According to the orthodox Freudian view, patient complaints indicate a problem not with the therapy, but with the patient, a result of negative transference, in which childhood conflicts with parents are projected onto the therapist. But most experts now agree that such doubts can signify real problems with the therapy and need to be carefully examined.

Research by Lester Luborsky, a clinical psychologist at the University of Pennsylvania and author of *Who Will Benefit from Psychotherapy?* published this fall, provides more reason to treat the matter with some urgency. He has found that up to a tenth of all patients may actually be harmed by therapy—their problems get worse or they end up frustrated or unhappy with the course of treatment.

In the past, the lack of objective guidelines made it difficult for patients to know what should happen at what point in therapy. While there can be no universal timetable, recent studies have shown that the most noticeable improvements tend to occur toward the beginning of treatment. As therapy continues, it takes longer for changes to occur, because the problems being dealt with are more deep-seated. The most profound changes, which affect longstanding personality characteristics, are the slowest.

These conclusions are based on studies involving 2,431 patients done by a research team led by Kenneth I. Howard, head of clinical psychology at Northwestern University. Howard found that for people in once-a-week therapy (the frequency of visits for 90 percent of patients), there is a striking pattern of improvement, a negatively accelerating curve.

Using statistical methods to describe the overall improvement of patients (rather than improvements in any one symptom), the researchers developed a way to predict their recovery: 10 percent of patients improve before the 1st session; 20 percent have improved after the 1st session; 30 percent after the 2d session; 40 percent after the 4th session; 50 percent after the 8th session; 60 percent after the 13th session; 70 percent after the 26th session; 80 percent after the 52d session, and 90 percent after the 104th session.

That final 90 percent figure is considered a "ceiling effect" beyond which little additional improvement can be expected. The reason psychotherapy does not help everyone, and those who are going to improve will almost certainly have shown at least some progress within two years.

The study found that 10 percent of patients show improvement after making an appointment, even before seeing a therapist. This may simply be relief at having done something concrete about getting help. Or it may reflect a spontaneous remission, the clearing up of problems without outside help.

Another study, by Howard and Marc A. Zola, a psychologist at the Institute of Living in Hartford, examined which of ninety common patient complaints clear up, on average, at what point in treatment. Their findings, reported at a meeting of the Society for Psychotherapy Research, are based on checklists filled out by 351 patients, in which they noted their symptoms before starting treatment and at various stages in therapy.

The first eight sessions of therapy mark a "remoralization phase," in which acute symptoms of distress tend to dissipate rapidly and the patient regains at least a guarded sense of optimism. Many symptoms clear up in these first sessions, changing little more, if at all, throughout the rest of treatment. These problems include difficulty controlling impulses, such as the urge to smash things or getting into frequent arguments; trouble thinking straight, concentrating or making decisions, or feeling "blocked" in finishing things; being demoralized, feeling inferior or being lonely, even when with friends.

During this phase, the therapist "helps the patient settle down and establish a working relationship," says Howard. "The patient should get the message that he's not alone with his troubles, that there is some hope, that he's found someone to help."

In the next phase, which lasts roughly from the second month of treatment to the sixth, there is a "remobilization" of the patient's ability to handle life. At this point many symptoms of anxiety and depression tend to abate, such as lack of energy, hope or interest in life and feelings of fearfulness or nervousness.

The last phase, from six months onward, is largely "preventive," according to Howard. In this stage therapy focuses on habitual personality patterns that cause self-defeating reactions to life, such as feelings of worthlessness, mistrust and self-blame. Therapy during this phase is intended to help the patient find ways to prevent a recurrence of his or her symptoms.

"This is the phase in therapy where patients are trying to understand themselves better, not just looking for the relief of some troubling problems," says Howard. "The focus shifts to the recurrent patterns in a person's life—the failed relationships, for example."

Although these findings are not meant as a standard for measuring progress in any specific case, they may reassure some people who are impatient with the pace of therapy, and may raise doubts in others. Doubts—about the therapist or the therapy itself—can arise at any time in the course of treatment. Even though such feelings are common, patients are often reluctant to discuss them for fear of sabotaging the experience, especially in short-term therapy, which can be fewer than twelve sessions. "There's a wish to keep things happy, because if it got too negative, therapy might end before the negativity is resolved," Lester Luborsky says of shorter therapy.

"Patient misgivings represent one of the most thorny problems for patient and therapist alike," says Dr. Robert S. Wallerstein, a psychiatrist

at the University of California, San Francisco School of Medicine and president of the International Psychoanalytical Association. "Sometimes it means that these two people just don't work well together," he says.

If doubts occur at the first meeting of patient and therapist, experts say that it's wise to shop around, and advise consulting two or three therapists before settling on one. Howard has found that a patient's first impression of a therapist is usually accurate. If at the first session the patient feels that the therapist is apprehensive unsure of himself or inattentive, it is a good indication that the treatment won't be productive. "If the therapist strikes you from the start as not connected to you, it's a warning you'll have to spend lots of time and energy forming a good working relationship, as opposed to finding a therapist where you click," Howard says.

That is not to say that for therapy to work patient and therapist must immediately feel perfectly attuned to each other. Sometimes when a first session seems "virtually perfect," Kenneth Howard notes, the following sessions are a letdown by comparison.

In a study by Howard in which patients evaluated their therapy after each session, in those cases where a therapist struck a patient as "off" from the beginning and where that perception stuck, the results of the treatment were generally poor. When patient and therapist became more attuned to each other as time went on, the outcome tended to be positive, even if the patient's first impression was not favorable.

The key to productive therapy, according to Lester Luborsky, is the formation of a good working alliance. If the patient feels understood by the therapist, has confidence that the therapist can help and feels that they have similar ideas about how treatment should proceed, the relationship has a good chance of yielding positive results.

Even in successful therapy, however, patients sometimes have misgivings. In such cases, Dr. Wallerstein says, "the feelings may be a symptom of precisely what the patient is in therapy to resolve." These feelings fre-

quently emerge after six months or so, once the problem that brought the patient to treatment has receded. In the foreground at this time are issues between patient and therapist that represent patterns of conflict that sometimes go back to the patient's childhood.

"The issues are the same ones that have to be negotiated in any intimate relationship: hostility, trust, dependency and sexuality," says Howard. "When they emerge, they are expressed as a conflict with the therapist. Whether therapy ends at this point depends on the willingness of client and therapist to confront what's going on. Some patients suddenly see their therapist as a malevolent force trying to keep them dependent, or as being angry or disappointed with them."

Candor between patient and therapist increases the likelihood that treatment will be successful. It's crucial that the patient discuss negative feelings with the therapist, and work toward a resolution. If that doesn't happen, the therapy can founder. Dr. Wallerstein says that "Many abrupt endings the therapist can't account for are due to the patient having deep misgivings he could not bring himself to mention."

What happens after doubts are raised is a telling sign of whether the working relationship is a sound one. While some therapists welcome a patient's expression of doubts, others feel threatened which is likely to inhibit future communication. "If a therapist gets defensive about a patient's misgivings, that puts a sharp limit on the treatment," says Dr. Wallerstein. "You want to be free to say whatever is on your mind to your therapist."

If things don't improve once doubts are aired, it's probably better for the patient to find another therapist. Researchers at Payne Whitney Clinic in New York found that dissatisfied patients made more progress when they switched therapists rather than staying with one with whom they felt unhappy. "Too many patients feel that if they don't do well, they're failures as patients, rather than seeing that the particular match just did not work out," says Luborsky. Few patients realize that they are free to consult with another therapist if they have serious doubts about their treatment.

Most consulting therapists insist that the patient first discuss his doubts with the current therapist. Then the consulting therapist will meet separately with the patient and the therapist, and recommend either that therapy continue or that it be stopped.

When to terminate therapy can be a point of disagreement between patient and therapist. Early in treatment most patients feel better to their therapists, according to Howard's research. He found that, in general, patients rated themselves as more improved than their therapists did. It was not until after six months of treatment that patients' and thera-pists' ratings of progress dove-tailed more often then not.

How, then, can a patient know when therapy is completed? Luborsky advises that if the patient feels that the problems that brought him to treatment are under control, and if he believes that the gains can be maintained without the therapist, then it's time to discuss terminating the treatment. The patient should review his original goals with the therapist and decide if they have been met.

Often, however, the prospect of ending therapy raises insecurities about being on one's own. Therapists say that it is quite common for symptoms to recur as a patient faces the end of treatment. If they do, the patient and therapist should discuss why the problems have reappeared, and usually they will wane.

Therapy is as much an art as a science. Unlike surgery, where success is clearly defined, the results of psychotherapy are highly subjective. Although studies have yielded general guidelines with which to gauge the progress of treatment, therapy is still an individual experience with periods of both rapid and barely discernible change, and with times of confidence in the process and of doubts.

"Patients need to be reminded over and over that when therapy is working, there will be times they don't feel it is helping them at all," says Luborsky. "It is those times that can be very fruitful, if you talk them over with your therapist. What may seem like the low point in therapy may actually turn out to be the most productive."

Breaking Bad Habits: New Therapy Focuses on the Relapse

December 27, 1988

In news that should hearten anyone whose New Year will bring resolutions to break bad habits, researchers say lapses do not necessarily mean that the effort is doomed. Rather, they say, learning to overcome lapses is emerging as one of the most important parts of such efforts, whether they are trying to eat less or to give up smoking.

"For any habit you want to change, the key to success is not just stopping, but keeping from relapsing," said Howard J. Shaffer, a psychologist at the Center for Addiction Studies at Harvard Medical School. "You can learn from a slip how to keep it from happening again."

Overcoming a relapse is the focus of a new treatment approach being used by therapists for patients with a wide range of addictions. In addition to obvious applications, like alcoholism, overeating and drug addiction, the new techniques are being used with cardiac patients who must adopt a healthier way of life and also with sex offenders.

The researchers said they learned about some of the methods from people who broke self-destructive habits on their own, without professional assistance. Researchers say that 90 percent of those who have quit smoking, for example, did it on their own. But for most of them, it took several attempts.

The new approach differs in emphasis from that of groups like Alcoholics Anonymous, which stress the need to avoid lapses altogether. "In A.A. people feel that if they slip and have a drink they're lost entirely, back to day one," Dr. Shaffer said.

"That attitude in itself can sometimes be enough to turn a slip into a full relapse, since it can lead to the attitude that if you've had one drink, you're off the wagon, so you may as well keep drinking."

Despite the difference in outlook, relapse prevention is often used along with treatment programs that involve Alcoholics Anonymous-type groups, said G. Allan Marlatt, a psychologist at the University of Washington who is an expert on breaking habits.

The approach is receiving wide recognition as a useful addition to virtually any of the dozens of therapeutic approaches now used to change self-defeating habits. Researchers have found that most treatment approaches for all kinds of addictions have comparable long-term success rates and that they are all made more effective when techniques of avoiding and overcoming relapses are added.

"The key is what happens after the formal treatment ends and the patient returns to his regular life," Dr. Shaffer said.

The importance of focusing on how people cope with temptations after they have changed a habit is highlighted by a study at Stanford Medical School, published by Oxford University Press. In that study, people who had gone through one of five different treatment programs for alcoholism were studied for two years after completing the programs. A careful analysis of what contributed to their success or failure in staying dry was done by the researchers, Rudolph Moos, John Finney and Ruth Cronkite, all psychologists at Stanford.

"The results suggest that how people cope with stress after their treatment has a great deal to do with how well they will succeed," Dr. Finney said. "Relapse prevention is one of the most promising approaches these days."

The focus on relapse prevention has come largely from the work of Dr. Marlatt and a fellow psychologists at the University of Washington, Judith R. Gordon. Theirs is a common-sense approach drawing on such homely wisdom as "forewarned is forearmed." But it not only prepares people to prevent relapses but also helps them take advantage of any slips rather than becoming demoralized by them.

"A slip is an error in learning, not a failure in willpower," Dr. Marlatt said. "The belief that a slip means you have no willpower or are addicted is a self-fulfilling prophecy. If you think it is so, then you act that way. But people who recover from habits they want to change treat slips very differently. They see themselves as having made a mistake they needn't repeat. And recovering from a slip gives them a stronger confidence in their ability to resist temptation."

Dr. Marlatt sees relapse prevention as applying to any habit people want to change. It was inspired by studies in the early 1970's that found relapses in about three-quarters of those treated for addictions as diverse as smoking, alcoholism and heroin. The studies showed that two-thirds of the relapses occurred within ninety days of the end of treatment.

"About 20 percent of people can kick a habit on the first try, but most people need several attempts, no matter what the habit," Dr. Marlatt said.

In research with Susan Curry, a psychologist at the University of Washington, Dr. Marlatt and Dr. Gordon studied 123 heavy smokers who were trying to quit. The participants had smoked for an average nineteen years and most had already tried to quit three or more times. The study was reported in the October 1988 issue of *The Journal of Consulting and Clinical Psychology*.

A key to Success

The researchers found that those who succeeded in quitting tended to attribute their relapses to something in the situation rather than a personal failing.

"The successful quitters focused on what they might have done differently, rather than on thoughts like, 'This just proves I'm addicted to nicotine,' " said Dr. Marlatt. "Those who went back to smoking tended to treat their first lapse as decisive. They felt guilty, blamed themselves for the lapse instead of the situation and saw the lapse as due to something in themselves they could not change, like a lack of willpower."

Many of those who eventually succeeded in quitting often had episodes when they smoked some cigarettes. But they were able to return to abstinence. "They saw themselves as having made a mistake they need not repeat," said Dr. Marlatt. "For example, one man smoked when he went to a bar with an old friend who had come to town. He said afterward, 'That taught me I have to be particularly vigilant about smoking when I drink.' "

Part of the training in relapse prevention programs encourages people to identify those situations in which they are most likely to encounter temptation. Often the pressures are . social, being with friends who gamble or getting into family arguments.

Emotional Roots of Lapses

Often the triggers are emotional. The triggering emotions are most often anger or frustration for men and depression for women, according to Dr. Marlatt.

In the training programs, one focus is on anticipating such situations, and finding more positive ways to deal with them. For instance, one of Dr. Shaffer's patients who was trying to stop using heroin decided not to walk down a particular hallway at work, because someone with whom he had used heroin had an office there.

Advising people just to say no is not enough, Dr. Shaffer said. "You need to rehearse exactly how you'll handle the situations when temptation is greatest," he advised. "At holiday parties, where there will be people plying you with rich foods, or alcohol, or even drugs, how will it be to refuse, and just what will you say?"

With his patients, Dr. Shaffer often plays the role of the person offering the temptation. He asks some patients to anticipate how they will spend every part of the day, virtually minute by minute, to identify what risky moments they face. Then, they can plan how they will deal with them.

"Habit change depends on increasing your awareness of just where in your life the temptations come from, and finding skillful ways to handle them," Dr. Marlatt said.

One of the more novel applications of relapse prevention is with sex offenders, especially child molesters who receive psychological treatment in prison and are then paroled. The programs are being tried in California and in Florida.

"They've had to redefine what they mean by lapse in working with child molesters," Dr. Marlatt said. "If they commit the offense, it's already too late. So they count a lapse as simply having a sexual fantasy of the offense."

One principle in the relapse prevention training is to treat any slip as an emergency that needs to be dealt with immediately. People going through the program are often given a small card they can take out for guidance. The card is described in *Relapse Prevention*, a book edited by Dr. Marlatt and Dr. Gordon and published by Guilford Press.

The card advises that as soon as a lapse occurs, the person should stop and look carefully at what has just happened, and realize the need to take specific steps to assure that the slip does not undermine the effort to change the habit.

Card holders are advised that feelings of guilt and self-blame are likely, and they should allow it to pass until they become calm. They are reminded that a slip is a chance for learning, not a total failure. Card holders are then asked to remind themselves of the reasons they were trying to change the habit.

Then they are urged to review the situation that led to the lapse, paying special attention to their mood, who they were with and what they were doing, and if there were any early warning signals that they might use in the future to prepare themselves to ward off temptation.

They are then instructed to make an immediate plan for recovery from the slip. "Throw away the rest of the pack of cigarettes," the card reads. "Pour out the remaining booze from the bottle."

Then, the card says, leave the scene of the slip. It urges the card holder to call a friend or psychotherapist for help, and to think of specific ways to avoid the slip from happening again.

The antidotes often take the form of a "positive addiction," finding something like regular exercise or gardening that the person can turn to when they feel most vulnerable to the old habit.

Dr. Shaffer, who has studied cocaine users who stopped the habit on their own, said, "The general principle is that you find the sequence of events that led up to your habit in the past, and you interrupt it."

Perhaps most important is to keep trying instead of giving up. "Most people have several slips and lapses before they finally kick a habit," said Dr. Marlatt. "It's like mountain climbing; you may need several attempts before you reach the top."

Researcher Reports Progress Against Autism

June 17, 1986

Using an intensive behavior modification program and training parents to continue treatment at home, U.C.L.A. psychologists say they have been able to transform a large proportion of autistic children into apparently normal children.

According to a report in the *Journal of Clinical and Consulting Psychology,* nineteen autistic children were treated for up to six years in the program at the University of California at Los Angeles. Nine were able to enter first grade and blend into normal classes, a success rate of close to 50 percent. Eight others attended special classes for children with language problems in regular schools. Only two needed to be in classes for the autistic.

"If you met them now that they are teenagers, you would never know that anything had been wrong with them," said Ivar Lovaas, the psychologist who directed the study. For instance, one now has an I.Q. of 130 and hopes to study meteorology at the Air Force Academy.

Autism, which emerges by the age of two and one-half in about five of 10,000 children, is marked by an indifference to others; severe retardation; problems in speaking, such as echolalia, in which the child repeats the words just spoken to him, and bizarre habits such as arm-flapping or rocking for hours on end. The disorder, whose exact causes are unknown, is considered lifelong, although about one in six autistic children become socially adjusted by adulthood.

Many programs for autistic children use behavioral modification methods. What sets the U.C.L.A. program apart is the intensity of training. Each child received forty hours a week of individual treatment from a specialist trained in techniques of behavior modification, and the treatment was continued by the child's parents at home and by teachers in preschool programs. In effect, the children received years of continuous therapy. The therapy puts a huge demand on the child's family, as the parents must be alert to the child's behavior to be able to respond appropriately.

The responses include praising appropriate speech or actions, ignoring bizarre behavior, putting a child who became aggressive in a room alone for a time-out period, or responding to undesirable behavior with a loud "no." Sometimes stronger punishment is used. "We give the kids an occasional smack on the butt if they get too far out of hand," said Dr. Lovaas.

Others who use behavior modification with autism say that even this level of punishment is unwarranted. However, the U.C.L.A. program does not use extreme punishments, called "aversives," like those that were the focus of controversy at a Providence, Rhode Island, treatment facility after the death of a student who was bombarded with static noise.

In the U.C.L.A. program, John McEachin, a graduate student, found that the nine children who are now in normal classes do not differ in any way from normal children on extensive tests, at the age of fourteen, on interpersonal relations, emotional stability, social skills or intelligence.

Experts on autism have greeted the U.C.L.A. success with cautious enthusiasm. "If true, these results are absolutely extraordinary," said Leon Eisenberg, a child psychiatrist at Harvard Medical School.

A range of treatments now in use continue to show modest success, particularly with autistic children who are relatively bright. But over the years reports of outstanding success in treating autism, with approaches ranging from psychoanalytic therapy to drugs, have each been later found to be an inflated claim.

Diagnosis by Other Clinicians

Dr. Lovaas's work appears to have avoided some of the pitfalls that invalidated others' claims. He has been careful to select children for treatment who have been diagnosed as autistic by independent clinicians, and to compare the children he treated to others whose disorders were as severe.

Of forty autistic children who received treatments lasting just ten hours a week, instead of forty, only two were able to blend into regular classes. Eighteen attended special language classes in regular schools, and twenty-two—more than half the group—remained in classes for the autistic.

There are several different patterns of autism and the U.C.L.A. treatment may not work with all of them. For instance, autistic children whose symptoms are combined with severe retardation—with an initial I.Q. below thirty—do not seem to gain significantly from the U.C.L.A. treatment, according to Dr. Lovaas. While some autistic children have normal intelligence, only about 30 percent have an I.Q. of seventy or more. The average for people in general is one hundred.

The average I.Q. of children in the test and comparison groups was, originally, about fifty—considered moderately retarded. Those who showed the greatest improvement in the test group, though, had a pretreatment I.Q. averaging about sixty and a final I.Q. averaging one-hundred and five.

Contact With Other Children

The treatment usually began by the age of three. Its aim was to get the children to stop their more bizarre and disruptive behavior, make contact with other people and begin to imitate what they saw others do. The second year emphasized helping the children to learn to talk and play with other children; most of the autistic children were enrolled in a regular preschool where the teacher was willing to carry out the treatment regime.

The program was flexible. In one case, when a young child had trouble finding playmates, workers from U.C.L.A. came to his house on Saturdays to put on parties for the children in the neighborhood, making him a social star of sorts.

The children who made enough progress were enrolled in ordinary kindergarten classes. The successes in the program were all among these children, who were promoted along with their classmates.

To avoid stigmatizing the children, the researchers did not inform the schools that the children had been diagnosed as autistic. "If we had to admit that the child had a problem, we'd say that it was 'language delay,' " Dr. Lovaas said. "And to pre-

vent suspicion we changed our name from Autism Clinic to Clinic for the Behavioral Treatment of Children."

Imitating and learning from normal children is crucial to the autistic children's progress and to the treatment's success, Dr. Lovaas said. "It's the kiss of death to be in a class with other autistic kids," he said. "You won't learn anything useful."

'A Spirit of Cooperation'

A similar philosophy is adopted by a Japanese program for autistic children, who are enrolled in small numbers in nursery school with normal children. The normal children help the autistic ones participate in a rigorous program of daily exercise.

"There is a spirit of cooperation that seems to normalize the autistic kids considerably," said Bernard Rimland, director of the Institute for Child Behavior in San Diego, who recently observed the Japanese program. "The normal kids lead the autistic ones around by the hand."

Dr. Rimland, an authority on autism, believes that both behavior modification and the Japanese approach—as well as supplements of vitamin B6, a treatment he favors—work in part by improving the autistic child's ability to pay attention to the environment. "If you can't pay attention, you can't learn," he said.

One of the key elements in the U.C.L.A. program, Dr. Lovaas believes, is the intense involvement of

parents. In a pioneering attempt at treating autistic children in the early 1970's, Dr. Lovaas used behavior techniques to treat autistic children for two years. A stipulation of his grant required that he stop after two years and repeat the process with a new group of children. "It was heartbreaking to stop," he said, "but it helped me discover what would make the treatment work better."

In a follow-up study, he found that while the children had made strong gains during treatment, those who were sent back to mental institutions regressed to their earlier levels. But those who went to live with parents, who continued the training, were still making progress. "The training only really works if you get the parents involved," he said.

Some experts on autism, though, question the approach for many or most families of autistic children. "The risk is that it puts the family in a pressure cooker," said Eric Schopler, editor of the *Journal of Autism and Developmental Disorders*. "It's an intense burden on the family—they give so much time, energy and money, which may shortchange other children in the family. For many families the cost of the training may just be too great."

Still, Dr. Lovaas, who has devoted the better part of two decades to developing and testing his treatment, is enthusiastic. "I'm positive now that autism need not be chronic if you take young autistic children and give them an intensive reorganization of their life year-round," he said.

Aid in Day-to-Day Life Seen as Hope for Schizophrenics

March, 19, 1986

Innovative programs scattered around the country are now offering the first rays of hope in decades for millions of tormented victims of schizophrenia, which has become the nation's worst mental health problem.

"We've learned that if we have the will to provide decent care for schizophrenics, their condition could be sharply improved," said John Talbott, a former president of the American Psychiatric Association.

But other experts say the growing ability to cope with schizophrenia is not being matched by a broad, coordinated effort to apply it. That failure, they say, is enormously costly to the nation both in the money spent for excessive hospitalization and in the shattered, unrepaired lives that result.

Schizophrenia's victims can be completely disabled by unsettling delusions or an inability to think clearly; they may find themselves shouting back wildly at imaginary voices or sinking, emotionless, into deep apathy.

Most of the new approaches in treating the baffling disorder focus on practical help for patients and their families in managing everyday problems: diminishing the stress that sets off some of the most disruptive and painful behavior, as well as teaching skills needed to achieve friendships, jobs and success in negotiating a bureaucracy to obtain the government benefits that any sick or poor person is entitled to.

"The environment in which the person lives has become the key factor in treating schizophrenia," said Dr. Samuel J. Keith, who heads the schizophrenia branch of the National Institute of Mental Health.

The trend reflects the inability of scientists thus far to discover the root causes of the disorder as well as the failure of powerful drugs to ameliorate some of the most prevalent symptoms.

But the innovative approaches to the handling of schizophrenia are demonstrating dramatic improvements in patients' return to mental stability.

A recently completed thirty-year study of hospitalized schizophrenics who had been given up as hopeless, but then were released in a program that closely manages and monitors their lives, has found that two-thirds of them are now living normal lives in the community, half of them without any signs of the disorder.

There are a range of treatments that, taken together, offer new hope.

Family management, the fastest growing of the new approaches, encourages the patient's family to keep stresses in the home minimal and teaches family members how to handle the day-to-day difficulties of living with a schizophrenic.

A full spectrum of community services—ranging from hiring neighbors to help look after schizophrenics to twenty-four crisis teams whose members will move in for days at a time with a schizophrenic in crisis—has proven capable of keeping all but a small minority of schizophrenics out of psychiatric hospitals while speeding their improvement. And when schizophrenics are helped to get the government funds due them, they need not live in shelters or on the streets.

Promise Comes amid Research Optimism

The promise of the new family and community programs is strengthened by recent research findings that portray a far more positive long-term prognosis for many schizophrenics than is commonly assumed, even by many of those who treat them.

For example, in an article in *The Archives of General Psychiatry,* a team of researchers at the University of Pittsburgh published results of a study showing that teaching the families of schizophrenics how to care for them can drastically improve the course of the illness.

It is not yet clear whether the new programs might not prove too expensive or unwieldy in some urban settings where social services, under the best of circumstances, are often mired in bureaucracy.

Some schizophrenics continue to be treated individually by psychotherapists, usually in combination with drugs, and with varying degrees of success. While there are some promising developments in psychotherapy, for the vast majority of schizophrenics the hope lies in the new approaches.

One of the factors behind it is a radical new understanding of schizophrenia itself. That the disorder goes far deeper than had been thought and that recovery does not end when the more obvious symptoms—the delusions and hallucinations—stop.

Effective treatment, it is now thought, requires an ongoing, dogged effort to help a person overcome the apathy and other problems created by the longlasting emotional and other deficits, and to rebuild crumbled social relationships.

One of the more inventive methods used, called "network therapy," constructs a support system for former hospital patients who otherwise would be isolated and alone.

"These are people who have been

in and out of the hospital for the last ten years and whose natural network of family and friends has gradually eroded," said Paul Wagner, a clinical social worker who directs the Mount Tom Institute in Holyoke, Massachusetts, one of several agencies that provides such services.

Network therapy begins with a series of meetings to which you invite absolutely everyone who knows the person and might help him," he said. "It might be a distant relative, some old friends, the grocer, maybe some neighbors. Everyone meets and you tell them the person's whole story. There stories are very tragic, very moving. By the end, just about everyone wants to help somehow.

"Each person does a small part," Mr. Wagner added. "One neighbor says he'll call more often, someone else volunteers to bring him to church. When you put it together, you have a treatment plan. Since we began network therapy in 1982, not a single person in the program has been readmitted to the hospital."

An important factor in this success, according to Mr. Wagner, is a crisis team available twenty-four hours a day. It not only makes house calls to help resolve crises, but also has access to families in the area who keep an extra bedroom available for the emergency team, where a person in crisis can stay and be treated for up to a month.

There is great interest among professionals in teaching families better ways to care for schizophrenic members, at least until they can live on their own. "There's hardly a place in the country where, in the last three years, they have not begun to use some form of family management," said Dr. Talbott. "It is an idea whose time has come."

Carol Anderson, a psychologist at the University of Pittsburgh who is one of the primary developers of the family management approach, said, "We emphasize that schizophrenia seems to be due to a biological vulnerability that is triggered by stress. Most families have some private theory about what caused it, often one that makes them feel guilty, like their child falling out of bed. They're relieved to learn that no one single life event causes schizophrenia."

Guides to Creating a Helpful Environment

The training, which Dr. Anderson describes in detail in *Schizophrenia in the Family* (Guilford Press), typically begins with a one-day session for families in which a member is being treated for schizophrenia. Families are told that because schizophrenics are easily overstimulated and distracted, they should avoid extremes of conflict and criticism on the one hand, or extreme enthusiasm on the other. They are also advised to create an attitude of "benign indifference" toward many of the symptoms of schizophrenia.

But families are also urged to set reasonable rules for the patient, so as "not to confuse the need for low stimulation with permissiveness." Even the most stable of families would be hard-pressed to deal with a member's insistence that the television screen be covered with aluminum foil to thwart eavesdropping.

Families are also urged to let patients withdraw for a time when they need to do so, for example, taking meals alone or staying in their rooms when company comes. At the same time, it is crucial that burdened family members maintain friends and sources of pleasure outside the home.

Research done by Dr. Anderson shows a one-year relapse rate under 10 percent in patients treated using family management. For patients who received only drug treatment the relapse rate was 50 percent. According to the reserchers, similar patients who receive no treatment at all have a relapse rate of 60 to 80 percent in the first year after leaving the hospital.

"The main rationale for family management is to calm the emotional climate and offer the family support, not point fingers or try to change the family dynamics," said Christine McGill, a social worker. She is training the staffs of hospitals engaged in a major five-year, $5 million study of family management being conducted by the National Institute of Mental Health. The study, now in its first year, is under way at four hospitals, including the Payne-Whitney Clinic in New York City and the Long Island Jewish-Hillside Medical Center in Glen Oaks.

A major goal of that study is to determine the extent to which dosages of the drugs used to treat schizophrenics can be lowered as families become more adept at handling the patient. The drugs, called neuroleptics, can have serious side effects, such as loss of muscular coordination. The standard treatment is to maintain patients with chronic symptoms on the drugs for years, but many experts now believe that family management and similar support can allow symptoms of schizophrenia to be controlled with intermittent or much lower doses of the drugs, or even no drugs at all.

With the proliferation of family management, Dr. McGill cautions, often what is offered to families is simply a one-day training program. "They neglect the crucial part, the contact with families to help them through the large and small crises," she said. "You need to make a minimum two-year commitment to help a family after a member has had a schizophrenic episode."

Programs for Those Outside the Family

For the several hundred thousand schizophrenics across the country who need continuing treatment, there is a longstanding Federal plan for a spectrum of community services. The plan, dating back to the 1970's, was to be a replacement for the "warehousing" of chronic patients in large state hospitals. But few states, it is now widely acknowledged, allotted sufficient funds for the community programs.

One notable exception is a highly successful program that began as an experiment in Madison, Wisconsin.

"We started by moving a large group of patients out of the state hospital into town, and moved the staff right along with them" into the community, said Leonard Stein, the psychiatrist who directed the project. "When we evaluated the needs of each patient we found that they had been coming back to the hospital because, for example, they got into trouble with a landlord and were evicted, or they didn't know how to get their social security benefits and got very upset."

Compared to patients who were treated in the hospital as a part of the usual follow-up treatment, the patients in this program had one-tenth the rate of relapse, had far fewer symptoms of schizophrenia, and were generally more satisfied with their lives. Moreover, the cost per patient in the community program was about $15,000 a year, while a full year in the hospital would cost $70,000.

Despite the success of the Wisconsin experiment, very few states have allocated the funds that would set up similar programs. One of the rare exceptions is a community-based program in western Massachusetts, created as the result of a legal action taken in behalf of patients at the state hospital in Northampton. In 1972 the hospital had 1,400 patients; now it has just over 200, a very small number for a region with 800,000 residents.

The network therapy at the Mount Tom Institute is part of the Massachusetts program. Among the other unusual services offered there is "respite care," where a family who is caring for a schizophrenic member can, when a particularly difficult crisis occurs, have the patient stay in a supervised house for a few days, or have mental health worker come and stay with the family to help them out.

In addition, specially trained families are available who will take in schizophrenic patients from other families for anywhere from a week to two months.

Such services are part of a concerted effort to keep patients living in the community, even when they are having psychotic episodes. "The state hospital is the last resort, not the first resort," said Steven J. Schwartz, the lawyer whose suit created the system.

The key to the Massachusetts program is case management, the assignment of around thirty patients to a service coordinator whose task it is to see that they get whatever help they need. This means, for example, that if someone is too confused or apathetic to find an apartment, the service coordinator will do it with him, and help him move in. And if an expatient needs looking after in his apartment, the service coordinator might hire neighbors to keep an eye on him.

New York Program Is Often Copied

Finding a group of friends and a job is seen by many mental health experts as key steps for those who have suffered from schizophrenia for many years. The most copied program that focuses on these needs is Fountain House in New York City.

"We start with the assumption that schizophrenia is a condition that isolates people and destroys their confidence," said Jim Schmidt, the director. "We give them a place to go where they are welcomed, even celebrated. They are not here to be treated or trained; it's a clubhouse."

Dozens of business have entry-level jobs reserved for Fountain House. Members try these jobs part-time, at first accompanied by someone from the staff who will do the job if the member fails at it. If the member succeeds, in six months he moves on to another job, until he is finally able to get a full-time job on his own.

There are now nearly 200 programs nationwide based on the Fountain House approach to getting former patients employed again. But while many communities have one or another part of the services offered in western Massachusetts or by Fountain House, programs with the entire range are few and far between.

"People are only just becoming aware that community treatment can be successful, if done right," Dr. Stein said. "There is no real alternative to a community program; the old hospitals are enormously expensive. And this works."

Nondrug Therapy Eases Panic Attacks

August 26, 1986

New psychotherapy techniques for treating panic attacks may be as effective—in some cases, more effective—than drugs now used for the problem, researchers reported today.

The standard drug treatments for panic have several drawbacks, psychologists told reporters at the annual meeting of the American Psychological Association in 1986. The drawbacks include a high rate of relapse when the drug is stopped; some degree of panic recurs in 30 percent to 90 percent of patients, the researchers said. Another drawback is that while most patients who suffer panic attacks are women, some of the drugs are not suitable for those of childbearing age because of possible side effects. In addition, the drugs available do not help about a quarter of patients.

In contrast, said Larry Michelson, a psychologist at the University of Pittsburgh Medical School, "psychological treatments for panic have no known side effects, a very low rate rate of relapse, are inexpensive, and have longlasting effects."

However, noted George Clum, director of the Anxiety Disorders Clinic at Virginia Polytechnic Institute and State University, "the drugs offer more immediate relief from panic than do the therapies."

In studies reported at the meeting, the new therapies for panic reduced the number of attacks suffered by patients from an average of nine a month before treatment to none afterward. The treatment lasted from nine to fifteen weeks.

In panic attacks, people experience extreme anxiety and intense physiological arousal; the heartbeat, for example, can rise to more than twice the normal rate in a matter of seconds. One prominent characteristic is that the person develops an intense fear of the symptoms themselves, believing that they mean imminent collapse or even death.

Anxiety disorders including panic are the most prevalent psychiatric complaints in the general population. About 25 percent of people experience panic attacks once or twice in a three-week period, according to a study done at the University of Manitoba. When the attacks occur once a week or more, it is diagnosed as "panic disorder," a psychiatric problem. The problem typically begins when a person is in his twenties.

Although the attacks may last just a minute or two, the average length in people who have sought treatment is about an hour, according to data presented by Michelle Craske, a psychologist at the Center for Stress and Anxiety Disorders at the State University of New York at Albany. For some people, the panic can wax and wane for days.

In a study by Dr. Michelson with people with agoraphobia, who become so panicked at the thought of going out in public that they become housebound, the patients were treated for twelve weeks with therapy designed for agoraphobia. Most of the patients had been suffering from panic attacks for ten to fifteen years and had been housebound for about half that time. Most had been treated previously with drugs and general psychotherapy for an average of two years, with little or no benefit. After Dr. Michelson's treatment, only 25 percent had panic attacks, and these were less intense and less frequent than before.

A similar study was reported by Dr. Craske. While the patients had suffered one or two panic attacks a week before the treatment, of the thirty-two who completed the study, only two had a panic attack, and they had just one each over six months.

The research reported today uses a range of techniques, including changing the way people think about their symptoms, and muscle relaxation paired with deep breathing, said Dr. Michelson.

Dr. Clum and Janet Borden, for example, taught patients to vividly imagine situations that make them feel panic until they actually induce an attack. Then the patients are helped to perceive their symptoms more realistically, so that, for instance, they do not think a racing heart means a heart attack.

One benefit of the therapies seems to be that patients learn to use them on their own after treatment ends. Dr. Craske reported that patients who had been cured of panic attacks continued to show a reduction in general anxiety six months after treatment had ended.

Dr. Michael Liebowitz, director of the Anxiety Disorders Clinic at the New York State Psychiatric Institute, suggested in a telephone interview that panic might best be treated with drugs in combination with behavioral therapy.

Sex and the Sexes

The course of love can be charted—or at least major parts of love, such as commitment, passion, and intimacy. Each unfolds at its own rate over the course of a loving relationship. And part of the difficulty in relationships is that what brings a couple together in the first place is not what will keep them together. Read why in "Patterns of Love Charted in New Studies."

What holds a marriage together? According to the data in "Marriage: Research Reveals Ingredients of Happiness," love alone is not enough. The ability to talk over problems is more important than how much a couple are in love or how happy the couple were before the marriages, the data shows.

And when it comes to finding out just what happens in a marriage, there are two answers, his and hers. The differences between a husband's and a wife's version of what is happening is as great in a happy marriage as in a distressed one. One of the main gaps, according to "Two Views of Marriage Explored: His and Hers," is in how important husbands and wives feel emotional intimacy is in a marriage.

Couples who fight are not necessarily the ones who will separate, according to findings in "Want a Happy Marriage? Learn to Fight a Good Fight." Arguments—if waged well—can actually nurture a relationships. But if couples don't know how to argue productively, their fights can sink the relationship.

One of the saddest miscommunications between the sexes has to do with how interested in sex a woman is while on a date. Sometimes that misunderstanding leads to a man forcing sex on a woman, in what legally is a rape. "When the Rapist is not a Stranger" describes the factors at play in date rape.

Unusual sex fantasies are more usual than you might think. And fantasies do not necessarily reveal your sexual orientation; many gay men and women, for instance, have sexual fantasies about the opposite sex. "Sexual Fantasies: What Are Their Hidden Meanings?" explains which are the most common fantasies, and when they are healthy and when not.

When Freud called women's psychology a "dark continent," he was expressing his puzzlement. For decades psychological theories slighted women, focusing for the most part, for instance, on male patterns of development. But that has changed, as is explained in "Psychology Is Revising Its View of Women."

One of the differences between men and women is in how they regard their own bodies. Both sexes distort their sense of their bodies, but in opposite ways. Men tend to think of their bodies as being in better shape than they actually are, women do the opposite. Read about it in "Dislike of Own Body Found Common Among Women."

Patterns of Love Charted in New Studies

September 10, 1985

Researchers charting the course of love are beginning to put some order into an area that has long been regarded as chaotic and undefinable.

The emotional turbulence of love and marriage, the research suggests, can be traced partly to the way habits of the heart are shaped in childhood, and partly to the inevitable changes over the course of even the most successful relationship.

"People don't know what they are in for when they fall in love," said Robert Sternberg, a psychologist at Yale University who is one of those doing the new research. "The divorce rate is so high not because people make foolish choices, but because they are drawn together for reasons that matter less as time goes on."

What brings a couple together, Dr. Sternberg is finding, almost inevitably recedes into the background as the relationship matures. And those qualities that matter most later on, his research suggests, are rarely the ones that loom large in the early stages of the match. In his view, the major components of love are intimacy, passion and commitment. While a relationship can manage to survive with any one or two of these qualities, Dr. Sternberg argues, the fullest love requires all three. However, each blossoms at its own pace, and follows its distinct course.

"Passion is the quickest to develop, and the quickest to fade," Dr. Sternberg said. "Intimacy develops more slowly, and commitment more gradually still. All of this means that no relationship is stable, because the basic components change at different rates."

Many turmoils of romantic love, other new research is showing, are a direct legacy of the partners' childhood bonds with their parents. That premise, of course, has been a mainstay of psychotherapists since Freud. But the research offers an important empirical test that, in broad strokes, supports otherwise untested, but common, assumptions made by therapists about the troubles that crop up in people's most intimate relationships.

The research is showing, for example, that children who grow up feeling rejected by the parent of the opposite sex are prone as adults to extremes of jealousy, anxiety and depression in their love life. But that psychological legacy can be diminished if a person understands the origins of his or her feelings, according to the researchers.

"We're confirming in our research what therapists have been saying for years," said Phillip Shaver, a psychologist at the University of Denver.

The work sheds light on two psychological puzzles. One is why people whose lives are otherwise well-ordered and successful can be so infantile—easily hurt, jealous, anxiously demanding—in their romantic relationships. The other is why a couple who seem so in love at the outset of their match can founder as time passes.

Dr. Sternberg's studies show how love can founder with time. In research on relationships that had lasted from just one month to as long as thirty-six years, he was able to identify the specific elements that increased and decreased in long-lasting couples.

The intimacy of the patterns becomes more crucial, particularly to women, as successful relationships endure, according to Dr. Sternberg. In general, both partners find it increasingly important to understand each other's wants and needs, to be able to listen to and support each other, and to share common values. And intimacy tends to maintain a gradual growth, although it may seem to recede into the background of the relationship.

"In a strong marriage, the emotion of intimacy will seem to fade as the partners become more familiar with each other," Dr. Sternberg said in an interview. "But it is there in a latent form, and emerges strongly when the relationship is interrupted by travel or illness—or death."

Passion, which peaks in the early phases of the relationship, declines to a plateau. Still, passion continues to matter to the long-term success of a relationship. According to Dr. Sternberg, "A man continues to care about his wife's physical attractiveness; the more attractive he feels she is, the more successful the relationship in the long run."

While a strong emotional commitment is essential to a long-term relationship, commitment alone does not bode well, according to Dr. Sternberg. "You have to work constantly at rejuvenating a relationship," he said. "You can't just count on its being O.K., or it will tend toward a hollow commitment, devoid of passion and intimacy. People need to put the kind of energy into it that they put into their children or career."

While Dr. Sternberg's theory may explain some of the vicissitudes of love, other investigators are probing into people's childhoods for clues. One view emerging from the new work is that romantic love in adulthood and the infant's love toward his parents are one and the same response seen at different points in life. Dr. Shaver reported data showing that the main patterns of love recognized in infancy hold true for adults, too.

Developmental psychologists, notably Mary Ainsworth at the University of Virginia, have classified infants according to the bonds they form with their parents, particularly with their mothers in the first year or two of life. Infants who feel their mother is available and responsive are most secure. But those who feel insecure about being loved fall into one of two patterns: some become anxious and clinging, while others react by with-drawing and avoiding reliance on anyone.

Dr. Ainsworth has found that about two-thirds of infants fall into the secure category, while the rest can be classified in equal proportions as anxiously clinging, or as withdrawing.

The same rough proportions, Dr. Shaver reported, hold true for adults, in terms of their romantic relationships. In a study of 540 people between the ages of fifteen and eighty-two, Dr. Shaver found that just over half fit into a secure style of romantic love, and the others split evenly between anxious clingers and those who tend to avoid romantic ties.

Those who are secure describe their love relationships as happy and trusting, while the anxious lovers report that they frequently become obsessed by their lovers, are prone to intense jealousy, and undergo extreme emotional highs and lows. The avoidant types, by comparison, shy away from intimacy.

The origins of these different styles of loving, Dr. Shaver believes, lie in childhood. For example, in recalling their childhood, people who were anxious lovers, when compared with the secure ones, tended to report that their mothers were emotionally intrusive, while their fathers were demanding and distant, and that the relationship between their parents was unhappy.

While psychotherapists have long made similar claims about the childhood origins of adult romantic problems, their theories suffer from a pitfall that also applies to Dr. Shaver's data. It is based on the recall of the person himself, and so may be biased

by his present outlook. In other words, people who are anxious about their love relationships as adults may be prone to recall their parents with similar anxiety.

That problem was overcome by other data reported by Carl Hindy, a psychologist at the University of North Florida in Jacksonville.

Dr. Hindy, who began his research while working with Conrad Schwarz at the University of Connecticutt, was able to study 192 men and women whose early family histories were known in unusual detail. Each of the people studied—as well as their mothers, fathers, one of their siblings, and a best friend—had undergone several hours of tests and questions about the person's early years and present relationships.

One pattern Dr. Hindy studied is what he calls "anxious attachment," a term borrowed from the British psychoanalyst John Bowlby's work with infants. Its common symptoms are extremes of depression when a relationship ends or of jealousy when there is an interloper, clinging to the partner while trying to extort signs of affection, and feeling that one never gets enough love and attention.

"Such people fail to develop stable expectations for love and affection in childhood, and grow up chronically anxious about what they fear will be a rejection from their partner," Dr. Hindy said. "They depend on the partner for emotional stability; their moods fluctuate with how loved they feel. Since they have no stable sense that others will like them, they are constantly searching for reassurance. They will even threaten to leave just to get an affirmation of their partner's love."

"When I've treated men like this in therapy, I've found that they put pressure on the woman to reciprocate dates and gifts with love," Dr. Hindy said. "Underneath, they are narcissists who want their partners to pay tribute to their perfection. But their intense fear is that they are not lovable as they are. So they try to extort love, and the harder they try, the more anxious they get."

Dr. Hindy's research reveals that those who are anxious in this way share common childood experiences

with those who seem to be their exact opposite; people who are quite calm in the face of a relationship, becoming neither jealous when it is threatened, nor depressed when it ends. That detached reaction, Dr. Hindy finds, is more common in men than in women.

"People who seem detached in their love relationships," Dr. Hindy said, "seem to have more hearty defenses; they avoid becoming vulnerable by shunning strong emotional ties altogether." Both those who are anxious and those who are detached have had similar experiences in childhood, according to Dr. Hindy's research.

In general, Dr. Hindy found that people with problems in adult love relationships tend to have had rejecting or hostile parents, or parents who gave them highly inconsistent and unpredictable affection—loving one moment, distant the next. But within that broad description, Dr. Hindry was able to detect more specific relationships between childhood experiences and adult difficulties in love.

The parent of the opposite sex seems crucial. For example, men who become overinvested in their lovers, and who complain that their affection is not sufficiently returned by their partner, had mothers who were relatively uninvolved with them as children.

For women who are similarly overly invested in their partner's reactions, however, it is the fathers' treatment that seems to have been crucial; their mothers were quite positive toward their daughters, while their fathers were detached or even hostile toward them.

"You are not doomed by your childhood," Dr. Shaver said. "These patterns can be changed if a person gains insight into them."

Other experts on marital relationships welcome the new research, but they also express some reservations. "Love is a jigsaw puzzle, and this is one important piece," said John Gottman, a psychologist at the University of Illinois. "But you have to keep in mind other things—such as a couple's ability to communicate with each other—which can be as important for the success of a relationship as their childhood experiences."

Marriage: Research Reveals Ingredients of Happiness

April 16, 1985

In the psychological web that is marriage, there is no sure way to know which threads are crucial for happiness and which are illusory. But new research is revealing some of the hidden ingredients of happy marriages.

Such elements as a couple's ability to talk over problems effectively, the research shows, are more crucial to compatibility, and are often more telling in the long run, than even how much a couple is in love. Such findings are being used as the basis for educational programs for couples who are about to be married.

To be sure, there is no single formula for marital compatibility. For every rule of thumb that psychological studies suggest, there are bound to be marriages that defy it.

But, although general prescriptions for marital happiness are elusive, the new research highlights broad patterns that distinguish between those marriages that thrive and those that wither. For example, long-range studies have found that one of the strongest predictors of success after five years of marriage is how well a couple communicated before they married. But, according to the same studies, how happy a couple were before marriage was unrelated to how long the marriage lasted. "What counts in making a happy marriage," said George Levinger of the University of Massachusetts, "is not so much how compatible you are, but how you deal with incompatibility."

Early marital research focused on finding the personality profiles of individuals who would fit together best. Over the years that effort was largely abandoned; researchers found no clear relationship between personality traits and marital happiness.

Although the prevailing view among some psychotherapists is that marital difficulties result from psychological problems in one partner or the other, the consensus among most marital researchers is that personality is less crucial to marital success than is the nature of the relationship itself. As the late Nathan Ackerman, a pioneering family therapist put it, even two neurotics can have a happy marriage.

As long ago as 1938, Lewis Terman, a Stanford University psychologist who was better known for his studies of intelligence, published findings he hoped would bring clarity to what he called "the chaos of opinion on the determiners of marital happiness."

Dr. Terman discovered that most of the opinions of the day on what was required for a happy marriage were dead wrong. For example, his research found little or no relationship between the frequency of sexual intercourse and marital satisfaction.

That finding has held up over the years. In a 1978 study of 100 happily married couples, it was found that 8 percent had intercourse less than once a month, and close to a quarter reported having intercourse two or three times a month. Most couples reported having intercourse one to three times a week. Two of the couples had no intercourse, while for one couple the rate was daily.

Moreover, one-third of the men and two-thirds of the women reported a sexual problem, such as difficulty getting an erection in men and difficulty reaching orgasm in women. And both men and women complained of such difficulties as inability to relax and a lack of interest in sexual activity. Even though the cou-

ples with sexual complaints reported being dissatisfied with their sex lives, they still felt their marriage to be "working" and happy.

The precursors of later marital success or failure can be detected in the earliest stages of a marriage, according to Howard Markman, a psychologist at the University of Denver. Writing in *Marital Interaction* (Guilford Press), Dr. Markman reports on a study in which twenty-six couples were regularly observed while discussing their problems over a period of almost six years, beginning just before their marriage. By the end of the study, eight of the couples had separated or divorced.

The best predictor of the couples' satisfaction after five-and-a-half years of marriage was how well they communicated before the marriage.

'Private Language' of Couples

Other research has found that happily married couples seem to develop a "private language," a set of subtle cues and private words that have meaning only to them. Researchers at the University of Illinois found that in happy marriages husbands were much better than were strangers at understanding exactly what their wives meant. But in distressed marriages, strangers were as adept at understanding messages from wives as were their own husbands.

Likewise, happily married couples show a high degree of responsiveness to each other in sharing events of the day. The absence of such responsiveness can lead to heightened tensions, according to John Gottman, the leader of the research group at the University of Illinois. Dr. Gottman said he believes the friendship built up through such day-to-day exchanges makes couples willing to go through the difficulties of repairing their relationship when it becomes strained.

One of the striking differences between the satisfied and distressed couples in the University of Denver study was in how they viewed the way they talked over their problems. The wives were aware of stress even when it was not readily apparent to others, but the husbands weren't.

In a series of studies, Dr. Markman and his colleagues had objective observers and the partners themselves rate how "positive"—by which Dr. Markman means friendly—or "negative"—that is, hostile, the spouses were during discussions of problems.

In unhappy couples, husbands seemed oblivious to the hostility of their wives in some of these conversations, although objective observers noted it.

The wives were sure their husbands were hostile, although the observers said the husbands, for the most part, did not seem to be especially difficult during these encounters.

The husbands' seeming lack of hostility was consistent with the widely observed tendency among husbands to avoid confrontation while wives seem more ready to engage it.

But why did the wives in these unhappy couples see the husbands as hostile? Dr. Markham suggests that the wives tend to be more sensitive to trouble in a marriage than husbands. Evidently, they were reading the true stress in their marriage into their husbands' behavior even though the behavior did not overtly reflect it.

"This does not mean that wives are the cause or the victims of marital distress," said Dr. Markman, but rather that the wives are better barometers of problems in the marriage than are the husbands.

In general, women are more comfortable with confrontation because—in happy marriages, at least—they more readily can end the fight by switching from a hostile stance to a conciliatory one, according to Dr. Gottman.

Husbands, in Dr. Gottman's research—even happy ones—were less able to make this switch in the heat of an argument.

In unhappy marriages, the wives no longer seemed willing to play this role, according to Dr. Gottman.

Men Withdraw, Women Argue

As the emotional tone of a marriage becomes more negative, men are more likely to react by withdrawing, while women are more likely to escalate emotional pressure, becoming more coercive and argumentative. The result is often an escalating cycle of pressure from the wife and withdrawal by the husband, a cycle that happily married couples seem better able to prevent.

"All couples go through ups and downs in marriage," Dr. Markman said in an interview. "But it's those couples who don't communicate well whose marriage is more likely to be the victim of such a difficult period."

Couples planning to marry who were trained by the University of Denver group in a range of marital skills were, after three years, still as happy as they were just before their marriage. But other couples who did not receive the training showed "dramatic declines in overall satisfaction," Dr. Markman said.

'Inevitable Push-Pull in Marriage'

Occasional tensions, of course, are inevitable in any marriage. A psychoanalytic view of marriage holds that each partner unconsciously gravitates to someone whom they see as fulfilling a deeply held need. The two most prominent of these needs exist in a state of tension, the desire for intimacy, on the one hand, and the need to establish one's identity as a separate person on the other. Marriage thus becomes a forum for the negotiation of a balance between these conflicting urges.

"There's an inevitable push-pull in marriage," said Michael Kolevzon, a professor of social work at Virginia

Commonwealth University. "As a couple's intimacy increases, you often see a corresponding increase in their desire for distance. How satisfied they will be in the marriage depends to a great extent on how they communicate these needs."

"Anger is one means this balancing act is negotiated in marriage," Dr. Kolevzon added in an interview. "Sometimes it's a way to ask for distance, I'll get angry with you so I can justify being alone for a while. Or with some people their anger is actually a plea for intimacy. They build up to an angry confrontation so it can resolve into intimacy as an affirmation that their spouse loves them despite their faults."

Programs Teach Marital Skills

The new research is leading to programs for couples who are about to be married. The programs are designed to strengthen those skills that seem to help couples weather the stresses and changes that challenge a marriage. These programs teach a range of marital skills that concentrate on communication, including these:

—The couples are taught to focus on one topic at a time and to make other preoccupations clear, such as "I may seem angry because I had a bad day at work."

—They are also trained to "stop the action" until the partners cool down when repetitive cycles of conflict begin. One of the major signs of distress in a couple is escalating hostility, often in the form of nagging that provokes an angry responses. The escalation seems unstoppable once begun.

—By being specific in criticizing or praising a spouse's actions, the couples learn how to prevent nebulous complaints that often trigger arguments. Thus, a spouse might say, "When I see your coat on the floor, I feel you are not doing your share around the house and I feel taken advantage of," instead of "You're a slob."

—The couples also learn to edit what they say, so as to avoid saying things that would needlessly hurt a spouse. "It's especially unproductive to dredge up past events and old grudges during a fight," Dr. Kolevzon said.

Two Views of Marriage Explored: His and Hers

April 1, 1986

Every marriage, researchers are discovering, is actually two marriages: his and hers. The differences suffuse even the happiest of relationships between husbands and wives.

Some of the new research suggests that, paradoxically, the differences need not be divisive, but can be sources of marital growth.

Psychologists say that couples who openly acknowledge these differences improve their chances of avoiding strife. And those who seek to free their marriages of such male-female differences are better able to do so if they are aware of how powerful, though largely hidden, the differences are.

One of the great gaps between husbands and wives is in their notions of emotional intimacy and how important they feel it is in a marriage. For many men, simply doing such things as working in the garden or going to a movie with their wives gives them a feeling of closeness. But for their wives that is not enough, according to Ted Huston, a psychologist at the University of Texas at Austin who has studies 130 couples intensively.

"For the wives, intimacy means talking things over, especially talking about the relationship itself," Dr. Huston said. "The men, by and large, don't understand what the wives want from them. They say, 'I want to do things with her, and all she wants to do is talk.' "

While women expect more emotional intimacy than their husbands do, "Many men seem to feel they've fulfilled their obligation to the relationship if they just do their chores," said Robert Sternberg, a psychologist at Yale University who has studied

couples. "They say, 'I took out the garbage; now leave me alone.' "

In courtship, Dr. Huston has found, men are much more willing to spend time talking to women in ways that build a woman's sense of intimacy. But after marriage, and as time goes on, the men tend to spend less and less time talking with their wives in these ways, and more time devoted to their work or with buddies. The trend is strongest in marriages that follow traditional patterns, and most of the current research suggests the traditional patterns are still prevalent despite two decades in which these conventional attitudes and mores have been assailed for the stereotypes they breed.

"Men put on a big show of interest when they are courting," Dr. Huston said. "But after the marriage their actual level of interest in the partner often does not seem as great as you would think, judging from the courtship. The intimacy of courtship is instrumental for the men, a way to capture the woman's interest. But that sort of intimacy is not natural for many men."

As with all such differences, there is a lesson to be learned. The starkness of the husband's apparent change in behavior after marriage can lead to disappointment, demands and acrimony—in short, a relationship in trouble. Dr. Huston suggests that in more successful marriages there is a middle ground in which the couple share experiences that naturally lead to more intimate conversation.

"You can't force intimacy," Dr. Huston said. "It has to arise spontaneously from shared activities."

Husbands' and wives' differing

stances toward intimacy signify deeper disparities between the sexes in the view of Carol Gilligan, a psychologist at Harvard University. Dr. Gilligan says young boys take pride in independence and are threatened by anything that might compromise their autonomy, while young girls tend to experience themselves as part of a network of relationships and are threatened by anything that might rupture these connections.

"Boys, as they mature, must learn to connect, girls to separate," said Kathleen White, a psychologist at Boston University, who, with her colleagues, is the author of an article on intimacy in marriage in the April 1986 issue of *The Journal of Personality and Social Psychology.*

In adulthood, this means women tend to be uncomfortable with separateness, while men are wary of intimacy. Some psychologists have proposed that one lesson teenage boys learn from their girlfriends is how to be emotionally intimate, a lesson that can extend into marriage, particularly for those who never really master it.

The more comfortable a husband is with intimacy, Dr. White's research shows, the more satisfied with the marriage is the wife likely to be.

Changing View Toward Parents

Another telling finding is that marriage typically makes a woman draw closer to her parents, while a man often becomes more distant from his. For a woman, closeness to her parents ranks among her most important expectations, the new research shows, while husbands tend to rank a warm association with either set of parents comparatively low.

For the men, the marriage evidently supplants earlier closeness to parents. What the men often seem to be saying, according to Dr. White, is, "I don't need my parents anymore; I have my wife."

But for women, Dr. White has found, the marriage seems to offer a crucial footing from which they can set aside earlier rebelliousness and make peace with their parents, particularly their mothers, and develop a new warmth.

Other factors may be at work, too. "Because many husbands focus their lives outside the marriage, on their work or their friends, many wives have a sense of being abandoned."

Dr. Huston said. "They turn to their mothers for an intimate involvement they do not get from their husbands."

Other research has found that wives place more emphasis than their husbands do on preserving ties with both sets of parents, not just their own. Some experts say a couple that blends the stances of the wife and the husband toward their parents can find a healthy balance in which independence and family ties coexist.

The disparities between husband and wife in such areas as intimacy and family ties are part of a wide range of differences that men and women bring to marriage, according to many experts.

Differing Sets of Values

Some of the starkest evidence of these differences has come from a study by Dr. Sternberg of people seventeen to sixty-nine years old, some of whom have been married for as long as thirty-six years. The men in the study rated as most important in their marriage their wives' ability to make love and the couple's shared interests. But the wives listed marital fidelity and ties to family and friends as most important. The wives were particularly concerned with how well the husband handled both sets of parents, especially hers, and also how well the couple got along with each other's friends.

Dr. Sternberg's study found evidence that the double standard still holds for many couples. Wives said fidelity was very important for both spouses; husbands said it was more important for wives than for husbands.

Perhaps the most dramatic difference is in evaluating the relationship. "The men rate almost everything as better than do the wives," Dr. Sternberg said. Men have a rosier view of love-making, finances, ties with parents, listening to each other, tolerance of flaws and romance.

"The only thing the women rate better than the men is the couple's degree of fidelity," Dr. Sternberg said.

Wives generally complain more about the state of their marriage than husbands do. Jesse Bernard, a sociologist, has proposed in *The Future of Marriage* (Yale University Press) that this is because marriage is harder on women than on men. Dr. Bernard, citing a wide range of studies, says the "psychological costs of marriage seem to be considerably greater for wives than for husbands."

Other marital experts, though, say wives appear to suffer more than husbands because women are more willing than men to admit their problems. Men often feel it is "unmanly" to admit depression or anxiety.

According to John Gottman, a psychologist at the University of Illinois who has studied happy and unhappy couples, wives are more willing to complain about problems in marriage than men are, and this is particularly so among unhappy couples. Men generally try to avoid conflicts in marriage, he has found, while women are more willing to confront them.

"Men and women have different goals when they disagree," Dr. Gottman said. "The wife wants to resolve the disagreement so that she feels closer to her husband and respected by him. The husband, though, just wants to avoid a blowup. The husband doesn't see the disagreement as an opportunity for closeness, but for trouble." Dr. Gottman believes this is because men are more vulnerable than women to physical stress from emotional confrontations, at least as he reads the research evidence.

The preferences that draw couples together also show a major, and perhaps unsurprising, difference between the sexes; women, by and large, place great importance on a man's earning potential, while men place great stress on a woman's attractiveness, according to Dr. White's study in *The Journal of Personality and Social Psychology*.

Some psychologists say that one lesson to be learned from the differences is that each partner in the psychological alliance that is marriage can be enriched by learning from the other. In this view, marriage offers a unique opportunity for psychological growth. "Men and women," said Dr. White, "need to take on each other's strengths."

The differences also point to what people mean when they say that it takes work to make a marriage work. Those who are complacent about the differences between spouses, who see no need to accommodate the partner's perspectives, may be putting the marriage at risk, the experts say.

"It's too easy to portray the expressive wife as good and the stoic husband as horrible; in fact, they are just different," said Carol Tavris, a social psychologist whose book *The Longest War* (Harcourt, Brace Javonovich) reviews sex differences.

"While you want to understand the differences, it is probably futile to try to change your partner to be just like your best friend," Dr. Tavris said. "It's better for husbands and wives to develop a sense of humor and tolerance, and to accept their mates as they are."

Want a Happy Marriage? Learn to Fight a Good Fight

February 21, 1989

What's the difference between a marriage that gets happier as time goes on and one that grows more miserable? In many cases it is fights, according to a new study that pinpoints exactly which kinds of arguments help a couple grow closer and which split them apart.

Ways of smoothing things over that seem to keep the peace in the short term, the study indicates, can undermine the relationship in the long run. This is particularly true of ignoring deep disagreements or pretending that they don't exist.

The conventional view that a couple's satisfaction with their marriage predicts how happy they will be in years to come was also challenged by the study. Paradoxically, those couples who were unhappy, but fought well, tended to have become much happier by the time they were contacted again three years later.

Although the findings may seem self-evident, they took the researchers themselves by surprise because they contradict the prevailing wisdom among professionals and are prompting more research.

There are those couples who are so well attuned that they rarely, if ever, fight over their differences. And there are other couples who simply do not fight, despite their grievances. In other research, psychologists have found that such couples are typically composed of partners who both are agreeable in all spheres of life, marriage among them.

But the findings on fights apply to the large majority of couples who have some degree of conflict in their relationship.

The study of marital arguments contradicts longstanding findings that had shown that couples who were more prone to arguments were the least satisfied with their marriage. The studies that led to those findings, however, failed to distinguish among the kinds of fights that couples have or to follow the course of the marriages to see whether they got better or worse.

The new study shows that certain kinds of fights can improve some marriages, and draws a clear distinction between the kinds of arguments that nurture a relationship and those that sink it. Arguments in which one or the other partner becomes defensive or stubborn, or whines or withdraws, are particularly destructive. Those fights in which the partners freely express their anger while not letting the intensity escalate out of control bode well for the future.

The findings, published in the February, 1989, issue of the *Journal of Consulting and Clinical Psychology,* are from the first study to analyze closely the specific emotional maneuvers during actual arguments between couples and then to track down those same couples three years later to see how satisfied they were with the marriage.

"We had assumed, like everyone else, that what made a couple happy now would make them happy in the future; we were surprised by what we found," said John Gottman, a psychologist at the University of Washington in Seattle who conducted the study with Lowell Krokoff, a psychologist at the University of Wisconsin.

"We were puzzled to find that the patterns that made some couples complain they were dissatisfied led to improvements in the relationship as time went on," Dr. Gottman said. "I thought at first there was an error in our techniques it went against all prevailing wisdom. Marital therapists rarely recommend that couples have a fight, and rarely saw couples who wished to."

Fights With Value

The most fruitful fights, the study showed, were those in which the partners felt free to be angry with each other, felt they made themselves understood to their partner, and finally came to a resolution involving some degree of compromise. Such fights, according to Dr. Gottman, give a couple the strong sense that they can weather conflict together.

But few fights follow this pattern; many couples rely on emotional ploys that are destructive to the relationship. The study found that among the most frequent destructive maneuvers during fights were the following:

● *Defensiveness or making excuses instead of taking resonsibility for a problem.*

● *Telling partners what one wants the other to stop doing as opposed to what the partner might do more of.*

● *Erroneously attributing blameworthy thought, motives or feelings to the other.*

● *Stubbornness.*

● *Contempuous remarks or insults.*

● *Whining complaints.*

But what of couples who never seem to fight? Other research has found that in marriages where both partners have little hostility toward the world in general, fights rarely if ever occur. When such couples are brought into a laboratory for research, investigators have found it virtually impossible to provoke an argument, according to a study by Timothy Smith, a psychologist at the University of Utah.

But in couples where either partner tends to be cynical or hostile toward the world in general, fights are easily provoked, Dr. Smith found. In such cases the more hostile partner is able to trigger an angry response even in a generally easygoing spouse.

Coming to the Surface

Fights are predictable during the second phase of marriage, after the initial romantic period, according to Harville Hendrix, a marital therapist in New York City who is the author of *Getting the Love You Want*, published by Henry Holt & Company. "During that period, the conflicts surface as couples negotiate unresolved childhood issues and needs they bring to marriage," he said. "If they have the tools to resolve those issues, then the conflicts fade during the next phase."

But in some marriages, the absence of fights may augur poorly for a couple. "In some marriages where there is an agreement not to fight, things are fine as long as their lives go well," said Dr. Gottman. "But if something bad happens, they are too brittle to handle the problem."

Dr. Gottman added, "Couples who have healthy fights develop a kind of marital efficacy that makes the marriage stronger as time goes on." In recognition of the usefulness of healthy fighting, a project at the University of Denver, led by Howard Markman, a psychologist, has been training couples in the skills that help them handle conflict well.

In keeping with Dr. Gottman's results, Dr. Markman found that those couples who learned how to argue productively were less happy at first, as their differences were aired, but became progressively more satisfied. After six years, the divorce rate was half that of a group of comparable couples who had not had the training.

Wives tend to have a special role in orchestrating a couple's fights, Dr. Gottman's study found. "Wives are the emotional managers of most marriages," said Dr. Gottman. "The wife is usually the one who brings up disagreements and makes a couple confront their differences. Our results suggest that a wife's anger is a valuable resource in a marriage."

This role is a delicate one, Dr. Gottman points out. "She has to be able to express her anger, but do it in such a way that it doesn't drive her husband away make him withdraw, or defensive, for instance."

The best response for a husband whose wife is starting a fight, Dr. Gottman said, is to "let her know he's listening, show respect for the disagreement, and acknowledge that there's something there that should be dealt with," along with being mad right back, if that is what he is feeling.

Even though anger can be productive, couples need to keep it within bounds. "Fights in which tempers or feelings like fear and sadness get out of hand bode poorly for a couple," Dr. Gottman said.

"I suspect that wives whose marriages improve are careful not to let the argument get out of hand; they keep the lid on," said Dr. Gottman. "But they don't in marriages that deteriorate."

One of the ways partners can de-escalate a fight in progress, Dr. Gottman said, is to paraphrase what a partner has said and look for a solution rather than disagreeing. Another is to suggest a compromise.

The idea that couples should be encouraged to learn to fight by certain rules in order to strengthen their relationship was popular during the 1970's, part of the movement that also fostered "encounter groups." But that idea has become passe among marital therapists, according to Richard Simon, a marital and family therapist and editor of the *Family Therapy Networker,* the leading newsletter in the field.

"Most marital therapists downplay the idea of having better fights these days," Dr. Simon said. "They tend to see fights as symptomatic of something else in the relationship. Many therapists try to shift the couple to a more positive focus, finding solutions. The basic attitude is that encouraging fights simply makes it more likely a couple will fight."

Still, some therapists welcome the findings. Dr. Gottman's study "fits our clinical observations we find that certain kinds of fights help couples clarify and resolve their differences," said Aaron Beck, a psychiatrist at the University of Pennsylvania Medical School who has written *Love Is Not Enough,* published by Harper & Row. "Stating what you're mad about and feeling that what you've said has been heard gives you the feeling you will be responded to by your mate."

"The worst kinds of fights are those in which partners resort to character assasination and blame; it just leads to a dead end," Dr. Beck added. "But when you state a concrete, specific complaint, then there is a good chance it will lead not just to a resolution, but to an improvement."

For example, it is unhelpful to make the charge that a spouse is "a slob" when what is meant is "it brothers me when you leave the cap off the toothpaste."

Dr. Beck finds that the note a fight ends on is particularly important. "If the fight leads to an escalating cycle of retaliation, it leaves the partners with a sense of hopelessness. But if it ends at a good point, it leaves them optimistic about their marriage and each other."

When the Rapist Is Not a Stranger

August 31, 1989

Researchers trying to understand the relative frequency of rape between acquaintances are focusing their attention on the radical differences in how men and women interpret each other's interest in a sexual encounter.

Surveys have found that as many as one in four women report that a man they were dating persisted in trying to force sex on them despite their pleading, crying, fighting him off or screaming. In one survey of women on thirty-two college campuses, 15 percent had experienced at least one rape, and 89 percent of the time it was by men the women knew. Half the rapes occurred during a date.

By better understanding what leads to such rapes, researchers hope to be able to offer guidelines to women and men that will help to lower the risk of their occurrence.

Some research points to the pernicious effects of the sexual double standard that holds, as one psychologist put it, "that nice women don't say yes, and real men don't listen to no." Other studies focus on what makes certain men more likely to force themselves on an unwilling woman, or if there are factors that make a woman more likely to become the victim.

While rape between strangers has long been the subject of scientific study, largely because of the accessibility of convicted rapists, the research on rape among acquaintances has been slower to develop.

"Most acquaintance rapes are never reported, let alone prosecuted, and few men admit to having forced sex on a woman," said Dr. Andrea Parrot, a psychologist at Cornell University. "It makes it difficult to study."

Despite the high proportion of women who have experienced forced sex, very few men admit to having been involved in such acts. In one survey of 1,152 male college students, just seventeen admitted to using physical force to have sexual intercourse with a women when she did not want to.

There is wide agreement among researchers that many men and women involved in instances of forced sex do not realize that, legally, the encounter usually meets the legal definition of rape. Researchers say this, along with factors such as shame, account for the vast underreporting of such incidents.

"When men are asked if there is any likelihood they would force a woman to have sex against her will if they could get away with it, about half say they would," said Dr. Neil Malamuth, a psychologist at the University of California at Los Angeles. "But if you ask them if they would rape a woman if they knew they could get away with it, only about 15 percent say they would."

Those who change their answers do not seem to realize that there is no difference between rape and forcing a woman to have sex against her will, Dr. Malamuth said. The difference is in the words used to describe the same act. Many women, too, share the confusion, and so many may not realize that they have been raped.

Specific definitions vary from state to state, but researchers consider a sexual encounter to be rape if a man forces a woman to have sex against her will or without her consent. The woman need not explicitly protest; women who fear for their lives or safety during a rape often seem to comply. But the researchers say it can be considered rape if the woman does not explicitly consent.

Some women are unable to consent because, for instance, they have passed out while drunk. A sexual encounter may also be considered rape if force or the threat of force is used, Dr. Parrot said.

Some of the research on forced sex points to the influence of the sexual double standard.

"The double standard labels women who are free about having sex as loose, but sees sexually active men as studs," said Dr. Charlene Muehlenhard who, with Marcia McCoy, presented data at the 1989 annual meeting of the American Psychological Association in New Orleans.

Influence of Double Standard

Like many people, the researchers had assumed that the double standard had eroded as the status of women changed. But from the data accumulating on rape among acquaintances, little seems to have changed.

One result, Dr. Muehlenhard said, is that woman who do not want to appear to be loose offer "token protest, in which the woman says no, but means yes."

In a survey of 610 women published last year, Dr. Muehlenhard found that more than a third had, at least once, put up such token resistance when they actually wanted to have sex. Women who believed their dates hold to the double standard were most likely to use the tactic of a false protest, presumably not to seem "loose."

The trouble is, Dr. Muehlenhard

says, that men tend to see all such protests as token resistance, a no that really means yes. Indeed, she says, the scenario where a forceful man continues a sexual advance despite a woman's protests, until she melts in compliance, is commonly depicted in films and books.

"This sexual script sends men the message that they should not believe women's refusals," Dr. Muehlenhard said. "This can lead to rape in some instances. Men can easily forget that most often no means no. If a man wants to avoid rape, he should believe what a woman tells him."

The double standard also creates pressures on men to force themselves on women, Dr. Muehlenhard said. "The problem is that we give men the message that if you're not sexually active, there's something wrong with you," she said. "At the same time, we tell women they will seem loose if they give in too readily."

In another study, published in 1989 in The Journal of Sex Research, 63 percent of men said they had sex when they did not want to, Dr. Muehlenhard found. "Sometimes it was because a woman made sexual advances and the man felt he would look bad to her—seem shy, afraid or gay—if he didn't go along," she said. "Some were instances of peer pressure from other men, such as at a party where others are having sex."

To be sure, factors other than the double standard are at work in rapes of acquaintances. In The Journal of Sex Research, Dr. Malamuth reported on a series of recent studies intended to identify attributes that make some men more likely than others to force sex on a woman.

Dr. Malamuth used a combination of questionnaires about attitudes toward sex. He also observed the reactions of men to stories depicting sexual incidents. While the men read the stories, a sensor detected the degree of their sexual arousal.

The men who were most likely to become aroused by a story in which a woman was forced to have sex despite protests tended to share other attitudes. One of these was the idea that dominance itself was a motive for

sex; they agreed with statements like "I enjoy the conquest." Another is hostility toward women, as expressed in sentiments like "women irritate me a great deal more than they are aware of."

A third, not surprisingly, is an acceptance of sexual violence. For instance, they might agree with the statement, "Sometimes the only way a man can get a cold woman turned on is to use force."

Differences between men and women in how they perceive a romantic encounter also contribute to rapes of acquaintances, according to research by Dr. R. Lance Shotland, a psychologist at Pennsylvania State University. In a study published in 1988 in The Social Psychology Quarterly, Dr. Shotland and Jane Craig, a research associate, found that men tended to interpret a woman's actions on a date, even such innocuous acts as speaking in a low voice or smiling, as indicating that she was interested in sex. Women, however, tended to see the same behaviors as simply being "friendly."

Other research has shown that men, particularly younger ones, tend to have difficulty discriminating between what women do that is merely friendly, and what indicates sexual interest. A woman drinking, coming to a man's apartment or wearing "sexy" clothes, for instance, all tended to be seen by men as indicators that the woman was interested in sex, while women did not agree, Dr. Muehlenhard found in a 1985 study.

In a 1979 California study, 43 percent of men of high school and college age said that by the fifth date it was "acceptable" for a man to force sex on a woman, and 39 percent of the men said it was acceptable if the man had "spent a lot of money on her."

Assumptions like these about the acceptability of sex are at play in gang rape, a rare event that occurs disproportionately on college campuses, where most cases go unreported, according to Dr. Chris O'Sullivan, a psychologist at Bucknell University. In a study this year of twenty-three incidents of gang rape, she found that the men involved seemed to think that what they were doing was

"O.K.," most often because they regarded the woman as promiscuous.

In virtually all the incidents, the raped woman was known by one or more of the men. Most of the rapes involved fraternities, or football or basketball teams.

The women who are raped by these groups are, in the men's eyes, distinguished from the women they date in terms of respectability. One man involved in a gang rape by football teammates, told Dr. O'Sullivan that the woman "had not, in fact, been raped because she had dated two of them previously," and had hurt the men's feelings by indiscriminately having sex with each of them.

'Respectability' as Factor

Women who socialize with the men on an equal footing, on the other hand, are unlikely to be victims of group rape, Dr. O'Sullivan said, both because of their "respectability" and because they understand the mores of the men's groups. Thus, women who date fraternity members learn not to go upstairs to a bathroom in the fraternity house unless another woman accompanies them, and that getting drunk at a party is taken as a signal of availability.

As a gang rape proceeds, according to other research, as each successive man takes his turn the woman is increasingly seen as "a whore" who deserves to be raped.

In research published in 1983, Dr. Shotland and Dr. Lynne Goodstein found that even when a woman protests that she does not want to have sex, both men and women tended to fault the women if she did not resist at the beginning of the encounter.

Research by Dr. Muehlenhard on effective tactics to avoid date rape show that the woman should make clear early in the encounter that she is not interested in having sex. Other effective approaches were physical resistance, screaming and claiming to have a venereal disease. But the single most powerful tactic of all was the statement, "This is rape and I'm calling the cops."

Sexual Fantasies: What Are Their Hidden Meanings?

February 28, 1984

Researchers know that sexual fantasies tell much about one's sexuality, but just how much they tell has been debated for decades.

The most recent evidence, while it by no means ends the debate, sheds light on several important aspects of the issue: what the fantasies say about one's sexual orientation, what the most common fantasies are, when they are healthy and when pathological and what they indicate about a couple's relationship. The latest contribution to the issue is from the Masters and Johnson Institute in a 1984 article on their treatment program for dissatisfied homosexuals. Researchers at the institute believe that whether a person has homosexual fantasies or heterosexual ones cannot be used as an indication of actual sexual preference. They cite evidence showing the frequency of homosexual fantasies among heterosexuals and heterosexual ones among homosexuals.

In the February 1984 issue of *The American Journal of Psychiatry,* Mark Schwartz and William Masters report a survey of 120 men and women, half of them homosexual and half heterosexual, showing that people's sexual fantasies can be at odds with their sexual orientation. Among both men and women who are homosexual, for example, heterosexual sex ranks as the third most common sexual fantasy. For heterosexual men and women, homosexual encounters rank fourth and fifth most common, respectively. Among heterosexual men and women, the most common fantasy involved replacement of their usual partners.

People tend to be selective in their recall of their own fantasies. To get a full record, David Barlow, director of the Sexuality Research Program at the State University of New York at Albany, asked people to carefully monitor their fantasies for several weeks.

"We find," he said in an interview, "most people have about seven or eight fantasies a day, although the range can be from none to forty and up."

"Among heterosexuals about three-quarters of fantasies are of 'normal' lovemaking, and about 25 percent are sexual variations—sadomasochism, homosexuality, group sex and the like," he said. "The normal pattern of sex fantasies includes a certain amount of unusual sex."

Dr. Schwartz and Dr. Masters report a similar variety of sex fantasies in the people they studied. Fantasies of group sex, for example, were the fifth most common among both homosexual and heterosexual men, while fantasies of forced sexual encounters were first among homosexual woman and second among heterosexual women. For heterosexual men and women, observing other people's sexual encounters was the third most common fantasy.

Extrapolating from Dr. Barlow's data to the lists reported by Dr. Schwartz and Dr. Masters, the fantasies at the top of the lists were by far more frequent than those at the bottom.

While the content of a sexual fantasy does not make it abnormal, its frequency can indicate a psychological problem. Dr. Barlow reported that in people with psychiatric problems, such as rapists and child molesters, the frequency of fantasies is extremely high, often a constant obsession throughout the day.

How much does the actual content of a fantasy matter? Many sex therapists argue that it does not matter much as long as it proves useful for a couple in lovemaking.

Dr. Schwartz, for six years director of research at the Masters and Johnson Institute and now a marital and sex therapist in New Orleans, said in an interview, "If a man loses his arousal while making love with his wife, and uses a fantasy to get it back, then lets go of the fantasy to focus on the lovemaking again, it's irrelevant what the fantasy is about. It's a helpful bridge back to making love, and increases the couple's intimacy."

"But if he keeps the fantasy in mind all during their lovemaking, it can increase the distance between the partners rather than bring them closer," he said.

Bernard Apfelbaum, directors of the Berkeley Sex Therapy Group, said, "It's important to look at the content of a sex fantasy during lovemaking for what it suggests about what's missing in the sexual encounter."

"For example," he said, "a man may say that while making love with his wife he had a fantasy of Raquel Welch in a bikini. On closer scrutiny, what is important in the fantasy is Raquel Welch's attitude, 'She's aroused by him, uncritical, accepting.' That's really a message about what he's missing from his wife. That's material to use in therapy for the couple."

"A sex fantasy can be a clinical barometer of the difficulties a person has with intimacy and emotional closeness," Dr. Schwartz said. About a third of women have had a history of some kind of sexual trauma, he said, and as a result, during lovemaking they may dissociate, separating their feelings from their acts. This sometimes takes the form of a sex fantasy that creates a psychological distance from their partner.

Problems With Intimacy

"Sex fantasies," Dr. Schwartz said, "can reveal such problems with intimacy. For instance, during lovemaking with his wife, a man's fantasies could range from imagining his wife, to fantasies about his secretary, to watching someone else make love, to the sort of impersonal sex that's in porno movies. Each of those fantasies along the gradient represents a increasing psychological distance from the relationship."

"The danger," Dr. Schwartz added, "is when people use a fantasy to maintain or increase the distance between them. After thirty years of marriage, a man or woman may replace the spouse with someone else in their fantasies. If he or she has to fantasize someone else while making love, then the relationship needs help."

Other sex therapists do not agree that such fantasies necessarily indicate that a couple is in need of therapy. "If a man fantasizes about his secretary after twenty years of marriage, that's not at all uncommon," Dr. Barlow said. He, like many other sex therapists, believes that, if a twenty-year fantasy helps in lovemaking, then there is no harm in it.

Nor does he believe that fantasies are always acted out. "It is not uncommon for a woman to tell us that she can get aroused by an attractive woman, although she would never want to have sexual relations with a woman." And by the same token, the Schwartz and Masters report shows that the fantasy of a forced sexual encounter, such as rape, does not mean that a person would necessarily enjoy acting it out in real life, although it ranked as the first or second most common fantasy among all groups.

"For most people who have a fantasy of rape," Dr. Barlow said, "it's a very idealized, even romantic act, something like the rape scene in 'The Fantastiks,'" perhaps somewhat styl-

ized and removed. "In our research, we find that if you play a tape for them of a realistic description of a real rape, with all its pain and violence, they don't get aroused. The meaning of a fantasy like that may be more symbolic than real; for many women who have guilt about sex, it can be a way of giving themselves permission to enjoy it."

Some Fantasies Reveal Troubles

"But if, say, a man has to have a fantasy of severe sadism before he can be aroused at all, then it's a psychological problem," Dr. Barlow said. "Such a habit of compulsive, obligatory fantasies are more likely to lead to someone trying to act them out. And that can mean trouble."

"If the fantasy is something like a role reversal or cross-dressing, and the wife is sympathetic, then it's fine," he continued. "But if acting out the fantasy brings harm to others, as with rape fantasies, then it's a problem. Or if the fantasy is of something like transvestism, and the wife is not accepting, then the person has to decide between his sexual preference and his marriage."

"When we treat someone like that," he said, "we don't consider them cured until the fantasy changes to a more desirable one. You have to look both at their behavior and their fantasies. Fantasy patterns, are a primary indicator of a person's sexual orientation." Many men who have had homosexual fantasies settle into a heterosexual preference.

Only homosexuals who are distressed by their sexual orientation are given a psychiatric diagnosis and considered in need of therapy.

"In our therapy program," Dr. Schwartz said, "we try to change the person's sexual behavior. When that changes, the fantasy change will follow. For example, a homosexual man may be dissatisfied with the shallowness of his relationships with his male lovers, and decide he wants to be with a woman. If he forms an intimate sexual relationship with a woman, his fantasy pattern will change."

The Masters and Johnson approach

to fantasy is in stark contrast to the psychoanalytic view, in which fantasies are even more important than actual behavior in determining a person's true sexual orientation.

In a paper given at the 1984 meeting of the American Psychoanalytic Association, Dr. Richard Isay contended that a person who has homosexual fantasies, but does not actively engage in homosexual activity, is homosexual—even if his homosexual fantasies are unconscious.

"What one does is not necessarily what one is," Dr. Isay said in an interview. "It's quite possible that those patients who changed their sexual behavior to a heterosexual pattern through the Masters and Johnson program did not change their deepest fantasies or their true preference. They may have gone through the change just because of social pressures, or even to please the therapist."

"A therapist ignores the patient's fantasy life at great risk," Dr. Isay continued. "If you induce a patient to change his sexual behavior, but ignore his fantasies, you risk leaving him socially stranded in a marriage he won't want, or his becoming severely depressed. If the change produces no problems in the long run, then the patient was probably not really a homosexual in the first place. But a therapist can't make that judgment without taking his fantasies into account."

The dispute about sexual fantasies is likely to continue until more and better scientific data on them are available.

"The problem," Dr. Schwartz said, "is that we have very, very little good research about people's sexual fantasies. If you base your conclusions on a sample of volunteers, they are self-selected and the results are biased. If you ask a random sample, people lie a lot. And a clinical population just is not representative."

"Our knowledge of sexual fantasies is about where our data on masturbation was fifty years ago, pre-Kinsey," he said. "We don't really know what the usual, normal pattern looks like. There are probably large numbers of people who think they're abnormal, but as we get better data, we'll probably find that the normal range of people's fantasies is even more diverse than we realize now."

Psychology Is Revising Its View of Women

March 20, 1984

Women's psychology, which Freud called "a dark continent," is finally being widely and energetically explored.

Women have been the missing and misunderstood sex in psychology, in the view of a large group of researchers who seek to remedy that omission. Psychology, they contend, has been seeing life through men's eyes. And the new evidence that has emerged goes a long way toward demonstrating that they are right.

While prompted by a feminist motive—to expunge psychology of sex biases—the new effort is distinct from much of the protest a decade ago in that its underpinning is scientific research. Most of the researchers involved are women, which raises the possibility that in purging psychology of male bias, an opposite one may be substituted. However, one expert, Joseph Pleck, an authority on the psychology of sex roles, sees their research as an essential corrective, "Although feminist theory guides their research," he said, "it doesn't warp it. Their work is sound, and they bring an essential balance to the field."

Carol Gilligan, a psychologist at Harvard who is one of those at the vanguard of the movement, said, "This is not a separatist psychology. We're revising mainstream theory. At a time when efforts are being made to eradicate discrimination between the sexes in the search for social equality and justice, the differences between the sexes are being rediscovered."

The research accepts the proposition, although it is still debated among some social scientists, that women tend to nuture, to mother.

And it examines the consequences. The psychologists say this nurturant quality gives women a different outlook on life from that of men, an outlook, they contend, that leads to important moral judgments that seem deficient from a male point of view.

The outlook also leads to self-sacrifice that seems "masochistic" from a psychoanalytic perspective. And finally, the studies show, the nurturant nature leads to a greater susceptibility to experiencing deep stress in the lives of loved ones as if it were their own.

In one sense, however, the new research is not discovering truths about women so much as it is affirming what feminists have been saying for some time. The evidence does indeed point to social training that makes men and women psychologically different. But, surprisingly, the research suggest that the training does not tend to occur in the first six years of life, as many theorists and parents had assumed.

Some of the studies have come up with other surprising insights. For instance, juggling the multiple roles of wife, mother and worker actually seems to lessen stress, contrary to predictions that the increase in working mothers would multiply stress problems in such women.

Dr. Gilligan notes that what some psychological theories take to be women's deficiencies are in fact mere differences from men.

Her work is at odds with that of Lawrence Kohlberg of Harvard, who elaborated on a theory of moral development formulated by Jean Piaget, the late Swiss psychologist. Dr. Kohlberg's data seemed to show that the

moral development of women was stunted. They tended to progress only part way up the hierarchy of development. They got to the point where they made judgments based on caring about others but never made it to the higher level that involved abstract principles.

Dr. Gilligan did not object to Dr. Kohlberg's hierarchy as it applied to men. But, she noted, the work was based on research with males, whose development became the accepted pattern against which women were judged.

Mother's Care Cited as Key

Dr. Gilligan's research, as described in her book *In a Different Voice* (Harvard University Press), suggests that the key difference between men and women stems from the disparate experience children of each sex have of the care they get from their mother.

For girls, Dr. Gilligan said, basic identity comes from experiencing themselves as like their mothers; for boys, forming a basic identity demands seeing themselves as opposite to their mothers.

Girls emerge from this experience with a strong inclination to sense other people's needs and feelings as their own, much like a mother caring for her children. Boys, on the other hand, assert their separateness from their mother, defining themselves more in terms of accomplishments in the world. This appears to be true even in these changing times.

The result, according to Dr. Gilligan, is that men are threatened by intimacy and have difficulty with relationships, while women are threatened by separation and tend to have difficulty establishing a strong identity apart from their personal relationships.

This key difference means that women are far more concerned with the other people in their lives than are men. That overriding concern, in Dr. Gilligan's view, is incorrectly seen in Dr. Kohlberg's theory, and others as well, as a failure to mature morally.

"The very traits that traditionally have defined the "goodness" of women, their care for and sensitivity to the needs of others," Dr. Gilligan writes, are those that mark them as "deficient" in Dr. Kohlberg's theory. This interpersonal basis for women's moral judgments, she concludes, offers an alternative conception of maturity, that women simply order human experience in terms of different priorities than men do.

Related findings on stress suggest that the importance that women place on relationships may have health costs. Illness is usually linked to stressful periods in life. Men, research shows, are more likely to become ill when their lives go through periods of major changes, such as an accident or a divorce. Women carry that burden, too. But the new research reveals that because they care so much more about others than men do, they tend to experience the troubles of those close to them as their own, adding to their personal burden of stress.

In the view of many feminists psychologists, the most explicit bias against women has been in psychoanalytic theory. Freud himself confessed bafflement at understanding the psychology of women.

Research on the social influences in women's lives has provided ammunition for challenges to psychoanalytic interpretations of female psychology. For example, Jean Baker Miller, a psychoanalyst, has criticized the theory that women who assert themselves suffer from "penis envy." Such thinking, she said, reflects the attitude of a dominant social group—men—toward a subordinate one.

The most recent challenge to the psychoanalytic view of women is an article in the March 1984 issue of the *American Psychologist* by Paula Caplan, a psychologist in Toronto.

Dr. Caplan attacks the notion, most fully articulated by the late Helene Deutsch, that women are innately masochistic. Calling the theory of female masochism a "myth," Dr. Caplan asserts that it is a mistaken interpretation of the social forces that shape women's outlooks.

When Freud observed that women seemed to put the needs of others ahead of their own, he described them as "moral masochists," who were self-sacrificing because of an unconscious guilt.

Dr. Caplan, echoing Dr. Gilligan's belief that psychology has chosen to see pathology when there is merely difference, writes, "Daughters are supposed to be nurturant, selfless (even self-denying), endlessly patient." Not only have they been blamed for responding to the training of society, she said, but it appears that another injustice has been done.

Dr. Caplan notes that this nurturant trait is a mature, even laudable, way of being. If women act that way, she said, it is pointless to see it in terms of an unconscious guilt, when there is a more straightforward explanation.

One of the first studies to map women's lifelong course of development is being conducted by Grace Baruch and Rosalind Barnett at Wellesley, who describe their initial results in the recently published book *Life-prints: New Patterns of Love and Work for Today's Woman* (New American Library).

"We were motivated by reading theories like Erik Erikson's stages of adult development and Daniel Levinson's research on men at midlife," Dr. Baruch said in an interview. "It seemed to us that what they said just didn't match what women experience. Women's developmental patterns are much more varied than men's. For example, Erikson says the formation of identity in early adulthood is followed by the capacity for intimacy. But many of the women we talked to described just the opposite

progression, with the sense of identity arising more strongly in midlife."

Motherhood as Source of Distress

One of the more surprising findings from the study was that motherhood was a main source of distress, while working was a key to well-being. Contrary to the stereotype of the happy homemaker, women with children who did not work were more unhappy than women who had children and worked.

"The greatest sense of well-being." Dr. Baruch said, "is among women who have high-level jobs, are mothers and are married. Juggling these multiple roles does not stress women. Work seems to be a buffer against the stresses of motherhood because it offers a sense of mastery of a sort that raising children does not."

For years there has been a debate over how much of the psychological difference between men and women—in aggression or math skills, for instance—is due to biology and how much to society's training.

A promising study that addresses this question is being done by Carol Jacklin and Eleanor Maccoby, who are looking at hundreds of children in Los Angeles. Dr. Jacklin, now director of the Program for the Study of Men and Women in Society at the University of Southern California, wrote a widely cited review of psychological sex differences in 1974 with Dr. Maccoby when both were at Stanford.

That review concluded that there were only a handful of differences between the sexes that stood careful scrutiny, among them that girls are verbally brighter than boys, while boys are more aggressive. At the time, however, there was no way to tell if such differences were due to biology or were learned as children grew.

The study now under way, Dr. Jacklin said in an interview, is designed to sort out which, if any, differences are biologically based, and to discover how they are caused. The children studied all had their hormone levels assayed at birth, have been tested repeatedly, and have been regularly observed interacting with parents, friends and teachers.

Although much data remains to be sifted, by the time the children entered first grade only a handful of sex differences had emerged, among them that boys are less timid than girls, while girls' I.Q. scores are higher on entering school. A relationship between the level of male hormones and aggression in boys, which has been observed by other researchers, has not been found in this study.

"Contrary to our expectations and to prevailing wisdom," Dr. Jacklin said, "in the first six years there was hardly a sign that parents treat boys and girls differently, save for the fact that fathers—but not mothers—gave their children sex-typed toys, like guns for boys and dolls for girls."

"We took Freud too seriously when we looked for big differences before age six, I think," she said.

Dislike of Own Body Found Common Among Women

March 19, 1985

Of all the ways people experience themselves, perhaps none is so primal as the sense of their own bodies. Yet that sense, researchers are finding, is prone to psychological distortions that can have profound effects on how people view themselves and their world.

Women, for example, tend to distort their perceptions of their bodies negatively. Men, just as unrealistically, distort their perceptions, though in a more positive, self-aggrandizing way, according to a study published in *The Journal of Abnormal Psychology*.

Another researcher, Thomas Cash, said in an interview, "About one-third of people, particularly women, report being strongly dissatisfied with their bodies; this is true even among people who are, objectively, quite attractive." Dr. Cash, a psychologist at Old Dominion College in Norfolk, Virginia has developed a therapy for people whose body image is unrealistically negative.

In the current view of many authorities, the importance of the body has often been overlooked in psychological theories. Seymour Fisher, a psychologist at Upstate Medical Center in Albany, who has been a pioneer in research on body perception, says theories of behavior cannot afford to omit "the powerful impact of the immediate experience of one's body in every situation."

The body image is so crucial to a person's very sense of self, psychologists say, that distortions in it can have significant effects. These, they say, range from enhancing or impairing one's general sense of well-being to creating a susceptibility to mental disorder. And the researchers are finding that this image is remarkably plastic, changing as circumstances change, as moods shift, for instance, or as a person encounters different sorts of people.

While the study of the body image has now become a fertile area of research, the field lacks a cohesive, generally accepted theory. Moreover, researchers have undertaken its study with widely varying agendas. For instance, psychologists involved in physical rehabilitation are trying to understand the role restoration of the body image plays in recovery from devastating injuries. Psychotherapists, working from a psychoanalytic framework, are finding relationships between early impairment in people's body image and the psychiatric symptoms they develop later in life. And social psychologists are discovering that body image plays a crucial part in people's self-esteem.

Several studies have found that women are far less satisfied with their bodies, particularly their weight, than are men. Women, for example, weigh themselves more frequently than men do, describe themselves as fat more often and diet more.

One major difference between how men and women feel about their bodies centers on the middle of the torso, from hips to abdomen, according to a national survey. Women tend to be least satisfied with that zone of their body, while men tend to be more satisfied.

New research by April Fallon and Paul Rozin of the University of Pennsylvania shows that both men and women tend to be unrealistic about how others perceive their bodies, but men distort that perception positively, while women do so negatively. The study, based on measures of close to 500 college-age men and women, is reported in *The Journal of Abnormal Psycholgy*.

Women in the study tended to rate their own bodies as heavier than those they felt men found most attractive. Moreover the women indicated that their ideal body weight was even thinner than that they thought men liked most.

When the men were asked what woman's body they found most attractive, however, it was heavier than what women thought to be ideal, and was also heavier than what women thought men liked.

The men's ideal body for a woman, though, was lighter than most women felt their own bodies were, a finding the researchers said gave a realistic basis to the women's desire to be lighter.

The men exhibited no such quandary about their bodies, or at least admitted to none. There was, on average, no appreciable difference between how they rated their own bodies, what they felt their own ideal body would be and what they thought women liked in a man's body.

But all the men's ratings were heavier than the man's body the women indicated was the most attractive to them.

Dr. Fallon and Dr. Rozin believe, as do many other experts, that the dissatisfaction women report with their own bodies, especially as compared to men's almost unrealistic satisfaction with their own bodies, may account for the higher rates among women of disorders such as anorexia nervosa and bulimia, which hinge on extremes of eating and dieting. About 90 percent of those who suffer these disorders are women.

"Men's preferences can account for only part of this pursuit of thinness," the researchers note, particularly since women's ideal body size is so much thinner than that preferred by men. Among the factors the researchers propose as giving women a skewed sense of the ideal woman's body are the extremely thin models used in fashion magazines and advertisements.

Dr. Fisher is, perhaps, the major theorist of body image. In a book to be published later this year by Lawrence Erlbaum Associates, Dr. Fisher elaborates a view of the psychology of the body image that he has been developing for more than twenty-five years.

"People are endlessly engaged in defensive strategies to cope with body experiences which are complex, confusing, and even alien," according to Dr. Fisher.

Research by Dr. Fisher and others has shown that people's sense of their own body is remarkably plastic. For example, the experience of failure has been found to make people feel smaller, as does being in the presence of a person in authority. And the more people pride themselves on their intellectual activities, the larger in size they estimate their head to be. Dr. Fisher concludes that "there is a constant process of feeling that one's body is growing larger or smaller as different life conditions are encountered."

The fantasy life of boys—but not girls—is rife with damage to the body, Dr. Fisher observes. This early difference, he proposes, is reflected later in life in how members of each sex handle anxiety about the body. Men, he has found, are more prone than are women to disturbances in their body image. For example, in one study in which men and women heard tape recordings with subliminal messages, including hostile and depressed themes, the men more often experienced a disturbance in their sense of body boundaries.

People's daily rituals for caring for their bodies—the long shower, specific exercises—Dr. Fisher believes,

serve to maintain a comforting sense of body security. So do clothes of a texture or tightness a person especially likes, or rubbing the skin with favorite lotions. These techniques, he feels, reassure people of the security of the body's boundaries.

Such theories of body image are becoming increasingly important to an understanding of the psychological reactions of people who suffer devastating injuries. Myron Eisenberg, a psychologist at Case Western Reserve University, and John Mayer, of Stanford University, are studying how people with disabilities such as spinal cord injury, view their bodies.

"Many of these patients seem to have lost touch with the sense of their body," Dr. Eisenberg said. "They have a chaotic body image." Rebuilding the body image may play a key role in making a psychological adjustment to such injuries.

Others have found that people with longstanding physical handicaps mentally separate the injured part from the rest of the body, and often express overall satisfaction with their body despite the handicap.

How people feel about their bodies, particularly how attractive they feel themselves to be, varies with mood. For example, people who are mildly depressed evaluate their bodies negatively, according to a report in the *Journal of Clinical and Consulting Psychology.*

Such negative views are in sharp contrast to the "illusory glow" that people often bring to such comparisons. "People who are not depressed, by comparison, see themselves on average as more attractive than others rate them to be," said Dr. Cash, one of the authors of the study.

Even so, Dr. Cash has found that there is often little connection between how attractive people are and how attractive they feel they are, particularly among women. "A woman who seems quite unattractive can be quite content with her body, while another who is highly attractive can be so obsessed with every little flaw in her appearance that she feels ugly."

Women, Dr. Cash believes, are more susceptible to such feelings because appearance is so much more central to their overall feelings about

themselves than it is for men. On the other hand men put much more emphasis on physical fitness in shaping their body image than do women.

Dr. Cash is developing a treatment program tailored to those who suffer from intensely negative feelings about their bodies. So far, all those treated have been women.

"Women have come for treatment who were extremely attractive," said Dr. Cash. "But that's the outside view, not how they see themselves."

The program includes having the women look in a mirror and note the irrational thoughts that spring to mind. "Many will think, I'm so ugly I can't stand to look at myself, or will be obsessed with some small imperfection, such as the shape of her nose or the size of her hips," said Dr. Cash. "They'll generalize that detail to their whole appearance, and ignore the ways they are attractive."

Typically, Dr. Cash reports, the women compare themselves only to the models in magazines or the actresses they see on television and in movies, rather than to the women they see in ordinary life. "They've fallen prey to the creeping standards of beauty in our society," he said.

The Freudian view has held that the body is the core of a person's psychological identity. "An infant develops his very sense of reality by coordinating his inner world of body sensations with the outer world," according to Joseph Lichtenberg, a psychoanalyst who has written on the topic in *The Journal of Psychoanalytic Enquiry.*

"Children will deny their inner reality so as not to lose the parent's love," he added. "There's the old joke where the mother tells the child, 'I'm cold, put on your sweater.' At its worst this kind of interaction leads to a lifelong unrealistic sense of one's body and one's self."

That people so often are out of touch with their bodies, in Dr. Fisher's view, can be traced to early childhood. Young children "quickly discover they are not supposed to touch, think about or refer to certain body parts, which are presumably bad," according to Dr. Fisher. The consequence, in his view, is that for many people the experience of their own body is either quite distorted or filled with guilt, or both.

Building on psychoanalytic theories of the body's significance, Daniel Brown, a clinical psychologist at Harvard Medical School, has proposed that impairments in the development of a person's body image at crucial junctures can lead later to specific susceptibilities to mental disorders.

"Neurotics seem to have had a failure in the development of their body image during the Oedipal years, roughly between three and five," according to Dr. Brown. "It leads them to have extremely erratic attitudes toward their body, or parts of it, either extremely negative or positive."

"People who suffer from personality disorders, such as narcissism, frequently don't see their body and themselves as the same," Dr. Brown said in an interview. "They seem to have had a disruption in body image during the phase where infants develop an autonomous sense of self, around age two."

"In psychosis there is the most extreme collapse of the body image, as though they had regressed to early infancy before the integrated body image forms," Dr. Brown added. "Psychotic patients often have a bizarre sense of their bodies, feeling parts have split off, or that it is falling apart."

Social Psychology

We all make excuses from time to time. But there are some people who go beyond the ordinary variety of excuse and rely on excuses to a point that is self-destructive. Just why and when they become self-defeating, is told in "Excuses: New Theory Defines Their Role in Life."

Some groups work together like clockwork, while others are torn by dissension or sapped by lethargy. The ingredients of the chemistry that can lead to group to work well depend on a balance of two main dynamics: a sense of solidarity and a focus on the task at hand, according to findings discussed in "Why Meetings Sometimes Don't Work."

The roots of prejudice are to be found, in part, in normal ways people divide the world up into categories and stereotypes. While these habits of cognition save us some trouble in most situations, they can become the basis for the kind of thinking that leads to inter-group prejudice. " 'Useful' Modes of Thinking Contribute to The Power of Prejudice" tells how an understanding of the underpins of prejudice can lead to some solutions.

What leads someone to risk his or her own life to help save a person in distress? The roots of altruism are coming clearer from a study of a unique group of altruists: men and women who hid Jews from the Nazis during World War II. If they had been caught, they themselves would have been killed. "Great Altruists: Science Ponders Soul of Goodness," describes research aiming to understand what set these people apart.

The U.S. attorney general issued a report on pornography stating that exposure to pornography leads to sexual violence. While the report was purportedly based on data from social psychologists, many of the researchers who did key studies objected to the attorney general's conclusions. Read why in "Researchers Dispute Pornography Report on Its Use of Data."

The realities of urban life are as varied as there are people in a city, according to the findings in "Scientists Find City Is a Series of Varying Perceptions." Whether residents feel safe or not, or whether a city is too noisy or crowded, has as much to do with their perception of the facts as the facts themselves. New techniques for studying how people perceive a city are playing a role in urban design.

Beauty is in the eye of the beholder. But the attractive female face may be more than a subjective impression. According to data in "Equation for Beauty Emerges in Studies," the standards of female facial beauty may spring from signs that a woman is young and healthy. And, like the preference of women for a mate with great earning ability, facial beauty may have played a role in evolution.

Excuses: New Theory Defines Their Role in Life

March 6, 1984

A team of psychologists has formulated the first comprehensive theory of one of life's pervasive ploys—excuses.

The theory explains how to distinguish benign excuses from destructive ones, how children learn to become adept excuse-makers, when excuses are symptoms of a psychological problem and what personality type is most prone to overusing excuses.

One of the most compelling findings suggests that as many as 20 percent of American adults overuse excuses to a point that may be detrimental to their emotional health.

The garden variety—white lies that prevent hurt feelings ("Sorry, I can't make the party, I'm all tied up")—are so common, the research team says, because they are a social lubricant vital to the smooth operation of daily life. But the new theory takes excuses out of the realm of the trivial and shows them, in many instances, to bespeak a greater, hidden human fragility.

Based on experiments and on studies of how people use excuses, as well as a broad range of related scientific findings by other researchers, the theory is described in a new book intended for professional readership, *Excuses: Masquerades in Search of Grace,* published by John Wiley & Sons.

It is written by Charles R. Snyder, along with Raymond Higgins and Rita J. Stucky, all of the University of Kansas.

Excuses, the researchers point put, take many subtle and devious forms. At their worst, they are chronic evasions of responsibility borne of irrational fear. These excuses prevent insights into one's own problems and thus stand as a barrier to healthy change in personality.

Unlike excuses that help to resolve real tensions, pathological ones often use feigned pretexts or unreasonably exaggerate the facts.

According to Dr. Snyder, there are three key signs of harmful excuses: blatant excuses; those that are broad-ranging, and those that are not easily reversed. He has developed a checklist of questions to consider in evaluating whether an excuse indicates an underlying problem.

While these guidelines are meant for therapists to use with their patients, they apply as well to judging excuses in other realms, such as work or with children.

Chronic excuse-makers use them to avert any admission of fault, and at all costs. The theory suggests that underlying their desperate diversionary tactics is the fear that their personality is so fragile that a single blow to its defenses, no matter how slight, has the power to destroy them.

Phillip Zimbardo, social psychologist at Stanford University, welcomed the new approach to excuses. It dovetails with extensive research of his own on shyness.

"This approach," Dr. Zimbardo said, "has important links to ways people sell themselves short, from shyness to fear of failure. It's an apt way to call attention to how people handicap themselves. Most people can find some areas of their lives where they do this, for example, when you won't even try something unless you're sure you'll do it perfectly."

"Some people stake their whole identity on their acts," he said. "They take the attitude that 'if you criticize anything I do, you criticize me.' Their egocentricity means they can't risk a failure because it's a devastating blow to their ego."

A major category of pathological excuse-making involves using a debilitating condition as a global excuse for any and all failures in life.

This tactic, which Dr. Snyder calls "self-handicapping," has a double payoff: it cushions failures while enhancing any successes. Thus the baseball pitcher who complains of a sore arm before a game is protected if he does poorly, but praised all the more if he pitches well despite the bothersome arm.

Psychological handicaps, such as alcoholism or phobias, can work in the same way. Carried to extremes, one sees people who lead lives contorted so as to justify their excuses.

"Some people," Dr. Snyder said "use problems like test anxiety, shyness or even hypochondriacal disease symptoms as excuses to avoid situations where they fear failure. Self-handicapping can offer an all-purpose out."

"For example," he said, "people who have had a history of psychological traumas sometimes employ them defensively when they think they're being evaluated. 'I've had a hard life' is a handy, universal excuse."

Common Personality Type

According to the theory, the people most prone to pathological excuse-making are a fairly common personality type. Dr. Snyder estimates that as many as one out of five people fall into this category.

By the same token, there is a group who are much less prone to excuse-making than are most people, even when faced with a situation that typically calls for an excuse.

These people, by failing to make excuses when finesse and thoughtfulness call for them, would seem at risk for social disasters, although they may often be saved by the strength of social convention. "Research shows," Dr. Snyder said, "that if someone fails to make an excuse when one is expected, people will do it for him. Not making a proper excuse is too much of a threat to the social fabric for most people to let pass."

The prime index for identifying those most and least prone to excuse-making is a personality continuum that gauges people by the degree to which they see the events in their lives controlled by themselves or by outside forces.

Those who see themselves in control view people's misfortunes as resulting from their own mistakes. Such people are less likely to make excuses. They see themselves as responsible for their failures and successes, and are willing to take whatever blame there may be for what they do.

On the other hand, those who view their lives as under the sway of outside forces see misfortune as a result of bad luck. They look to factors beyond their control to explain successes and failures. As a consequence, when they fail, they readily put responsibility on something or someone other than themselves—they make an excuse.

Julian Rotter, the psychologist on whose research Dr. Snyder bases part of his theory, comments, "Although a particular group of people are most likely to justify their failures by blaming others, just about anyone can behave this way from time to time."

Fragile Regard for Self Worth

Those most likely to make excuses are particularly mistrustful of other people, have a fragile regard for their own worth and are highly sensitive to criticism.

People in this group, according to Dr. Snyder, are most prone to abusing excuses in general, and so most likely to be among those who could benefit from therapy for it.

People who overuse excuses do so automatically, without fully realizing what they are doing. In treating such a person, Dr. Snyder recommends that a therapist first help the patient to become more aware of his excuse-making, but not blame the patient for them. As the patient becomes more aware of the situations that trigger his excuses, he will find that they are not so threatening as he may have thought.

The goal of therapy then becomes either to strengthen those skills for which the patient may have been making anticipatory apologies, thereby bolstering his sense of worth, or simply to get the patient to take more responsibility for his strengths and weaknesses.

"Our presumption," Dr. Snyder said, "is that once the factors that motivate excuses are resolved, excuses cease to be a problem."

According to the theory, people owe much of their excuse-making talents to their parents. In teaching them such essential social skills as politeness and consideration of others, parents inadvertently teach the elements of excuse-making.

For example, a parent often comforts a crying child by making excuses for him or her ("Mommy knows you didn't mean to do it") or demands an excuse when a child has done something wrong ("Why did you put the cat in the freezer?"). This is by no means bad. These social skills will be essential in adulthood.

Developmental psychologists have identified the stages in children's mastery of this ploy. The excuses preschool children make are usually rather flimsy. The need to protect one's self-image and the ability to make sophisticated excuses does not ordinarily emerge until between the ages of six and nine years.

The theory ties the emergence of image-protecting excuses to the development of self-criticism during those years of life. In general, six-year-olds are critical of their friends' behavior, but not their own, and so see no reason to make excuses for it. But by the age of seven, many children have begun to worry about what other people think of them, and by eight most children also are concerned about meeting their own standards. The emergence of these concerns sets the stage for excuses.

Full-fledged self-criticism develops at about the age of nine, and with it the motive for making excuses when those standards are not met.

As the child grows older, his skills as an excuse-maker improve with changes in his thinking. Preschool children reason differently from older ones. A younger child, for example, may be aware of the seriousness of an act of wrongdoing because of its consequences, but does consider the intentions of its perpetrator. Older children, though, include intent in judging an act's morality.

One implication is that the younger children will merely deny the act ("I didn't do it") while older children makes a more elegant excuse ("I didn't mean to").

All-Purpose Cover Story

Although the new view of excuse-making may well have an impact on the practice of psychotherapy, therapists will already be familiar with much of it. Rationalization, in psychoanalytic parlance, is a prominent defense mechanism that provides a cover story for a multitude of sins. Excuses, in the new theory, are seen as a variety of rationalization and the intent is to help therapists focus more clearly on its many manifestations.

Even psychiatric symptoms themselves can be excuses, as has long been observed. Alfred Adler, writing in the early part of the century, proposed that patients' symptoms, from phobias to depression, were ways of excusing themselves for life's failures. This, said Dr. Adler, accounted for the tenacious resistance of patients in therapy to giving up their symptoms—their treasured excuses.

Why Meetings Sometimes Don't Work

June 7, 1988

Researchers studying the effectiveness of groups are drawing conclusions that may change the way many executives view their work habits. Among these are findings that meetings are too often a poor way to get the best out of people and that one of the most destructive forces in a group can be the participant who is trying harder than everybody else.

Groups can work well, the studies show, when there is a balance between a sense of solidarity and a focus on the task at hand and when the task is appropriate to the group. But one recent study demonstrated that, contrary to many executives' belief, groups are not as good as one person working alone when it comes to brainstorming for innovative ideas.

These surprising findings are among the latest in a long line of studies trying to elucidate the complex interactions among people in groups, interactions that often make the sum seem so different from the parts.

Factors That Undermine Group Efforts

The work is pinpointing many of the factors that undermine group efforts and suggesting guidelines for making groups work more smoothly. For instance, the main factor in unproductive business meetings is one of the most fundamental, having the wrong people present.

That finding is from a study by Lynn Oppenheim, a psychologist at the Wharton Center for Applied Research in Philadelphia. Dr. Oppenheim's study involved more than 200 top and mid-level managers at eight different organizations. Senior managers in the study spent an average of twenty-three hours a week in meetings, and middle managers spent eleven.

Having the right people present does not mean just including those who are needed, her study points out, but also excluding those who are not.

One common breach of this principle is in having too many people present, including "dead weight"—people not directly involved in the matters under discussion, or not close enough to them to help. Those at the meeting may then spend too much time explaining background that everyone else there knows, or may be sidetracked onto some other subject.

Another miscalculation occurs when managers call meetings for things that can better be done individually with each of the people there. Executives in Dr. Oppenheim's study said 20 to 30 percent of meetings could have been handled better by phone or through a memo.

A common type of fruitless meeting, according to Dr. Oppenheim, is when a manager calls a meeting to be briefed by subordinates whose work depends little or not at all on what the others do. While a manager may feel this is an effective use of his time, his subordinates will usually resent what seems to them a waste of their time.

A Focal Point of Power Struggles

Another major force that can sabotage meetings, often unrecognized by those who attend, is that meetings are a focal point of power struggles. In one corporation Dr. Oppenheim studied, in which two companies had been merged, there was a battle at managerial meetings over what should go into the minutes. Executives from each of the formerly separate companies had formed factions, each wanting its version of decisions to be recorded for circulation to those not present.

In such situations, a manager would do well to acknowledge the opposing forces that are weighing down the meetings and deal with the conflict either in the meeting or outside of it, management experts say.

Calling a meeting is a political act in itself, and those who accept the invitation or decline are making a tacit judgment about the place of the convener in the power politics of the organization, Dr. Oppenheim noted.

Meetings are usually not meant to do real work but to initiate or control it. Thus the success of a meeting does not necessarily depend on what goes on while the group is together.

Another mark of a good meeting is that all participants, not just the leader, get something out of it.

How Each Benefits

"Meetings are called for the leader," Dr. Oppenheim said. "A meeting you loathed may have been very productive from the leader's perspective. But a good leader runs a meeting that also is productive in some way for each person there."

"People who felt well served by a meeting are more likely to cooperate with the leader in the future," Dr. Oppenheim said.

Certain elements make a meeting seem particularly productive to its participants, Dr. Oppenheim's work indicates. One is the sense that the meeting has a definite objective; a common complaint is that meetings do not seem to have a clear purpose. Another mark of the productive meeting is that it has a tangible outcome, usually a decision for action.

While people also feel better about attending a meeting where the leader keeps the group focused, leaders who are too forceful in controlling a meeting can undermine their own efforts, Dr. Oppenheim said. Others who have studied the workings of groups, including group meetings, agree.

"Authority in a group should be benign," said Robert F. Bales, professor of psychology emeritus at Harvard University and a pioneer in the study of groups. "When a group is dominated by an authoritarian leader, it tends to create resistance, and even revolt. If the revolt is not open, it will take the form of withdrawing interest."

In Dr. Bales's research, the most effective groups were those in which there was a balance between building a sense of solidarity among members and on getting the group's task accomplished. Thus the time a group's members spend getting more comfortable with each other—joking or hanging out," say—is, within limits, as important to productivity as time spent following the agenda.

Brains and Affability

The importance of the balance between building solidarity and working on a given task is reflected in one of the most recent findings on group effectiveness. A study by Robert Sternberg, a psychologist at Yale University, shows that the most effective groups have a balance among members of a group between intelligence, on the one hand, and social abilities, on the other. A group strong in either intelligence or affability alone, he finds, is handicapped.

"Every group has an intelligence," Dr. Sternberg said. "The group's I.Q. is not just a simple addition of the I.Q.'s and talents of everyone in the group. It is the interplay of their intellectual abilities with their personalities and social skills."

Dr. Sternberg has sought to explore why some groups—whether a committee, a jury or a flight crew—are so effective at what they do, while others limp along. While that question has long fascinated social psychologists and other students of group dynamics, Dr. Sternberg had addressed the question in a new way, examining how the intellectual and social traits of each member interact in the group's chemistry.

In a study published in the journal *Intelligence,* Dr. Sternberg, with Wendy Williams, a graduate student at Yale, tested volunteers on their personality traits, intelligence and social abilities. The volunteers were then given thirty minutes to perform a task.

One task was to come up with a marketing plan for introducing an imaginary new non-sugar sweetener; another was to come up with a land use policy that would preserve farmland in an area that was rapidly becoming suburbanized.

The groups that came up with the best answers all had at least one member who was particularly high in I.Q. as well as members who were especially creative and some who were quite practical. That mix—of intelligence, creativity and practicality—was a basic ingredient of group effectiveness.

But those elements in isolation were not enough to make a group outstanding. In addition, the group members had to have a high degree of diversity of both experiences and points of view. "If a group sees things only from one perspective, there is the danger that no one will spot a simple flaw in their plan," Dr. Sternberg said.

An even more important trait of successful groups, making them highly coordinated, was that most people in them had the same levels of persuasiveness, expressiveness and assertiveness. If any member of a group was far stronger than the others in any of these traits, it tended to undermine the group's success. But if the group lacked these abilities their efforts also faltered.

"The group average matters more on these traits because if one person is too good at them, he will take over the group," Dr. Sternberg said. "It produces a lack of harmony and coordination."

That harmony allows a group to capitalize on the intellectual and creative abilities of its most talented member, the Yale study indicated. In those groups where the traits that make for harmony were strong in all members, having an outstandingly talented member helped the whole group. But in those groups where the ability to coordinate was poor, the group effort was not helped by having someone so talented.

'Eager Beavers' as Handicaps

By the same token, even a single group member who is out of step—particularly an "eager beaver" who is too earnest in fulfilling the group's mission and who steps on the toes of others—can undermine the group.

Earlier work on groups sought to distinguish between those tasks for which groups generally perform better and those at which a person working alone will excel.

"In general, any task at which a fine coordination is required, and lack of coordination will cause problems, is best done by an individual rather than a group," said Norbert Kerr, a psychologist at the University of California at San Diego.

Some research does suggest that there can be some benefit in sharing ideas with other people while trying to generate fresh approaches; Dr. Sternberg, for instance, found that the groups he studies did better at generating original solutions to the problems he posed than did people working alone.

But the review of studies found that the advantages of groups are too often overridden by the difficulties members have in coordinating efforts, so that some people in the group fail to contribute as much as they might. The review, by Michael Diehl and Wolfgang Stroebe, psychologists at the University of Tubingen in West Germany, was published in a 1988 issue of the *Journal of Personality and Social Psychology*.

"The fact that only one person can talk at a time seems to reduce the number of ideas each person volunteers," Dr. Kerr said.

'Useful' Modes of Thinking Contribute to the Power of Prejudice

May 12, 1987

In seeking to understand the tenacity of prejudice, researchers are turning away from an earlier focus on such extreme racism as that exhibited by members of the Ku Klux Klan to examine the pernicious stereotypes among people who do not consider themselves prejudiced.

A troubling aspect of the problem, researchers find, is that many stereotypes seem to be helpful in organizing perceptions of the world. Recent studies on this cognitive aspect, amplifying on earlier work, are proving useful in explaining the tenacity of prejudice as a distortion of that process. One finding is that people tend to seek and remember situations that reinforce stereotypes, while avoiding those that do not.

Another troubling conclusion of the research is that simply putting people of different races together does not necessarily eliminate prejudice. For example, Walter Stephan, a psychologist at the University of Delaware, found in a review of eighteen studies of the effects of school desegregation that interracial hostilities rose more often than they decreased at desegregated schools.

Overt, admitted bigotry is on the decline, studies indicate. Yet they reveal that a more subtle form of prejudice, in which people disavow racist attitudes but nevertheless act with prejudice in some situations, is not declining.

Such people justify prejudiced actions or attitudes with what they believe are rational, nonracist explanations. To those who have felt the sting of racial discrimination, the phenomenon is well known. An employer, for instance, may reject a black job applicant, ostensibly not be-cause of his race but because the employer says he believes the person's education and experience are not quite right. Yet a white applicant with the same qualifications is hired.

Part of the difficulty in eradicating prejudice, even in those who intellectually see it as wrong, stems from its deep emotional roots. "The emotions of prejudice are formed early in childhood, while the beliefs that are used to justify it come later," said Thomas Pettigrew, a psychologist at the University of California at Santa Cruz, a noted scholar in the field. "Later in life you may want to change your prejudice, but it is far easier to change your intellectual beliefs than your deep feelings."

"Many Southerners have confessed to me, for instance, that even though in their minds they no longer feel prejudice against blacks, they still feel squeamish when they shake hands with a black," Dr. Pettigrew added. "The feelings are left over from what they learned in their families as children."

Psychoanalytic theories, too, point to the importance of childhood experience. "We distinguish between the familiar and the strange early in infancy," said Mortimer Ostow, a psychoanalyst and professor of pastoral psychiatry at the Jewish Theological Seminary in New York. "Then in childhood, when we join groups, we learn to draw boundaries between us and them. By adolescence the group identity becomes even more important, and out-groups become the place to deposit our own faults."

The classic psychoanalytic literature on prejudice notes that a person's own sense of insecurity is often reflected in the need to find an outgroup to despise, with the person's most loathed personality characteristics pushed onto someone else—thus, the "filthy" Jews or blacks, or Italians or whites. New work is adding to the theories.

Dr. Ostow and other psychoanalysts have studied people in treatment who explored their own anti-semitic prejudices. "The inner dynamics are surprising," said Dr. Ostow. "We find that there almost always was a time in the past when the prejudiced person was attracted to the other group. The prejudice is a later repudiation of that earlier attraction."

Often the attraction occurs in childhood or adolescence, according to Dr. Ostow. The child becomes fascinated by strangers, particularly by people in a group other than that of his own family. At the same time, though, the child may experience this as a betrayal of his family. The child then pulls back from the fascination, often after a rebuff or disappointment, or when he feels guilt at betraying his family. When the attraction happens later in life, the turning point is often rejection by a lover.

"The prejudice that forms symbolizes a loyalty to home and its values," said Dr. Ostow. "But it is built on a deep ambivalence."

Much of the recent work on prejudice has moved from a psychoanalytic view to a cognitive one, in which most prejudice is seen as the byproduct of the normal processes whereby people perceive and categorize one another. To a large extent the new work builds on that of Gordon Allport, the late Harvard University psychologist and author of the 1954 classic, *The Nature of Prejudice.*

Dr. Allport proposed that the roots

of prejudice included the tendency to label people according to their membership in a group. Such labels, Dr. Allport observed, take on a "primary potency," whereby the individual is seen in terms of the group stereotype—Chinese, say—rather than in terms of his specific character. Some current work elaborates on this aspect of Dr. Allport's work, as well as on his proposal that specific kinds of contact between people of different groups could reduce their negative stereotypes of each other.

Dr. Allport proposed that beneficial contacts would, for instance, be cooperative ones between people who are of equal status, that allow people to get to know each other personally. Other kinds of contact—between people who are not equal in status or power, such as between an upperclass homemaker and a minority-group domestic employee, for example—would tend to reinforce prejudice.

Many psychologists now believe that school busing and some other desegregation efforts have often failed to foster the beneficial sorts of contacts. Where they have occurred, however, prejudiced has lessened.

Too often, research has shown, children of different ethnic groups in newly desegregated schools fail to mix socially, instead forming hostile cliques. This, together with the frequent perception that one group is lower in status than the other, can intensify racial stereotypes.

On the other hand, in cases where children are more likely to work together as equals to attain a common goal, as on sports teams or in bands, stereotypes do tend to break down. And new experiments are being tried to foster such beneficial interactions in the classroom.

'We All Need to Categorize'

The new explorations of the cognitive role of stereotypes find them to be a distortion of a process that helps people order their perceptions. The mind looks for ways to simplify the chaos around it. Lumping people into categories is one.

"We all need to categorize in order to make our way through the world," said Myron Rothbart, a psychologist at the University of Oregon. "And that is where the problem begins, we see the category and not the person."

The tenacity of people's stereotypes, both innocent and destructive, is a result of the pervasive role of categorization in mental life. And the stereotypes tend to be self-confirming.

"It is hard to change people's preconceptions once they are established," said Dr. Stephan, who is one of those doing the new research. "Even if you present people with evidence that disconfirms their stereotypes—an emotionally open and warm Englishman, say, who breaks your image of the cold, reserved English—they will find ways to deny the evidence. They can say, 'He's unusual,' or, 'It's just that he's been drinking.'"

In a study of a recently desegregated school, Janet Schofield, a psychologist at the University of Pittsburgh, found that many of the black students thought the whites considered themselves superior. When white students offered help to black students, the blacks often spurned the offers, seeing them as a confirmation of the attitudes they attributed to the whites.

And research by David Hamilton, a psychologist at the University of California at Santa Barbara, shows that people tend to seek and remember information that confirms their stereotypes. So, a black who sees whites as haughty and unfriendly may notice more and remember better the whites who have acted that way than those who were warm and friendly. And if, for example, white people avoid black people, there is little opportunity for receiving information that might upset their stereotypes.

Subtle Forms of Bias

Even people who profess not to be prejudiced often exhibit subtle forms of bias, according to research by the psychologists Samuel Gaertner of the University of Delaware and John Dovidio of Colgate University.

Many national surveys have shown, for example, that the racial attitudes of whites have become markedly more tolerant over the last forty years. But other research suggests that "although the old-fashioned, 'redneck' form of bigotry is less prevalent, prejudice continues to exist in more subtle, more indirect and less overtly negative forms," Dr. Gaertner and Dr. Dovidio assert in *Prejudice, Discrimination and Racism,* published by Academic Press.

"People who believe they are unprejudiced will act with bias in some situations, but give some other, rational reason to justify the prejudiced act," Dr. Gaertner said in an interview.

According to research by John McConahay, a psychologist at Duke University, this more subtle form of prejudice is marked by ambivalence and exhibits itself most often in ambiguous situations where racism does not seem to be at issue. In one experiment Dr. McConahay found that whites who scored highest on a test of this subtle racism tended to reject more black applicants than white ones for a hypothetical job, though the applicants' qualifications were identical.

Some experts say social or historical facts play a role in justifying prejudice. Thus in the Southwest, negative stereotypes of Hispanic people fit traits often ascribed to migrant laborers, a role many Hispanic people held for decades. Years after such roles end, Dr. Stephan has found, the specific stereotypes still prevail.

"America is full of realities from 350 years of discrimination against blacks that make blacks, in the minds of some, seem to be at fault when actually they are victims," said Dr. Pettigrew.

"There are, for instance, very few black professors at Harvard, where I taught for many years," he went on "Why? The prejudiced person attributes that fact to something about blacks, rather than to something Harvard or about the means by which tenure decisions are made."

Great Altruists: Science Ponders Soul of Goodness

March 5, 1985

It was still dark that morning in 1942 when the Gestapo rousted from bed the Jews of Bobawa, a Polish village. In the confusion, twelve-year-old Samuel Oliner slipped away and hid on a roof, still in his pajamas. The next afternoon, when he dared to look around, the ghetto was silent. The Jews of Bobawa, murdered that day, by then were lying in a mass grave in the nearby countryside.

Samuel found some clothes in an empty house and, skirting German patrols and Polish looters, fled to the country. There, after walking for two days, he found his way to the farmhouse of Balwina Piecuch, a peasant woman who had been friendly with his family. Mrs. Piecuch knew, when Samuel knocked at the door, that she would be shot if the Germans found her harboring a Jew. Without hesitating, she took Samuel in.

Balwina Piecuch taught Samuel the rituals of Polish Catholic life—how to go to confession, how to pray, catechism. With her help, Samuel posed as an impoverished Polish stable boy in search of work and a place to live. Thus Samuel survived the war.

Exemplars of Human Goodness

By some estimates, there were as many as 200,000 Jews who, like Samuel Oliner, were saved from the Nazis by non-Jewish rescuers. In Berlin 5,000 Jews survived through the combined efforts of tens of thousands of Germans, many of whom fooled the Gestapo by moving Jews from hiding place to hiding place.

Now, in a remarkable project, re-searchers are reaching into the caldron of good and evil that was World War II to retrieve for study those exemplars of human goodness, the non-Jews who, like Mrs. Piecuch, risked their lives to help Jews survive the Nazis.

The director of the project is Samuel Oliner, now a sociologist at Humboldt State University in Arcata, California.

"We want to find the common threads among those few who helped, and the differences between the rescuers and those others who might have helped but chose to look the other way," Dr. Oliner said in an interview. He heads the Altruistic Personality Project, in which researchers working in the United States, Canada, Europe and Israel will conduct, if funds allow, detailed interviews with 400 people who rescued Jews during the war.

Strong Sense of Self-Worth

Dr. Oliner and his associates, who have already interviewed 140 rescuers, believe they are racing the clock to reach the rest before they die. On the basis of the interviews he has conducted already, however, he has reached some preliminary conclusions about the characteristics of the rescuers.

In broad strokes, his findings are in accord with the views of such humanistic psychologists as Abraham Maslow and Erich Fromm, who saw a strong sense of self-worth and security as the psychological base from which people could reach out to help others.

To be sure, there is no single, all encompassing explanation for the rescuers' acts. Indeed, some saved Jews for selfish reasons, they were paid or bribed. Most sheltered people they knew or with whom they had ties. But many rescued complete strangers.

Dr. Oliner's research project is part of a broad search under way to understand what leads an individual to help when others turn their backs on a person in need. While that question is one that theologians and philosophers have sought to answer for thousands of years, psychologists of late have made intensive efforts to provide their own insights.

Spurred by Murder of Kitty Genovese

Ironically, the current research on altruism was spurred, in large part, by a tragic instance of its absence, the 1964 murder of Kitty Genovese as thirty-eight neighbors in Kew Gardens, Queens, looked on without calling the police for help. The incident galvanized psychologists, who realized that they had no ready explanation for why these neighbors refused to help, or for contrasting acts of human kindness.

Psychoanalysts have proposed several psychological motives for altruism. One view, for example, holds that those who help others to their own detriment are masochistic. Another sees altruism as an effort to expiate unconscious guilt or shame. For example, Erik Erikson attributed Mohandas Gandhi's humanitarianism, in part, to such guilt.

Behaviorists, on the other hand, have explained altruism in terms of the reinforcement people get from making themselves feel good by doing good. Behavior geneticists have studied twins to see if there is an inherited temperament that predisposes some toward acts of kindness.

Sociobiologists offer an entirely different analysis of altruism, noting that it is seen, too, in animals. For example, in several species of primates, members of one troop will raise an orphaned youngster from another troop. Some sociobiologists argue that altruism is a survival strategy in evolution, since helping others who share one's genes is a form of reproductive success. But such theories, in Dr. Oliner's view, do little to explain what impelled the rescuers he is studying to risk their lives—and often their families' lives, too.

What can be said, for example, of the motives of the S.S. officer who concealed a Jewish couple until the end of the war in his living quarters directly above the S.S. Center in Berlin? Or, for that matter, what drove the Belgian countess who not only hid 100 women and children on her estate, but also cooked kosher food for them?

Of most interest to the researchers is the contrast between these rescuers and the vast majority of non-Jews who also could have saved Jews, but did not. Dr. Oliner has so far interviewed twenty non-rescuers, and plans to talk to 180 more.

The preliminary findings from his project, and results from a variety of other studies, converge on the formative experiences people have in childhood, which seem to make them, many years later, more predisposed than others to come to the aid of the distressed.

On the basis of this preliminary data, Dr. Oliner has identified a key cluster of the factors that seem to be at play in the rescuers as a group. There were, in his view, three elements that combined to lead the rescuers to their acts of kindness and heroism.

Foremost among them was having compassionate values. In most cases, these values seem to have come from someone in the person's childhood who embodied them. Perry London, a psychologist at Harvard University who studied a group of rescuers now living in Israel, concluded that "almost all the rescuers" had a strong identification with a parent who was a "very strong moralist."

But, Dr. Oliner points out, espousing such values was in itself not enough. The rescuers were also distinguished by a sense of competence. They saw themselves as in control of their lives. Moreover, they also seemed inclined to take calculated risks.

And, finally, the rescuers had to have at their disposal the wherewithal to put their values and sense of competence into action. For some that meant a special expertise, such as being an expert skier who could escort Jews across the snow-covered Alps to Switzerland; for others, it simply meant having a home large enough to have a hiding place and having family and friends who supported the rescue effort.

Though Dr. Oliner cautions that these findings are preliminary, they dovetail with results from several other diverse studies of altruists.

In an approach similar to that taken by Dr. Oliner, Nancy McWilliams, a psychoanalyst, has conducted intensive clinical interviews with five people who have dedicated their lives to helping others. Although exploratory, Dr. McWilliams's research is instructive because her subjects represent an extreme of altruism; they include a woman who cares for the children of lepers in the Far East, and a man who runs an international adoption agency for crippled or otherwise unwanted children.

She began her study because she was dissatisfied with the psychoanalytic theories of altruism that saw it as pathological. "These are the kind of people who don't show up in psychotherapists' offices," she said. "They're not neurotic or depressed, they have good relationships and a sense of humor about themselves."

She found a common pattern in the early development of those she studied. Most had suffered the loss in early childhood of a warm and nurturant caretaker, such as the death of a mother. And in every case there was a "rescue" by someone in their lives who they felt saved them by replacing the lost person. For some it was a housekeeper; for others an older sibling or their father.

"As children, they idealized that person," Dr. McWilliams said. "He or she became their model for altruism. Moreover, most grew up in families with strong religious values. Many of them feel a sense of 'doing God's work,' as one put it, though none is observant now."

One of the most detailed theories of the roots of altruism is that proposed by Ervin Staub, a psychologist at the University of Massachusetts. Writing in *The Biological and Social Origins of Altruism and Aggression,* a collection of articles by several experts published in 1985 by Cambridge University Press, Dr. Staub reports evidence that altruism requires more than just compassionate values and the psychological and practical competence to put them into effect.

"Goodness, like evil, often begins in small steps," Dr. Staub said in an interview. "Heroes evolve; they aren't born. Very often the rescuers made only a small commitment at the start—to hide someone for a day or two. But once they had taken that step, they began to see themselves differently, as someone who helps. What starts as mere willingness becomes intense involvement."

Dr. Staub cites the example of Raoul Wallenberg, the Swedish diplomat who used his status to save hundreds of Hungarian Jews. "The first person Wallenberg rescued was a business partner who was a Hungarian Jew. Soon, though, Wallenberg was manufacturing passes that made Jews candidates for Swedish citizenship, and so protected them from the Germans. As his involvement grew, it got to the point that he was exposing himself to great risks by giving out the passes to Jews waiting in line for Nazi deportation trains."

But there is a special kind of person who is more likely than most to take that first step to help, and to stay with the effort to the end, the altruist.

"There is a pattern of child-rearing that seems to encourage altruism in later years," said Dr. Staub, who is studying the roots of altruism in childhood. "A warm and nurturant relationship between parent and child is essential, but not enough in itself. The same holds for having parents who espouse altruistic values—it's important, but not sufficient."

From his own research and that of others Dr. Staub has identified a particular style of disciplining children which seems essential for children to learn the lessons of altruism.

"The parents who transmit altruism most effectively," he said, "exert a firm control over their children. Although they are nurturant, they are not permissive. They use a combination of firmness, warmth and reasoning. They point out to children the consequences to others of misbehavior—and good behavior. And they actively guide the child to do good, to share, to be helpful."

Children who have been coached to be helpful, or who engaged in altruistic projects such as making toys for poor, hospitalized children, Dr. Staub has found, are later more altruistic when a spontaneous situation in which they can help others arises.

There may be quite specific interactions between parents and children that cultivate such altruism, according to results from a major series of studies by Carolyn Zahn-Waxler and her colleagues at the National Institute of Mental Health.

The beginnings of altruism, her research shows, can be seen in toddlers as young as two years. At that age altruism typically takes such forms as trying to make an upset playmate stop crying by offering toys or food, or otherwise consoling him.

Whether a child displays altruism seems tied to how the mother or other caretakers treat the child in key moments, particularly times when another person is in distress. For example, according to Dr. Zahn-Waxler, children who were more often altruistic had mothers who tended to explain to them the consequences of hurting other children, and to do so with great feeling, with an admonition such as, "I don't like to be with you when you act like that."

When the mothers gave a calm, unemotional admonition, it did not seem to lead the children to be altruistic. Nor were the children of mothers who frequently handled the child's transgressions by simply telling them, "No! Stop!" without explaining why.

Some mothers Dr. Zahn-Waxler studied, particularly those who blamed their children for mistreating playmates, induced a guilt-ridden altruism in their young children. These children often feel they have caused hurts that were not their doing.

On the other hand, the young children of chronically depressed mothers seem to be particularly sensitive to the distress of other children, Dr. Zahn-Waxler finds. While they are not overly guilty about the distress, they are preoccupied by it.

A healthier kind of altruism, she believes, is that produced by "the nurturant but moralizing parent who arouses the child to concerned action."

Researchers Dispute Pornography Report on Its Use of Data

May 17, 1986

The Attorney General's report on the social effects of pornography has drawn expressions of dismay and shock from some of the researchers on whose work the report's conclusions are largely based.

The report, made public in July, 1986, states that exposure to pornography plays a role in causing "sexual violence, sexual coercion or unwanted sexual aggression." A copy of the draft was made available to *The New York Times* earlier this week.

In the 211-page introduction, the Attorney General's Commission on Pornography calls for Government action against the pornography industry, including stricter penalties for violation of laws on obscenity.

Objections to Conclusions

But the researchers who provided key data for the report denied Friday that the panel had established a direct causal link between most sexually explicit material and any act of sexual violence.

"These conclusions seem bizarre to me," said Edward Donnerstein, a psychologist at the University of Wisconsin who is one of the nation's leading experts on the effects of pornography. Some of the major conclusions of the panel are based in part on his research.

The researchers interviewed did say, however, that their work established a link between viewing some types of pornographic movies and the development of callous and demeaning attitudes toward women.

Several of the main researchers

charged that major conclusions of the commission resulted from a biased reading of inconclusive, complicated and often contradictory evidence, ignoring some research findings and emphasizing others.

The panel acknowledges that their conclusions were based on more than just the social science evidence. Some members of the panel are planning to offer dissenting opinions.

In general, the researchers said their data indicated that rape and demeaning attitudes toward women might be more strongly associated with violence in the social environment than with explicit, but nonviolent, depictions of sex in pornographic literature or films.

"It is the violence more than the sex—and negative messages about human relationships—that are the problem," said Dr. Donnerstein. "And these messages are everywhere."

The experts are also indignant because the report has come out before they could attend a meeting called by the Surgeon General, Dr. C. Everett Koop. At the request of Attorney General Edwin Meese 3d, Dr. Koop has invited twenty leading social scientists, including a half dozen of the principal researchers, to meet for four days at the end of June to review research on the effects of pornography.

Complaint About Timing

The experts say they had been led to believe their consensus, as reached at the June meeting, would be forwarded to the Attorney General for use in the report. But the report is already done.

"The panel seems to have deliberately released its findings before we could meet, because they were afraid that the social scientists' conclusions would contradict theirs," said Murray Strauss, a sociologist at the University of New Hampshire who is one of the researchers invited to the June meeting. "I dispute their conclusions, because they are not in accord with my understanding of the scientific data."

Allen Sears, the executive director of the commission, said the panel did not rely only on the research of social scientists but, instead, sought a wide range of testimony from law-enforcement officers, members of the clergy and others. "Science does not give the complete answer," said Mr. Sears.

Ted Khron, a special assistant to the Assistant Secretary for Health who is working with the Surgeon General, said that even though the pornography commissioners had evidently completed their work, the June meeting would be held anyway and its conclusions would be made public.

"If they have closed up shop when we come to our conclusions, we'll pin them on the door like Martin Luther," he said. "We'll issue a report even if our conclusions differ from the commission's. It's a refreshing example of democracy in action."

Research is Contradictory

Most of the key researchers whose work was regarded as central to the commission's conclusions, according to its staff members, testified at hearings in Houston last September.

Not all commissioners agreed with the report. One, Dr. Judith Becker, director of the Sexual Behavior Clinic at the New York State Psychiatric Institute, said, "I've been working with sex offenders for ten years and have reviewed the scientific literature, and I don't think a causal link exists between pornography and sex crimes." She said she would write a dissenting opinion.

The researchers interviewed said that their own testimony was contradictory on several key points, particularly on the behavioral effects of nonviolent pornography, and that they looked forward to sorting out these differences at the meeting next month.

A major flaw in the method by which the panel came to its conclusions, said some of the experts, is in confusing correlations with causes, running afoul of basic scientific principles.

"There are eleven different factors that are correlated with rape, but none of them can be taken to be a cause of rape," said Dr. Strauss. In comparing the incidence of rates from state to state, Dr. Strauss said, none of the eleven factors "accounts for more than about 5 percent of the difference between states in their rape rates."

The main controversy is over the panel's conclusions regarding what it calls "degrading" pornography, a category whose boundaries are blurred and, some experts say, overly general. Sexual materials are considered degrading, according to researchers who have used the term, when it depicts people in a demeaning or dehumanizing way, or portrays unequal power in a sexual relationship.

'Some Causal Relationship'

It is with regard to such pornography, the panel's report notes, that the conclusions reach far beyond the empirical evidence. The panel report concludes that substantial exposure to such pornography "bears some causal relationship" to sexual violence and coercion.

Research by Dolf Zillmann, a psychologist at the University of Indiana, has found that viewing several hours of "stag" films over several weeks lowers men's respect for women and lessens their commitment to relationships with women. But Dr. Donnerstein of Wisconsin and his colleagues had men view up to ten hours of films considered degrading, and found no appreciable effects on attitudes toward rape or other violence against women, and no loss of sympathy for rape victims.

Some experts charge that the panel has ignored important data that are not in keeping with their conclusions. For instance, a study by Beryl Kutchinsky, a psychologist at the Institute of Criminal Justice in Copenhagen, reported in April, found that in those European countries that have abandoned all restrictions on sexual materials, rape rates over the last ten to twenty years have declined or remained constant.

A conclusion by the commission that violent pornography is a cause of sexual violence is seen by researchers as having some basis—though an arguable one—in the empirical evidence.

Laboratory studies, mainly by Dr. Neil Malamuth of the University of California at Los Angeles, Dr. Donnerstein and his colleague Dan Linz, have found that some men become more accepting of sexual violence after viewing films that depict such violence. For instance, in one study, some men who viewed films in which a woman falls in love with a man who sexually assaults her became more accepting of the idea that rape victims secretly want to be raped.

Other research has found that similar attitudes toward women are prevalent among men who have committed sexual violence, such as raping their dates. But no study has as yet found the direct causal link between viewing depictions of sexual violence and committing such violence that the panel concluded exists.

At the panel's hearing in Houston, Dr. Malamuth suggested that approval of sexual aggression toward women was necessary, in most cases, but not sufficient in itself to lead a man to actually become sexually aggressive.

Scientists Find City Is a Series of Varying Perceptions

December 31, 1985

In a sense, social scientists find, the city does not exist. There is no such single entity, but rather many cities, as many as there are people to experience them. And researchers now believe that the subjective reality is every bit as important to understanding and fostering successful urban life as the concrete and asphalt of objective measurement.

Although most earlier approaches to assessing the quality of city life led researchers to consider such factors as noise levels and density, the new work shows that how people actually perceive their environments is as important as the environments themselves.

"The images that people hold in their minds reflect multiple realities," says Edward Krupat, a social psychologist at the forefront of the new approach.

The studies have profound implications both for city dwellers and for city planners and administrators, in leading more contented lives and in designing and operating cities. Spurred by the research, urban planners and architects are using techniques that anticipate, in the planning stages, varying human reactions to a project. Computer simulations of walks or drives through developments are being used, for example, to test reactions to design options.

The studies indicate, too, that a mayor, for example, can no longer assume that the city he perceives that he is running is quite same as the one that his voters think they live in.

Among the areas most actively investigated at present are how children's mental maps change as their minds mature, how people's images of a place reflect the level of crime there, and how people's images of their neighborhoods affect the success of redevelopment.

The usefulness of the new approach has been brought home by such studies as one finding that the likelihood of being robbed was twenty times greater in Washington than in Milwaukee, but Milwaukee residents felt only slightly safer than Washingtonians.

"If a person believes a place is unsafe, it makes little difference that there is no danger by all objective indicators, he will not go there, "Dr. Krupat said. In a sense, part of the city ceases to exist for that person.

The potency of people's images of their surroundings was shown in a study of tenant groups who had received money to restore run-down and partly abandoned apartment buildings in Harlem. The researchers found that a group's success depended partly on whether some tenants had positive memories of the past in that part of the city.

"The older people, particularly the women who had an image of Harlem based on the 1920's and 1930's, were the glue that held together the groups that were successful in restoring the buildings," said Susan Saegert, a psychologists at the City University of New York graduate center, who studied the rehabilitation effort.

"That image of a robust, appealing Harlem gave them a sense of what things could be like again, a sense the younger people did not have," she said, "It let them stick it out until the buildings they lived in had been brought back to something like the Harlem they remembered." The newly shaped reality was directly dependent, in that case, on the perceptions of the people who shaped it.

The subjective nature of the city is evident in mental maps people create of cities they inhabit. Certainly the most famous mental map is that of the world as seen from New York City, drawn by the cartoonist Saul Steinberg for a cover of the New Yorker magazine. His map showed the West Side of the city in great detail, and beyond it a virtually empty America with a few sparse landmarks, such as Chicago. Any New Yorker can testify that this perception of the world is common here.

In their research, psychologists are asking people to draw similar mental maps. These freehand drawings are full of distortions and blind spots, but it is these very inaccuracies that psychologists find so valuable. They offer a sort of urban Rorschach, an insight into the personal meanings and experiences a person finds in a city.

"The images of those sections of the city that people use most and with which they are most familiar are more complete and fine-grained, while people may be barely aware of the existence of other sections," according to Dr. Krupat, whose book *People in Cities* (Cambridge University Press) reviews much of the recent research.

Combining of Basic Elements

The study of people's mental maps of the city was pioneered by Kevin Lynch, an urban planner who sought a way to analyze the key elements of a city. The drawings, he found, were highly personalized, but could be combined in terms of certain basic elements. These included major travel routes like rail lines or streets; city districts, such as SoHo, recognized as having a common character; and landmarks, especially notable elements such as the Empire State Building or Grand Central Station.

Urban planners have used the technique to analyze and compare cities. In one study, for example, residents of Los Angeles, Boston and Jersey City were asked to draw their cities. Boston was found to evoke detailed images, while Los Angeles and Jersey City were found to have few distinctive features in people's minds.

Drawings of Paris made by more than 200 Parisians from all parts of the city reveal the less than perfect links between a city's image and its reality. The research, by the late Stanley Milgram, a social psychologist at the City University of New York, demonstrates the highly personal nature of people's mental maps.

A twenty-five-year-old commercial agent's drawing gave prominence to the university district he had only recently left and to the modern skyscrapers at the city's edge—a feature notable by its absence in the maps of older Parisians. A fifty-year-old woman who had spent much of her life in a single neighborhood depicted its streets in scrupulous detail, ignoring most of the rest of the city. A butcher's map showed not only his home neighborhood, but also the area where the stockyards and slaughterhouses are situated. And an architect depicted not the city as it is, but the ideal, well-landscaped Paris he wished it to be.

Egocentricity of Children

Gary Moore, an environmental psychologist at the University of Wisconsin in Milwaukee, has found that young children's mental maps are highly egocentric, featuring streets and landmarks of personal significance, with little resemblance to actual geography. Older children have a larger frame of reference, organizing their maps around key landmarks like schools or shopping centers, but with little overall coordination. Still older children's maps resemble those of adults, with more complex drawings that show, for example, several different routes to a given place.

Newcomers still learning their way around a city follow the same general progression, but in weeks or months, rather than the years that children take, according to Dr. Krupat.

In a child's reality, a locale is typically marked by dangerous or "scary" zones to which parents are generally oblivious. In research reported in *Children's Experience of Place* (Irvington Press), Roger Hart has found that young children describing their neighborhoods mentioned such landmarks as funeral parlors, empty stores and abandoned houses as scary, and places with "big boys," "gas tanks that might blow up" and "quicksand" as dangerous.

Their parents were for the most part unaware of these treacherous places. When asked what their children might consider dangerous, the parents mentioned such things as busy roads, but named almost none of the other dreaded landmarks their children listed.

Subjectivity in Distances

The subjective reality of the city has a marked effect on how people estimate distances, research has shown. If a place is subjectively close, people are much more likely to go there than to a place that may actually be more accessible, but does not seem so. A study in Britain found that people felt stores toward the center of town were "closer" than those that were in fact closer but on the out-skirts of town.

Another factor distorting distances is the complexity of getting some where. Researchers at Ohio State University found that the more turns and major intersections on the way, the farther people felt the place to be, regardless of actual distance.

People's sense of a city relies greatly on their friendships there. Karen Franck, an environmental psychologist, compared how quickly newcomers to New York City and to a small town made friends. The newcomers to New York, she found, were slower to find friends; it took them about eight months to catch up to the number of friends made by the newcomers to the small town.

Reporting in the *Journal of Social Issues,* she concluded that urban friendships were no less numerous nor intimate than those in small towns but were slower to develop. She notes that one initial obstacle to urban friendships is the "urbanites" practiced air of outward indifference that makes it difficult to anticipate who will react positively and who will not" to the chance of friendship.

On the other hand, according to Dr. Krupat, once inside a network of friends in the city, a person's possibilities for friendships multiply far more greatly than they can in a small town. In that sense, the city has many more opportunities for friendship.

These social bonds, even just nodding acquaintances, play a key role in people's sense of security in the city and in maintaining local order. People feel more responsible for what goes on and are more likely to intervene or seek help when needed. "As local social ties increase, it becomes easier to discriminate between strangers and people who belong," says Ralph Taylor, a psychologist in the Department of Criminal Justice at Temple University, who directed a series of studies in Baltimore.

Link to Crime Rates

He found that when the psychological meaning of a place, particularly people's sense of attachment to it and to people there, is of major import in determining the level of crime. In neighborhoods where residents have few acquaintances, crime rates rise, as do people's fears.

The subjective approach to urban study is supplying answers to the question of whether cities are necessarily stressful. The answer seems to depend largely on what level of stimulation a person prefers. Many city dwellers, psychologists point out, are drawn there in the first place because of the pace and excitement. And the way a person adapts to such stimulation—that is, how much stimuli will be seen as stressful and how little as boring—may determine his reaction to either an urban or a rural setting. Urbanites seem able to handle more stimuli than residents of small towns, according to Daniel Geller, a psychologist at Georgetown University.

Newcomers from small towns to a city like New York generally find urban life overwhelming at first, but once they adjust their hometowns tend to strike them as too slow, say researchers at Pennsylvania State University. Likewise, students from small towns in a study done at the University of Michigan felt Ann Arbor was less safe and more cosmopolitan than did students from larger cities.

As people who come to the city adjust to life there, Dr. Geller notes, they no longer feel overwhelmed by it, but tend to seek out the novelty and excitement it offers. Furthermore, the monotony of small-town life may be refreshing for a vacation but can itself be stressful in a long stay.

One practical application of the new approach is in allowing a test of proposed changes in a city, such as a major development project. Kenneth Craik, at the University of California at Berkeley, is using architect's scale models to produce an audio-visual simulation of a walk or drive through a proposed development.

Such simulations, according to Dr. Craik's research, are so close to reality that alternative designs can be tested before construction. Such simulations were used in planning the development of the Berkeley waterfront and are now being used to weigh alternative plans for several municipal projects, including the redevelopment of Times Square.

Equation for Beauty Emerges in Studies

August 5, 1986

The beauty of the female face, it appears, is mathematically quantifiable. Moreover, new research is identifying why the emerging equation can attempt to define what has for so long been thought of as strictly subjective.

In the last two decades, psychologists have come to realize that physical attractiveness, in males as well as females, carries with it an impressive array of social and psychological benefits—from getting more attention from teachers in childhood, to earning more money in adulthood.

Researchers are now attempting to determine precisely what constitutes attractiveness, and what makes it is so compelling.

While much of this research has thus far focused on the female face, psychologists are now also studying the features that make a man's face attractive. But, in mating, a man's looks matter less than his social status and wealth, according to David Buss, a psychologist at the University of Michigan, who has studied characteristics most commonly sought in a mate by men and women and has studied the role of attractiveness in human evolution.

In an article in *The American Scientist*, Dr. Buss reported that the sexes agree for the most part on what they seek in a mate. In general, men and women say they value kindness and intelligence most, and agree on the importance of an exciting personality, good health and creativity. But for men, the physical attractiveness of a partner is significantly more important than it is for women, according to Dr. Buss. And for women, generally, a mate's earning capacity is a greater consideration than it is for men.

One explanation for these differences, in Dr. Buss's view, lies in the evolutionary advantages those preferences hold for each sex. In evolution, signs of beauty in a woman are cues that she is young and healthy—thus at the peak of her reproductive ability—and therefore desirable, according to Dr. Buss. These factors were of great importance through most of human history; in the past more women died in childbirth than do now.

For a man, physical appearance is not as great a signal of his reproductive value, however, age imposes fewer constraints on a man's capacity for reproduction. But a man is in a better position to further the survival chances of his offspring if he has access to resources or power, and so it has been to women's advantage to seek mates who had these capabilities, Dr. Buss argues.

"So there is a selective advantage in evolution for those men who can best distinguish among women to find a mate who is at her peak reproductive powers," says Dr. Buss. "There would be an advantage to women whose physical make-up most closely resembled the signs by which men recognised a woman's health and fertility."

The attractive female face is just such a sign, according to research reported in *The Journal of Personality and Social Psychology* by Michael Cunningham, a psychologist at the University of Louisville in Kentucky. In a series of experiments, Dr. Cunningham asked 150 white, male American college students to rate the attractiveness and social attributes of fifty women from pictures of their faces. Twenty-seven of the women were finalists in the Miss Universe contest. Though most of the women were white, seven were black and six were Asian.

Dimensions and proportions of what was regarded as attractive emerged with remarkable consistency and precision from Dr. Cunningham's research.

Elements of the perceived ideal of the attractive female face included: eye width that is three-tenths the width of the face at the eyes' level; chin length, one-fifth the height of the face; distance from the center of the eye to the bottom of the eyebrow, one-tenth the height of the face; the height of the visible eyeball, one-fourteenth the height of the face; the width of the pupil, one-fourteenth the distance between the cheekbones; and the total area for the nose, less than 5 percent of the area of the face.

Dr. Cunningham's data describe an ideal, not an actual face. Nor can they be regarded as anything suggesting absolute beauty; rather they are measures of a developed standard, a way to describe the images that a culture, in this case white American culture, defines as attractive.

Very small differences in these ratios made a large difference for attractiveness. For example, the ideal mouth, Dr. Cunningham found, was half or 50 percent the width of the face at mouth level. If that percentage varied by as little at ten points, his research subjects found the face much less attractive.

Personality and Dimples

Of course, a woman's personality and intelligence may matter to an individual man far more than her face whether he will find her attractive. Moreover, any given man may be drawn to a particular feature—dimples and freckles, say, or a strong, classical nose—that the ideal lacks.

But the purport of the Cunningham research is that there is strong agreement on what constitutes facial attractiveness, though the specifics of the ideal may vary from culture to culture.

Dr. Cunningham believes his research holds clues to just why the specific facial patterns of female beauty he identified hold such social and psychological power. The large eyes, along with a small chin and nose, he says, are facial features that typify a newborn. The high wide cheekbone and narrow cheeks, though, are signs that a woman has reached puberty. And the high eyebrows, dilated pupils and wide smile are all signals of positive emotions: interest, excitement and sociability.

"The infant like features draw out in them the same caretaking response a baby would; they make a woman seem cute and adorable," said Dr. Cunningham. "But the signs of maturity signal that a woman has reached childbearing years, which adds a sexual dimension. And the sociable emotions signal personality traits that people are drawn to."

A 'Compelling' Combination

"The sum total of the features signify someone who is slightly young and helpless, though sexually mature and friendly," Dr. Cunningham added.

"And men find that combination compelling."

Research continues to show that being attractive carries a pronounced psychological advantage in life, that a powerful stereotype applied to attractive people equates their beauty with goodness. "Most people assume that good-looking men and women have nearly all the positive traits," according to Elaine Hatfield, a psychologist at the University of Hawaii who has reviewed the research on the social psychology of attractiveness in her book *Mirror, Mirror . . .* published by the State University of New York Press.

Other people, for example, tend to assume that beautiful women and handsome men are warm, sensitive, kind, interesting, poised, sociable and outgoing, and will have good jobs and fulfilling lives.

These social perceptions are one of the benefits of cosmetic facial surgery, according to judgments made of photographs of men and women before and after their surgery. Those who underwent the surgery were seen by others afterward as more self-assertive, intelligent, likable, and able to succeed than they were before the surgery, according to research reported in the journal *Plastic and Reconstructive Surgery.*

The positive treatment of those with an attractive face begins from infancy, with parents tending to give more attention to cuter babies, and continues through life. The teachers of attractive children tend to assume they are more intelligent and popular than their peers. Such expectations psychologists believe, become part of a self-fulfilling prophecy.

Whatever the reason, good-looking

people have been found, on average, to end up in jobs with higher pay and prestige than do their less attractive competitors.

In one study, girls in high school were rated for attractiveness and fifteen years later the more attractive women were found to be in families with significantly higher net income than were their less attractive classmates.

Of course, looks alone do not guarantee success. For instance, the more handsome men in the West Point Class of 1950 rose to higher ranks while at the Academy than their less attractive classmates did, according to a report in the *American Journal of Sociology,* by Allan Mazur, a sociologist at Syracuse University. However, as the cadets' careers continued in the military after graduation, looks helped less and less in promotions and other factors came to the fore.

While there is no sure evidence that the specific features identified in his research have seen as attractive through history, Dr. Cunningham believes that in cultures as ancient as that of classical Egypt women were using cosmetics to mimic or emphasize these features, just as modern cosmetic facial surgery does today.

Some experts disagree with the arguments for the evolutionary advantages of attractiveness. "I'm skeptical of these evolutionary arguments because there is a huge leap from the data to the explanation," said Ellen Berscheid, a social psychologist at the University of Minnesota, who is a leader in the research on attractiveness.

Attractiveness in women should matter less in dating and marriage as women gain more equal footing with men in positions of power and success, according to Dr. Berscheid.